# NEOLITHIC EUROPE

BRIDGET AND RAYMOND ALLCHIN *The Rise of Civilization in India and Pakistan*
DAVID W. PHILLIPSON *African Archaeology*
CLIVE GAMBLE *The Palaeolithic Settlement of Europe*
ALASDAIR WHITTLE *Neolithic Europe: a Survey*

CAMBRIDGE WORLD ARCHAEOLOGY

# NEOLITHIC EUROPE: A SURVEY

## ALASDAIR WHITTLE

*Department of Archaeology,*
*University College, Cardiff*

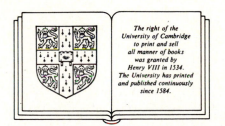

The right of the
University of Cambridge
to print and sell
all manner of books
was granted by
Henry VIII in 1534.
The University has printed
and published continuously
since 1584.

## CAMBRIDGE UNIVERSITY PRESS

CAMBRIDGE

NEW YORK   NEW ROCHELLE

MELBOURNE   SYDNEY

Published by the Press Syndicate of the University of Cambridge
The Pitt Building, Trumpington Street, Cambridge CB2 1RP
32 East 57th Street, New York, NY 10022, USA
10 Stamford Road, Oakleigh, Melbourne 3166, Australia

First published 1985
Reprinted 1988

Printed in Great Britain at the University Press, Cambridge

Library of Congress catalogue card number: 84–23844

*British Library cataloguing in publication data*
Whittle, A. W. R.
Neolithic Europe: a survey – (Cambridge world archaeology)
1. Neolithic period – Europe
1. Title
940.1   GN776.22.E8

ISBN 0 521 24799 3 Hardcovers
ISBN 0 521 29870 X Paperback

WV

# CONTENTS

# FIGURES

# PREFACE

The dangers no less than the difficulties of writing an account of a period as long and of an area as large as this are obvious. Among the difficulties are counted the number of different languages in which the evidence is published, and the gradually swelling flood of publications. Among the dangers the risk of superficiality looms the largest. At times during the writing I have felt like following Dr Johnson in seeing myself as a harmless drudge or in being surprised that the task was being done at all, even if not done well. However this is the last hint of apology for this work. The invitation from the Cambridge University Press in 1981 to submit proposals for a survey of Neolithic Europe was welcome and readily accepted. The resulting task has been challenging and endlessly interesting, and I hope the reader can share this sense of discovery and excitement. There are four main justifications for the book apart from this. First, there is an obvious need for more works that will serve to introduce students and general readers to the intricacies of various prehistoric periods. The subject is not yet ready for text books and this is not intended as such. It is however a wideranging, interpretative introduction which I hope will lead the reader on to a more detailed study. Secondly, as research develops and becomes more detailed from region to region there remains a need at the highest level for synthesis, on the one hand to draw together those aspects of the period in different regions which are in fact in various ways linked, on the other hand to remind one of the endless variety of development in prehistoric society which may be missed if one sticks too narrowly to a single region. Thirdly, an attempt at synthesis need not entail an abandonment of critical standards, and the third justification rests on the continuing need to assess the varying nature of the evidence across Europe. Finally, the ultimate concern of the book is with Neolithic society, and it seems to me that as many tests as possible are required of our emergent interpretations and theories concerning social change and development.

The label 'neolithic' is derived from the Three Age system of division of the past and is only loosely used here. The account covers developments in various areas which could strictly be labelled as Chalcolithic or belonging to the Copper Age. The central European term of Eneolithic, with its connotations of specific historical development, is also avoided because development is too varied to be covered adequately by one simple label.[1] In addition chapter 2 surveys selected examples from the Mesolithic or Epipalaeolithic phase of the post-glacial period. In all the account ranges from the eighth to the late third millennium bc in uncorrected radiocarbon chronology, and generally I advocate that phases be expressed in such terms rather than in those of the Three Age system. The account ends at different stages of the third millennium bc in different parts of Europe. Thus in south-east Europe it goes down to around 2500 bc, but elsewhere to around 2200 bc. This division was made in south-east Europe on the grounds that after that date one is dealing with new developments especially in the Aegean which are beyond the scope of this book. In the other areas of Europe I have preferred to end the account before the horizon of the Beaker cultural complex. The area covered is self-evident, except that I stray little into the USSR except for its far north-west briefly in chapter 2 and Moldavia and the Ukraine in chapters 3, 4 and 5. Neither much of Scandinavia nor the Mediterranean islands receive the attention they deserve, but space has been limited. One could also wish to bring northern Africa more into the Mediterranean scene.

The uncorrected radiocarbon chronology has been used throughout not only for convenience but also because a European dendrochronology is now pending, and it seems better to delay a final calibration of dates until the European dendrochronology is achieved, covering the whole of the post-glacial period. The kind of correction that will be necessary is of course well known. According to the scheme of Clark 2000 bc should be 2520 BC, 3000 bc 3785 BC, 4000 bc 4845 BC and the last point 4550 bc should be 5415 BC.[2] The ending of the scheme at this date illustrates the difficulties which would ensue for an account of this kind from use of the calibrated chronology throughout. There is no space here for the quotation of individual dates and their standard deviations, but the reader will need no reminder of the importance of these, and of the need for constant checking of the reliability, associations and significance of dated samples.

Each part is introduced by short sections on environment, the nature of the evidence and material sequences and chronology. The reader who wishes to avoid this detail should simply proceed to the main sections.

*Cardiff*
*February 1984*

# ACKNOWLEDGEMENTS

A work of this kind incurs many debts. My first acknowledgement must be to all those whose research is used in this synthesis, including those earlier archaeologists whose efforts we often now criticise. I have received much invaluable help from a number of British colleagues. Andrew Sherratt, Bob Chapman, Jim Lewthwaite, Lawrence Barfield, Stephen Shennan, Nick Starling and Richard Bradley have read all or parts of the book in draft form, commented critically on it, and supplied much-needed advice and information. Many colleagues abroad too numerous to mention have also supplied information, references and illustrations. I have also been helped by the good advice of Robin Derricourt of Cambridge University Press, both in the planning and in the execution of the book, and by the copy-editing of Pauline Leng. Needless to say, the faults that remain in the book are my own responsibility.

I am very grateful to the British Academy and the Bulgarian Academy of Sciences for arranging a short-term exchange visit for me to Bulgaria in 1982, and to the British Academy and the Czechoslovak and Slovak Academies of Science for arranging a short-term exchange visit to Czechoslovakia in 1983. Both visits provided me with invaluable opportunities to see material and sites at first hand, and to discuss many problems with those most involved in their resolution. I thank all those colleagues who gave their time to me, and especially Dr Kančo Kančev for guiding me so expertly round Bulgaria. I am also indebted to University College for a grant to attend the 1983 conference at Montpellier on the Early Neolithic of the West Mediterranean. I should like to thank all the staff of the Ashmolean Museum library in Oxford for their unfailing help; the inter-library loan staff of the Arts Library, University College, Cardiff, for their help in the long search for foreign publications; and the Department of Archaeology of the National Museum of Wales for access to its European literature. In my own department, I should particularly like to thank Sabina Thompson for so efficiently and accurately typing the manuscript and for learning word-processing in order to do so, and Howard Mason for so expertly drawing the illustrations, maps and charts, often from very unpromising originals or rough versions. Alison Powers has read and patiently edited the manuscript to the benefit of its grammar and sense, and Peter Price has given invaluable help with editing and word-processing. They cannot be thanked enough.

Finally, I should like to thank Peter and Liz Whittle and Nick and Natalie

Bicât for their hospitality on my frequent visits to the library in Oxford, and my family for all their support and encouragement.

Acknowledgement is due to the following for their permission to reproduce the illustrations indicated: CNRS, Paris 2.2; K. Bokelmann 2.6; National Museum, Copenhagen 2.7, 6.11, 6.23; J. Jacobsen 3.3; National Bank of Greece 3.4, 5.10; Rijksmuseum van Oudheden, Leiden 3.18; I. Pavlů 3.19, 3.20; M. Oliver 3.26; Pitt Rivers Museum, Oxford 3.27; S. Tinè 3.28; J. Courtin 3.31; Srpaka Knjizerina Zadrugen, Belgrade 4.2, 4.3; Institute of Archaeology, Sofia 5.8, 5.14, 5.16; M. Gimbutas 5.15; Somerset Levels Project 6.19; R. Mercer 6.20; Archaeological and Ethnographic Museum, Lodz 6.22; Commissioners of Public Works, Dublin 6.24; Statens Historiska Museet, Stockholm 6.28; J. Vaquer 7.5; Athlone Press 7.16.

# ABBREVIATIONS

| | |
|---|---|
| EN | Early Neolithic (subdivided A–C) ⎱ conventional divisions |
| MN | Middle Neolithic (subdivided I–IV) ⎰ of Scandinavian sequence |
| IE | Indo-European |
| LBK | *Linearbandkeramik* or Linear pottery |
| LW | Langweiler |
| MK | Michelsberg |
| SOM | Seine–Oise–Marne |
| TL | thermoluminescence |
| TRB | *Trichterrandbecher* or funnel-necked beaker |
| VNSP | Vila Nova de São Pedro |

# CHAPTER I

# INTRODUCTION:
# APPROACHES TO THE EVIDENCE

> Once a coincidence was taking a walk with a little accident, and they
> met an explanation – a *very* old explanation – so old that it was quite
> doubled up, and looked more like a conundrum.
>
> Lewis Carroll, *Sylvie and Bruno Concluded*

The period covered by this book is a long one. The main span of time
considered is almost 4000 radiocarbon years long, and longer therefore in
absolute chronology. In addition I briefly survey the preceding phase of the
post-glacial period, which is of uncertain absolute duration, but at least
another 2000 years long. The timescale offered is therefore considerably
greater than is available in other disciplines. Within this timespan it is
evident from the many and varied sources of evidence that the abiding
characteristic of the human societies which are the subject of archaeological
enquiry was a propensity to change. Such change took place at greater and
slower rates, and in differing degrees and ways, but is everywhere apparent.
One must also stress at the outset that, despite the great distance in time of
the period covered here from our own era, the evidence for it is in many areas
of Europe abundant and this evidence has long been studied, in some parts of
Europe indeed on a systematic basis since the latter half of the nineteenth
century. We may therefore emphasise these three aspects of the Neolithic
period in Europe (as here defined[1]): the period was long; there were many
changes during it – in environment, technology, subsistence, exchange,
burial, ritual and indeed in the whole sphere of social relations; and the
evidence available for study is despite its many imperfections rich and varied.
One question remains to be asked: what are we to make of it all, what does it
all mean? The very varied kinds of response that one hears and reads indicate
that there is no simple answer to such a deceptively simple question.

This is no place for a history of the study of the Neolithic period in Europe
as such,[2] but a historical perspective can at least set this question in context.
It is worth noting the development of two aspects, first the basic collection of
evidence and its ordering in correct chronological sequence, and secondly the
kinds of historical and sociological interpretation made with this evidence. It
will be evident that the first aspect has been subject to more continuous
development than the second, and this is a cause for concern.

Systematic investigation of European prehistory began in the nineteenth
century. By the beginning of the twentieth century many outstanding sites of
the Neolithic period were known and already partially investigated. For

example, the Siret brothers had been active at Los Millares in south-east Spain; Lagozza and Swiss lakeside settlements had been observed and investigated; many of the great megalithic monuments of western Europe had been noted and explored; central European settlements and cemeteries were coming to light, as at Lengyel and Řivnáč; a little tentative work had been done on the great tells of the Balkans; and Tsountas for example was at work on the great Thessalian sites of Sesklo and Dimini. Chronology both relative and absolute was far from perfect of course but the basic orderings of Worsaae, Thomsen and Montelius were widely accepted. The Czech prehistorian E. Neustupný has noted[3] how much of the basic central European chronology was known to Palliardi, a rich amateur investigator in Moravia at this time; another good example is the durability of Müller's scheme for the development of Danish Single-grave culture burials and artefacts.[4]

There were of course many problems still unsolved, and the great syntheses of Childe from the 1920s onwards[5] can be taken as a measure of the continued accumulation of data, of the expansion of excavation and research, and of the improvement in relative chronology from region to region, even though absolute chronology tended to now be based on cross-dating ultimately with the eastern Mediterranean world. If we jump to the 1950s we find further improvements, notably in the scale of excavation and in the development of radiocarbon dating. Bulgarian archaeologists for example had begun to excavate considerable slices of their tells before the Second World War, and after it this trend was accelerated in the Balkans, particularly in Bulgaria and Romania. In central and western Europe, there had been extensive pre-war excavations at the Linear pottery site of Köln–Lindenthal, but their scale was then exceptional. After the war the vast excavations at Bylany, begun in the 1950s, set new standards for the investigation of early agricultural settlements, and were soon followed by extensive excavations of similar sites in Dutch Limburg.[6] The discovery and application of radiocarbon dating are well known, as are also the controversies surrounding its gradual acceptance by archaeologists, and indeed the remaining problems of calibration or correction. There was a sustained rearguard action against it in some quarters, but the nettle was grasped with increasing conviction and the implications of the method for freeing much of European development from the eastern Mediterranean and for a general lengthening of the timescale found clearest expression in papers by Neustupný and Renfrew in the late 1960s.[7]

Other developments have continued from the 1960s into the present decade. Two are particularly worth noting. Systematic surveys for settlement evidence, for example in Thessaly, southern Poland and southern Italy, have greatly increased the amount of known sites and allowed for the first time systematic comparisons between different periods in any given area.[8] Secondly, alongside the much older technique of pollen analysis, there has developed a more systematic concern for the recovery of seeds and bones from excavated sites, which again has greatly increased the quantity and quality of subsistence data available, made valid comparisons possible and indeed provoked much thought about the way in which economic resources were used at different periods.[9]

These developments have not been uniform, however. Systematic sieving for seeds and bones for example is still not widely practised. Another development, the greater use of numerical methods for sampling and analysis, has also been extremely varied. There are also considerable differences in the way research is organised and supported financially in the different countries of Europe, though in all cases there is a recurrence of state organisations, museums and university departments.[10] This diversity now presents considerable variety in the nature and quality of the evidence, which is a theme followed throughout the book, and which creates many difficulties for wide synthesis of this kind.

More profound difficulties lie in the realm of interpretation. However much better the data continue to become, these problems are likely to remain, unless there is a corresponding impetus to expand and refine the range of archaeological theory applicable to the Neolithic period. We come back again to the question – what are we to make of it all? It is difficult here to generalise about the kinds of interpretation offered in past and indeed present research, but at the risk of over-simplification two broad past traditions may be outlined. It would be naive to attempt to force all recent developments into either of these two traditions. For example some specific work concerned with subsistence, economy and settlement has been largely independent of both. The first tradition outlined has had major concerns with formal description and categorisation, and little concern with interpretation. The 'formalist' element goes back to Montelius and beyond; the 'minimalist' element has emphasised the difficulties of creating history out of material evidence alone. One example of this is the alleged ladder of reliability of inference according to which we are supposed to have decreasing confidence in inferences as we move from the consideration of technology and economy to the examination of society and religious or spiritual matters.[11] It is a conceit of much of the so-called 'new archaeology' of the last 15 or 20 years, a reaction to this negative approach, that most prehistorians before the 1960s lurked in this slough of prehistoric despond. In fact there has been a second and much more positive tradition. A willingness to attempt social or historical interpretation from the available archaeological evidence can be traced back into the nineteenth century, no less than can other elements of archaeological development. Obvious examples are Nilsson's and Morgan's schemes of social development from savagery to barbarism to civilisation, however quaint we may now find them. Interest in Indo-European language and society, and also Marxist theory, have provided other possibilities since the same date, for example of attempting to trace the emergence of patriarchal society.[12] There have therefore been theories of social development, even if often inexplicit and long fossilised, but one has only to read Childe's varied works from the 1920s to the 1950s, for example, to realise the vigour of this tradition. For Childe and many others the culture concept was of major and lasting importance. Taken over by Childe from the German anthropological tradition, in essence it seeks regularities in the archaeological record, such that recurrent artefactual and other evidence is grouped together to form an archaeological culture. This in turn is regularly (though not necessarily) equated with the existence of a distinctive group of people and, if there is distinctive skeletal evidence, with a 'race'.[13] With the general concerns of this tradition with change and with social interpretation, much of the changing archaeological record has been read as a timetable for the arrival and departure of different groups and peoples. Because of the reliance of relative chronology on the eastern Mediterranean in the pre-radiocarbon era, there was also a strong tendency to derive change from the outside, and particularly from the east. Copper metallurgy and megalithic monuments are two classic examples so treated, but the extent of this approach should not be exaggerated; Childe again for example suggests many other examples of internal social change.

With the first tradition there can be perhaps in the end little debate; far greater possibilities for improvement and development lie with the second. It is important not to underestimate the strengths of this second tradition. In its more ambitious forms it presents models for interpretation of the archaeological record and for the explanation of change which simply cannot be ruled out of court altogether. After all, recent ethnographic work for example in East Africa has repeatedly emphasised regularities, patterning and boundaries in material culture and suggested that certain artefacts can be diagnostic for the identity of certain human groups.[14] It would also be exceedingly foolish to deny the reality in later prehistoric or 'protohistoric' times of greater and lesser population movements, adjustments and displacements, as also to deny that change – whether technological, economic or social – can *never* come from outside. Indeed the shift to cereal-based cultivation, the staple theme of the Neolithic period, may well have to be explained in this way, even if the argument has to be longer and more complicated than in the earlier decades of research.

What must however be recognised is that the conventional assumptions of this tradition have been increasingly challenged over the last 15 to 20 years, that they cannot automatically be accepted and that we have now before us a wider and I think more exciting range of explanatory possibilities. This is the essence of the so-called 'new archaeology' beginning in the 1960s. A few brief examples will suffice here to illustrate this. First, there have been many suggestions of locally developed rather than externally derived or diffused changes. Notable examples are plant and animal domestication, copper metallurgy, and megalithic constructions; the latter two are now widely accepted as local developments within Europe, owing little or nothing to the eastern Mediterranean or south-west Asia. Partly this re-orientation in explanation was connected with the revolution in chronology provided by radiocarbon dating, but was also due to an explicit concern with detailed explanation. Secondly, the culture concept has itself been increasingly examined. It is clear that on a purely descriptive level a definition such as Childe's is excessively vague, and that in reality there are widely varying situations of regularity and distribution of artefactual and other evidence. Groupings may be tight in one case, ill defined in another, overlapping (or 'polythetic' in the jargon) in others. Stemming from ethnographic work there has also been the recent important suggestion that material culture must not be seen as a passive reflection of social reality, but that it is itself an element fully involved in the web of social relations and is actively employed by people in the maintenance or transformation of social orders.[15] There are several good examples of the application of this sort of idea in the horizon immediately after the last period covered by this book in central and western Europe, the horizon of Bell beakers, and the idea can just as well be applied in the preceding Corded ware horizon and others earlier still.[16] The basic notion here is that the Bell beaker culture need not be the archaeological remains of a distinct, self-contained human group, but a special status assemblage specific perhaps to only a certain part of the population or certain special spheres of life such as ritual and burial.

There have been other important developments too, some indeed within the 'new archaeology' itself. Much of this can now be seen as excessively positivist and systemic, and seeking categorisations of society which are likely to be too simple. For example there is a long tradition in archaeology of inferring social reality, especially social difference, from the burial record. Childe was aware of the dangers of this procedure, and an important paper in 1969 by Ucko reminded archaeologists of them.[17] However one strand of the new archaeology, particularly in the USA and Great Britain, devoted itself to the formulation of principles by means of which social differences could be traced in the burial record, basically on the assumption that the greater energy, effort and material wealth expended on a person in death, the greater his or her social importance in life. This kind of approach is also widely followed in Europe, if not always with such explicit principles.[18] However a recent restatement of the interpretative difficulties has emphasised that death and burial are events to be considered within the continuing web of social life, that burial may be radically affected in its form by such notions as purity or impurity rather than by the social position of the deceased alone, and that burial can be variously used to mask, distort or invert social reality. As one example, collective burial could be seen to project an ideology of cooperation at odds with the reality of social differentiation.[19] The interpretative dangers are obvious and enormous.

We are faced therefore, paradoxically, with a situation in which as theory improves practice becomes more difficult. We cannot assume that a simple relationship exists between people and material culture, nor that change is most likely to come from outside a society, nor that the trajectory of change over time was simple or unilinear.[20] Nor do external suggested sources of change such as environment, climate or population growth have in themselves alone great explanatory value for understanding change. The environment is better seen as constraining rather than as directly determining human action, and population behaviour is probably best seen as itself symptomatic of the nature of social relations rather than as a determinant of them. In coming to frame alternative approaches, moreover, one must now seek to combine both local and non-local factors. It is important for example to examine at a local level possibilities or opportunities for change and development, be they in the sphere of technology, subsistence or social differentiation. Considerable use for example is made in later chapters of the idea of internal conflicts of interest within communities and societies. Such imbalance, stress or 'contradiction'[21] is not in itself a profound or original concept, but it does provide one way of thinking about the internal dynamics of change in a society, and the area of conflict may be wide, from substistence and production, to the spheres of exchange, status and ritual.

However it would be myopic to insist that the local scale of analysis alone is sufficient, and there is anyway just as much vagueness in the definition of 'local' as pointed out above in the definition of the culture concept. Cultures in the archaeological sense do underline the fact that individual sites or areas are often part of wider phenomena. We must seek to combine the local and the non-local in explanation. Indeed the scale and nature of interaction at a non-local level may have profound consequences for social relations at a local level. One significant hypothesis advanced in parts of later chapters is that the ability to interact at long range with other elite groups was an important element in creating and maintaining internal social differentiation by the third millennium bc. Nor, as emphasised above, can such factors as technological diffusion or some population movement be automatically dismissed in every case.

The general nature of the rather broader theory advocated should be clear, and we must now examine the evidence in its light.

# CHAPTER 2

# EARLY POST-GLACIAL BACKGROUND, 8000–6000 bc

## *Environment*

The post-glacial period in Europe traditionally is considered to begin towards or at the end of the ninth millennium BC, a date established by varve chronology in northern Europe as long ago as the end of the last century, and prima facie supported by more recent radiocarbon dating.[1] This chapter surveys developments in early post-glacial Europe in the 2000 radiocarbon years before the first establishment of cereal-based economies (Fig. 2.1). This period has been variously labelled Epipalaeolithic or Mesolithic, depending on the emphasis given to continuity from the later glacial period. The term Mesolithic is used here in the first place with chronological reference only and the term early post-glacial is also used as a synonym; the nature of human

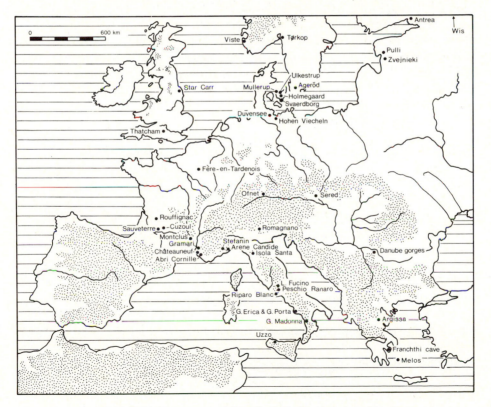

**2.1** Simplified location map of the principal sites mentioned in chapter 2

activity within it remains to be discussed. It is worth stressing too that the
starting point is to some extent arbitrarily chosen. It marks the final retreat of
late glacial ice sheets and the beginning of more or less uninterrupted
temperature rise. This process had however begun as early as 16000 bc, and in
the Allerød interstadial, dated to much of the tenth millennium BC, forest
conditions and fauna were to be found as far north as Denmark; continuous
occupation of southern coastal parts of Norway may have been possible from
this date. Further south, though the final cold phase of the Younger Dryas
period undoubtedly reduced the extent of deciduous forest in areas such as
the Pyrenees or Provence, continuous closed woodland can be traced in
pollen diagrams in Greece back to well before 10000 bc. In the southern
Carpathian basin, the Younger Dryas period is not marked in forest changes
but in sediments and rodent faunas.[2]

The dominant factor to be considered in the post-glacial environmental
changes was a rapid rise in temperature. Evidence for the general trend comes
from various sources, such as the distribution of sensitive flora and fauna, and
isotopic measurement of pelagic and lake sediments, but is generally consistent. The initial rise seems to have been rapid, and starting at 9°C, present
day summer temperatures may have been reached within a millennium, and
maximum temperatures of up to 2–2.5°C higher than today within two. The
spread of hazel and other warmth-demanding species matches finds of the
warmth-demanding European pond tortoise (*Emys orbicularis*) in northern
Europe from the seventh millennium bc onwards, indicating July
temperatures at least 2°C over those of today. A similar trend is seen in an
isotopic study of lake sediments on Gotland in the Baltic (though the detailed
chronology rests on extrapolation from few radiocarbon dates) and indeed in
similar studies on the Greenland ice core and on deep sea cores. A rise in
winter temperatures may have been at least as important, though fewer
estimates of these are available. A late glacial January mean temperature in
Denmark estimated at between −2° and −8°C on the basis of the presence of
both plants *Pleurospermum austriacum* and *Armeria maritima* provides a
base line from which to calculate. The trend remains to be established in
detail. Reference to a cold snap in the early post-glacial period in the western
Mediterranean and the Alps and northern Europe is not made in most of the
Mediterranean. Use of flora and fauna as indicators must take account of the
ecological conditions of their immigration into fresh areas; established birch
and pine woods may for example have slowed the colonisation of hazel
northwards. Interest in climate in a wider sense is of long standing, and goes
back to late nineteenth- and early twentieth-century investigations by the
Scandinavians Blytt and Sernander into wet and dry phases supposedly seen
in the history of peat deposits. Their research, though before the days of
pollen analysis, produced labels still used for the stages of the post-glacial
vegetational succession. The first or Pre-Boreal period is thought to have been
at first dry but increasingly wet in the north, followed by the second or Boreal
period with more arid conditions, marked especially in northern Europe by
shrinking lake margins.[3] Evidence further south is more varied. Greek data

suggest that a Mediterranean climate like that of today predominated over the entire post-glacial period until late antiquity. In the western Mediterranean, pollen analysis in Provence suggests greater humidity in the Boreal period than further north, though the probably more reliable sedimentological evidence both in this area and in eastern Spain does allow far greater dryness in the seventh millennium bc. Detailed local sequences rather than broad generalisations are now required.

The first effect of these changes to be considered is sea-level rise produced by melting of the ice sheets. This can be seen around the coasts of the whole of Europe. In Greece, short-term tectonic movement can probably be discounted and there is a rapid rise from −80 to 120 m in the late glacial period to about −6 m by 4000 bc, seen for example in the Cycladic site of Saliagos, with subsequent slow rise to present levels. Detailed investigation in the western Mediterranean matches this general picture. Sea level off the south French coast was about 60 m below present level at around 8000 bc; there was a brief stabilisation around 50 m in the eighth millennium, with further rapid rise, to past −26 m at around 5000 bc, and to −3 m by around 3000 bc. Not all the data agree, since there may be a time lag between submergence and the formation of datable covering deposits. Loss of land in the Mediterranean will have been considerable, especially in the shallower northern part of the Adriatic though to a lesser extent around the steeper west Italian, French and Spanish coasts. The loss of space may partly have been offset from the point of view of exploitable resources by the continued formation of fresh lagoons, rich in fish and shells.[4] In northern Europe account must be taken of the movement of the earth's crust as well as of an increase in the volume of seawater. The classic case of the Baltic illustrates the interplay between these two factors. In the late glacial period the Baltic was a freshwater lake, dammed by low sea level and the icesheet. In the early post-glacial rapidly rising levels formed the Yoldia Sea with an entry over central-southern Sweden. Subsequent recovery by the land relieved of the weight of ice led to damming again, forming the Ancylus Lake from the mid eighth to the mid seventh millennia bc. Further sea rise renewed contact with the sea, creating the Litorina Sea.[5] The southern part of the North Sea basin was steadily submerged, aided by tilting of western parts of the British Isles. Britain was insulated by 6000 bc. Land loss again must have been considerable.

The second effect to consider is that of vegetational change. The establishment of forest in many areas precedes the beginning of our period. Oak forest seems to have been present in southern areas like Greece from the start. In southern France mixed oak woodland was already well established in some lowland areas by the eighth millennium bc and expanded further in the seventh at the expense of pine, and grassland, which retreated to higher altitudes. Forest trees now included conifers, deciduous and evergreen oak, lime, Aleppo pine and wild olive. For northern Europe, in Scandinavia and the British Isles for example, the general trend is clear and has been repeatedly established where peat deposits are available for pollen analysis. The late glacial environment was tundra with only occasional stands of trees such as birch. As temperatures rose birch forest spread rapidly, followed by pine. After about 7000 bc hazel became a more important forest component, with birch and pine still well represented. From the later seventh millennium bc the mixed oak forest was beginning to replace this, with species such as oak, ash, elm and lime being important constituents, and this type of forest was dominant by the sixth millennium. In intermediate latitudes the process of change was of similar character but probably took place rather more quickly, depending on the extent and distribution of late glacial refuges. In detail, the changes were varied both from region to region – as has been well established in the British Isles and in southern Scandinavia; factors such as geology, soils, topography, climate and altitude being responsible – and within each region. Present-day ecological zonation in the Mediterranean shows Aleppo pine and evergreen oaks up to 500–700 m, deciduous woodland from 500 to 1000 m, and beech, fir and other pines from 700–900 m to 1500–1800 m. Detailed pollen analysis can even reveal micro-variation in early post-glacial woodland over a small area.

These various changes are best denoted by local or regional stages. Many British and Irish palaeobotanists for example use only local stages in describing particular pollen profiles. Regional schemes are available for Ireland, Britain and parts of southern Scandinavia amongst others.[6] Despite their convenience, it is unfortunate that there is still widespread use of the Blytt–Sernander labels Pre-Boreal, Boreal, Atlantic and so on, since there cannot be exact correspondence between different areas, and since even in the area of their origin, southern Scandinavia, there is no consistency in their application because they have different criteria in each region.[7] Further south in Europe, the use of these zone labels, though frequent, can be more confusing still.

The third effect to be considered concerns the changes in resources, both animal and plant. The glacial megafauna began to become extinct in the Bølling and Allerød interstadials of the late glacial period. Giant deer are only found in Denmark until the earlier eighth millennium. Reindeer, the major food staple of cold parts of Europe in the late glacial period, moved northwards following the displaced subarctic zone, though some may have lingered on the north European plain for part of the eighth millennium bc and herds may have survived in the mountains of southern Norway for longer. As in the warmer phases of the late glacial period, other herbivores better suited to grassland and forest grazing and warmer temperatures took their place. Elk, aurochs or wild cattle, red deer, roe deer and pig were of particular importance for people in northern parts, as sources of meat, fat, marrow, skins and bone and antler for tools. Those five species today have very varied habits and habitats, a diversity which may have more than compensated for the loss of large concentrated reindeer herds. On the basis of present-day patterns of animal behaviour one would predict that red deer and wild cattle were gregarious, while elk were rather solitary and pig and roe were found dispersed in small groups; seasonal fluctuations if they followed present patterns would result in greater red deer dispersal in summer with separation between the sexes. Other animals of the early post-glacial environment such as lynx, fox, marten, or beaver would have provided furs and skins, and the latter meat as well. Wolf and dog would also have provided skins and meat, and dogs are generally considered to have been domesticated by this period. Warmer conditions presumably hastened the return of freshwater fish such as the pike and the sheat fish, the latter today spawning near the surface when temperatures reach 18°C. The same warmth may also have encouraged greater numbers of bird species, though some may have equally tended to migrate north towards the tundra for summer feeding. Plant life on land and in water was radically enriched, offering a vast supply of food not available in late glacial cold phases; Eskimos in subarctic Alaska used to eat about a cupful of berries per year. Sea fish and marine mammals were presumably less affected; there is evidence from south-west Norway for the presence of whales, seals and sea birds from about 10000 bc. The opening of the Baltic however would have distributed such resources more widely.[8]

Further south such changes would have become progressively less marked. Elk drop out of the faunal record, though the other four herbivores are well represented in southern Europe, with the addition of ibex and chamois in southern and mountainous areas. The distribution of these species may have been affected by environmental change. For example, the increase of numbers of ibex and chamois at sites in the Danube gorges between 10000 and 8000 bc is seen as a response to greater snowfall in early post-glacial winters, forcing these animals off the mountains.[9] There is a classic controversy over the question of sheep in the western Mediterranean in the early post-glacial period. It is difficult to distinguish sheep from other caprines such as ibex and chamois if few bones are available. Sheep bones are well attested from the Neolithic period onwards but the earlier situation is hard to reconstruct. One school of thought has it that sheep were present in central and southern France from the Upper Palaeolithic into the early post-glacial period surviving in the late glacial in oak woodland refuges. But the sites in question are ones like Gramari, Vaucluse, in the south of France, with very few bones, no sealed stratigraphy and doubtful radiocarbon dates. Early post-glacial sheep have also been claimed in eastern Spain but are not mentioned in Italy. Other evidence suggests that present-day mouflon in Corsica and Sardinia, supposedly descendants of indigenous stock, are feral; the implication is that sheep in the western Mediterranean are of Asiatic stock and therefore introduced. The date of such an introduction may lie at the beginning of the Neolithic around 6000 bc, on the basis of recent excavations in southern France. The importance of sheep therefore is less perhaps as an early post-glacial resource, more as an indication of developments at the beginning of the Neolithic period, as we shall see in the next chapter.[10]

River fish such as carp and sea fish such as tunny were also to be found in southern Europe; their distribution and density may also have been affected by temperature change, as the increase in fish in the two levels at Cuina Turcului in the Danube gorges between 10000 and 8000 bc and the appearance of large sea fish at the Franchthi Cave in southern Greece around

7000 bc suggest. Plant food, in the form of seeds, roots, tubers, nuts and berries, would also presumably have been abundant. Annual seed-bearing grasses could have been an important resource well before 10000 bc, though the evidence is sparse. It has often been assumed that the ancestors of cereals, the so-called noble grasses, were restricted in origin to the Near East. Even today when plant distributions may have changed considerably wild einkorn (*Triticum boeoticum*) is found in south-east Bulgaria. Wild barley (*Hordeum spontaneum*) is present along the north coast of Africa. There seems no good reason to exclude most of the Mediterrean from cereals' preferred habitat, and sporadic finds at the Franchthi Cave from about 10500 bc support this. Large grass or cereal pollen grains from Icoana in the Danube gorges just before 6000 bc may also testify to this aspect of indigenous European resources.[11]

It is important to see these various changes as interrelated factors of the ecological setting. For example, red deer and other herbivores prefer foods such as grasses, sedges and young browse, which would have been abundant in the varied forest conditions particularly of northern Europe in the first two millennia of the post-glacial period. The silting of lakes and river courses, as well as the rise of sea level, would also have produced substantial areas of high-quality grazing for herbivores. Hazel woodland in the seventh millennium would have offered its own sources of plant food. The increase in exploitable biomass in the early post-glacial period must have been considerable, particularly in northern compared to southern Europe. Biomass has been seen as reaching its maximum at the point of intersection of ecological niches that are different from each other. From this point of view the early post-glacial period covered in this chapter offered not major constraints for human activity but abundant opportunities.[12]

*Material culture: chronology and groupings, 8000–6000 bc*

Material culture surviving on most early post-glacial sites consists of flint and other stone tools of various kinds. Tools interpreted as knives, scrapers, borers and engravers are very widespread, and may have performed basic domestic tasks. Tools interpreted as axes are generally restricted to northern Europe and are seen as performing various heavy duty tasks. Small chipped flake and blade segments – 'microliths' – are interpreted as projectile points, generally as the tips and barbs of arrowheads; varieties of these are ubiquitous (Figs. 2.2 and 2.3). Different combinations of these elements are found on different sites. In conditions of favourable preservation such as, notably, in countries round the Baltic, a range of tools in wood, bone and antler is also found, which for the most part can be fitted into these three categories. All these tools have been used also to provide the basic chronological and cultural framework for the period. Long stratigraphies are largely restricted to southern Europe, and detailed investigations of these are comparatively rare. Radiocarbon dating has been unevenly applied; its lack is felt particularly in central and eastern Europe. In northern Europe it has been possible to relate assemblages to the environmental record to compensate for the lack of

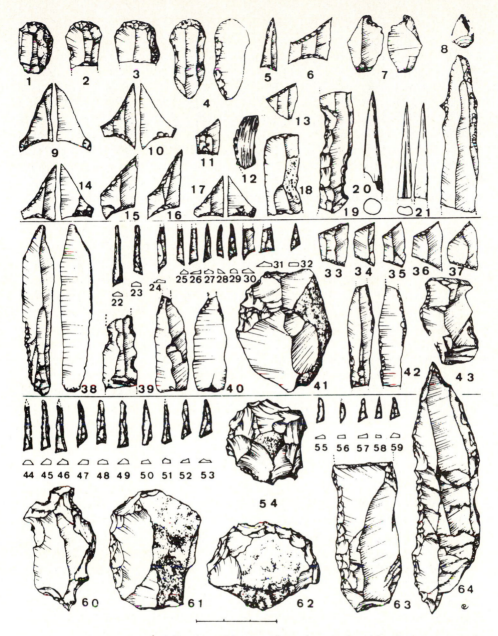

**2.2** Succession of flint assemblages in the early post-glacial levels at La Baume de Montclus, Gard, south of France. Bottom, layers 22–17 middle Montclusien; middle, layers 16–15 upper Montclusien; top, layer 14 middle Castelnovien. *After* Escalon de Fonton

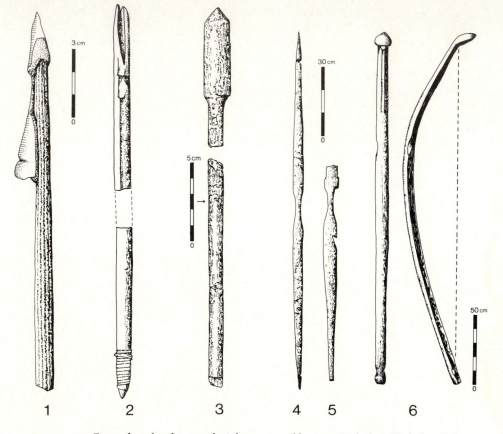

**2.3** Examples of early post-glacial arrows and bows. 1 Loshult; 2 Vinkel; 3 Holmegaard IV; 4–5 Holmegaard; 6 Wis. *After* Rozoy and Andersen

stratigraphic sequence, but this method too involves uncertainties. Typological schemes can be most criticised for being applied too widely beyond their
area of origin. Broad interregional correlations need to be tested rather than
assumed. The inappropriate use of labels such as 'Sauveterrian' or
'Tardenoisian' for assemblages far away from Sauveterre-la-Lemance in the
Dordogne or Fère-en-Tardenois in the Île de France has obscured such
problems. As when describing the environment, we must start with local,
descriptive schemes. From a functional point of view, the imbalance between
stone and organic tools in the archaeological record must be recognised as a
serious drawback, as must the lack of sufficient detailed research on what
specific artefacts were used for and how long they lasted.[13] There seems to be
considerable continuity with artefactual traditions of the late glacial period.
Even where there is much change in the early post-glacial period there is little
need to explain this by reference to substantial population shift. Some
population movement may indeed have taken place, such as of reindeer
hunters into the mountains of southern Norway, but the more generally

appropriate hypothesis is of continued adaptation by the local population. Small stone projectile points or microliths are not a direct response to forest and forest fauna, but to the development of bows, which can be traced definitely in the late glacial to the Ahrensburgian culture of the cold Younger Dryas phase and possibly to the Hamburgian culture of the Oldest Dryas phase.[14] Changing flint projectile points may reflect better bows or better arrows. At the same time some aspects of their morphology seem due to fashion or cultural choice since many forms are interchangeable, either replacing each other in stratified sequences or being found together, as at the Scanian site Ageröd I:B around 6000 bc.[15] Likewise the distribution of stone axes is extremely curious (Fig. 2.4). Contact across the southern boundary of this distribution is demonstrable, and there was no less forest in central and southern Europe, perhaps even more. Had stone axes been vital for or provided clear advantages in forested conditions, they would surely in the absence of alternative tools have been diffused southwards. It is possible therefore that their functional role in the north is misunderstood or over-estimated, or that alternatives further south have not been recognised.

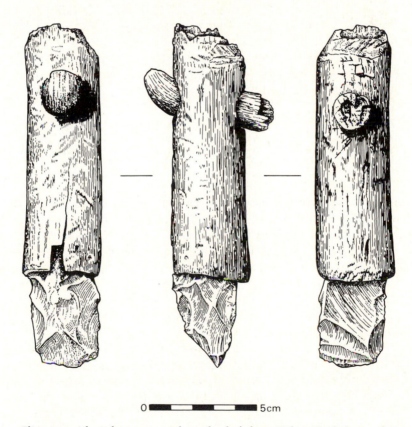

0 ▮▮▮▮ ▮▮▮▮ 5cm

**2.4** Flint axe with antler mount and wooden haft from Hohen Viecheln, northern Germany. *After* Schuldt.

Concerning specific tools, the clearest (and most often discussed) changes during the early post-glacial period are to be seen in microliths. Late glacial types of points had disappeared virtually everywhere by 7000 bc. Obliquely blunted, non-geometric microliths appear in several areas by or before 8000 bc (such as southern France, northern Italy or southern Scandinavia) with clear forerunners in late glacial assemblages. Geometric forms such as triangles and crescents are also of early appearance, but become particularly common after 7000 bc. Specialised trapezoidal forms, while of early origin also, become popular in several areas (the British Isles and east of the Danube were largely excluded) around or soon after 6000 bc.

In eastern Europe, the dating of development is particularly lacking. In the Danube gorges, two levels at Cuina Turcului dated to 10000 and 8000 bc have assemblages of backed blades and points, denticulated flakes and other tools: labels such as Epi-Gravettian or Romanellian testify to the late glacial tradition. Towards 6000 bc sites such as Icoana and Ostrovul Banului have a range of tools, more in quartzite than in flint, such as scrapers, knives and irregular pieces with microliths lacking; some points of bone and antler including biserially barbed ones are known.[16] The introduction of geometric industries to eastern Europe is poorly dated. The assemblage of Sered' in Slovakia, datable only by pollen analysis to a period of mixed pine and oak forest illustrates this. In the stratified and radiocarbon dated sequence of the Franchthi Cave in southern Greece simple geometric microliths appear in the seventh millennium bc. Trapezes made on broad blades are amongst the forms found in Thessalian 'aceramic Neolithic' sites such as Argissa dated around 6000 bc.[17]

Change in Italy is better dated, but its pace is varied and regionalised. As in eastern Europe, some assemblages remain in the late glacial tradition for some time, as in Calabria, Campania and Liguria, with backed blades and points prominent. Radiocarbon-dated sites like Romagnano in the Adige valley near Trento or Isola Santa in Tuscany show the appearance of geometric microliths such as triangles and crescents alongside backed points from soon after 8000 bc. Specialised tool assemblages with notched and denticulated forms occur; one such is dated at the Latium site of Riparo Blanc to the mid seventh millennium bc. Trapezoidal microlith forms make their appearance in the Adige valley around 6000 bc. The development is restricted in geographical scope, this horizon being absent in Liguria, but present in Provence.[18]

Stratified rock shelters and small caves in south-east France provide another area where the general sequence is reasonably clear though several recently excavated sites await full publication and radiocarbon dates are still relatively sparse. The transition from late glacial traditions is particularly clear, in local terms from Valorguien assemblages with backed points to Montadien assemblages with smaller, geometric microliths including triangles, crescents and obliquely blunted forms. The sequence of Abri Cornille-Sulauze, Istres, Bouches du Rhône, provides perhaps the best example, though it is not itself radiocarbon dated. Trapezes and rhomboids are added in the early eighth millennium on the basis of a single date from Ponteau-Martigues, Bouches du Rhône, though they are not yet common. The later part of the sequence is less clear in detail in this coastal area. Castelnovien assemblages with a dominant trapeze element are well documented in the sixth millennium, as at the type sites Châteauneuf-les-Martigues, Bouches du Rhône. The radiocarbon-dated sequence here however does not go earlier than this. Further inland in the Vaucluse, Gard and Aveyron *départements*, development may have followed a different course. The stratified and dated (but not yet fully published) site of Baume de Montclus, Gard, still has geometric, triangular microliths in levels of the early sixth millennium, with trapezes added in the mid sixth millennium and becoming dominant soon after. This may be contrasted again with the Dordogne where the stratigraphy of sites like Cuzoul, Sauveterre and Rouffignac shows triangular and other microliths going back probably to at least the late eighth millennium; some trapezes were again an early feature (in the classic Sauveterrien area!).[19]

Much further north, a detailed typological sequence has been proposed for the Maglemosian culture of Denmark, its six supposed stages lasting from around 8000 bc to around or after 6000 bc. The long struggle to establish the correct sequence for the Danish Mesolithic is worth noting. Its general characteristics as outlined here and in chapter 4 seem now secure, with a transition in the early post-glacial period from tanged point assemblages to ones including obliquely blunted, triangular and crescentic microliths, end scrapers, distinctive core types, and axes, mainly of the core variety. There is also a variety of antler and bone tools, with the barbed bone point standing out as characteristic. In detail however, the proposed sequence is less secure. It is based on differences in microliths, scrapers and cores. For example obliquely blunted microliths are held progressively to drop out, while triangular microliths become more asymmetrical, and handled and keeled cores exemplify late stages in the sequence. Some fixed points are provided by pollen analysis and radiocarbon dating, as at Mullerup, Verup, Ulkestrup and Svaerdborg, but stratigraphic succession is largely lacking, many earlier investigations provided scanty pollen analysis, and radiocarbon dates are still far too few. There is room for overlap between supposedly successive stages as the Scanian example of Ageröd shows, and also for regionalisation. For example there are no stage 5 sites from Brinch Petersen's list in either the Aamosen area of northern Zealand or Jutland; those cited are from southern Zealand. There is controversy over the end of the sequence and the extent of contact or overlap with the succeeding Kongemose culture. There are radiocarbon dates from Ulkestrup just before 6000 bc, and Kongemose around 5600 bc. The former is assigned to stage 3. What happens in the interval is uncertain. This is not to deny the reality of artefactual change through time – detailed study of stratified artefacts of Ageröd I in Scania again provides perhaps the best example, with gradual changes in the style and abundance of particular types – but to emphasise the difficulty of establishing valid regional chronologies.[20]

In the British Isles typological dating is undeveloped, and a simple distinction between Earlier and Later assemblages is made, with the boundary before 6000 bc. Few sites have been closely dated by pollen analysis or radiocarbon. An early, perhaps abrupt, transition from late glacial traditions is evident, on the basis of radiocarbon dates for sites in the Kennet valley at Thatcham Berkshire. Star Carr in Yorkshire, dated by one radiocarbon sample to the mid eighth millennium bc, illustrates the problems of detailed chronology. As will be discussed again below, the duration of occupation of the site is unclear, though stratigraphic separation between worked timbers and artefacts suggests use over a number of years. Flint types such as obliquely blunted and triangular microliths, burins, and scrapers do not appear to change during the occupation of the site, but some stratigraphic separation between coarse, medium and finely barbed antler points is apparent. It is therefore unwise to take the assemblage as static or representing a clearly defined period.[21]

## Approaches to early post-glacial communities

Many accounts of human society at this time have assumed rather than documented a particular subsistence basis, namely hunting and gathering, and asserted that a combination of environmental and technological factors such as resource fluctuation and an inability to produce food had a determining influence on both daily life and society as a whole. Research on this period has often been carried out with the behaviour of recent hunter-gatherers firmly in mind. Such people are widely documented in general terms and particular groups have been closely observed, to such an extent that on occasion they are influenced in their movements by their accompanying anthropologist. Recent hunter-gatherers tend to subsist in harsh, marginal environments. Their exploitation of resources is often parasitic, though it may be regular and orderly. Seasonal resource fluctuation entails mobility of settlement and imposes constraints on population aggregation and growth, and by extension, it is believed, affects or determines social organisation resulting in small autonomous family units linked only with wider kin and breeding groups and supportive alliances.[22]

From these sorts of approach, many prehistorians have tended to derive one particular model for early post-glacial communities, of generally small mobile social units, carefully cropping fluctuating resources and adapting their own numbers safely to the capacity of those resources to support them, and with rather fluid though important social relations beyond the immediate, more or less egalitarian group. Greatest attention perhaps recently has been paid to the fine adjustment of resource use season by season. This model will be discussed here, but will be also supplemented by alternatives involving greater stability of settlement and control over food resources, so that having reviewed case studies of subsistence it will be possible to view environmental and technological factors not so much as determinants but as constraints on social arrangements. This view too can be supported by a wider use of the ethnographic record, where we find for example !Kung bushmen prolonging population aggregation for social reasons, and other settled people with high population, personal property and permanent leaders, based on rich, natural or wild resources.

Hunters and gatherers face risks, like all people, from fluctuations in the supply of resources on which they depend. Fluctuations in this period could have come both over a number of years, and annually through the amounts of exploitable plants, animals and other resources varying from season to season, with late winter and early spring being particularly difficult times. A common assumption for this period is that by and large hunter-gatherers did not store food, and were therefore reliant in each season on what was seasonally available. In the first model therefore the response of hunter-gatherers is seen as a careful adaptation to this situation. This would take a number of forms. Communities would tend to make full use of the range of resources in their environment. The timing of their exploitation and its level, and human mobility to arrive at the point of maximum seasonal abundance are particularly important as well as a safe deliberate adjustment of human numbers by birth spacing and other forms of birth control. Far from living a catch-as-catch-can existence, hunters are envisaged as making every effort to cull animals systematically and not to endanger future breeding success. It is unfair to generalise but many such models envisage a rather low overall contribution to the diet from fish and plant foods; Jochim for example assigns these an arbitrary value of about 15 per cent. In the archaeological record close attention is paid to differences between 'base' and 'extraction' camps, their size and location, resources used and season occupied, in order to construct 'schedules' of resource use.[23]

Another model which deserves greater emphasis also predicts a parasitic or non-food-producing subsistence basis but much greater stability of settlement based on an abundance of natural resources. Such resources could have been rich indeed. For example animal densities could have exceeded levels reconstructed purely from modern case studies and the extent of animal movement through the seasons over their habitats may also have been reduced in the past as compared to the different circumstances of the present. Red deer are an obvious case in point. Particular resources may have fluctuated in their seasonal abundance, but certain sites or areas could have been within reach of a steady supply of successive alternatives. Coastal and marine areas would offer both migratory and stable resources. In this sort of favourable situation, the imperative need for mobility, so often assumed, would be greatly or completely minimised.[24]

The main element of a third model is some degree of control over the food supply, combined with either mobile or stable settlement. The technology of such control is not complicated. Forest can be cleared by fire or axe to produce regenerating browse which is particularly attractive to herbivores, thus affecting their movements. Men and dogs may also be able loosely to herd animals from area to area; it has been claimed that animals' fear of man is a learned not innate characteristic. Breeding, though direct control is harder, could easily be influenced by selective culling. Use of trees and plants could be varied; selective clearance to encourage hazel, selective weeding of areas of favoured plants and deliberate sowing are all possibilities which do not deserve to be discounted a priori. The notions of horticulture and arboriculture are apposite. Storage of meat and plants, especially by drying, is not complicated and need not involve extensive below-ground facilities. Control of these kinds could have eased life in a mobile round of settlement or provided a basis for permanent settlement. The motive for applying such control, which is likely to have been more labour intensive, could have been varied, either to avoid or reduce subsistence stress, or to intensify food supplies to allow settled life, and to enhance status and social standing.[25]

Particular cases must now be studied to see which of these models, or which combinations of them, are most appropriate in different areas in the early post-glacial period. In passing to these from general problems, specific difficulties recur in interpreting the archaeological record at each site which are worth emphasising. The size of individual sites is hard to recover without extensive excavation. Even with this knowledge, it is hard to predict whether artefact clusters represent huts or structures, or exterior working areas or middens. Certain activities may be localised or occur more or less indiscriminately. The definition of what constitutes a site is a problem in itself. Are the concentrations in one locality, as at Ageröd or Svaerdborg, several sites, or one with spatial segregation of activities and people? Season and duration of occupation are very difficult to establish reliably (especially if food was stored). As for matters of subsistence, a lot of plant use need not have involved processing which would produce durable carbonised remains. In the absence of genetic changes with morphological effects, as is believed to result from selective breeding, control over animals is hard to prove. Particular proportions of red deer of different age and sex, interpreted by some as showing selective culling or more, are seen by others as easily explicable as the result of logistical tactics of killing, butchering, transport and use.[26] The balance between different parts of the diet is difficult to quantify, as is the contribution of stored food.

## Subsistence: case studies

The occupation of the Franchthi Cave in the Argolid of southern Greece goes far back into the Upper Palaeolithic.[27] The limestone cave lies not far above present sea level (see Fig. 3.3). Excavations have been limited to four soundings in the interior (but with stratified radiocarbon dated deposits up to 11 m deep), four at the entrance, and exploration of the adjacent shoreline, where deposits are exclusively Neolithic. The size of the site, and fluctuations in size are thus impossible to recover. There is considerable continuity between the Upper Palaeolithic and the Lower Mesolithic levels (8300–7250 bc), with red deer, cattle, pig, land snails, marine molluscs, small sea fish, pulses, barley and oats represented in both. Environmental change is probably responsible for the replacement of ass and goat by a greater concentration on deer in the Mesolithic levels, and the appearance of wild pear and greater numbers of pistachio. Age and sex data however are not yet available. The cereal remains are particularly interesting. They are not abundant at first but become later (from 9000 bc in one trench, 7000 bc in another) 'important components of the Mesolithic assemblage'. In the absence of morphological change, it is not clear whether they are 'wild' or 'domesticated'. It is probably more important to quantify how much they were used. Present-day stands of wild cereals can give prolific yields; one researcher was able to harvest a kilo in only an hour and estimated that a family could gather far more than a year's supply in only three weeks.[28] Contemporary use of morphologically unchanged cereals in village communities is documented in the Levant, as at Tell Abu Hureyra and Mureybit.[29] In the Upper Mesolithic levels large fish are found with vertebrae comparable in size to those of tunny weighing several hundred pounds. Obsidian from Melos, some 130 km south-east, is also found in quantity from this level, showing an undoubted sea-going capacity. The change is difficult to interpret. It might mark the rise of sea level to a point where regular marine exploitation was economic from that particular site, or the date of reintroduction of tunny to the area, or some need to exploit more resources or rather an increased scale of social movement and interaction. The stratified deposits in the cave are deep, and preliminary reports do not mention major hiatuses, apart from rock falls, so that it is possible that occupation of the site was both prolonged and more or less continuous. The site could be seen as a successful long-stay base, but the lack of knowledge of other sites in the area makes this hard to test.

That site is unlikely to be unique. Several coastal sites are known on Sicily of the early post-glacial period. Preliminary details from the investigation of the Grotta dell' Uzzo on Cape S. Vito are reminiscent of the Franchthi Cave. There is radiocarbon-dated occupation from the ninth millennium to beyond 6000 bc. Exploited resources include red deer and pig, roe deer, fox and other furred animals, birds, shellfish, crabs and fish of several species including tunny. Fishbones become more numerous in the Later Mesolithic levels. The Mesolithic deposits are some 3 m deep. Here again permanent rather than mobile settlement seems likely or possible from the rich concentration of resources.[30]

Inland at the Danube gorges the same possibilities of abundant resources and development of control over them exist. A large series of sites is known, due especially to rescue in the 1960s in advance of hydro-electric damming schemes. Most of the sites were near the pre-dam water level; one or two were on islands in the Danube (Fig. 2.5). Many of the sites had suffered damage, and their size is hard to reconstruct. Two levels at the rock shelter Cuina Turcului are separated by a sterile layer and dated to around 10000 and 8000 bc. Very varied resources were exploited with pig, beaver, ibex and chamois most numerous in the first level, and ibex, large bovines and chamois in the second. Red deer and polecat are added in the second. The incidence of ibex and chamois has led to suggestions of winter occupation, but this does not preclude use of the site at other seasons as well. Also represented in the remains are birds, tortoises, molluscs and fish. Fish bones are dominated by

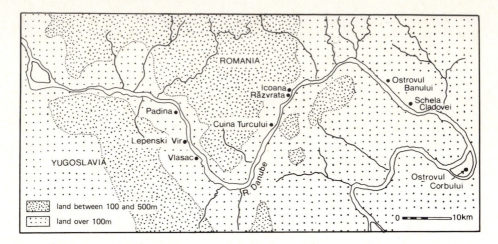

**2.5** Simplified location map of the principal sites of the Danube gorges. *After* Srejović and Letica

those of *Abramis brama*, but also include *Cyprinus carpio*, *Exon lucius*, and *Stizostedio lucioperca*. They are much more numerous in the upper level. At a later date in the area, in the seventh millennium bc (on the basis of radiocarbon dates for Icoana: chronological problems for the area recur in chapter 4), sites like Icoana, Răzvrata and the island site Ostrovul Banului show the continued importance of river fishing. Species include those mentioned above and *Acipense ruthenus*, *Huso huso*, *Lencius cephalus* and *Silurus glanis*. Molluscs and birds are found again. The animal remains have been most studied at Icoana, and split into three categories of exploitation: the non-regular hunting of nine different species of furred animals, as well as of chamois and cattle; the large-scale exploitation of red and roe deer; and the selective killing of pigs, including many juveniles under a year old. Pigs were killed all year round, and the deer bones, which were much broken up and therefore likely to underrepresent juvenile bones, do include calves of 6–11 and 11–14 months, indicating summer and winter occupation. Pollen in coprolites from Icoana includes large grass or cereal species over 35 nm, with an evident size increase through the stratified levels up to around 6000 bc. Perforated antler tools on this and other sites have been seen as hoes or digging sticks. The further possible extension of cereal ancestors into Europe is important, though there are no reports of direct recovery of plant remains in the excavations. Hearths, huts and burials (to which we will return) further give the impression of reduced mobility or permanence in an area beside a river full of fish which offered possibilities for cultivation on alluvial deposits, with game in the hinterland and in the wider basins of the gorges, amongst which the pigs could have been under some sort of control.[31]

How far this area is typical of eastern Europe is unclear. Sites are relatively sparse in lower-lying areas, though represented on coasts and in highland areas; there may be some increase in the number of open-air Later Mesolithic sites. Lack of research and post-depositional environmental changes have obscured much of this important area.[32]

The Italian peninsula offers a proportionately greater number and variety of early post-glacial sites. The diversity is significant. Faunal remains include prominently red deer, and pig, with cattle, ibex, roe deer and others represented. Shellfish, fish and birds have also been recorded. The location and size of some sites indicate an element at least of mobile settlement, since it is not likely that small, high-lying or fairly inaccessible sites such as Romagnano in the Adige valley, the Grotta di Peschio Ranaro in Latium or the Arma dello Stefanin in inland Liguria were permanent bases. There are also sites in areas where resources may have been more concentrated through the year, such as the Fucine Lake basin in the Abruzzi, but remains on sites here such as the Grotta Maritza and Grotta Punta are dominated by small animals, fish and birds. Such a lack of the range of larger game may suggest selective or seasonal exploitation. There are also a number of present-day coastal sites, such as Arene Candide in Liguria, Grotta Erica and Grotta Porta di Positano in Campania, and Grotta della Madonna, Praia a Mare in Calabria which may have sufficiently diverse resources around them for the need for mobile settlement to be much reduced. Herbivores and other animals are again represented, together with land snails and birds. Marine shellfish were collected in the upper levels of the Campanian sites, presumably as the shoreline advanced inland closer to them, and other sites of late eighth and earlier seventh millennium bc date show use of the same resource. There are few records of sea fish but the validity of this absence is doubtful. Pollen analysis has not been sufficiently practised for there to be evidence of human interference with vegetation, and details of the age, sex and morphology of the recorded fauna are scarce. A steady reduction during the late glacial period in the size of red deer points to the unhelpful nature of the morphological criterion for changes in man–animal relationships.[33] There seems to have been a similar range of possibilities in southern France and eastern Spain to that in Italy, but evidence for subsistence is less developed in these areas than for material culture. Inland and upland sites are well represented but the coastal aspect is largely unrepresented till around 6000 bc. Red deer, roe deer, pig, cattle, ibex and horse are variously represented (for the question of sheep see above p. 11), and rabbit is found amongst smaller game, together with a variety of land snails. Bones recorded at the rock shelter Baume de Montclus above the River Cèze in the Aude were largely of fish.[34]

In north-west Europe, there is a wide range of sites, though coastal sites are not found till around and after 6000 bc. Some of these sites, in England, Germany and Denmark are famous for their quantity of organic remains preserved in waterlogged conditions. The better quality of the evidence however deserves more critical interpretation than it has often received. The actual number of sites with good organic preservation is low, and of these some were excavated long ago (though to high standards for their day, such as Mullerup in Zealand) and others remain largely unpublished, such as Holme-gaard IV or Ulkestrup, also on Zealand. Probably none have been completely excavated.[35] Their chronological range is uneven, so that our first detailed example, Star Carr in Yorkshire, England, must alone represent the eighth millennium bc.[36] That it has been seen as a winter base camp, an all-year round industrial site and an all-year hunting stand indicates the difficulties of interpretation. Set in birch–pine woodland, the site lay on a gravel spit at the edge of a lake, on the western edge of the North Sea basin which has been envisaged at this date as very rich in resources of all kinds. An area of about 200 m² has been excavated, including a brushwood platform straddling the junction between the reedy edge of the lake and higher ground, but the edge of the settlement has only been reliably outlined on the western side. The site was evidently used over a considerable period of time, since remains were stratified over a height of 16–46 cm during which occupation antler points changed from being finely to coarsely barbed, and at least one lens of organic mud separates charcoal spreads, but the exact span has not been established. The season of occupation has been variously interpreted. The excavator relied on the presence of shed red deer and elk antler to establish definite times, in April and January respectively (on the assumption that shed antler is quickly eaten or otherwise destroyed in the wild unless collected by man, and that such collected antlers were not stored for later use) and on the presence of unshed, mature red deer and elk antler to lengthen the winter occupation from September to April. Unshed roe antler, on the animals from April to October, was supposed to come from those killed in early autumn. A much broader approach is necessary. Shed antler might be collected and stored for later use; roe antler on the site suggests summer as well as winter occupation, as do calf bones (all the more since much of the bone on the site had been broken for marrow, a situation in which young animals would be likely to be archaeologically underrepresented because of their more slender and more easily broken bones) and perhaps some of the smaller animals such as hedgehog and some of the migratory birds such as crane and stork. There is no evidence that occupation was continuous, or that the same season is represented in each putative reoccupation.

The range of tools on the site seems compatible with 'domestic' or base-camp activities, though the quantity of broken antler points has been seen as reflecting craft manufacture practised as an aid to alleviating boredom in waiting at a hunting stand. The further argument for this viewpoint that there is no functional separation of different activities, as reflected in the distribution of different tool types, is not conclusive in the light of observations among !Kung bushmen that it is the social context in which an activity is carried out, not the nature of the activity itself which determines where material remains are deposited. Star Carr raises the question of what constitutes a site – the immediate concentration of material remains or the rather wider use of a particular concentration of resources – since other sites around the lake are known.

The inhabitants of the site exploited a range of large herbivores – elk, aurochs, red deer, roe deer and pig – and smaller fur-bearing animals such as fox, marten and beaver, the latter of which can also be eaten. Estimates of relative numbers have been produced to show that red deer provided three-fifths of the meat at the site, but there is a danger that deer have been overcounted by using the antler as a criterion, and elk and aurochs could anyway provide far more meat per individual than red deer. Amongst the red deer the largest proportion is represented by adult males, which suggests that exploitation was selective and avoided endangering the breeding success of the population. The common assumption has been that such herbivores were hunted, either individually or in drives, and domesticated dog at the site (which may also have been eaten) supports this assumption, as do also animal bones from the site with claimed lesions from hunting wounds. These cases are supported in their turn by the late glacial elk skeleton from Poulton-le-Fylde, Lancashire with a barbed point in its lower leg, and the aurochs skeleton pollen-dated to the Pre-Boreal period from Vig on Zealand with flint microliths embedded in it, from more than one episode of wounding.[37] Other forms of relationship could be envisaged, involving human influence on deer movement and even loose herding, though specific evidence for these must be cited from a later period (see chapter 4). Many plants available at or near the site would have been nutritious, such as the yellow water lily (*Nuphar lutea*), common reed (*Phragmites communis*) and bog-bean (*Menyanthes trifoliata*) or fat hen (*Chenopodium album*) and nettle (*Urtica dioica*), but no proof is available from the excavation that they were so used. Many of these sorts of plants may have been processed and eaten in ways that would leave no trace of their use, for example through carbonisation. Fish are absent from the site, which may be due to inappropriate recovery techniques in excavation; a genuine absence of fish from inland waters early in the post-glacial period; differential decay of fish bone; cultural avoidance of fish; insufficient need to use all available resources; processing on a separate part of the site; or to seasonal factors. The range of possibilities illustrates the very real problems of interpreting sites of this kind and period.

Star Carr has often been connected with contemporary sites in adjacent uplands on the North York moors and further off in the Pennines. These sites, many of which lie over 300 m above sea level, are generally small and their flint assemblages have a preponderance of microliths amongst finished tool forms, though some areas have a considerable density of such sites. It is plausible therefore to regard them as summer hunting stands or camps. A model has then been reconstructed of mobile settlement for the region, with upland summer movement following deer herds and winter sojourn in the lowlands avoiding the worst of the weather and exploiting concentrations of game. Hunting in the summer in the uplands may however have been a minority occupation, perhaps as sport or status activity with low chances of success, since Star Carr indicates summer use of the lowlands, where the greatest variety of resources would remain concentrated. It is even possible to envisage a sufficient abundance for the need for mobile settlement again to be much reduced.

For sites in north-west Europe with a range of organic preservation in the seventh millennium bc one must turn to Zealand and north-west Germany

**2.6** (**a**) Birch-bark flooring from settlement area no. 8, and (**b**) hazelnut roasting hearth from settlement area no. 6, at Duvensee, northern Germany. Photo: Bokelmann

(Figs. 2.6 and 2.7).[38] Sites from contemporary coastal areas are missing, since the shorelines of the Ancylus Lake and early Litorina Sea, and of the North Sea, were below the present ones. The rather numerous sites of this period reflect inland settlement. The range of site locations is quite varied in the only slightly undulating landscape, but the majority have been recovered beside or near swamps, river courses and lakes. This is particularly striking in north-west Zealand where well-known sites with organic preservation such as Mullerup, Vinde–Helsinge, Øgaarde, Hesselbjergaard and Ulkestrup are but part of a large string of sites along the Halleby Aas watercourse, which stretches some 40 km from Tostrup to the coast, incorporating the Aamosen swamp (with open water at its centre) and the Skarridsø and Tissø lakes. Other well-known sites such as Holmegaard in central and Svaerdborg in southern Zealand are also beside lakes. Such locations can be best explained by considering the resources available around them. These sites were in ecotones, or the boundaries between different ecological zones so that within reach were both the fish, fowl, mammals and plants of wet ground, and the animals and plants of drier ground. The attractiveness of waterside grazing to large herbivores in the now increasingly closed woodland should be stressed and the larger the water system, the more grazing there was along its margins. Variations in precise location have been noted, as at Holmegaard where site v

2.7 Early excavations in progress (1917–18) at Svaerdborg, Zealand. Photo: National Museum, Copenhagen

is just outside the swampy margins while others lie on small islets or peninsulas. Sites like this have been found closely spaced as also at Svaerd-borg where sites I, II and III are only 300–400 m apart. Their size varies from the 140 by 110 m of Svaerdborg I to the 50 m² of Svaerdborg II, to the smaller areas still of some of the Holmegaard fishing sites or the elk kill and butchering site at Skottemarke. Duration varies too, from the single season of occupation claimed at Svaerdborg VI, to the more complex stratigraphy of Svaerdborg I. The renewal of a hearth up to five times within a possibly roofed structure at Duvensee in Holstein has also been used as an indicator, but like the rest of the evidence it is imprecise. The existence of well-built structures in the area can also be taken to support less rather than more mobile settlement but again it is unclear whether they were in use for a season or for longer. At Duvensee there were mat-like settings of birch and pine bark, in one case forming a 5 m square. Fires were lit on spreads of sand within this flooring. At Ulkestrup there were remains of two similar settings, the better-preserved having a floor of sheets of pine bark up to 2 m long and 0.5 m broad, and forming an area of 6.7 by 4.5 m. This in turn was paved with smaller pieces of elm, birch and pine bark and set with a single hearth. There were similar traces at Holmegaard IV. Whether or how these were roofed is unclear, though there is a consensus that they probably were. Concentrations of flint debris at Svaerdborg II and several other sites have been taken to represent similar structures. There is space at Svaerdborg I for many such structures. Certainly there was artefactual debris on the Duvensee floors, but dis-tinguishing between floor or hut areas and midden or working areas outside them is difficult. Evidence for seasonality is imprecise too. Fish bones (such as pike at Holmegaard, Hohen Viecheln and Svaerdborg, which is most easily caught when spawning in the late spring flood water, or sheat fish (*Silurus glanis*) at Holmegaard and Øgaarde which spawns near the surface when temperatures reach 18°C, and roe deer calves (at Svaerdborg and Hohen Viecheln) indicate summer occupation. Winter occupation has been less well defined. Holmegaard V is seen as a winter site from its location, and its lack of fishbone and barbed points compared with its neighbours. At Hohen Viecheln, there was shed and unshed red deer antler, and no shed roe antler, but the evidence is incomplete. There were only two fragments of elk antler and elk and aurochs skulls were not found, these larger animals perhaps having been butchered somewhere other than on the site (teeth and lower jaws are represented however). The decline of elk in the seventh millennium bc as its preferred habitat changed also meant a greater use of red deer antler for tools, which has also tended to destroy this potential source of evidence for seasonality. Hazel nuts, found on many sites, occasionally in quantity as at Duvensee and Ulkestrup, are conventionally seen as autumn indicators, but they can be stored for longer, making them imprecise as indicators.

As elsewhere, faunal remains generally show a wide range of herbivores and other animals being exploited, though proportions vary, affected in part by location and season no doubt, and also by off-site butchering and on-site bone loss through bone splintering, dog scavenging and decalcification.

Svaerdborg I with high proportions of roe and pig is a little unusual, but the wider local context is unclear; a wide range of species were recorded at Svaerdborg II but in insufficient quantities for relative proportions to have any validity. The available evidence suggests again a structured exploitation, as for example of adult red deer, though distinction between male and female was not possible with mandibles, and the possibility of a range of man–animal relationships exists here as in the English case already considered. Pike were taken in quantities as at Svaerdborg; almost half those recorded at Hohen Viecheln weighed 4 kg and over. Land and water birds are well represented. Plant use remains problematical. Hazel was by now abundant; surges in hazel values detected in pollen analysis in England, but not noted so far in Denmark, may reflect deliberate clearance to encourage its spread. It is difficult to know whether water plants are present on sites because of their use by man as well as their ecological situation. A large cache of yellow water-lily seeds beneath the archaeological layer at one of the Holmegaard sites is often cited as evidence of their use, but might be flotsam.[39]

There is one scrap of evidence for contemporary use of the Baltic and North Sea. There is a bone of grey seal (*Haliochoerus grypus*) from Svaerdborg. Whether from a sealskin or a carcase it does show inland settlements of the later seventh millennium bc in touch with the sea, either down the connecting Dana River to the Kattegat or more probably by this date to the closer Litorina Sea. Grey seal give birth ashore in winter.[40] This raises the possibility of seasonal movement, but it would also be surprising if coastal resources were not exploited all year round. Two possibilities can then be suggested: that the coast and inland were largely separate zones of exploitation with much reduced movement of settlement within each zone; or that they were related, with some degree of movement inland in summer when resources were more abundant in that zone.

Other areas of northern Europe may also have had sufficiently concentrated resources for permanent settlement to be considered from an early date. The Viste Cave in south-west and Tørkop in south-east Norway, occupied respectively from about 6000 bc and from the seventh millennium bc show such a range. Sites in the eastern Baltic area such as Antrea, Zvejnieki and Pulli and also Wis further north, have an exciting range of organic preservation.[41] Elk was an important resource in this area, but its solitary, shy nature and seasonal movement may have severely constrained the possibilities of stable settlement for the communities exploiting it.

## Society: new models

The evidence reviewed suggests that patterns of settlement were varied. Stability is likely in parts of the Mediterranean and possible in parts of northern Europe. The most important consideration to emerge from this survey is the freedom to abandon environment and technology as prime determinants of all aspects of society and to consider wider approaches to the nature of society. For if human communities were to be seen as essentially

parasitic in their subsistence and unable despite careful adaptation to produce any surplus, as necessarily mobile in response to the round of seasonal
resource fluctuation, as consequently dispersed and thinly populated and
unable to maintain any aggregations in their numbers for any length of time
for fear of threatening the available food supply, then various consequences
might follow for their social relations, the likelihood of which is reinforced by
observation of recent mobile hunter-gatherers. The basic social unit in these
cases is the family, which is part of a genetically necessary breeding network,
which if closed may have a minimum requirement of about 400 members and
can be called a band. Families, kin groups and bands also take part in various
alliances, designed to spread a web of mutual obligation and help. It is
generally believed that such societies lack private ownership of resources and
in some cases lack claims to particular territory, leadership or other forms of
internal differentiation, and the ability to solve internal disputes and conflicts other than by the parties splitting up. Note that not all these observed
features of recent mobile hunter-gatherers need follow from their mode of
life; property, territory, leadership and dispute solving could all be compatible to some extent with the constraints of mobility. Moreover, if a much
more sedentary way of life can be envisaged, with some degree of control over
resources, surplus food supply and food storage, alternative possibilities for
society emerge. It must also be recognised that such features may be
themselves the products of particular social relations.

In either case, rather different societies to those of recent mobile hunter-
gatherers can be envisaged, in which leadership and other kinds of differentiation, and property and resource ownership, would be more strongly developed. Interpretation of the early post-glacial period is further complicated by
the difficulty of choosing a 'social baseline' for the period. Late glacial
communities with their clearly defined major resources could have had
dominant groups or individuals within them. On the other hand the bow has
been seen as favouring the establishment of smaller self-sufficient social
units. Resource abundance and diversity in the early post-glacial period may
have made the achievement of social pre-eminence or dominance difficult.
The starting point must therefore considerably affect the nature and development of social relations in the early post-glacial period.[42]

When predictions of this kind come to be matched with observations, there
are a number of features which can be considered, some of which support in
my opinion the likelihood of sedentary settlement and social differentiation
in at least parts of Europe. Although social cohesion is necessary in all social
formations, indicators of an increased sense of group identity are particularly
interesting clues in this respect. Ritual treatment of animal remains could be
one way in which hunters or herders expressed their own social cohesion and
claims to resources. Such behaviour goes back to the late glacial period and
the ritual drowning of reindeer carcases at such sites as Meiendorf. Red deer
masks formed of shaped skulls and antlers, as found at Star Carr and Hohen
Viecheln, and the deliberate re-shooting of elk carcases, as seen in the careful
study of lesions on elk bones from Skottemarke on Lolland and Favrbo in

Zealand can be seen as in the same tradition. The alternative argument that the Star Carr frontlets were practical hunting aids does not take sufficient account of the extent to which they were altered, especially by laborious attenuation of the beam of the selected mature examples. Had light masks been required, the skulls of younger stags could easily have been selected. The interpretive danger in these cases is to press examples of spiritual needs or beliefs into a specific social role. The same may be observed of art, in the form of decorated tools and ornaments in northern Europe and in the fixed form of rock-shelter paintings and engravings in eastern and northern Spain some of which probably belong to this period. But it is tempting all the same to assume that such art has some social role or meaning to the extent of reflecting an increased sense of awareness of self and group or in the case of fixed art of territory. It is difficult to estimate how widespread such practices were. Engravings in central French rock shelters in the Tardenois area and decorated bone tools in the Danube gorges widen the distribution, making it more likely that the surviving examples are accidentally preserved by conditions of geology and organic preservation.[43]

Artefact types have regularly been treated as guides to group boundaries. It is fairly clear that at this period there were no sharply defined boundaries between recurrent assemblages of artefacts or archaeological cultures. The regional approach to such groupings has already been outlined. Treatment of the late glacial period in southern Scandinavia has referred to a basic widely spread technocomplex of shared tool types and technology.[44] There is debate in the early post-glacial period whether material culture in Scania is Maglemosian in the same sense as in Zealand and Jutland. Differences between coastal and inland areas in southern France are usually based on a much more restricted range of artefact types, principally microliths. Artefactual differentiation in Italy has been seen as related to different functions and activities. Gradual change between regions is significant, for it suggests that the basic range of material culture was not of prime importance in expressing group identity. It is possible that had a wider range of artefact types survived, this picture would change, though styles of barbed point in northern Europe for example are widespread like other non-perishable items. Attention has therefore usually been given to individual artefact types which do change more markedly from region to region, especially the points. In the late glacial period 'social territories' have been defined on the north European plain and in southern Scandinavia on the basis of differences in tanged point manufacture, and much regional differentiation has been attempted on the basis of microlith styles in the early post-glacial period. This approach cannot easily be dismissed. Ethnographers have observed that most of the cultural matter that is at any one time associated with a human population is not constrained by the existence of ethnic or group boundaries, and that particular items may be selected for significant roles in relation to that boundary.[45] The problem for the archaeologist is of knowing which items are significant. It may be questioned how microliths played such a role. Alternative types were in contemporary use, and fashion may have played a part in their changing distributions. Many differences evident to the typologist, and no doubt deliberately created by their makers, would have been obscured when microliths were hafted, bound with fibre and mounted with resin.[46] If however microlith styles were actively used in the definition of group identity and territory, their abundance would certainly have made them efficient in this role. Fluctuation in style from area to area could thus have largely local significance; taxonomically archaic types could be reused at will – to the confusion of the archaeological typologist – as long as the essential message of difference was clearly conveyed and received. The scale of areas with similar projectile points seems much reduced in the early post-glacial period compared with the late glacial period, and smaller territories of this kind are compatible with greater group definition, high population, and less open breeding networks. Long-distance movement of raw materials such as obsidian and flint can also be considered. Two striking examples are the transport of Melian obsidian to the Franchthi Cave from the later eighth millennium bc, and the dispersal of chocolate-coloured flint from restricted sources in central Poland over parts of the country. Both involved however rather small quantities of material. Such movements can be interpreted as the result of exchanges between separate people. There is just sufficient data in the chocolate flint case to suggest a core area of greatest use, with some dispersal beyond this. This might be compatible with 'down-the-line' exchanges, of short range at each transaction.[47] It would then be legitimate to seek a social context for such exchanges, which might also be seen as part of the process of group definition. The practice is limited however on the available evidence for the early post-glacial period. In the case of chocolate flint, dispersal is also reduced in this period compared with earlier and later periods. There is also the possibility with this scale of movement that it reflects not exchange but deliberate and independent procurement by outsiders.

Another possible indicator of group identity is burials, though some of the general difficulties of interpretation have been outlined in chapter 1. Formal human burial can be traced far back into the Palaeolithic period, but with one or two notable exceptions most early burials are not found together in any quantity. One or two per site are typical. This pattern continues in the early post-glacial period. There are a number of individual burials from southern and eastern France for example, and others from Italy. Examples are a woman aged about 50 buried on her back with red ochre under her skull, under a stone cairn at the Vatte di Zambano rock shelter in the Adige valley around 6000 bc, and an adult man in the Grotta Maritza. Such burials are not known everywhere. They are lacking in the British Isles, and in southern Scandinavia only stray human remains have so far been found on settlements, such as Mullerup, Svaerdborg I, Øgaarde and Vinde–Helsinge, just as stray remains have been found in several French sites. It is possible that excavation particularly of open settlements as opposed to caves or shelters has been too limited, as the striking later example of Vedbaek in Zealand demonstrates, as discussed in chapter 4.

The marked variation on this general pattern is a series of sites with more numerous burials, found in the Mediterranean and eastern Europe. Examples include the Franchthi Cave; Icoana and Schela Cladovei in the Danube gorges; the Grotta dell'Uzzo, Sicily; and Arene Candide in Liguria. At the latter both adults and children were buried with ornaments of animal teeth and sea shells, and pebbles covered with red ochre, from the late glacial period onwards. In the Grotta dell'Uzzo eight burials also with simple grave goods have been found, and in the Franchthi Cave there are preliminary reports of several skeletons, one of which at least was in an undisturbed grave with goods and red ochre. It is unclear how many of these burials were deposited at the same time, but the greater regularity of use of the sites for burial is striking. In the case of 20 burials of both adults and children at Schela Cladovei there is a little more information. The burials were arranged, some in rectangular graves, with their feet towards a hearth. Two graves contained red ochre and some had grave goods such as one with five bone points. There was evidently some sequence since some of the earlier burials were disturbed by later additions. The chronology of the sites is also open to question but these burials precede several alterations of the hearth and an overlying layer with Criş material culture, and have been assigned to the seventh millennium bc. Padina may offer a similar case in the same area. A possible example from further north is at Ofnet, in Bavaria, where almost 30 skulls were found together in two pits apparently dug from a thin Early Mesolithic level in a stratified cave deposit but the date and even the attribution to the period have been strongly doubted.[48]

It is tempting to link these more collective burials or longer-used burial sites with an increased sense of territoriality and group identity, in which the greater number of burials reflects not only longer stays at particular bases but perhaps also an enhanced social role for burials which through careful disposal of the dead and regard for ancestors supported claims to territory and resources. This much is speculation, and can be disputed on theoretical grounds as exaggeratedly functionalist, but it is noticeable that the examples of this change in burial practice have been cited from those parts of Europe where there were the greatest indications of permanent settlement, in the Mediterranean and one area of eastern Europe. It is plausible though far from certain that the two suggested developments are related.

Is it possible to seek further signs of development, particularly of internal social differentiation? There are no clear indications from the burials cited of particular age or sex groups being afforded more elaborate treatment than any others. It is possible that selection itself for formal burial was a sign of differentiation, given the low numbers recorded against the likely original population, and if social relations were expressed through kinship, the appearance of more numerous burials could reflect an increased dominance or importance of particular kin groups as well as the suggested greater sense of group identity. The presence amongst the burials of young women and children can be used to support the attainment of social position by birth rather than by individual achievement in life. It is difficult however to take this last stage of the argument much further (a problem that recurs in later chapters) since collective burial may represent the community as a whole rather than specific groups or families within it. Many other social possibilities remain in the realm of speculation. It is important though to shift from viewing environment and technology as prime determinants to seeing them as constraints, for this radically widens relevant social possibilities. From this perspective there are many plausible assumptions to be seriously considered about the social context of production in the early post-glacial period, not just involving enforced cooperation at a barely achieved subsistence level, but also surplus and storage, territoriality, private property, and resource ownership with an ethic of acquisition rather than of sharing. Such a distinction has been made between the herding and hunting modes of production, which emphasises again the importance of social relations over and above techniques of subsistence.[49]

These considerations will constantly recur as the shift to new resources which begins about 6000 bc is discussed in the following chapters. A final specific possibility is differentiation between sites. Large long-stay bases have generally been considered as a function of ecological abundance, but it may equally with this different perspective be profitable to consider them as socially pre-eminent sites, of uneven social access, whose occupants were able not only to control or manipulate resources roundabout but to exploit them socially for the strengthening of alliances and obligations. Such a context could make sense of features such as the apparent over-hunting of aurochs seen in the unusually well-preserved and numerous calf bones at Ulkestrup on Zealand; behaviour which would not fit the model of restrained, scheduled resource exploitation.[50] What is lacking in such possibilities is clear definition of change, both within these two millennia and compared to the late glacial period. If the period is a continuation – socially speaking – from the previous one, such social features could be seen as general conditions of this kind of way of life. If they are new developments however explanation of the change is called for. As throughout the book, this kind of historical explanation will be seen to be very difficult to sustain, once factors such as environment, technology or population are rejected as external prime movers of change, and this problem is returned to throughout the book.

# CHAPTER 3

# THE ESTABLISHMENT OF AGRICULTURAL COMMUNITIES

## 3.1 First farmers in south-east Europe, 6000–4000 bc

*Environment*

The trend towards climatic amelioration evident in the early post-glacial period is generally considered to have continued in this period, and the Atlantic period, beginning in the mid sixth millennium bc, is often seen as warmer and wetter than the preceding period; the more detailed suggestion is also made that winters were warmer and summers cooler and wetter. Most of these generalisations are based on palaeobotanical evidence from central or north-west Europe, and there is little specific evidence from within our area (Fig. 3.1). Thus changes in soil composition at the stratified settlement of Anza in Yugoslav Macedonia were explained climatically by reference to synthesis of palaeobotanical data from much further north. On the northern boundary of our area, on the Great Hungarian plain, such comparisons are more valid. Limited pollen analysis is compatible with the suggested trend, as well as revealing several oscillations, as also suggested by Frenzel. Further south in Greece there seems to be no evidence for major climatic fluctuation over the entire Holocene until late antiquity, and one may envisage a prevalent Mediterranean climate as today.

It is likely that forest development reached its climax over most of the area in this period, though pollen analysis is again sparse. A shift in the lower Danube area from Late Boreal forest steppe to Atlantic forest has been cited, and forest was already well established in Greece by the beginning of this period. Pollen analysis from Lake Balaton, though not closely dated, shows a heavy tree cover; one exception to the general pattern, apart from local variations everywhere, may have been the Great Hungarian plain, where pollen analysis suggests a mosaic of floodplain, marsh forest and forest steppe vegetation, the latter supported also by finds of wild ass and bustard from contemporary settlements.[1]

Sea level continued to rise, as discussed in the previous chapter, and is witnessed by the submergence of late fifth millennium bc deposits on the Cycladic island of Saliagos at 6 m below present sea level. A post-glacial transgression of the Black Sea into the lower Danube area which reached 5 m above present sea level has been proposed for an uncertain date before the fourth millennium bc, on the basis of terrace formations and a lack of Early Neolithic settlement in the area. There is however little accompanying

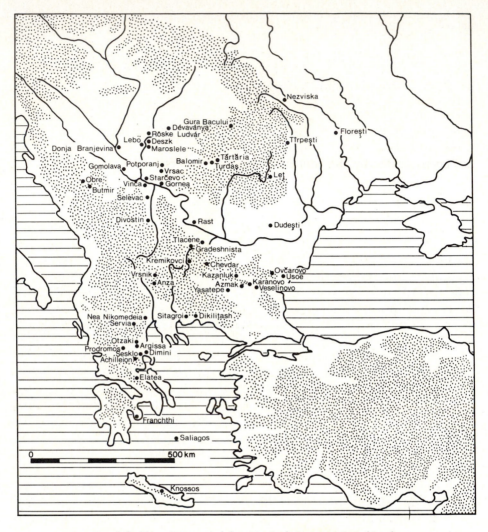

**3.1** Simplified location map of the principal sites mentioned in chapter 3.1

sedimentological data and the suggested episode seems ill at ease with the Mediterranean evidence.[2]

In this setting, soil resources were to be of ever greater importance in this period. At the risk of overgeneralisation, it is likely that soils were at the peak of their post-glacial fertility and that a wide range of easily workable soils was available, as is discussed in more detail later. There has been considerable change in the area however since the period in question, and the reconstruction of contemporary soil state in an area where buried soils are generally lacking is obviously difficult. Research has made clear the extent of post-Neolithic deposition, as in Greece and Bulgaria but specific problems remain, as at the Greek Macedonian site of Nea Nikomedeia or concerning the chernozems of the Great Hungarian plain.[3]

## The nature of the evidence

Research in parts of our area such as Romania is over 150 years old. More systematic excavation and a clear recognition of the Neolithic period generally dates to the early part of this century, as in Romania or the Aegean. An example is Tsountas' work at Dimini and Sesklo in Thessaly. The tradition of research is thus well established, but its maintenance has been uneven, steady in Greece, but erratic in areas like Bosnia after very early investigations at Butmir. Since the Second World War a further imbalance has been created by the concentration of extensive settlement excavations in Bulgaria and Romania especially. Not only is the geographical coverage of the period thus uneven, but the quality of excavation has varied enormously; few investigations can match the range of techniques applied by international teams at Anza, Selevac, or Gomolava in Yugoslavia or Achilleion in Thessaly.[4] There remains plenty of scope for further improvement, since in the range of past excavations one notes the limited extent of excavations;[5] the lack of detailed recording of the contexts of artefacts rather than their typological characteristics; the poor recovery of bone and plant remains;[6] and the slow rate of publication.[7] There is also a tendency to use individual sites, such as Karanovo in central Bulgaria and Vinča in Yugoslavia near Belgrade, as representative of the development of whole areas.[8] In addition, many excavations have been opportunistic, as of the river-damaged sites of Argissa in Thessaly and Gomolava in Srem, and rather few have been selected after systematic survey of a given area.[9] While surveys are becoming more common, as in Thessaly, the Sava valley or the Great Hungarian plain, previous site selection has tended to favour the most obvious or well-known sites in a landscape.[10]

## Chronology

Compared to the early post-glacial period, the greater abundance of identified settlements, the generally greater depth of stratified deposits and the greater frequency of excavation, have made the establishment of relative chronology region by region easier (Fig. 3.2). Many problems remain. It cannot be assumed that the sequence at one site will be repeated endlessly at others; indeed the keynote of the comparatively well-researched area of Greece with many stratigraphies is regional variation from an early stage.[11] The lack of similar stratigraphies further north, in parts of Yugoslavia, Romania and Hungary, has led to the formation of typological rather than stratigraphical sequences, with more than a casual reference to southern sequences.[12] The identification of stratigraphic hiatus is hard to establish except where there is a clear humus level; thus a gap is suggested between levels 2 and 3 at Karanovo, but between 1 and 2 the gap may have been very short or non-existent. In limited excavations it is dangerous to assume that such breaks were ubiquitous on the site, as the differences within the investigated parts of Anza show. Thus square II at the site contains only periods Ib, III and IV. The

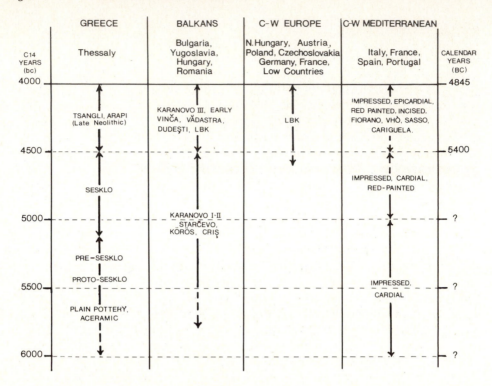

| | GREECE | BALKANS | C-W EUROPE | C-W MEDITERRANEAN | |
|---|---|---|---|---|---|
| C14 YEARS (bc) | Thessaly | Bulgaria, Yugoslavia, Hungary, Romania | N.Hungary, Austria, Poland, Czechoslovakia Germany, France, Low Countries | Italy, France, Spain, Portugal | CALENDAR YEARS (BC) |
| 4000 | | | | | 4845 |
| | TSANGLI, ARAPI (Late Neolithic) | KARANOVO III, EARLY VINČA, VĂDASTRA, DUDEŞTI, LBK | LBK | IMPRESSED, EPICARDIAL, RED PAINTED, INCISED, FIORANO, VHÒ, SASSO, CARIGUELA. | |
| 4500 | SESKLO | | | IMPRESSED, CARDIAL, RED-PAINTED | 5400 |
| 5000 | | KARANOVO I-II STARČEVO, KÖRÖS, CRIŞ | | | ? |
| | PRE-SESKLO | | | | |
| | PROTO-SESKLO | | | IMPRESSED, | |
| 5500 | | | | CARDIAL | ? |
| | PLAIN POTTERY, ACERAMIC | | | | |
| 6000 | | | | | ? |

**3.2** Simplified outline chronology of the main areas discussed in chapter 3, c. 6000–4000 bc

situation at Karanovo is based on excavation of about 1700 m², but the unit is treated in the preliminary reports as uniform.[13]

The widespread application of radiocarbon dating promises to be the best solution to many of these problems. As well as a careful choice of samples, large series of dates are needed from individual sites. So far these are available only from several sites in Greece, chiefly the Franchthi Cave, Sesklo, Argissa, Achilleion, Elatea, Sitagroi, Servia and Nea Nikomedeia; three sites in Bulgaria, Azmak, Karanovo and Chevdar; three in Yugoslavia, Anza, Obre II and Selevac (with two dates so far only); and one site in Hungary, Deszk–Olajkút – hardly an impressive tally.[14] Individual dates are more common.

Despite these drawbacks the discussion that follows makes the working assumption that a useful subdivision of the period can be made at around 4500 bc, on the combined basis of stratigraphic evidence and radiocarbon dates.

*Material sequences, 6000–4500 bc*

The only properly investigated site in Greece with stratigraphic continuity between the Mesolithic and Neolithic periods is the Franchthi Cave in the Argolid (Fig. 3.3).[15] As we have seen in the previous chapter, excavation

**3.3** The present setting of the Franchthi Cave, southern Greece. Photo: Jacobsen

within and just outside the cave has been necessarily limited; a number of cuttings has also been made on the shore below the entrance to the cave, to the extent of about half the previous area opened. The beginning of the Neolithic period is defined artefactually by the addition of polished stone axes, stone grinders and a variety of bone awls and shell and stone beads to assemblages in which blade tools continue uninterrupted, and by the appearance of simple monochrome pottery, in the form of globular bowls and footed cups. It is possible that there was an 'aceramic' phase of brief duration but the preliminary reports are contradictory. The difficulty was compounded by a probable stratigraphic hiatus in cuttings G and H, and the necessity of abandoning cutting A because of the danger of rockfall. Cutting F provided a continuous stratigraphic sequence with little or no pottery in the earliest Neolithic level. The settlement was apparently extended to the shore from the beginning of the Neolithic, and contains the earliest pottery on the site. These changes are radiocarbon dated to around 6000 bc, though uncertainty remains about their exact synchroneity.

At a small number of other sites, mainly in Thessaly but including also Knossos on Crete, Early Neolithic levels but without pottery have been stratified beneath levels with pottery, and such preceramic sites are candidates for being amongst the earliest Neolithic sites in Greece, a possibility reinforced by the dates of around 6000 bc from Knossos and Argissa and the date only a little later from the Sesklo acropolis though accompanied by two rather later ones.[16] There is direct stratigraphic continuity between these levels and overlying ceramic levels at several sites such as Argissa, Sesklo, Knossos and Soufli Magoula. Gediki however has an intervening sand layer. Excavation has necessarily been limited. The focus of excavation at Argissa for example was an area of only 11 by 6 m, though traces of preceramic levels were claimed to be visible, but without excavation, at the base of the mound over a distance of 85 m, having been made available by river destruction. Traces at Sesklo were observed over an interval of 125 m. These levels do not appear to be the result of transient occupation. At Argissa they are 30–45 cm or thicker, and contain various pits and shallow oval scoops cut in the subsoil, and at Sesklo similar scoops and the possible foundation of a wall, to which we will return later. Such levels are in fact not aceramic, since fired clay figurines were recovered at Sesklo and Knossos as well as small clay studs at Sesklo. It is also possible that pottery was part of the assemblages. Sherds were recorded in the lowest levels at Argissa for example, though their numbers declined markedly to only a handful. The excavator considered these to be intrusive, via later postholes. Achilleion too on preliminary observation was thought to contain preceramic levels, which further excavation disproved. The stone assemblages are sparse. Flint, chert and obsidian probably from Melos were used for blade tools. At Argissa chert and especially obsidian were used for small blades and segments, scrapers, borers and simple trapezes on broad blades. (It is noticeable that there are very few cores.) There were no heavy stone tools, except one granite object, possibly the butt of a polished axe. Stone tools are also found.[17] While these assemblages are undoubtedly early in the Greek Neolithic sequence, it remains to be established whether they are earlier than others with ceramics and whether they really have an independent status, a point to which we shall return in discussing subsistence.

At other sites in Greece and in the subsequent levels of those already mentioned, greatest attention amongst the assemblages conventionally is given to pottery. The classic sequence is that from Sesklo and other sites in Thessaly, partly known from early excavations and subsequent analysis and refined and expanded by subsequent excavations (Fig. 3.4).[18] At sites like Argissa and Sesklo an early horizon of plain pottery is recognised, consisting of hemispherical and globular bowls and jars, with round or flat bases, sometimes with ring bases, and simple rims and lugs. The succeeding 'Proto-Sesklo' phase includes the first painted pottery, a variety of red motifs such as zig-zags, chevrons, triangles, and lozenges being painted directly on to the pottery or on to a covering slip. Pot shapes were now more varied. In the pre-Sesklo phase such painted pottery became much less common and monochrome pots again became prevalent with some also decorated with impressions. In the Sesklo phase there was a great increase in red-on-white painted pottery of varied designs on a wider range of pot shapes. Monochrome pot continued and later innovations included grey-on-grey ware, white-on-dark painted ware and scraped ware in which a covering red slip is scraped to reveal an underlying white slip. The most recent example of this sequence, and it is claimed the fullest, comes from the south Thessalian site of

**3.4** Painted red-on-white wares of the sixth and fifth millennia in Thessaly and central Greece. 1–2 early painted style from Thessaly; 3 solid style from Tzani Magoula; 4–5 Sesklo phase, Thessaly; 6 Chaeronea. *After* Theocharis

Achilleion, near Farsala, with the added advantage of a long series of radiocarbon dates.[19] The series begins with an early ceramic level in the mid sixth millennium bc. The pre-Sesklo level is classed as Middle Neolithic in contrast to normal usage and has no reduction in painted pottery, and the Sesklo phase begins in the late sixth millennium bc, continuing into the earlier fifth. The latest part of the phase is not dated at Achilleion; at Sesklo itself this appears to lie in the mid fifth millennium bc.

It is possible that the early monochrome ceramic phase was widespread, as far as southern Greece, and genuinely independent, but it may not have covered the whole of the country, for in Macedonia at sites like Nea Nikomedeia and Servia a monochrome phase is not apparent.[20] Small quantities of red-on-white ware were found at both sites, and a very small amount of white-on-red at Nea Nikomedeia. It is possible that these sites are equivalent to the proto-Sesklo phase of Thessaly. Radiocarbon dates at Servia start only in the very early fifth millennium bc for Sesklo-like ceramics, but at Nea Nikomedeia there are two of the mid sixth millennium bc, and even one of the late seventh. This last may be anomalous, since any good series of dates as from Achilleion seemingly inevitably contains one or two out of sequence. More dates clearly are needed but the distinct possibility of early northern variation must be admitted. Sites in western Thessaly too such as Prodromos with impressed pottery as well as monochrome and painted might also represent early variation. After the putative early monochrome phase variation is the keynote everywhere. One example already noted above is in the pre-Sesklo phase at Achilleion compared with Sesklo itself. Another is the pre-Sesklo phase at Otzaki, with a sequence of monochrome and variegated plain wares, followed by first nail-impressed then jabbed-impressed wares.[21] Further differentiation is evident further south in Greece in both the Early and Middle Neolithic in for example the early 'rainbow' wares of Corinth or the Middle Neolithic dark-on-light painted lustrous 'Urfirnis' pottery. It is interesting however that the transition to the Middle Neolithic phase of more elaborate painted pottery seems to be similarly dated in the Peloponnese as in Thessaly, on the basis of radiocarbon dates from the Franchthi Cave. The likely pattern of shortlived early uniformity followed by considerable region-alised variation in this relatively well-researched area is important, for it seems to emphasise the difficulties facing chronological schemes in areas to the north where there is greater reliance on typology alone.

Other items of material culture are regularly scarcer than pottery, especially in the earlier phases. Continuity in blade industries with preceramic assemblages is likely at both Argissa and Sesklo. The Franchthi situation has been noted, and Nea Nikomedeia too has a flint and blade industry, which includes one microlithic triangle and two trapeziform blade segments. The slightly later development of these assemblages has scarcely been commented on except for a trend to larger and more uniform tools, and an increasing

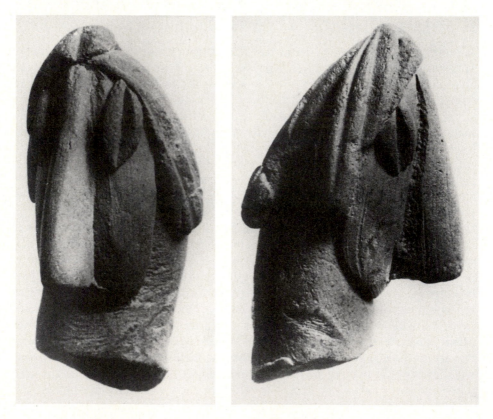

3.5 Head of a clay figurine from Sesklo, fifth millennium bc. Height 3 cm. *After* Theocharis

use of obsidian. Polished stone tools were few at the beginning, and the axe-adzes and chisels at Nea Nikomedeia for example were markedly small like those from most sites. Miniature stone axes and clay counterparts are also found, as at Achilleion. Greater quantities of heavy stone tools are recorded in fifth millennium sites such as Agia Sofia near Larisa.[22] Stone was also used for vessels, such as the greenstone ring-based dish in Achilleion phase ia, for stone studs or plugs, as at Nea Nikomedeia along with nail-like objects, and occasionally for decorated seals or stamps. These were more common in clay, at Nea Nikomedeia for example each with a different geometric pattern. Clay was also the medium for a very varied range of anthropomorphic figurines mostly of female figures, and also of animal figurines (Fig. 3.5). The female figurines are generally rather small, and consist of standing, squatting or sitting figures, with arms folded, on hips or outstretched, and with rather bland facial features but exaggerated lower limbs and sexual parts. Some are decorated with incised lines or painted lines. In the Sesklo phase, new elements such as eyes in the form of grains of corn, details of hair and face, and more painted decoration come in. A recent example of this increased elaboration is the lozenge-shaped face mask, about 4 cm long, which was attachable to a small clay pillar, from phase iiib at Achilleion (Fig. 3.6). Other clay objects include miniature tables or altars and house or shrine models (Fig. 3.7).[23]

As in Greece, so too to the north most sites dealt with in this chapter have no stratigraphic continuity with earlier sites. There is one group of sites however in the Danube gorges between Yugoslavia and Romania which

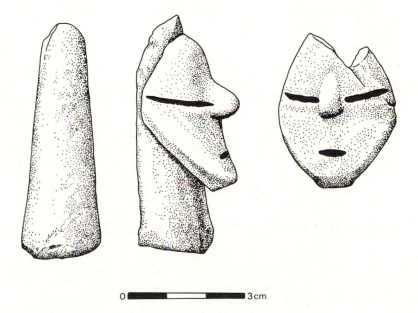

0 ▬▬▬▭▬▬▬ 3cm

**3.6** Clay face mask and pillar from a Sesklo phase level (iiib) at Achilleion, Thessaly, fifth millennium bc. *After* Gimbutas

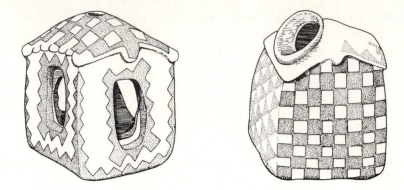

**3.7** Red-painted clay models of buildings from (left) Crannon and (right) Myrrini, Karditsa, Thessaly, sixth and fifth millennia bc. Height of both approximately 9 cm. *After* Theocharis

deserves attention, like the Franchthi Cave, for the superimposition of Mesolithic and Neolithic levels. Discussion of sites like Lepenski Vir, Padina and Vlasac is reserved for the next chapter since their stratigraphically pre-Starčevo–Criş levels are not clearly earlier than the Starčevo–Criş complex as a whole in the region. But as we have seen in the previous chapter, sites with probably seventh or very early sixth millennium bc levels such as Schela Cladovei or Ostrovul Banului have overlying levels with Criş material including pottery. Details on this material however are sparse, the absolute dates for these levels are not established, and there is anyway not the same kind of stratigraphic continuity as seen as the Franchthi Cave. Fuller investigations of sites of this kind would nonetheless contribute considerably to our understanding of material sequences.

As again in Greece the greatest attention in establishing material sequences in the Balkans has been paid to pottery, and particularly to the variation in decoration. Forms consist for the most part of hemispherical and globular bowls, pedestalled bowls, and necked jars. Three different sorts of ceramic tradition can be considered in the large area from northern Macedonia and southern Bulgaria to the Great Hungarian plain and northern Romania. First, there is a limited number of sites whose pottery is considered to have close connections with the early painted wares of Greece. In northern Macedonia the partially sampled site of Anza in the Ovce Polje basin has a long ceramic sequence, supported by numerous radiocarbon dates.[24] Its first phase, ia, in the later sixth millennium bc, includes fine wares with designs such as triangles, net patterns and curved lines painted in white-on-red, which are considered to be closely comparable with Nea Nikomedeia and equivalent to the Proto-Sesklo phase; phase ib is equated with the Sesklo phase, though it includes painting by white-on-red and other dark colours rather than Sesklo red-on-white, and specific motifs differ too. There are unpublished other sites to the north in the upper Morava valley with similar early pottery. Another example is the site of Gura Baciului in Transylvania with white-on-red painted and monochrome pottery in its earliest level, and other sites may be found scattered further north such as Donja Branjevina in southern Pannonia.[25] It remains to be established however to what extent these sites form a coherent group, and more importantly how close the similarities to Greek pottery are. It may be profitable to consider them as individual variants, or as variants on the next ceramic group to be considered, known after level 1 at the site of Karanovo in central-southern Bulgaria. A distinctive fine ware form here is the pedestalled bowl, and the most distinctive decoration consists of white-on-red paint in angular bands, triangles and spirals; incised and plastic decoration is also found (Fig. 3.8). Radiocarbon dates for the Karanovo 1 level at Azmak near Stara Zagora span the later sixth and earlier fifth millennium bc; no dates are available from the eponymous site itself from this level. Any direct derivation from the Proto- or Pre-Sesklo phases would be premature at this stage in view of the lack of dated sites. The exact extent of Karanovo 1 assemblages is unclear, though it appears to be largely restricted to central-southern Bulgaria. In western Bulgaria for example the site of Kremikovci has black-on-red as well as white-on-red painted pottery. In this area Karanovo 1 levels are succeeded more or less without a break at several sites by Karanovo 11 levels, dated by three samples from the eponymous site to the earlier to mid fifth millennium bc, whose pottery includes not yet more elaborately painted forms – as in the Greek sequence – but less painted decoration, replaced by incision and channelling. Large, open-footed bowls are a notable new form. The extent of these assemblages appears similar to the preceding.[26]

To the north lay the third ceramic tradition to be considered, the Starčevo–Körös–Criş complex, its regional names derived respectively from the site near Belgrade and river names in Hungary and Romania. Fine painted ware is

0 ▬▬▬▬ 5 cm

**3.8** Painted white-on-red fine wares from Chevdar, levels III and IV, central Bulgaria, sixth and fifth millennia bc. *After* Georgiev

much less common in this complex, being rare for example in the Körös group of south-east Hungary. Black-on-red painting is prevalent, in geometric and curvilinear patterns. Incised and roughened surface or 'barbotine' decoration is also found. Wide geographical uniformity has been claimed but variation seems a more likely keynote, as at Kremikovci, Anza in Macedonia and so on; its extent remains to be established. At stratified sites it is clear that styles changed through time, as at Anza, Tlacene or Gradeshnita in north-west Bulgaria, but uniform changes are not apparent. Sites further north with shallower stratigraphies have presented more problems.[27] Several schemes have been proposed for the internal chronology of the Starčevo culture, based essentially on the differing contents of closed pits at the eponymous site, and supported only partially by vertical and horizontal stratigraphy.[28] One scheme proposes an evolution from dominant coarse ware, to painted ware including white painting, to the decline of white painting, and finally an increase in painted pottery and roughened decoration. A similarly based scheme has been proposed for the Körös culture, based on the proportion of barbotine decoration, starting with none and ending with a lot.[29] The validity of these schemes in individual localities, let alone wider regions remains to be established. At any rate Hungarian archaeologists do not accept the implications of the Milojčić chronology that the Körös culture was a late development. Absolute chronology is not well established but available radiocarbon dates suggest that the Starčevo–Körös–Criş complex was in existence by the later sixth millennium bc. Anza II with Starčevo ceramics is thus dated by several samples, which match more isolated dates further north from sites such as Divostin and from Körös sites. It remains possible that Anza I with its more southerly connections was in fact contemporary with an already-established Starčevo tradition to its north, and that the change is one of cultural boundaries, rather than of innovation. This brief discussion has sought to establish the same sort of differentiation in the Balkans as seen in Greece, though it is poorly known. Differing rates of change, as in central-southern Bulgaria, should also be stressed.

Other material culture must not be overlooked, though its value as a chronological indicator is not yet established. Blade industries of flint chert and obsidian were prevalent. Obsidian, probably from a north Hungarian source occurs in quantity at relatively close sites like Gura Baciului but more sparingly further off. There is a recurrent microlithic element in such sites within the Criş culture which is suspected, without further proof, to have some connection with Mesolithic traditions (themselves very poorly known, as we saw in the last chapter). Stone axes were small and relatively scarce throughout the area; there is a slight increase in numbers in the Anza sequence, from three in phase I to seven and six in phases II and III respectively. Miniature axes, stone plugs and pendants, clay seals, figurines and miniature tables are amongst other items shared in common with Greece.[30] The question of local differentiation and regional uniformity in these items has been little explored, but it is evident that as well as local traits there are also traits with a very wide distribution from the middle Danube to northern Greece, such as rod-headed figurines with a decorative head-dress, found as far apart as Starčevo and Nea Nikomedeia.[31]

## Settlements

The social significance of this material must now be considered and in turning to this question one is struck by the fact that the vast majority of the material concerned comes from within a series of settlements. These did not necessarily all have the same role or status, but other activities such as disposal of the dead or formal ritual seem also to have been concentrated within settlements. An increase in size compared to Mesolithic sites is the first striking difference. A useful indication of the general trend is the extension of occupation at the Franchthi Cave down on to the present shore, already noted above. Most sites however are 'open' sites. A range from 0.4 to 0.8 ha is suggested for sites in Thessaly.[32] This can be estimated without total excavation on the basis of mound or tell size where occupation has been concentrated on one spot, and to some extent by the spread of artefacts on the surface as recorded by survey. Individual sites can however be hard to estimate; both Argissa and Nea Nikomedeia for example had been damaged before excavation, by river action and quarrying respectively. Some individual sites also do not fit the general pattern. It is claimed that Sesklo for example was some 10 ha in extent by the Sesklo phase, though excavation has been of much more limited extent. Differential growth is thus a second striking feature of Neolithic settlements. In central-southern Bulgaria excavation has been concentrated almost entirely on recognisable settlement mounds or tells. Some of these were in use throughout the period covered by this book and became eventually not only high but broad in extent. Karanovo for example is some 12 m high, covering an area of around 250 by 150 m, over 4 ha; Yasatepe is 4 m high with a basal diameter of 150 m; Azmak is 8 m high with a basal diameter of 80 m.[33] It is likely therefore that the final diameter does not reflect the extent of initial settlement. Excavation was possible over 1700 m$^2$ at Karanovo, and of the whole settlements at Yasatepe and Azmak, but there has been no clear statement of the extent of occupation in Karanovo I and II levels. Estimates of the number of houses have therefore varied considerably, from 15–30 to 60 or more.[34] There is a danger too that excavation has been concentrated on the most successful sites over a long period of time, and therefore the largest or fastest growing. Further north in the Starčevo–Körös–Criş complex settlements that became tells and continued in use in later periods are far rarer. One example is Vinča near Belgrade, eventually 9 m high and 6 ha in extent; the site is only partially excavated and the extent of the Starčevo features is unclear.[35] Anza provides further insight into these problems. The excavated samples suggested a maximum extent in phase I of 4.75 ha, and in II and III of 3.8 ha but the discontinuous nature of some of the layers has already been noted above, so that one should not assume that the whole area was equally densely occupied or built over. This probably applies to many of the tell sites already considered. Excavation of sites like Gura Baciului has been too limited to establish their size, though the impression is of smaller sites than Thessaly. Many Körös sites however are extensive, regularly spread over 300–400 m by 30–40 m at the edge of the floodplain; one example Dévaványa–Katonaföldek covers 800 by 50–100 m.[36] Though settlement layers accumulated on such sites, it is likely that they too had shifting foci and that the whole extent was not in contemporary use. As well as limited excavation, the chronological difficulties discussed above hinder a resolution of this problem.

A further difference between these and earlier post-glacial settlements is their assumed greater permanence, though this is difficult to prove in many cases and may not take sufficient account of the developments discussed in the last chapter. Animal bone assemblages have generally not been sufficiently closely studied to allow age patterns to be established in any detail, but there is scattered evidence of animals being killed at all stages of their first year or so when dentition provides some guide to seasonality. The best direct evidence for year-round occupation comes from the Körös sites in south-east Hungary of Ludaš–Budžak, Maroslele–Pana, Röske–Ludvár and Deszk–Olajkút, on the basis of the bones of migrant birds and of mammals which could be aged. The assumption that most sites were continuously occupied is based on the investment in the facilities such as housing which they contain and on the constraining needs of activities, particularly subsistence activities, carried out from them, but there is no justification for assuming that this is valid for all sites. The first structural features at many sites (such as Argissa and Achilleion) are ill-defined pits and scoops, the latter often referred to as pit-dwellings. It is possible that these are connected with more transient occupation, and are known because these sites were later chosen for more permanent occupation. Some preceramic sites in Greece could perhaps be explained as seasonally occupied bases. There is evidence from a west Thessalian ceramic site Prodromos both that the focus of settlement was scattered in the early stages, and that certain joints of meat are not represented at the settlement, possible indications of greater settlement mobility over the year for at least part of the community concerned than is often assumed. At preceramic Argissa however, all parts of the animal body were represented. Starčevo flood plain sites along the Sava valley have also been seen as seasonally occupied.[37]

It is also the case that most recognised sites seem to be occupied for considerable periods of time on the basis of the depth of their deposits and of the span of radiocarbon dates where these are available, though this feature may not provide such a strong contrast to the Late Mesolithic situation. The depth of deposit can be impressive; thus three building levels in level I at Karanovo in 0.6–1 m, two building levels in level II in 1.75–2 m of build-up. The volume however cannot be treated simply, and the nature of house construction (see below) amongst other factors must be taken into account when comparing regional differences and the Mesolithic situation.

Another development lies in the sheer numbers of known sites compared with the Mesolithic period. As will be seen later in this chapter and in chapter

5, settlement in this period was not ubiquitous, but the numbers of sites in areas where settlement is recorded are vastly increased. This implies that the density of contemporary settlement also increased, which is likely though difficult to prove. Indeed locational preferences may further serve to concentrate settlement in certain parts of the landscape. Where reasonable data are available, as in Thessaly, or in the area around Karanovo spacing of sites at around 5 km or less is apparent. Uniformity should not be expected in other regions since a range of factors is involved. Wider spacing is apparent in parts of the Morava and Sava valleys, where Starčevo sites lie from 7 to 10 km apart.[38] The problems of survey and chronology discussed above should be remembered, but undoubtedly the impression overall is of more numerous sites and of denser settlement within the areas occupied.

The layout of many of these settlements in Greece and central-southern Bulgaria was organised, as far as the usually limited scale of excavation allows us to tell. Little is known of very early levels with scoops or pit-dwellings at Argissa or Achilleion. At Nea Nikomedeia in the excavated portion of the site there is a cluster of six buildings around a larger building (Fig. 3.9). At Achilleion there are hints of gradually increased coherence of layout, but with closely spaced houses and adjacent communal areas or yards

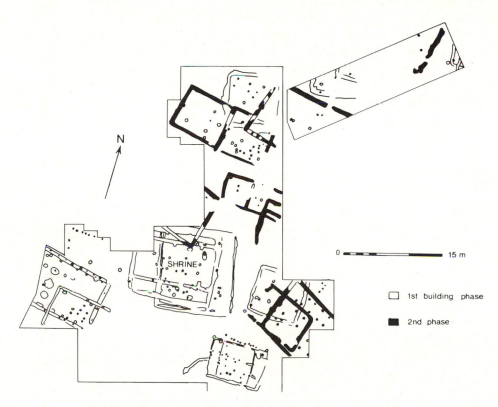

**3.9** Two phases of structures at Nea Nikomedeia, Greek Macedonia. *After* Theocharis

throughout. Similar development may be hinted at by the regular layout of
Sesklo phase buildings at Otzaki with closely spaced rectangular buildings
separated by narrow lanes. Sesklo itself in this phase is spatially differentiated, with an inner raised area or acropolis defined by a deep ditch, perimeter
retaining walls and an internal enclosure, containing one large building and
several smaller ones and a paved courtyard. In the outer area are other
buildings on a common alignment, again closely spaced and separated only by
small yards and narrow lanes. One or two sites may have well-defined
boundaries or even defences, such as Chatzimissiotiki with stone walls and
Soufli with a deep V-shaped ditch. Houses at Karanovo were for the most part
closely spaced, in an orderly arrangement on either side of lanes, with a few
more isolated. In the area excavated two wood-lined lanes were found in the
Karanovo I level, one running east–west and the other north–south; in the
Karanovo II level the overall layout and the lanes changed, with now a sand
and pebble covering. It is very difficult to tell how typical this form of
settlement was in its region. Such sites could have been exceptional, but
virtually nothing is known of other sorts of site in the area. Further north sites
seem to have been for the most part smaller and less organised, such as the
Körös settlement at Lebö with its house and surrounding pits, clay pits, and
scattered graves.

Within most of these settlements the basic architectural unit was the
single-roomed four-walled building. Exceptions are the pit-dwellings noted
in the early levels of some sites, and the tent-like structures claimed in the
northern part of the Körös culture. As hinted above, these sorts of building
may have been more common than the face value of the evidence suggests.
Walled houses varied in construction from area to area and indeed from level
to level within the same site (Fig. 3.10). The most common basic elements

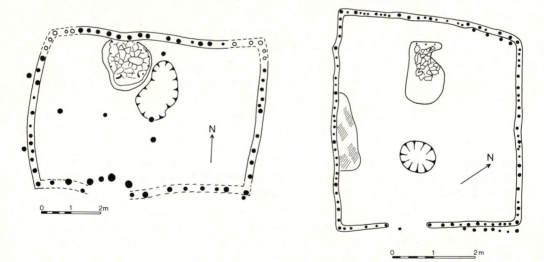

3.10 Houses and internal fittings from Chevdar, levels III and IV, central Bulgaria,
sixth and fifth millennia bc. *After* Georgiev

were a wooden frame with a daub or clay covering, with stone footings and mud brick more common in Greece. At Karanovo 1 houses were about 7 by 7 m, though the smallest was 5 by 3.5 m. It is interesting again that the feature of a wooden subframe, interpreted as damp proofing, was not found in the very earliest houses. There was an oven on the back or side wall of each house. Anza illustrates variation, from interconnected mudbrick rectangular houses 12 by 6 m in phase 1, to more free-standing rectangular buildings 8–10 by 4 m, with a timber frame of small close-set uprights and a daub covering, and some with stone footings. Occasionally, preserved details indicate that some houses at least were carefully built and furnished. Parts of a roof of roughly trimmed trunks and branches were recovered at Prodromos in Thessaly: house models have gabled roofs. There is evidence from Karanovo that the walls were painted red and white. A fragment of a clay house-model from the Körös site of Röszke–Ludvár has an animal head on one gable apex, and other models from Greece, from the Sesklo phase for the most part, have features such as smoke holes in the roof. Some buildings were two-storeyed. My two examples are from the Sesklo phase of Greece. House no. 11–12 at Sesklo had a pottery store or workshop in one of its two basements; some house plans from other sites such as Otzaki or Tsangli show also the feature of internal buttresses, suggesting that two-storeyed buildings were common. A basement store at Servia was evidently being used for plant storage when the house was burnt and debris from the upper floor collapsed into it.[39]

For the most part in this period there seems to have been little variation in the size of buildings within settlements. The later development at Sesklo already noted may be an exception. Another may be Nea Nikomedeia where the largest building, about 10 by 10 m with two internal partitions far exceeds in size the other two- and one-roomed buildings clustered around it.

Two similar methods of calculating the population of settlements have been used. Both rely on an estimate of how much living space people need. The simpler method is to suggest that one-roomed buildings of the size we have considered were occupied by a single family of say six persons, and multiply the known number of buildings on the site by this figure. The more sophisticated method is to calculate the amount of used floor space (as seen in excavated segments) as a fraction of the total area of a site, and then divide this by an estimate of how much space people need; a figure of 10 $m^2$ per person is often used. At Anza floorspace was estimated as 60 per cent of the total area used, but was used to produce a figure for houses rather than actual numbers of people. This caution is justified, for calculations of this sort are difficult. Variations in the estimate of house numbers in Karanovo 1 have already been noted; the upper figure might give a population of 300 or more, the lower much less. It is clearly difficult to establish the amount of space or houses in contemporary use. The use of space cannot easily be derived from ethnography as an independent variable; the social use of space in the past demands to be investigated in its own right. Naroll in fact suggested that floor area and settlement population are an allometric variable pair, whose growth is related in the form of a loglog regression, and that population could be very roughly calculated as of the order of one-tenth of floor area in square metres. Other studies have attacked both claims, tending to deny any constant figures. It may be less dangerous to return to the one house – one family equation (bearing in mind Yellen's observation among the !Kung bushmen that two adults and four children need not take up significantly more space than two adults), though this approach requires more total excavation, and is less practical therefore at the present stage. Another method is to consider the carrying capacity of the area around sites in confined topographical situations, such as Chevdar in a small basin of 250 ha in the Topolnitza valley. As we shall see, this could have supported 100–150 people, which provides an upper limit, but does not specify the actual site population, which could have been less.[40]

The evidence therefore ranges from sites with a single house to perhaps 60 or more. It was suggested that the area of Anza I could have held 200 houses, but there is no proof that all the space was used at an even density. On a very simple level of analysis, one may suggest that the range of site sizes could be divided into three types; the homestead with a single (nuclear or extended) family, the hamlet with a few families, and the village with upwards of say 50 people and perhaps reaching 200–300 in some cases. More detailed analysis of such variation is badly needed, and the status of the larger settlements particularly is of great importance, for the existence of local or regional centres at this early stage of our period would be a crucial development. Perhaps the most striking feature of all is simply the amount of variation that we can currently observe. I believe that this cannot ultimately be explained simply as the result of variation in the quality of resources available around each site, though good resources were a precondition for the maintenance of successful longlived sites, and that social relations as a whole rather than just the subsistence economy have to be taken into account. The first step however is to now consider the economic basis of these new settlements, believed to be on the whole both larger and more permanent than in the early post-glacial period.

## Subsistence and its social context

From the beginning of this period new food staples which were not native to the area were exploited along with resources previously in use. The new resources consist chiefly of a range of cereals, believed on the basis of morphological criteria to be domesticated and therefore deliberately sown, and of sheep and goats, believed to be domesticated and therefore closely husbanded by virtue of their appearance in an area where they had not previously been found. The cereals consist of wheats (emmer, einkorn and bread wheat) and barleys (two-row and six-row hulled and naked barley). Legumes which had previously been used in the area such as peas, lentils and vetches continued to be exploited, but probably as deliberately sown crops like the cereals, partly on the basis of the frequency of their occurrence and partly on the basis of morphological criteria for domestication. Other plant foods such as acorns, olives, pistachio, Cornelian cherry and plum continued to be exploited, probably in their wild state and as casual or incidental resources. As well as husbanded sheep and goats, pig and cattle were exploited; these are thought to have been also domesticated on morphological criteria, and especially on a reduction in size. Dogs were present and are believed again on the basis of morphological criteria to be domesticated. Other animals continued to be exploited such as morphologically unchanged pig, cattle, red deer and others, whose previous use has been examined in the last chapter. As far as the evidence and the means by which it was recovered allow us to say, the whole combination marks a significant shift in subsistence, the widespread adoption of mixed farming based on cereal agriculture and animal husbandry overtaking previous trends towards intensified animal and plant use.

The early distribution, combination and novelty of these various elements are key questions. It must be stressed again that they can only be resolved ultimately on the basis of recovery techniques of proven reliability, which have not been widely enough employed, and for that reason claims made here are liable to be changed by future research. For example, it was believed that wheat but not barley was exploited in central-southern Bulgaria but both species were recovered using systematic methods at sites such as Chevdar and Kazanluk. The same revolution in recovery techniques has also improved the recovery of animal bone, especially if small or fragmentary. The figures from Chevdar for example are astonishing, dry- and wet-sieving radically increasing the recovery rate compared to standard techniques with spade or trowel in the trench. On present evidence not all the staples mentioned above occur on individual sites; the present pattern perhaps is for one or two cereals and one domesticated animal species to appear dominant at any one site. Further problems of the archaeological representation of differential resource use are discussed below. These new elements appear to be widespread in our area from the beginning of the period, though it must not be assumed that they all appeared instantaneously in all parts. Problems of the chronology of the spread of agriculture are returned to below, but for the moment the case of the Franchthi Cave may serve to make the point. Even in that stratified sequence it is by no means clear that the introduction of wheat, barley and sheep and goats was simultaneous. The remains consist of substantial numbers of apparently domesticated sheep and goats and of finds in cultivated emmer wheat (*Triticum dicoccum* Schubl.), followed shortly by cultivated two-row hulled barley (*Hordeum distichum* L.). There is however no clear information yet on how synchronous these changes were; the preliminary plant report again mentions a possible stratigraphic break, which would of course mask any period of gradual transition. Despite the continued use of the site the excavator inclines to the view that these changes were in total sudden and introduced from outside. The preliminary report also indicates that cultivated lentils appear quite long after, around 5000 bc, and einkorn later still, around 4500 bc, even though by those dates they were known at other sites in Greece. Nor was the use of plants unvarying with time, as the case of Anza shows, where flotation and sieving were used in recovery. As well as emmer throughout phases I–III, einkorn was also present in small quantities (in the generally small samples) but absent from phase Ib, and club wheat (*T. compactum*) was present only in Ia. Sheep and goats were for the most part in terms of numbers at least the dominant animals (and of these two, sheep), but their representation varied like the cereals. In Greece and the southern Balkans with only one or two outliers at sites like Leţ in Transylvania and Körös sites in south-east Hungary like Röszke–Ludvár, they comprise at least 50 per cent of the faunal assemblages, measuring either the number of bones or the minimum number of individuals, and in several cases up to 70 per cent or more. At Anza for example they constituted between 62 and 70 per cent of individuals in phases I–III. At other sites in the Starčevo–Körös–Criş complex cattle and pig were apparently roughly as important numerically as sheep and goats, as at Gura Baciului. It is likely that these variations represent an adaptation to differing environment, sheep and goats being less suited to the more temperate conditions of the more northern parts of the Balkans. Their high numbers among Körös domesticated animals have been interpreted in terms of cultural traditions imported wholesale from the south, but it is likely that they were very well suited to the dry conditions of the Great Hungarian plain which were within a reasonable distance of the river-based settlements. The whole of Körös culture subsistence reflects adaptability, showing that we are not dealing with an inflexible agricultural system. Cereals were cultivated as well, and other resources available in the river valleys or their margins were heavily exploited. Wild animals (that is, morphologically unchanged), regularly comprise a significant percentage of the faunal assemblage (up to 35 per cent and in one case 62 per cent). Fish, especially catfish and pike were caught, including catfish estimated at near 200 kg. Lenses 2–3 cm thick consisting of fish-scales at Röszke–Ludvár may reflect large-scale processing and drying. Shellfish and snails were also regularly used. The stratigraphy of one pit at Röszke–Ludvár reflects the successive deposition of different resources, with first freshwater mussels stratified below forest animals in turn stratified below fish. It is suggested that these were used in spring, autumn/winter and summer respectively though the seasonal pattern is far from clear.[41]

The conventional view is that the elements of this subsistence economy were introduced, or in a minority view were adopted, from outside sources, in the Near East. On conventional criteria of domestication, cultivated wheats and barleys and domesticated sheep goats and pigs can all be documented in the Near East from Turkey to Iraq at earlier dates than in Europe, back to around 7000 bc, and stable settlements using morphologically unchanged cereals such as Mureybit in Syria can be dated around a millennium earlier. It is also a conventional belief that the precursors of domesticated cereals and sheep and goats were not generally available in south-east Europe, a further argument for introduction from outside. If the conventional view remains for the present dominant, it is nonetheless hard to support fully. The chronological disparity between the two areas is certainly suggestive but not conclusive.

The problems of present-day distributions of wild cereals have already been noted and in fact wild einkorn has been recorded in Greece and Bulgaria and wild barley in Crete and along the whole of the North African coast. The Franchthi Cave record already noted is important, showing wild barley, oats, lentils, peas and vetches in use in the early post-glacial period or before, and cereal pollen was recorded in the Danube gorges apparently a little before 6000 bc. It is striking that at Franchthi the first cereals recognised as domesticated come in abruptly, and that the first is a wheat, not previously represented. But local development of cereals from before 8000 bc in the Aegean – if not at this particular site – can hardly be discounted. Likewise with animals, domesticated sheep and goats have been claimed in the past in Mesolithic layers, at the La Adam Caves in the Dobruja region of Romania, on the basis of simply their presence in the area, but the layers in question are thin and not dated absolutely and the find is isolated and disputed.[42] On the basis of present radiocarbon dates cattle were domesticated (i.e. reduced in size) earlier in Greece, at sites like Argissa, than in the Near East, and the process of domestication therefore could both have been local and begun before 6000 bc, as discussed in the last chapter.[43] Some sites like Anza apparently show local domestication in progress, on the basis of the variation in size among the cattle. One must also note sites like Nea Nikomedeia where the cattle were not for certain domesticated by conventional criteria, though immature animals were numerous. The same applies for pigs at this site, and size varation is evident elsewhere. Those at Anza for example were small but those at Chevdar were large and not certainly domesticated on conventional criteria.

There is thus considerable evidence that the subsistence basis of this period was varied, though with widespread, recurrent elements in it. The source of the shift to cereals and sheep and goats, cattle and pig remains unclear, especially since morphological criteria for domestication of both cereals and animals remain subject to one major ambiguity, in that while the presence of morphological changes may reflect selective breeding, their absence does not rule out intensive human use and close control. The time scale required for genetic changes to work their way through a whole population is also not established, though likely to be considerable. But the appearance of these changes so widely in the archaeological record, whether the end or the beginning of a process, seems to mark the final establishment of intensive exploitation of plants and animals.[44]

How this was carried out however is not well known in detail, as the evidence for differing aspects of cultivation and husbandry shows. Even the location of sites has not received the detailed attention it deserves (Figs. 3.11 and 3.12).[45] The general pattern throughout the region is of sites near water or in areas of high water table, with fertile and workable soils available close to. It is likely that the needs of cereal cultivation were a major factor in this choice. Such regularities run through different sorts of environment such as the Thessalian plain, the Maritsa basin or the Morava valley despite local variations. They seem to extend to south-east Hungary, where Körös settle-

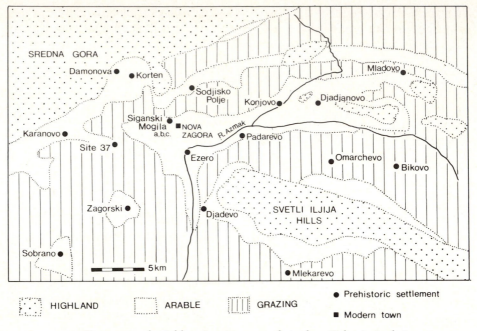

**3.11** Karanovo and neighbouring sites, central-southern Bulgaria, in their reconstructed environmental setting. *After* Dennell and Webley

ments in or at the edge of the flood plain probably exploited alluvial deposits on levees for cultivation, using the flood plain for fishing, hunting and grazing, and the chernozems of the drier more open plain for grazing rather than for cultivation. Regularity however does not imply uniformity, and variation is well documented too, from Starčevo sites in the Sava flood plain to Anza and neighbouring sites like Vršnik and Rug Bair in the Ovce Polje, a former lake basin in the upper drainage area of the River Vardar. It can be difficult to reconstruct the environment of particular sites. The excavator of Nea Nikomedeia for example saw the site as lying on a slight knoll at the edge of a marshy lake or inlet in an area of largely open landscape while another study suggests it lay at least 5 km from the Thermaic gulf and was an inland site on well-drained old lacustrine soils, in a mostly wooded environment. The scale of clearance of woodland for cultivation and grazing is poorly known, since pollen analysis has seldom been carried out close to settlements, though it is suspected to have been small. Pollen diagrams from northern Greece show little interference with climax forest, even when the sampling point as at Ginnitsa in the Macedonian plain is only 8 km from the settlement of Nea Nikomedeia. The absence of large assemblages of heavy duty stone tools may also indicate the limited scale of clearance and the concentrated nature of cultivation, though in areas such as around Karanovo the cumulative effect of several contemporary sites was presumably more considerable. The restricted scale of clearance suggests that cultivation may have been practised intensively in fixed plots, gardens or fields, though no

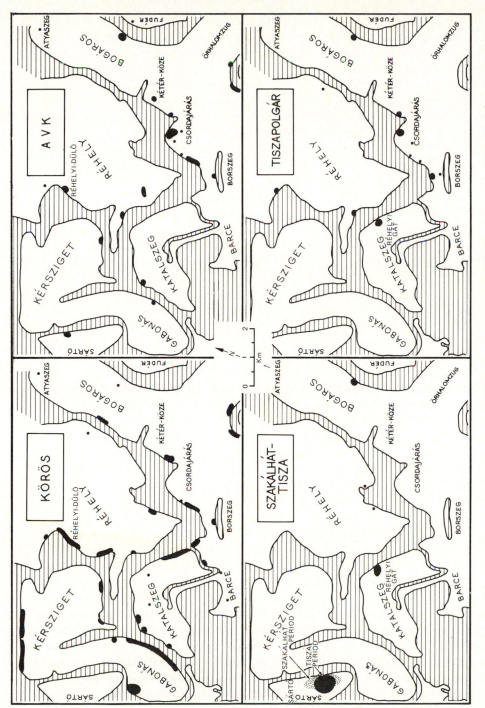

**3.12** Diagrammatic representation of the location and distribution of settlement in Dévaványa district, Körös basin, eastern Hungary, in the Körös and subsequent phases. Blank represents terrace, hatched flood plain. *After Sherratt*

direct evidence for these survives in this part of Europe (see chapter 6). With the dearth of pollen analysis it is impossible to estimate the role of shifting cultivation, in which plots are cleared by felling and burning the vegetation, used for a short period and then abandoned as yields decline. There seems to be considerable continuity at most settlements, and the concept of shifting cultivation has been derived from ethnographic observation in areas of generally poor soils in the tropics or northern Europe where the prime need is to transfer nutrients from vegetation to the soil in the form of ash, or to release nutrients in the soil by burning. It can be calculated however that even a small area, say with a 5 km radius around a site, would provide enough land for shifting plots for a settlement of even village size. The hypothesis of stable cultivation however is preferable. There is plenty of experimental evidence to show that reasonable yields can be maintained for long periods of time on soils of average fertility, even without manuring or fallowing, though weed control is critical; at Rothampsted in southern England for example continuous cropping of a leached brown soil still yields 70 per cent of the first three years' yield.[46] A performance at least as good could be expected from fertile soils of this period. There is no direct evidence on cultivation methods or tools, though it is commonly assumed that hoes or digging sticks were in use rather than ards or ploughs. There is little direct justification for this assumption.

Knowledge of actual crop use depends first on preservation, in most circumstances by carbonisation, and secondly on systematic recovery.[47] Since it has only recently been realised that there are different stages and kinds of treatment of crops after harvest which do not expose them all equally to the risk of carbonisation, knowledge of the nature of the deposit in which carbonised remains occur is necessary, and detailed study of this sort is in its infancy. There is no direct evidence at this stage for the sowing season, which would require careful study of associated weeds, but one might expect cereals to have been winter sown. We have a little more knowledge of crop composition. Numbers of samples evidently from an early stage in crop processing indicate that crops would have been accompanied by large quantities of weeds, and as harvesting is likely to have been selective the actual quantity of weeds in the fields is likely to have been greater. While small samples from various contexts and stages of preparation may show mixed crops, there is a striking series of larger samples, from Karanovo I contexts at Chevdar and Azmak and from a preceramic context at Knossos on Crete, which are dominated in each case by one cereal or legume, though accompanied by very small quantities of others. These deposits are largely free of weeds showing that they have been cleaned, but it is inconceivable that the processing itself would result in such crop purity, which must therefore reflect more or less accurately the original crop composition. The Bulgarian samples were from oven contexts suggesting also that the crops were being prepared for consumption or possibly storage, and not therefore the result of mixing. The significance of different species is little studied. It is possible that einkorn was at this stage mainly a minor component of other crops rather than a crop in its own right. The hexaploid bread wheat would have been better for baking than emmer wheat because it has gluten in its flour and can be used for lighter bread; naked barley is freer-threshing than hulled. Crop variety presumably also offered greater security from total crop failure if each species had slightly different characteristics. It is thought that wheats are generally more suited to heavier soils than barleys whose tolerance of soils and climate is generally greater.[48] Such diversity must underlie the agricultural adaptability already observed.

Careful study of plant remains also promises to yield information about crop rotation involving different species. The argument rests at Chevdar on the observation of commensals in mostly pure single-species samples. It is possible that this reflects not just slightly mixed seed at sowing but also the presence of relicts of former crops grown on the same land, and therefore a rotation of some kind involving at Chevdar emmer, barley and legumes. These suggestions are open to much further analysis, but they serve to reinforce the likelihood of stable cultivation in relatively restricted plots. It is unfortunate that this kind of analysis has not been repeated at other sites and that there is so little information about the precise contexts studied at Chevdar. The legume stored in pure amounts at Chevdar was the vetch *Vicia cf. sativa* which is a rich source of protein in its own right, though its cultivation is labour-intensive, and replenishes the soil with nitrogen. Short fallow and animal manuring are other possibilities to consider at other sites; a suggestion has been made for the Mediterranean that sheep and goats were more effective as providers of manure than of any other product.[49]

Study of plant remains also yields information about the care with which cereal and legume crops were processed after harvest, and some less clean samples may also be by-products, used for example for animal fodder. Information of this kind must also depend on the season when deposits were carbonised. The fire which destroyed one of the Sesklo phase levels at Servia may have happened soon after harvest because of the quantities of plant material observed over the site at this level, including in the basement discussed above heaps of einkorn, lentils and *Lathyrus sativus*.

There is no direct evidence for crop yields, and one must simply choose between varying estimates.[50] On the basis that Neolithic Bulgarian yields would have been lower than in medieval England and western Europe, one proposal is of an average yield of 400 kg per ha, with a third to a quarter kept as seed. Higher yields have been proposed for Neolithic Greece where settlement was concentrated on a restricted range of fertile soils, of up to 800–1000 kg per ha, and it has been stressed that lower quantities of seed corn would be needed than in the cold soils of northern Europe. The contrast is crucial, for the higher estimates propose far greater productivity and therefore potentially smaller areas required around each settlement to support its population. The higher estimates would also enhance the value of a sustained shift in subsistence practices to cereal cultivation compared to indigenous plant use. Certainty is unfortunately impossible, but the higher estimates do seem plausible. It is often estimated that an adult needs 2000–2500 calories per day, and one kilo of wheat can supply around 3000 calories, or rather more if only the edible portion is weighed. It can be seen from these figures that one adult can be supported for a year on the cereal produce of about 1 ha, on the more pessimistic estimates of yields, or about 0.5 ha, on the more optimistic. Even if allowance is made for half the arable land being under short fallow at any one time, even a village at the upper end of the size scale discussed above, say of 300 people, could be supported with the lower yields by a small area, which assuming an even distribution of arable land around the settlement could be fitted easily into a radius of under 2 km. Other resources such as animals exploited in conjunction with cereals or in areas beyond would further decrease this figure. These figures however supply only minimum estimates of requirements for production. They do not indicate the actual scale of production, and it is dangerous to assume that all the communities under discussion in this period were merely at subsistence level. The greater the productivity of cereal cultivation, the greater the capacity for surplus production and the use of food in social relations other than within the household or family group. Admittedly the visible storage capacity of houses and settlements is not great, being limited to pits beside houses in more open settlements, such as the clay-lined ones in Körös settlements or the earth-sunk pots within houses, for example up to 0.5 km high in Karanovo level II.[51] But since the visible capacity would hardly hold even the seed corn of a single family or household, the bulk of grain must have been kept in above-ground containers, in lofts and so on. The ritual emphasis given to hearths and therefore presumably food preparation and consumption, which will be discussed below shortly, may indicate the social importance of food at a level of production far above that required for the satisfaction of dietary needs.

Most discussions suggest that animals played a smaller part in subsistence than plants in this period, because they are higher in the food chain, and are less productive per hectare, especially in the more closed woodland of the period in which the amount of browse and grazing would have been less than in open grassland. This last observation may not apply to all areas, such as south-east Hungary. The already-discussed composition of herds leads on to a consideration of the products which the various species provided. Despite the abundance of animal bones in excavations this has received comparatively little attention. Detailed information about the age and sex of animals is required. An animal kept for meat is likely to be slaughtered at an earlier age than one kept for other products such as milk or wool, since after a certain age its weight does not increase while its food consumption stays constant.[52] Even properly investigated sites may yield very small samples which are inadequate for analysis, such as Chevdar. One of the best samples available is that from Anza. Unfortunately the bones from the site were highly fragmented, which may underrepresent the juvenile bones, and the analysis lumps together all four main phases of the site. However the data suggest that pig were killed mostly when young, and at least half of the sheep; goats were killed mostly when adult, like the greater proportion of the cattle. On the assumption stated above, it is likely that sheep could have been kept partly for wool and goats for milk, and cattle for milk, hides or simply accumulation. It must also be remembered of course that the species' weights are disparate since cattle would provide far more meat than sheep. Again diversity would provide some security, and further adaptability via the different species' different grazing habits. The obvious constraint on animal numbers would be the amount of available grazing, but with comparatively little required for cultivation this must be considered as virtually limitless. Husbanded animals are a mobile resource and can be moved to seasonally available grazing too. Upland cave sites occupied in this period may testify to this sort of movement. Dennell suggests that the provision of winter fodder would have been a more specific constraint but it is not clear how severe this would have been in the climatic conditions of the period despite the considerable forest cover. Extensive winter pasture in the floodplain is envisaged in the area of the Körös culture.[53] The age data discussed certainly show that it was possible to overwinter animals, though not of course in what quantities. Although relatively few animals may have been needed as a supplement to cereals for satisfying dietary needs and as an alternative security, this says nothing about the size of herds actually kept. If animals can be considered a form of capital, it cannot be assumed that they were not accumulated for their own sake, as the adult cattle at Anza hint. (Indeed given the uncertainties discussed about the morphological criteria for animal domestication it might be suggested that morphological change marks not the beginning of human control, but its intensification and direction towards social rather than purely dietary needs.) There is little further evidence on scale at this stage of research, though we will return to it a little later. One reason for this which must be stressed is that, as with cereals and plants, beside proper recovery techniques understanding of bone assemblages requires insight into the behaviour which led to their deposition and into the processes of destruction which may have subsequently distorted the deposited sample. One cannot assume that bones in all contexts throughout a settlement will provide an equally good sample of the whole animal economy, nor indeed since we are dealing with a mobile resource that any one site is a self-contained unit. There is little analysis of this kind in the area; contrast for example the contextual detail of the plant remains with the lack of context for the animal bones at Chevdar. The kind of analysis carried out at Prodromos is all too rare.

Neither cereal cultivation nor animal husbandry can be seen as independent forces in Neolithic society which in some way determined its form and development, and despite their undoubted importance attention should be focused on their use by communities within a social context, rather than on their performance outside and effect on such a social context. There are three useful examples of this viewpoint. Together cultivation and husbandry are likely to have been highly productive and adaptable, and we have seen good reason to believe that they could satisfy quite easily the dietary needs of even larger villages within a short distance of the settlement. If there were, as was argued in the last chapter, various incipient forms of indigenous experimentation with plants and animals, they were in this period subsumed by these new forms of exploitation. The difference perhaps is one of degree rather than of kind. It is generally assumed that the advantages of mixed farming were self-evident, in terms of greater reliability and security of food supply, ease of storage, and stability of settlement, offset only perhaps by the greater labour input required especially by fixed-plot cultivation. But the advantages of these forms of subsistence could only have been self-evident in a social context when more food and more permanent settlement (or easier means to maintain it) were already desired. The agricultural system whether derived *ex machina* from the Near East or at least partly developed within south-east Europe provided the means of satisfying these wants but cannot be seen necessarily as having created them out of nothing. Likewise it is often assumed that settlement expansion and population growth are natural consequences of the adoption of agriculture, virtually without reference to the nature of the communities which adopted it in its various forms. Agriculture may be seen as a precondition, not perhaps of settlement expansion or population growth in themselves, but at least of the rates of increase now discernible in the archaeological record, but it cannot be considered as an independent factor, since this does not specify how it was to be used by the communities practising it. That agricultural communities were expansive provides ultimately more insight into the nature of their social relations than into their subsistence basis. This claim can be accentuated the greater the role one allows for indigenous development at the beginning of the period. A positive response to changed constraints, say in the matter of birth spacing, may indicate a society where the creation of larger families and more kin was socially desirable from the point of view of mutual help, alliance and status. It is possible that some population increase was not consciously recognised, since anthropologists have noted that perception of population levels can be distorted, but the contrast with hunter-gatherers, amongst whom birth control is argued to be of great importance, is striking.[54] Finally we have seen even from a brief review of settlements that some reached a far larger size than others. Such differential growth is exemplified by Sesklo in Thessaly by the Sesklo phase. Another example is Knossos in Crete which grew steadily in size through the Neolithic period. Good arable and grazing may have been again preconditions for such success, but they do not by themselves explain why some sites were thus more successful than others. Such 'functionalist' explanation has been offered for the size and continuity of tells in central-southern Bulgaria.[55] The argument runs in essence that of the range of sites in the Karanovo area the longest lived settlements have the greatest percentage of usable arable within a given radius (2 km) around them, and in direct consequence were the most successful. This factor (though the correlations are by no means exact) may again be seen as a precondition for success, but others must be considered too. The larger the settlement the greater the potential for internal conflict, which could have been resolved partly by rules, ritual and other institutions, but partly also by the provision of extra space around the settlement to avoid conflicts over arable and grazing. The higher too the yields that may be argued for cultivation, the less critical the quantity of arable for basic subsistence needs, and the more possibilities it provided for surplus production. Such production discussed above may have been vital for the maintenance of large sites seen as social centres rather than purely as agglomerations of people, with such agricultural produce used as part of the network of social relations required to support such a nucleation without fission, rather than simply as food. Nor can the belief that each settlement whatever its size and status was self-sufficient, which underlies the argument, be accepted automatically, for uniformity and variation should be investigated rather than merely assumed. Further consideration of settlements and material culture provides some other ways of investigating the operation of Neolithic society and the internal differences it contained.

## Social differentiation and control

Throughout the evidence there is a discernible dichotomy at both local and regional levels between uniformity and differentiation. This feature may be a clue of considerable value to the nature of social relations in the period. At the local level, internal differentiation is not readily apparent within individual settlements in terms of either layout or material culture. Such significantly larger buildings as exist for example, can be interpreted as communal buildings, in the case of Nea Nikomedeia specifically as a shrine from the figurines and other artefacts it contains. Other examples where ritual artefacts are concentrated have been noted, as at Achilleion in phases II, III and IV, though not in markedly distinctive buildings, or at Anza in phase II. It is possible that social differentiation is only expressed in the control of ritual, as in these cases, but a shared ritual is apparent throughout most settlements. Its most common locus is the ordinary household, whose importance was bolstered by a number of features. Visible storage facilities are situated in or close to it. Such burials as are found occur within the settlement, and often in rubbish pits beside houses. The house itself could be well plastered and painted and its roof furnished with animal and other symbols. Inside, the hearth or oven was a focal point, and many figurines (where they occur) have been found in or close to houses, though lack of detailed publication precludes much further precision. Other ritual paraphernalia such as model clay tables have been found mainly in rubbish pits. The distribution of such equipment, and of other items such as the individualistic clay seals, within a settlement may ultimately prove a clue a internal differentiation, but on present published evidence this is not readily apparent. Still on a local level greater differentiation may be visible between sites in terms of their size, which has already been discussed, and their concern with ritual practice. It is claimed that figurines were present on only 20 per cent of settlements and even if this figure is revised upwards, it indicates differences in activity and role between settlements.[56] Again published information does not allow much further detail for any given area. It would be useful to know the scale and extent of the distribution of exchanged items such as obsidian from Melos and Hungary, of Aegean *spondylus* which occurs at sites like Karanovo

1 or Anza, or of pots exchanged between adjacent style areas, such as claimed at Servia in Macedonia from further north.[57] But while differences may be suspected, it is difficult at present to quantify them.

At a regional level there is uniformity of a sort in the shared character of much material culture from pottery to figurines to chipped stone assemblages. The scale of this uniformity and its significance are difficult to measure, and might only be comparable to the lithic 'technocomplexes' explored in the previous chapter, but the very generalised similarities cannot altogether be dismissed. Long-range contact of a more specific kind is apparent in some ritual equipment and in exchanged items. Two types of rod-headed figurines for example have a broad distribution from the central Balkans down into northern Greece and, though claims for a specific pantheon over the whole area have been widely doubted, there are sufficiently recurrent instances of certain animals for figurines and protomes on pots, of house models, tables and seals for one to believe in a considerable degree of shared ritual at a regional level, despite the danger in this sphere of mistakenly equating similarity in form with similarity in function. Long-range exchange of artefacts and materials such as obsidian, *spondylus* and pottery need not indicate shared identity of any kind but the contact over considerable distances is significant, as between Nea Nikomedeia and Melos. What is lacking again however is detail concerning the distribution of exchanged items, to investigate the kind of exchange taking place. Down-the-line exchange would reduce contact between communities to a much more local level than directed exchange. Contrasted with these various means of bringing communities together there is also differentiation between neighbouring areas. The most discussed example is pottery, which shows considerable regional variability over areas of differing size. The contrasting possible early phase of ceramic uniformity in Greece stands out as an exception to the general pattern. There has not been sufficient excavation or research to establish whether the boundaries between different styles are sharp or blurred, though one gets the impression that they are well defined in Greece at least. Figurines and seals are other items which also show variation on a regional scale.

The explanation of these various observed features and patterns in the material evidence is fraught with difficulty.[58] For example a hypothesis that greater differentiation of ceramic styles reflects greater stress amongst the communities concerned has been proposed, the Mediterranean example chosen supposedly showing wide early uniformity and later differentiation of styles over small areas. The hypothesis suggests that material culture is more actively used to define group identity when there is competition for space, scarce resources and so on. However the interpretation may be incomplete since it offers too little positive explanation for early uniformity, rather assuming that it just happens. This seems inadequate for the early monochrome phase in Greece for example. If stress is involved, one might have to differentiate between different sorts of stress. The stress of the pioneering or early stage of agriculture for example, when communities were dispersed and in a state of transition, could have led to a desire for contact over wide areas which found expression in material culture. But it may have changed later as population grew to a different, competitive kind of stress. Though interpretation is so difficult (in this case the danger is in assuming rather than proving that stress existed), the pattern of contrasts outlined above seem central to any broad interpretation of society. After a pioneering or transitional phase communities were widespread and well established. Larger settlements than had existed before were maintained and some increased. Internal uniformity bolstered by a common ritual may have been necessary for the operation of such nucleations and to suppress or conceal differences which would have threatened them. Long-range links with other communities through the medium of ritual and exchange could also have served to minimise difference. At the same time, competition between local communities is possible, difference being expressed in sites of different sizes and status, the most successful perhaps being those able to achieve the greatest surplus production and maintain the most ritual activity. Competition may also have been a factor regionally, with the identity of different regions being marked in material culture as a form of self-interest and self-protection. This in its turn as suggested above would be denied or concealed by cross-regional contacts.

## Origins

Having reviewed the evidence it remains to pull together the scattered discussion of the origins of these communities. Many writers have assumed on the grounds of chronology, material culture and subsistence that their origins lie in the Near East. Some even claim to be able to see a south–north spread after an initial establishment in Greece, though we have seen reason to doubt the quality of the evidence on which this rests. Against these kinds of arguments for direct colonisation one can note that chronological priority need not imply a causal connection, that similarities in material culture between south-east Europe and the Near East are vague, and that there is some evidence for local use of cereals before 6000 bc and for local domestication (by conventional criteria) of cattle and pigs, though not of sheep and goats, after this date.[59] The argument for indigenous adoption of external developments would be all the stronger if we knew more of the early post-glacial period in the whole area under consideration. It is not just a compromise to suggest that both processes were involved, both population expansion from outside, seen at its most probable in the case of Crete, and also local development and local adoption of external developments. The effect of neighbouring areas on each other was extensive, as will be seen throughout this book, with neither external influence nor local inspiration being by themselves sufficient explanation of what happened. Ultimately the discussion here is hampered by arbitrary geographical boundaries. There may be little good reason to separate south-east Europe from south-west Asia and the eastern Mediterranean generally. The nature of society and its effect on subsistence may have been broadly similar over the whole region, so that in the south-east we observe a process parallel to, even indivisible from, that observable in the rest of Europe. The only real difference may be one of timing, and even that is not securely established in the present state of research.

*Material sequences, c. 4500–4000 bc*

The chronology of this period is not well established, either in Greece or the Balkans. There is no exact synchronism between these areas. Though artefactual change is widely observable around the middle of the fifth millennium bc, the rate of change at its end is variable.

There are few radiocarbon dates for the transition to the Greek Late Neolithic and fewer series of dates. The Sitagroi series together with one date at Servia suggest a beginning by the middle of the fifth millennium, not incompatible with the slightly later date at Sesklo where there is stratigraphic discontinuity.[60] Other dates, from Franchthi and Saliagos in the Cyclades help to confirm this position, but the dates from Franchthi are of very variable quality and consistency at this level. The final phase at Achilleion, ivb, is not radiocarbon dated. Problems of synchronism are accentuated by the variety of stratigraphic situations at this point, with continuity at sites like Tsangli, Arapi or Servia, discontinuity at Sesklo and others, abandonment at Achilleion and new foundations like Sitagroi and other sites on the Thracian plain of northern Greece.[61] Proposed sequences reflect these difficulties. For example in the classic areas of Thessaly, to continue the example from earlier in the chapter, a generalised sequence was built up on the basis of several sites rather than a single site, but some components of it did not even have a secure stratigraphic basis in any one site.

These problems are particularly acute in the fourth millennium (chapter 5) but may well apply to the early part of the sequence. However sites like Tsangli and Arapi (not radiocarbon dated) have early phases of pottery radically different from the Sesklo phase. Painted pottery is common, especially matt-painted dark designs on lighter surfaces, in a variety of geometric and linear designs, but also polychrome ware of red and black on a light ground; both kinds of painting can be on the same vessel. Dark and grey wares continue too, with incised or rippled decoration. Further north Servia has fine black burnished rippled pottery and some painted pottery perhaps of Thessalian type in its assemblage; Sitagroi 1 has dark pottery quite like Veselinovo–Karanovo iii forms in central-southern Bulgaria but phase ii beginning before 4000 bc has a variety of painted wares with resemblances again in Thessaly. There are similar general problems in establishing reliable sequences in the Balkans. There is a mixture of stratigraphic situations. In Bulgaria there is a break between Karanovo ii and iii but continuity at Yasatepe. At Veselinovo itself excavation has been incomplete, and a Karanovo ii level is suspected. In the central Balkans there are almost 30 sites with material transitional between the Starčevo and Vinča cultures, but many more new Vinča sites. In Oltenia and Muntenia, Dudeşti culture levels

are not stratified above Criş levels, except perhaps at Tîrgşor. The deep
deposits of Veselinovo and Vinča sites contrast with these sites.[62] Radiocarbon dating has also been inadequately applied. There are only four dates from
four sites with Karanovo III material, and the succeeding, probably briefer,
Karanovo IV phase is undated. For the early Vinča culture there are 24 dates
from nine sites, but no single site has more than five dates; the Anza sequence
is more poorly dated at this point since there are only three dates for phase IVb
and phase IVa is undated. The vulnerability of individual dates is obvious.[63]
Nonetheless a recent synthesis of the Vinča culture has proposed an early
phase on the combined basis of radiocarbon dates and typology over a wide
area, as preferable to extrapolation of the stratigraphy of the eponymous site
Vinča over the whole area of the culture. Previously Vinča itself provided the
key stratigraphy, though this was very poorly published in detail, divided in
one scheme into four successive phases numbered A–D, the second and third
being further subdivided into two. Another combines the Vinča sequence
first with a Transylvanian variant named after the site of Turdaş (often
transcribed Tordoš) unsystematically excavated in the last century and then
with Pločnik, a southern Yugoslav tell; Vinča–Turdaş I and II are roughly
equivalent to Vinča A and B. There is one radiocarbon date from between A
and BI at the eponymous site. The new ordering proposes that the early phase
cover A–C at Vinča itself and regional variants elsewhere, the phase spanning
c. 4500–3900 bc.[64] Dudeşti chronology is founded, apart from typological
resemblances to Vinča–Turdaş material, on a closed pit find at Dudeşti itself
of Dudeşti and Linear pottery.

Although there is no uniformity over the Balkans as a whole, there is a
general shift in pottery, on which as in Greece attention continues to be
focussed, to dark wares, enhanced by burnishing and decorated by channelling, rippling or incision. (The area of the different Linear pottery culture from
the Hungarian plain north of the Carpathians to Moldavia and Muntenia is
discussed later in the chapter). Karanovo III or Veselinovo fine ware is mostly
undecorated, and the most distinctive form is the pear-shaped or cylindrical
beaker on legs or a flat base, with a handle with projecting upper terminal. In
the Vinča culture and its Transylvanian early variant, the Turdaş culture,
there were distinctive fine-ware globular and biconical lugged pots, footed or
pedestalled bowls, handled pear-shaped jars and shallow dishes. The thicker
fine ware was decorated with incisions and impressions (and also paint in
south-west Romania, as at Rast), and the thinner fine ware with channelling
or rippling. All tended to be well burnished (Fig. 3.13). Dudeşti pottery is
similarly decorated, with shouldered bowls being distinctive.[65]

Various origins have been proposed for these styles. Connections with the
eastern Mediterranean have been mooted for Greek matt-painted and polychrome wares. For the Balkans, Childe's theory of expansion from Anatolia
and Greece has been widely followed. A further use of the hypothesis is to
document developments within the Balkans; we read for example of the
northward 'march of the Vinča tribe' and that 'an eastern shock cannot be
denied' on Anza ceramics from the Karanovo area. For the most part however,

**3.13** Early Vinča pottery from Anza, phase IV. Yugoslav Macedonia, later fifth millennium bc. *After* Gimbutas

local development is to be preferred, and purely local antecedents for favoured shapes and fabrics are available in the preceding complexes; Vinča and Anza provide useful examples.[66] We will however return below to the difficult questions of how to explain both change and inter-regional similarities without recourse to the hypothesis of new population, when other evidence has been reviewed. The rate of change is interesting, for example in central-southern Bulgaria, where perhaps at the end of this period the poorly known Karanovo IV phase begins, on the basis of radiocarbon dates for III and V and of a suggested synchronism with late VInča–Turdaş. Rather than yet another population change, the material from Karanovo IV such as small pedestalled bowls with covering incised geometric decoration suggests a different rate of artefactual change from other areas.

As for material other than pottery, the general pattern seems to be of greater quantity and variety, as of chipped stone industries or of polished stone tools. Greater numbers are illustrated by the jump in the figures for Anza IV to 27 from six in the previous phase. In other sites especially of the Vinča culture plano-convex 'adzes' were developed. Figurines too were more numerous, the increase illustrated again by figures of 48 from Anza IV compared with 16 from II–III. Those in Bulgaria have a more conservative rod-headed form, while Vinča figurines have flat-topped triangular faces, with the body frequently incised; there is a double-headed example at Rast, found also at Vinča itself, and other varities including seated figurines up to 25 cm high. In Greece however there is a decline of figurines. Clay tables continue, as in Karanovo III and elsewhere, and other ritual innovations are Vinča lids incised with human or animal faces, and incised clay tablets (Figs. 3.14 and

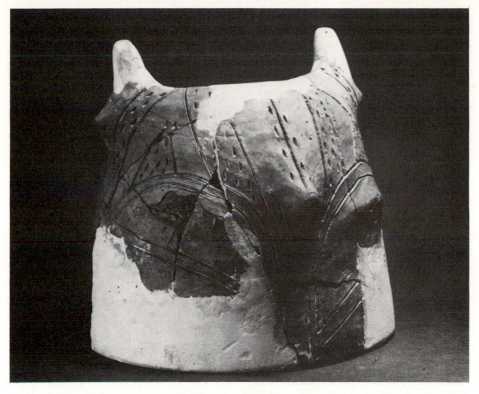

**3.14** Early Vinča animal lid from Vinča. *After* Gimbutas

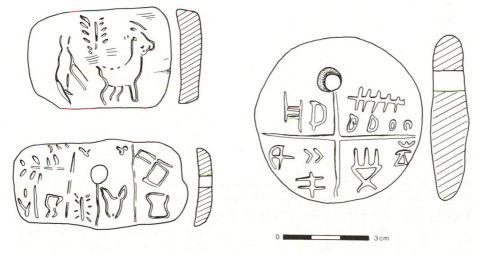

**3.15** Inscribed clay tablets from Tărtăria, Transylvania, Romania. *After* Gimbutas

3.15). Finds of the latter in an in-filled pit at a settlement called Tărtăria in Transylvania evidently dug from the Turdaş culture layer have provoked controversy.[67] There were three unbaked tablets, one circular and two rectangular, the former and one of the latter being perforated. These had incised signs on them, and the unperforated rectangular one had what appear to be representations of a goat and one other animal and a tree. In addition there were 26 schematic figurines of early Vinča type, two alabaster figurines, a clay 'anchor' and a *spondylus* bracelet. There were also the burnt bones of a mature adult. While this horizon was acceptable to some, the date of original publication should be noted; for many at this time Vinča was equated with Troy I, a position which was supported by alleged similarities between the Tărtăria signs and those of the Jemdet Nasr period in Mesopotamia dated around 3000 BC (i.e. in calendar years). An alternative response for those keen to assert the validity of the radiocarbon chronology was to maintain that the pit was dug from a later, Coţofeni, level at the site. It is however most likely that the finds should be accepted at face value since, on the one hand there are many vessels in early and late Vinča contexts and in fourth millennium bc contexts in Bulgaria with similar incised signs, many of them indeed discoveries made long before Tărtăria, and on the other there are other inscribed tablets only a little later in date than Tărtăria, as at Gradeshnitsa in north-west Bulgaria.

A final example of increasing artefactual diversity is the small number of worked copper objects in early Vinča contexts, such as the beads from Vinča, Selevac and Čoka, the fishhook from Gornea and the awl from Balomir. (The imprecision of the chronological evidence may be noted briefly again, since the single radiocarbon date from Gornea is early fourth millennium.) Similar trinkets in similar or even earlier horizons have been found in eastern Bulgaria at Ovčarovo and Usoe.[68] These artefacts may for the most part be made of native or pure copper, and simply beaten into shape, perhaps with the aid of heating or annealing. There is however a piece of copper slag in Anza IV which shows that copper was also smelted from its ores, probably oxide ores because these are easier to smelt. True metallurgy came to be of considerable importance in the fourth millennium and will be discussed at much greater length in chapter 5. No especial significance either from the technical or the social point of view should be attached to the early horizon of trinket manufacture. It finds a satisfactory place in the context of artefactual diversity in the later fifth millennium bc. Though copper finds go back to much earlier dates in the Near East, it is likely enough that this was an independent process in south-east Europe.[69]

### Settlements and their social context

A notable feature of this period virtually throughout our area is an expansion of the zones of settlement.[70] Much of the evidence for this claim has not been collected systematically, but proper surveys in Thessaly and in the Sava valley do confirm the trend. In Thessaly the process can be seen in the numbers of small new sites in the dry eastern plain, and in the Sava valley by the numbers of new sites founded in the early Vinča period, as for example at Gomolava. In the Aegean for example the beginnings of the settlement at Saliagos in the Cyclades have been radiocarbon dated to the late fifth millennium bc. In northern Greece, tell sites such as Sitagroi and Dikilitash begin in the mid fifth millennium bc. In the lower Morava basin excavation at Selevac has shown its foundation in the early Vinča period. On the Yugoslav coast sites of the Danilo culture seem to represent the absorption of peripheral hunters and gatherers by neighbouring farmers. On the Black Sea coast there are also clearer indications of settled communities, as in north-east Bulgaria. It has been suggested that there was an early phase of the Hamangia culture in the Dobruja with impressed pottery dating to this period or earlier; but there is no stratigraphic evidence to support this apart from the confused situation at La Adam.

In train with this change there are indications of larger sites in several areas. The evidence from Greece is inconclusive at this stage, and the problems remain of establishing site size at tell settlements, as in central-southern Bulgaria. A striking change at Karanovo and Yasatepe is the slightly larger house size combined with the division of house interiors into three, with a central 'living' room. Those at Yasatepe are set close together in rows. But while suggestive, these features contribute nothing directly to the question of overall size. The clearest evidence for larger sites comes from the area of the early Vinča culture. Anza in this phase covers a maximum area of 9–10 ha which might have contained some 400 houses if all used to the same extent, while Selevac covers some 80 ha, towards the upper limit for the culture. It is noticeable that the largest Vinča sites are unenclosed, while the tells are much smaller. Problems in the analysis of the extent of a site like Anza have already been noted and at Selevac it was suggested that the settlement 'drifted' uphill through the span of its occupation and that its area in the late fifth millennium bc may have been considerably more compact than the total extent of the site. Nonetheless it appears that some sites grew radically in size in the central Balkans.

Both settlement expansion and site growth can be taken to support the likelihood of population increase. It has been argued already that population level cannot be seen as an independent variable operating outside the context of contemporary society, but is one effect of competitive social relations at the level of both individual communities and regions. The increase of size (and perhaps therefore of population) at particular sites may not on its own testify to an overall increase of population but rather a nucleation or concentration, whether or not accompanied by a general increase of other sites in the area round about them. But the numbers of Vinča sites known make it likely that both processes were operating. It is probable too that some sites were differentiated from the rest not only by their size but also by their social role. Again in the Vinča culture there is suggestive evidence for an uneven distribution or concentration of ritual activities, beginning in the early Vinča period through perhaps clearer in the later. Certain sites like the large tells of Vinča or Tărtăria (6 and 3 ha respectively) or the vast 100 ha unenclosed site of Potporanj appear to have far greater numbers of figurines and other ritual paraphernalia than their neighbours. Another indication may be the large amount of obsidian at Vinča in early Vinča contexts, and also at Vršac and Potporanj, in contrast to the sparse amounts at most sites. Movement and consumption were selective. The evidence from elsewhere is less clear, though it may be significant for example that at Karanovo one of the internal divisions of some houses was used partly for figurines as if to emphasise this ritual aspect of life. It is also interesting that the fortunes of some sites fluctuated while others waned altogether. Sesklo does not have the same prominence in the earlier part of the Greek Late Neolithic as in the classical Sesklo phase. The occupation of Anza comes to an end around 4000 bc. The suggested cause of increased aridity in the Ovce Polje basin may be too specific, for if valid it should have affected many more sites than it appears to have done. It may be useful therefore to think in terms of a social failure of some kind, in terms of either a breakdown of internal cohesion or a replacement of and taking over of its role by other sites in the region. The same fate awaited sites like Vinča itself and Selevac in the earlier fourth millennium bc, as discussed in chapter 5.

It has been argued that the subsistence economy is embedded in contemporary social relations rather than an external force, and its operation might therefore be a clue to further social change of the kinds discussed. The evidence however is sporadic, and taken at face value shows little change. Staple crops and animals on the evidence of sites like Anza, Selevac and Gomolava were largely unchanged. Concentration on sheep and goats was maintained at Anza, on cattle further north. Similar crops were grown and animals husbanded at Sitagroi, with a continued emphasis on immature animals. Small clearances only are detectable in the surrounding plain of Drama, though they may increase in size in Macedonia. In Thessaly there is a gradual reduction in the numerical dominance of sheep and goats. Scattered evidence from the central Balkans may hint at other changes not yet widely detected because of inadequate research and recovery techniques. Flax, probably domesticated, was recovered at Gomolava, and whether used for oil or linen might indicate increased diversification of products. It has been suggested also that the large amounts of heavy soils such as chernozems and smonicas within a 2 km radius around several large Vinča sites such as Potporanj make the use of some form of plough likely in order to bring enough arable under cultivation to feed their populations. The find of a large fish vertebra at Potporanj, the site lying several kilometres from the nearest large river, could also indicate the lack of self-sufficiency of the bigger sites or at any rate a flow of food into them from sites in the area roundabout. If these are real changes they may emphasise differentiation between sites in the settlement pattern as a whole.

It may also be instructive to return to the broad pattern of material culture distribution. We have seen evidence for the expansion of the areas of settlement and for infilling in areas already settled, and some evidence for internal differentiation. At the same time there is, at least as far as pottery is concerned, considerable uniformity over wide areas, as in Greece. Over the rest of the Balkans, while neither differences within nor between regions should be minimised, there is also a general shift to dark pottery which has many points in common from region to region. If such similarities are accepted but the conventionally argued new populations rejected, one may have a further clue to the nature of social relations in this period. I suggest that expansion, internal differentiation and inter-regional contact are all connected, the role of the latter being to ease or conceal stresses or conflicts at the regional level. As far as one can see, boundaries between different regions are not particularly sharply defined though this has not been much researched.[71] Within different culture areas the role of uniformity in material culture may have been to provide internal cohesion and likewise to deny or conceal stresses or conflict. It may be no accident that a lot of the evidence for internal differentiation discussed has come from the Vinča culture in the central Balkans, which albeit with regional variation has the largest area of any at this period. If the hypothesis of new populations is rejected, material culture must be assigned social roles of this kind. How else could one explain the pattern of change from around 4500 bc, other than as implausibly random events?

All these changes should be seen as social developments, the effect of social relations at community and regional level, rather than as responses to external agents such as climate or the adoption of a uniform agriculture. The critical factor is how the societies in question used the resources available within the pattern of constraints facing them. The varied nature of society that has been seen is further testimony of this. I have also argued for the existence of various contradictions or conflicts in social relations at both local and regional level. Such contradictions can be argued to provide a dynamic source of change in society, and their importance will be seen in chapter 5 to be enhanced in the succeeding millennium and a half.

## 3.2 Expansion in central and western Europe, 4500–4000 bc

### Environment, 6000–4000 bc

This section covers developments in central and western Europe, from the Great Hungarian plain west to the Paris basin, and from the upper Rhine and Danube valleys north to the edge of the north European plain. Varied evidence suggests that this was a period of warmer conditions than those of today. Pollen analyses from central Europe have been used to suggest the existence of fluctuations within this pattern though their scale is hardly evident from such a source. The prevailing vegetational type was undoubtedly climax closed woodland, as indicated by analyses both on the fringes of the area as in the north Alpine foreland and less often within the lowland parts which were the focus of agricultural settlement, as in the upper Danube between Ingolstadt and Regensburg. Its composition may have varied, being lighter in the Great Hungarian plain, though sources of pollen are too few in the area for detailed study of this aspect. The section also briefly covers the eastern flank of the Carpathians in Moldavia and the Ukraine. Environmental evidence for that area is not abundant, but sufficient to suggest extensive woodland, perhaps with a mixture of coniferous or broad-leaved species in the major valleys such as the Prut and Dniester, and mixed oak forest along with some more open parts on the interfluves.[72]

*Indigenous background, 6000–4500 bc*

There is ample evidence for the continued presence of indigenous communities in parts of this wide area, as suggested by regional research in parts such as the Paris basin and Belgium, the lower Rhine, the north Alpine foreland, the upper Danube valley, or the north European plain between the Elbe and Oder (Fig. 3.16).[73] The evidence is discontinuous however, and the situation in areas such as Czechoslovakia and northern Hungary is much less clear, though geometric flint assemblages are found. Some suggested groups such as the Eger group in northern Hungary with its assemblages of heavy tools may in fact represent only large-scale stone extraction dating from later periods. In the absence of deep stratigraphies the chronological succession of flint styles has not been well established over the area as a whole. Geometric microliths are widely evident, including trapezoidal forms. In northern France, one of

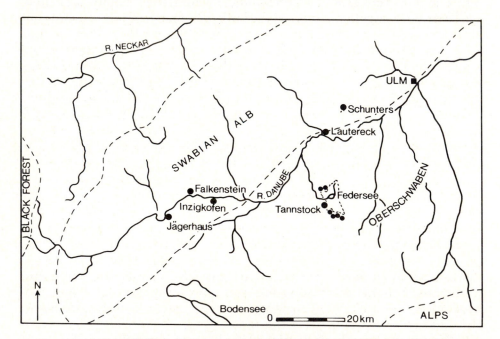

**3.16** Simplified location map of principal sites in the upper Danube valley, sixth and earlier fifth millennia bc. *After* Jochim

the best researched areas, it has been suggested that trapezes spread widely in the early sixth millennium bc, that the phenomenon was discontinuous, and that 'new' and 'old' styles could be found in contemporary association, as at Birsmatten in northern Switzerland. Birsmatten also illustrates the latter point. The need for local chronologies emphasised in chapter 2 still prevails. Assemblages with trapezes as at Sered' in the Pannonian plain in southern Czechoslovakia still await independent dating.

The nature of human settlement is unclear in this area, an important deficiency in recent research. Site locations, on the basis of the regional studies cited, seem to be quite varied with interfluve and upland sites recorded as well as the expected river- and lakesides (as in the Paris basin and the north Alpine foreland). The range and variations of site sizes however have been less well studied. Large sites do occur, such as the group of as many as 35 huts at Schötz–Fischerhausern in north-west Switzerland, though it is not clear how many were contemporary, and roughly the same number on the former shore of the Federsee Lake representing at least two different occupations.[74] It is possible therefore that many of the other sites under discussion were transient hunting sites rather than longer-stay bases. The prevalent model is of seasonally mobile groups, seen at its most sophisticated and explicit in the upper Danube valley, where a detailed annual round has been proposed.[75] On the basis of excavated sites such as Jägerhaus Cave, Lautereck and Tannstock on the Federsee (dating in broad terms to the Late Mesolithic but perhaps to the sixth as much as to the fifth millennium bc in more specific terms) and of ethnographic *comparanda* and animal behaviour, it is envisaged that large ungulates provided the bulk of human food while fishing and plant gathering were minor components of the subsistence economy. Winter groups may have been rather small and well dispersed in the upper valley, while summer nucleation is possible lower and including the Federsee. In fact the specific seasonality evidence at these sites is very poor, as indeed for any specific form of ungulate exploitation. Other possibilities therefore have to be considered. Within the large expanses of forest, settlement may have been concentrated on ecologically more diverse regions, such as especially the Federsee, the lakes of the north Alpine foreland (though Sakellaridis notes that there are as many non-lakeside sites recorded) and those of the north European plain. Less varied settlement may then characterise the foci of occupation with transient exploitation elsewhere. It is also possible that some degree of control over animal resources was established. The evidence is minimal, though high ivy pollen at Baulmes–Abri de la Cure, Lac de Neuchâtel at a level estimated at around 5000 bc could be connected with the provision of fodder. In the faunal assemblage from Nenzlingen–Birsmatten in the Birs valley of northern Switzerland, pig were mainly large immature specimens, but this detail from one site cannot support much weight of hypothesis. The lack of pollen analysis also makes it hard to see whether climax forest was regularly cleared.

Following the hypothesis developed in chapter 2 about the possible social role of stylistic variation of projectile points, it is of interest to note on the one hand the extremely varied pattern of development from region to region and on the other hand the now perhaps spatially more restricted zones of particular styles (though these are not closely dated) such as the Teverener, Hülstener and Nollheider groups between the Rhine and Weser. This may indicate more populous breeding networks or an increased concern with group identity and territory.[76] Either or both possibilities could in turn suggest the likelihood of increased pressure on resources in central-western Europe. Further examination of these aspects is however prevented by the lack of evidence for burial and exchange for example, which have been fruitful sources of speculation in other areas. We will return to the indigenous situation in discussing the origins of the striking developments of the second half of the fifth millennium bc in the area, for it may hold the key to their explanation.

### The Linear pottery culture, c. 4600/4500–4000 bc and after

In the mid fifth millennium bc there appeared in central and western Europe a new cultural grouping, distributed from the fringes of the Starčevo–Körös and early Vinča area west as far as the Paris basin and the lower Rhine, from the north Alpine foreland north to the fringes of the north European plain, and eastwards down the east flank of the Carpathians in the Ukraine and Moldavia (Fig. 3.17). It has been labelled after the characteristic incised linear

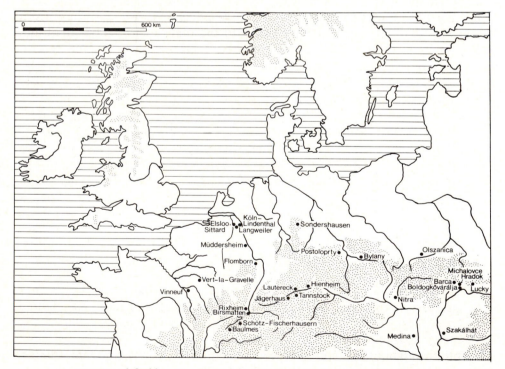

**3.17** Simplified location map of the principal sites mentioned in chapter 3.2

decoration of its pottery, some styles of which were very widely distributed within the cultural grouping.[77] Settlements of large houses with substantial timbers are characteristic except in the Great Hungarian plain and eastwards, generally located on fertile soils (usually loess) near water. Their subsistence basis was cereal cultivation and the husbandry of a restricted range of domesticated animals, principally cattle and pig. The rapid change implied by the appearance of these features has often been taken to represent swift agricultural colonisation, but the contribution of indigenous populations must as in south-east Europe be carefully considered. This debate forms the underlying theme of this section.

## The nature of the evidence and chronology and material sequences

Over this broad area the physical layout and formation of settlements were substantially different from those in much of south-east Europe. Some sites were occupied throughout the span of the culture but except in the Great Hungarian plain vertical stratigraphic accumulations of deposit are not found, partly due to the nature of house construction, partly due to the often dispersed form of settlement layout. Subsequent erosion of these 'open' settlements has been unkind; virtually without exception the buildings of these sites lack their original floors. Such sites provide therefore only very limited opportunities for observing vertical and horizontal stratigraphy, and radiocarbon dating has not been applied in earnest. Virtually only in Slovakia and northern Hungary are vertical stratigraphies available and these from caves or shelters in uplands peripheral to the main foci of settlement and development. On the other hand there have been notable extensive excavations of settlements, the speed of publication is relatively good and aspects of their environmental setting have been closely studied. Decorated pottery again forms the basis for chronological subdivision of the culture.[78] Given the nature of the stratigraphic evidence the most reliable typologies are likely to be the simplest. Thus in Hungary, Czechoslovakia and south-east Germany a basic threefold division into early, middle and late phases underlies proposed schemes and in the southern Netherlands, the lower and middle Rhine, as well as in Poland and east of the Carpathians a basic twofold division is envisaged between earlier and later phases. This basic framework can be checked to some extent by contact finds with subsequent cultures. This is further referred to in chapters 5 and 6. Regional variation is considerable by the late or later phases but at the risk of overgeneralisation, the basic trend in decorative change is from simple use of one to three continuous incised lines to the elaboration of the line with stops (the so called music-note) and of the band by infilling with subsidiary motifs between two lines and subsequently in the west to the breaking-up of the line and band into more fragmented linear motifs and the development of separate rim decoration (Fig. 3.18). Motifs throughout are both curvilinear and rectilinear. Forms are basically simple throughout including closed and semi-open bowls, and jars, though pedestalled forms are found in the early phase in central Europe and pear-

**3.18** Artefacts from an LBK grave (no. 83) at Elsloo, southern Netherlands. Photo: Rijksmuseum van Oudheden, Leiden

shaped closed bowls are common in the late phase. Finer and coarser wares are represented. In all regions the greatest decorative variation seems to have occurred in the later part of the sequence. Painting, so common earlier in the Balkans, was not used much beyond the Great Hungarian plain (apart from the late Šarka style of Bohemia), occurring in regional groups on the plain such as the Esztar and Szakálhát of the middle–late phases, and it may be remembered that by the later fifth millennium bc to the south unpainted wares were dominant in the area of the Vinča culture. Further elaboration and regionalisation can be seen in the highly incised fine ware of the Bükk group of north-east Hungary, with its own periodisation corresponding roughly to the late phases of the Great Hungarian plain, and its immediate successors.

More-detailed typologies have regularly been attempted. For example in the area of central Europe one particular style of simple incised line, occurring on flat-based bowls with organic temper, has been suggested to be the very earliest, and a distribution has been recorded from Czechoslovakia to Hessen and Baden-Wurttemberg.[79] This is without stratigraphic basis, though it does occur early in the suggested sequence at Bylany in Bohemia. In the core area of the eastern Linear pottery culture in and around the Great Hungarian plain, a detailed eight-stage sequence has been proposed, including a *Protolinearbandkeramik* contemporary with late Starčevo–Körös before the above early phase. This sequence is partly based on the vertical stratigraphy of cave sites such as Ardovo, Čertova Diera and Domica but its weakness is that no one cave site contains the complete sequence and that it relies on other, open sites (though with closed finds) such as Michalovče–Hradók, and Lucky and Barca III, representing respectively the first and second phases. A detailed sequence of a different kind has been proposed on the basis of the evidence for vertical and horizontal stratigraphy at the site of Bylany in Bohemia though work on the full publication of the site still continues. Some 4.5 of an estimated 22 ha have been excavated. Some eight main phases were proposed, further subdivisible into about three times as many, but direct vertical stratigraphy is in fact available only between the Orange and Grey phases in the middle of the sequence, and between the terminal Light Brown phase and its various predecessors. This problem persists further west. Thus at the large site of Elsloo beside the Maas in Dutch Limburg (where some 3 out of 10 ha have been excavated) out of 95 excavated houses relatively few directly overlapped. The response, followed also on the Rhine, has been to devise a ceramic sequence by seriating pits and decorated pottery, on the Petrie replacement principle that new types of artefacts tend to replace those currently in use and are themselves replaced in turn by yet newer types. This has produced a fourfold subdivision of the two main chronological phases in each region. Application of the same method at specific sites on the Aldenhoven plateau between Aachen and Köln has produced a reasonable but not exact match with the regional sequence.[80] The methodology is impressive but the underlying principle debatable. It raises the recurrent issue of whether variation is largely temporal, or whether it has other aspects, such as function or individual and group status. Little attention has been paid to the spatial analysis of differing decoration within sites except in one study of Elsloo and Hienheim, Bavaria (and this too on the assumption of steady replacement of styles through time), and in one study of Olszanica in southern Poland, here excitingly with the explicit assumption of faster innovation in some houses than others.[81] Considerably more attention could be given to the possibility of wider variation in decoration than the seriations allow, the social significance of which will be returned to later. The only site where a series of radiocarbon dates has been obtained is Elsloo. Nine out of 11 dates fall in the span 4500–4000 bc; one is slightly earlier and one slightly later. No one phase is thus dated by more than one or two samples, but it is noticeable that the internal phasing of the site is to some extent contradicted by the dates. It remains to be seen in other circumstances whether this was a test of the typology or of the radiocarbon dating. The blade industries of the culture have been partially documented, though little chronological development is apparent.[82] Some development of axes, adzes and perforated adzes has been suggested at Elsloo, and there too amongst the house types those with an internal central Y-configuration of posts have been suggested to be earlier than those without. The direct evidence really comes down to the cutting of house no. 25 by house no. 26, but the latter still has remnants of the Y-feature; there is also no difference in plan between the earlier no. 54 and the later no. 53, which overlap. The possibility remains that house plans did not change in the simple way proposed.

Finally on the question of origins (to be returned to later) there have been two schools of thought, one that Linear pottery culture was a development within the late Starčevo–Körös culture and that its extension and other features (including blade industries) represent the continued colonisation of temperate Europe by agricultural communities, the other that Linear pottery culture was an innovation of indigenous communities beyond the fringes of the Starčevo–Körös culture, in the suggested Szatmár group at the Great Hungarian plain and in the suggested Medina group of Transdanubia. For the present one may note the stratigraphic deficiencies of the former hypothesis, the varied nature of the pottery and chronological uncertainties about the latter two groups, and the assumption common to both that the origins of new developments are to be sought in or around the Great Hungarian plain immediately adjacent to previous agricultural settlement.

### Settlements: central and western Europe

Settlements of the Linear pottery culture are for the most part sites in a recurrent position in the landscape, generally in the lower part of the river valleys though on the whole seeming to avoid the low parts of the largest rivers and the floodplain itself.[83] Thus in Czechoslovakia, Bylany and other neighbours lie in rolling country dissected by small streams, Hienheim in Bavaria lies on a terrace 15 m above the Danube, Olszanica and other sites in southern Poland in the lower parts of tributaries of the Vistula, Langweiler 11 and its neighbours on the bottom of the little Merzbachtal in flattish country feeding the tributaries of the Maas, and Elsloo and its neighbours in Dutch Limburg lie on terraces of the Maas and its tributaries. The pattern is not invariable, but it is strikingly regular. For the most part too settlements are therefore sited close to well-watered soils, and as well as their proximity to alluvial deposits a remarkably strong correlation has been observed with the distribution of loess soils. Loess is a fine wind-sorted silt laid down in periglacial conditions which can form deep but discontinuous deposits in central and western Europe, from roughly the southern edge of the north European plain to the north Alpine foreland and extending into western France. It is rich in minerals, its structure is uniform, it is well drained and easily cultivated. Linear pottery sites regularly occur on the edge of patches of loess, through being close to water courses. Other favourable soils are found close to Linear pottery sites, but the relationship with loess is extremely strong; in a study of the Rhineland, only the Worms–Rheinpfalz area had less than 70 per cent of sites on loess soils, and a recent survey in central Germany suggests even higher figures.[84] The main constituents of settlements are timber longhouses, pits flanking these from which soil was dug for wall daub, storage pits at variable distances from the houses, and occasional lengths of fence or palisade (Fig. 3.19). Most longhouses are about 6–7 m broad, but range in length from 6 to 45 m. The extent of variation is less perhaps than evident at first sight. The main distribution at for example Bylany was between 6 and 20 m and at Olszanica between 6–8 and 12–26 m, and at the former only one example 45 m long was recorded. Five rows of large posts formed the basic

**3.19** Two LBK houses under excavation at Bylany, Bohemia, Czechoslovakia. Photo: Pavlů

frame of the house, which it is suggested on the basis of so many posts was not cross-tied, though no above-ground structural timbers have survived. At one (generally southern) end of some houses a concentration of posts has been taken to support a raised area, though the significance of a continuous bedding trench at the other is not clear. The original floor has not survived. On the analogy of a fourth millennium longhouse at Postoloprty in Czechoslovakia which contained four spaced pits interpreted as hearths it was proposed that there was one hearth per 6 m in all such longhouses. A more useful division has been made further west, of a central part of the longhouse which is freer of posts than its ends; this ranges in length at Elsloo from 6 to 16 m, at Hienheim from 5 to 19.5 m. Charcoal in the postholes of the central areas here indicate the former presence of at least one hearth, but the significance of the variation in size remains unclear.[85] Ethnographic comparanda provide an uncertain yardstick, and the same space available could house a nuclear family comfortably or an extended family with less room. The existence of lofts or first-floor rooms tends to be left out of these discussions. The extent of animal stalling inside longhouses is also unclear. Since the floors do not survive, differential artefact distribution (itself little recorded) is not likely to be of great help. Analysis of the organic content and phosphate content of a house at Hienheim revealed no internal variation, and analysis of the nitrogen content of a house at Olszanica produced an identical result.[86] It may be argued that there was little climatic pressure for regular winter stalling, and the occasional fenced enclosures beside longhouses, as beside the largest longhouses in the Green and Blue phases at Bylany, might be taken to bear this out, though there is of course no proof of the seasonal use of such pens. An alternative approach to the question of house size variation is to consider it as related to status. Thus at Elsloo, six to ten occupants have been posited per house (as appropriate to a small extended family) but the range of the central area, from 35 to 112 m² has been taken as related to the wealth and status of the family. There has not been much testing of this approach by looking at artefact distributions. This has been applied at Olszanica but the results are contradictory. Thus polished stone tools were found particularly clustered in the immediate area of house no. 6, a very large structure 41.5 m long. The rare pieces of imported obsidian at the site were also significantly clustered in pits beside the wall of another longhouse and sherds of imported Bükk pottery were found nearby as well. However the house in question was only 12 by 6 m. One may have to reckon with different functions for different longhouses (to which we return below) not directly expressed in all cases by their lengths.

This question should also be considered in relation to the variation in size of the settlements as a whole. In the crude terms of total numbers per site the variation can be considerable, from small clusters of houses to large concentrations, as seen in the contrast in Dutch Limburg between Geleen and Elsloo or Sittard, or in the other large examples already cited such as Hienheim or Bylany. It is certain that not all houses were contemporary, but the contrast and range in sizes must persist despite the overall reduction in numbers of houses in contemporary use. Relatively few houses actually overlap however (for Elsloo and Bylany see above) so that the numbers in contemporary use are uncertain. Another approach has been to consider the duration of timber such as oak. While a short house-life of only 15 years has been suggested many other authorities would allow at least twice as long and it seems possible given the weights of timber involved that many structures would have remained stable for a while even after substantial decay of their uprights at the junction with the soil.[87] This merely indicates the difficulties of putting precise figures to the numbers of houses in contemporary use in a settlement. For Elsloo the figure of 11–17 huts at any one time has been suggested, but for the much larger overall site of Bylany smaller units were proposed, thus seven or eight houses in the Green and Red phases when the site was considered to have been enlarged; each of these contained one 40 m longhouse (Fig. 3.20). The difference in interpretation can be partly explained by differing attitudes to the continuity of use of Linear pottery culture settlements. Soudský championed the view that settlements were cyclically used, abandoned and re-used, on the basis that pottery at the site showed discontinuous evolution. Storage pits with up to 15 layers of burning and relining were also taken to specify the likely duration of each occupation episode. The practice of shifting cultivation has been seen as a further motor in this movement. These criteria have previously been widely accepted, but

**3.20** General view of the excavations of the LBK settlement at Bylany, Bohemia. Photo: Pavlů

are now fiercely contested, at least in western Europe. It is dangerous to assume the nature of ceramic evolution, let alone on an incompletely excavated site. One cannot assume that each pit relining was an annual event, nor that pits themselves can be reliably assigned to individual short phases. Shifting cultivation is far from being the only likely form of cereal use in western and central Europe, and even its practice need not entail shifting settlement (as discussed further below). Even allowing for settlement drift and house replacement, the residential focus may not itself have changed much in many sites over long periods within the span of the culture.

The discussion so far has hinted at a longer life for houses than usually accepted, and potentially therefore larger groups of houses in contemporary use per site. It has also hinted at a hierarchy of sites in any area based on their overall size. This latter point however conceals considerable problems in defining what constitutes a site. These have been raised above all by the extensive excavations on the Aldenhovener Platte on either side of the small Merzbach stream. The overall pattern of houses is of substantial concentrations separated by short distances (Fig. 3.21).[88] The concentrations themselves, however, as at Langweiler II or at Langweiler IX can be broken down on the basis of stratigraphic overlap and of the refined ceramic typology proposed into a number of phases with much smaller numbers of houses in the use (Fig. 3.22). Langweiler IX is on a lower spur in the Merzbach valley. It covers some

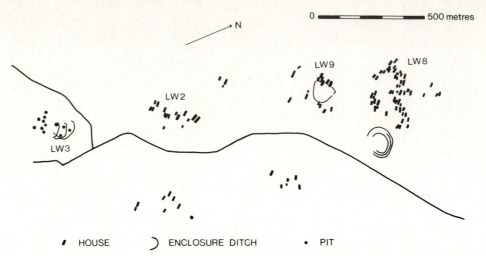

**3.21** Main excavated features of the LBK occupation of the Merzbach valley, Alden-hoven Plateau, near Köln, and the location of the main Langweiler sites. *After* Kuper *et al.*

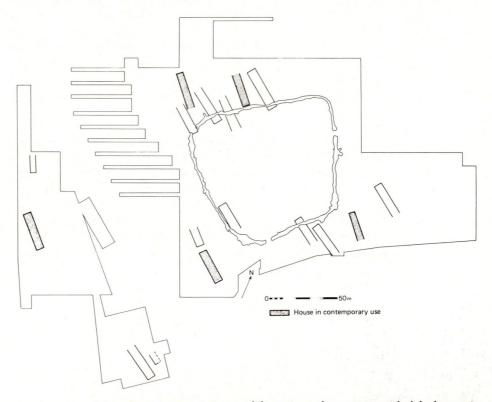

**3.22** Diagrammatic representation of the main settlement area and of the houses in occupation in phases I and II at Langweiler site IX, Aldenhoven Plateau. *After* Farruggia *et al.*

39000 m², containing 17 recognisable longhouses and another represented only by its flanking loam pits. The site could be divided into four spatial zones, each covering roughly the same area. One was abandoned early in the occupation, which lasted for most of the span of the Linear pottery culture in the area, and another was interrupted midway but in the other two there was suggested to be a succession of up to six houses, one (and exceptionally two) in each of the five main proposed phases. The average minimum distance between contemporary houses was some 140 m. Langweiler II by contrast was of shorter duration within the regional sequence. One possibility that these excavations raise is that the basic residential unit was the individual family (perhaps extended), each with its own area around it but cumulatively far from being in isolation. It is possible therefore that larger sites like Elsloo or Bylany, which appear to be villages rather than homesteads or hamlets, could in fact be broken down to some extent into loose concentrations of this kind of unit. The difference between sites would be marked only by a reduction in the minimum distance between houses, and in regions like the Merzbach the separation of individual sites may have little point other than archaeological convenience. Another possibility arises from considering the pattern of flint artefacts and pits recorded at Langweiler IX. While many artefacts and pits cluster around the houses themselves, a respectable proportion is to be found in the central area between zones 2, 3 and 4. One hypothesis is that the spatial organisation of the site reflects different residential units (on who knows what basis of age, sex, status and so on) which did indeed go together to make one whole, reflected in a central area used for pit digging, craft activities, rubbish deposition and so on. (With reference to the earlier discussion of Bylany, even the number of pits recorded, over 400, would not have provided the total grain-storage capacity needed for the settlement, some of which must be archaeologically invisible.) It is a great pity that similar artefactual distributions have not been recorded much elsewhere. The Langweiler IX plan is unusual, and one must avoid pushing its implications too far; allowance too must be made for regional variation (though Aldenhoven is only some 30 km from Elsloo). The point is clear however that much further research is needed in the differentiation of Linear pottery settlements.

Lengths of fence of palisade, and even shallow ditches as at Sittard occur within many Linear pottery culture settlement areas, though for the greater part of its span sites seem to have been essentially unenclosed. A number of sites have ditched enclosures in the later stages of the culture. Langweiler IX is a case in point, where a sub-rectangular enclosure of 0.6 ha with a V-shaped ditch and three entrances, seemingly replaced the scattered hamlet. The ditch itself was recut twice, in the second episode with a flatter base. Also in the Merzbachtal, there were four intersecting V-shaped semicircular ditches on a higher promontory at Langweiler III, and three concentric ditches at Langweiler VIII in the valley bottom, the outer one with a diameter of 130–140 m having a more V-sectioned profile than the others. There is no certain connection in the Merzbach valley between enclosures and longhouses and the former may replace the latter. However a little to the east, on the middle terrace of the Rhine at Köln–Lindenthal, there is a greater possibility that at least some of the successive ditched enclosures, to one of which may have belonged a palisaded enclosure, were contemporary with and enclosed long-houses of the middle and later phases of the culture.[89] The earlier warning about site differentiation is again relevant.

In the absence of systematic survey and extensive excavation, the overall density of settlement and its regional variations is difficult to establish. The areas of Elsloo and Hienheim may be taken as typical of the sort of pattern revealed by unsystematic survey and partial excavation.[90] In Dutch Limburg the evidence is impressive even on this basis, with sites clustered on the valley sides for the most part, with the larger sites 1.5–2 km apart and smaller sites at intervals of under 1 km. There may be elements of the same pattern in the less-well-explored Danube valley around Hienheim. The Merzbach excavations indicate that such patterns may be underrepresentations of the total evidence, since the picture has emerged there of more or less continuous settlement in hamlets or homesteads on low spurs along the valley bottom which was not appreciated till the advent of large-scale open-cast mining. Extensive and systematic survey in the loess uplands of Little Poland (though its procedural basis has not been clearly recorded) also suggests that the Aldenhoven pattern may not be a local phenomenon, since the bottoms of the smaller river valleys contain abundant traces of LBK occupation, ribbon-like linear distributions with similar small intervals between clusters (Fig. 3.23). Detailed maps in the same publication show larger concentrations sur-rounded by satellite sites at intervals of less than 1 km. Further excavation is needed; the already cited settlement of Olszanica for comparison covers over

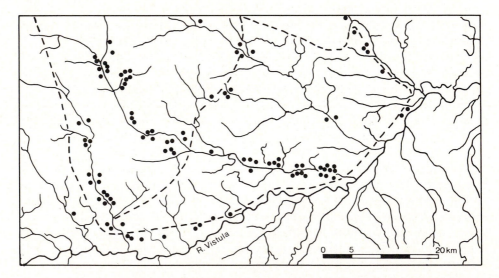

**3.23** Simplified map of the distribution of LBK settlement in southern Poland. (Dotted lines define subregions.) *After* Kruk

50 ha. If the model of dense occupation is correct, an interesting comparison emerges with settlement in south-east Europe. The difference may not be so much in overall numbers of people, but in their physical distribution across the landscape, and the different patterns therefore are likely to result as much from different social relations at family and community level as from the constraints of the various landscapes involved. Unfortunately there is only a little more pollen evidence in the loess areas of west-central Europe than in eastern Europe, and the locations of pollen profiles are not very close to the settlements in question. The closest bog to Hienheim was some 8 km distant. The pollen analysis here does not indicate extensive clearance. Woodworking axes and adzes are recurrent finds on Linear pottery culture sites but not abundant. Out of 113 graves at Elsloo 33 contained one or more of these tools. It is possible that many were wedges rather than actual cutting tools. A final point to note is the varying continuity of settlement from region to region. In this initial phase of agricultural settlement in west-central Europe some foci of settlement were more important than others, and as in eastern Europe infilling and expansion were a secondary phenomenon.

## Subsistence and the social context of production

Mixed farming appears to have been the subsistence basis of Linear pottery culture settlements. Few sites have been systematically sampled for plant remains and certainly none with internal spatial variation in mind. Wheat grains (of emmer and einkorn) have been recurrent finds in rubbish pits. Barley has been recovered in carbonised form only north and west of the Harz mountains though impressions of it on pottery stretch from the Rhineland to Czechoslovakia. This may indicate the inadequacies of sampling (or alternatively the movement of pottery). Peas, lentils, linseed and poppy were also cultivated. Quantities of edible wild plants are represented, such as chess (*Bromus secalinus*) and hazel, which were probably deliberately collected and eaten. The status of others such as fat hen is uncertain due to their low quantities except in the Rhineland where they occur more numerously; but here too they are considered as cleaning waste. The wheats seem to have been grown together, but separately from pulses. Some analysis, as at Elsloo and Hienheim and in the Rhineland, has been enough to establish the expected processes of crop cleaning and processing and to indicate that crops were infested with weeds of many varieties including tall climbers big enough to be harvested with the ear of grain. The presence in Linear pottery culture contexts in north-west Hungary of the weed *Agrostemma githago* L. has been taken to indicate winter sowing, though elsewhere it has been suggested that there was a spring sowing regime.[91] Because of the lack of pollen evidence little is known of the scale of clearance or the permanence and nature of cultivation. One model to have found increasing support recently is of restricted clearance centred on the valleys in which there were stable, fairly small plots or gardens intensively cultivated. Shade-tolerant weeds are prevalent in many floral samples. Well-watered loess could certainly yield steady returns, especially at the peak of its post-glacial fertility.[92] Simple rotation with fallow or nitrogen-fixing pulses would help to maintain yields too, to say nothing of manuring. An exceptional observation has been made at Langweiler IX of an area 4.6 ha in extent immediately to the west of the occupation focus which had numerous traces of redeposited black earth. This was suggested to be a main field area. Also in the Rhineland the repetition of assemblages of identical species has been taken to support the idea of fixed cultivation, though this has been disputed. There are no clear pedological reasons why at this date slash and burn cultivation need have been practised; parallels with the Tropics or recent northern Europe or America are in-appropriate. That does not exclude its practice for other reasons, including social ones, but it is unlikely that even this need have entailed shifting settlement, because of the large areas within even a 5 km radius around a settlement.

In many parts of its distribution the loess has been decalcified to varying depths since the fifth millennium bc, and the preservation of animal bone has been irregular. Thus in the Rhineland the site of Müddersheim stands out for its bone preservation, though this has been better in central Europe.[93] Systematic bone recovery has been little practised, if at all. The overall pattern that emerges to date is of the major importance of domesticated cattle, with pigs and ovicaprids being less numerous. This has generally been seen as an adaptation to the temperate forested environment of central and western Europe. These may not in themselves be sufficient reasons for such a shift compared to eastern Europe, though they are obviously necessary conditions. One possible exception points the way to social choice as a factor too; sites in Saxony and Thuringia in East Germany have quite high figures for ovicaprids, though lower than cattle, and two sites have ovicaprids dominant which cannot be so easily explained on an ecological basis, though it is claimed on the basis of molluscan assemblages that some open country and light forest were still present.[94] If the earlier suggestion of the role of ovicaprids as providers of manure is valid, their demise may reflect changes in cultivation methods and soil fertility. Cattle may have been kept for meat, though there is a suggestion of dairying in Poland, on the basis of age data and sieves. The alleged presence of oxen in central Europe raises the possibility of traction and its applications, such as timber moving and possibly already plough cultivation though there is no other direct indication of the latter. Morphologically unchanged indigenous forest animals such as deer, aurochs and boar were still represented in faunal assemblages, but generally constitute less than 10 per cent. They are usually assumed to have been wild and to have been hunted, which may be dangerous in the light of the discussion in chapter 2. At the same site, Müddersheim, different usage of morphological criteria has produced figures of 29 and 8 per cent 'wild' animals.

The balance between cereal cultivation and animal husbandry is as always difficult to reconstruct. On purely ecological grounds it is likely that cereal cultivation was more important, since on the one hand settlements seem to have been placed with its needs in mind and on the other animal densities are likely to have been lower in a mainly forested environment. But animals provide a mobile, flexible resource and could have been grazed far from settlements. Low numbers need not reflect lack of social value as the recent example of the mithan in Asia indicates.[95] The scale of production in both spheres may not be directly reflected in the archaeological record. The rarity of grain caches and the generally low number of earth-sunk storage pits in contemporary use for example need not preclude intensive grain production. We may refer again to the discussion of tell size and duration, land availability and social competition. Neither in Dutch Limburg, nor on the Aldenhovener Platte, nor in Little Poland, nor in central Germany are the larger and longlived LBK settlements distinguishable from small neighbours on grounds of the greater availability of good arable land. As in eastern Europe, high productivity could have been achieved within a short range of settlements, but if surplus production was necessary for larger sites and social pre-eminence, there were here equal opportunities to achieve it, which puts the basic reasons for social differentiation (if this is what the range of site sizes and durations in some way reflects) firmly in the sphere of social not ecological relations. Though individual settlements were often very long-lasting, many LBK communities did change to some extent. Within the long span of the culture population grew and settlement expanded. This can be seen in a number of ways. Individual sites such as Bylany and Elsloo increased in size during their occupation. The zones of settlement were extended, as for example on the western edge, into southern Belgium at a later date than Dutch Limburg or into the Paris basin at a later date than the Rhineland. Material culture in the later phases shows increasing regional diversity, plausibly interpreted, as argued below, as a result of more populous settlement. Further changes rooted in these beginnings will be followed in chapter 6, of which the generally late appearance to ditched enclosures in western Europe is a foretaste. To a certain extent such expansion can be treated in the abstract, as the result of settled life, high agricultural productivity and an empty landscape waiting to be filled, but ultimately it must reflect the nature of social relations within LBK communities, which allowed population to rise, practised intensive cultivation, undertook colonisation and the construction of new settlements. Though the nature and scale of production is well concealed in the archaeological record, this perspective certainly suggests a competitive social milieu.

## Other aspects of social relations

Other aspects of social relations are contradictory. The burial evidence for example does not provide any clear indication of social differentiation. This aspect of the evidence is geographically limited, since although scattered burials with limited grave goods occur in settlements in central Europe in graves or rubbish pits near the houses, separate cemeteries adjacent to settlements occur only sporadically there, as in the examples at Nitra in Slovakia or Sondershausen in Thuringia, whereas they are much more frequent on the Rhine and to its west, as at Flomborn and Rixheim in the Rhineland, Elsloo and Niedermerz in the Merzbach valley below the Lang-weiler sites, or Vinneuf in the Yonne valley of the Paris basin. Of these cemeteries only Nitra and Elsloo have been intensively analysed.[96] A general problem is again the variable preservation of bone; decalcification of the loess at Elsloo was 2 m deep so that bodies survived mainly as 'ghosts' with occasional traces of durable teeth enamel. Ageing and sexing were therefore attempted here on the basis of associated grave goods. Graves were usually simple rectangular pits, little differentiated, roughly on the same alignment and quite closely spaced. At Elsloo only four had a noticeably different alignment. Here and at Nitra there have been claims of internal spatial groupings, though this requires further discussion. Inhumation was the dominant rite. Elsloo provides an exception for 47 of its 113 recovered graves were cremations in much shallower graves, and it is possible that other cremations have been destroyed. A few occurred also at Niedermerz. The size of cemeteries varies, from the teens and twenties at Vinneuf, Rixheim and Aiterhofen, to over 60 at Nitra, and over 100 at Elsloo and Niedermerz. There may be a basic contrast between these comparatively well-investigated areas, and the smaller ones which as in the Paris basin may recur on a more individual basis per community. All ages and both sexes are represented where these data are available, though juveniles and children were under-represented compared to the structure of the living population, as in so much of the prehistoric burial record. Numbers of graves lack associated goods – some 29 at Elsloo, where fewer goods were also deposited with the cre-mations. There are typically half a dozen or so categories of grave goods, notably axes or adzes, complete pots and also sherds, both often decorated, flint arrowheads, flint blades, shell ornaments, and rubbing or grinding stones. The vast majority of graves have one or two or three of these categories only, though at at Elsloo more than one item in a category may be present. There are indications of differentiation in goods according to sex. Thus at Nitra adzes and with one exception shell ornaments occurred exclusively with men, at Aiterhofen arrowheads and adzes with men, querns and awls with women, and so on. The men in question with these goods at Nitra were judged to be mainly over 40 years old. Children and juveniles had very few goods in most cases. Four graves at Elsloo had over five categories of goods (nos. 1, 83, 87, 100), though they could not reliably be sexed. The most abundant grave assemblage at Rixheim (no. 14) belonged to a woman. Generalising one may state that although the sexes are often differentiated, there is no indication of the dominance of either sex, and graves without goods as well as the alternative rite of cremations serve further to impede straightforward interpretation. The cemeteries might in themselves indicate competition for land and the importance of descent for access to it (see also chapter 5); their contents may reflect balanced social relations with LBK communities, but could as well mask more competitive relations in life. The likely rarity of cemetery burial in the Elsloo and Niedermerz areas may be a further clue to this, with cemeteries located hypothetically next to dominant settlements but conveying in the details of mortuary rite a sense of communal cooperation and activity. The competing interpretative possibilities are not easily resolved. According to the regional sequence the cemetery at Elsloo was in use in the latter part of the site's occupation, after it had reached its maximum size, which may support the hints of concealed differentiation made here.

Several kinds of artefacts and raw materials were distributed over long distances within the Linear pottery culture in central and western Europe including shell ornaments, pottery, flint and obsidian, and axes and adzes of other hard rocks. *Spondylus* shell is the most spectacular indicator of this movement. It is found as simply perforated shell, otherwise little altered, or cut into bracelets and beads. Curiously it has not been studied in depth recently, so that it is not clear whether raw material was circulating as well as artefacts. It is rarely found in settlements apart from graves, but frequently occurs in these and the cemeteries already discussed (with the exception of the decalcified Elsloo and Niedermerz cases). The quantities are generally modest, as at Nitra but can be spectacular even at the far end of its presumed distribution as at Vert-la-Gravelle in the Marne. It is possible that some of the *spondylus* in question is of fossil origin or even wrongly indentified, but it is widely assumed that its ultimate origin lies to the east, either in the Aegean or the Adriatic, and that its distribution to the west is an extension of its use in the Balkans and Greece from the sixth millennium bc onwards.[97] It may be no coincidence that its occurrence in central and western Europe coincides with an increased circulation of artefacts in the Balkans as for example in the Vinča culture. Axes and adzes were generally manufactured out of hard, fine-grained rock. At Elsloo and neighbours rock types included amphibolites, basalts, quartzites and others, and Aldenhoven sites such as Langweiler 11 and 1x included more or less the same. The source of such material is not local, unless included in gravel deposits which is considered unlikely. The basalts may be derived from those of the Siebengebirge and Eifel hills, some 80 km distant, and the dark quartzites perhaps from the Ardennes, while the amphibolite is still unlocated; a previously suggested location in Silesia is doubted though a source within 200–300 km is possible.[98] There is no sign of the movement of raw material as opposed to finished product. Amphibolites at Hienheim were thought possibly to derive from closer sources in Bavaria and Thuringia. Obsidian in southern Poland probably derived from northern Hungary has already been referred to; flint too may have been distributed on a more than purely local scale, as again in the case of southern Polish chocolate flint found in some quantity as far away as northern Poland and Slovakia or possibly in the case of southern Dutch–Belgian flint deposits at Rijckholt–St Geertruid where sources mined certainly in the fourth millennium may have been exploited already in the fifth and may therefore already have been mined and widely distributed at this early date too.[99] The possibility of pottery movement has already arisen in connection with impressions of barley. It was tested, negatively, at both Elsloo and Hienheim. It might account for some of the alleged ceramic discontinuities at Bylany. Bükk pottery, as at

Olszanica, was imported from the area of the eastern LBK in northern
Hungary. On the north-west fringe of the LBK there is a category of decorated
pottery with organic temper called Limburg pottery. This occurs on the loess
in Dutch Limburg, in the lower Rhine and in the Aisne valley but is
considered to be an import from indigenous non-LBK communities to the
north of the loess.[100] All these data raise various possibilities for communal
and individual interaction, for exchange and trade, alliance and competition,
and ensuing contradictions. For example exchange between communities
may have cemented local relations but also enhanced the status of certain
groups within those communities. The difficulty is that there are insufficient
data for spatial differences to be studied, and too little of the material can be
seen in a definite context, much of the material being derived from rubbish
pits, or from graves, which have their own special problem of interpretation.
Olszanica as already seen provides a rare opportunity to see stone tools and
obsidian concentrated on two particular longhouses.

Whatever use was made of such movements for individual or group
interests, these certainly brought long-range contacts within the LBK. This
communal aspect of artefact movement is reinforced by other aspects of
material culture, especially decorated pottery, but also flint and stone tools
and house types. The early uniformity of decorated pottery has already been
emphasised and contrasted with later regionalisation, which even includes
painted pottery in Bohemia in the Šarka style. These developments are best
seen in terms of communal needs. In the earlier phase there was rapid and
widespread dispersal of population, and zones of settlement were not continuous; later settlement expanded, sites became larger. Uniformity in
material culture and even settlement form may have helped to reduce the
stresses felt by such pioneer communities. As population increased there was
less need for long-range alliance, and more need perhaps for the assertion of
local identities though artefact exchanges would still have provided a long-
range medium of interaction. There has been far less interpretation of
patterns of material culture at a local level. Only the spatial distribution of
decorated ceramics at Elsloo and Hienheim have been explored, with a view
to understanding local social relations. Unequally distributed decorative
traits were used largely with reference to the site sequence to explore the
incidence of innovation in the settlements; in each phase two or three houses
only seemed to be the focus of decorative change. This like house-size
differences might be related to internal ranking, though the correlation of the
two factors were not in fact closely tested in the study.

### The eastern LBK

In ceramic terms the eastern parts of the LBK have many similarities with the
LBK in central and western Europe, and both the Great Hungarian plain and
east Carpathian groups are generally seen as variants of the LBK as a whole.
Incised linear decoration is present in the former from the start, though with a
tendency to rectilinear rather than curvilinear motifs; music-note decoration

appears briefly in its earlier phase then disappears. Such style however characterises the fine pottery east of the Carpathians, generally considered to belong to the later phase of the LBK as a whole, which receives some support from two radiocarbon dates from Tîrpeşti in Moldavia and from contacts with contemporary and succeeding cultures around it. While the east Carpathian group seems to have rather simple decorated wares with ready parallels to the west, the idiosyncracy of the Great Hungarian plain must be stressed. For such a relatively small area there are proportionally more local variants than to the west and north, and painted decoration either on its own or in combination with incised lines survives in use into late phases (though largely abandoned in the earlier Vinča culture to the south).[101] Assemblages of flint and other stone tools have a certain uniformity across the whole LBK area but in most other aspects the eastern LBK is again strikingly different. Settlement excavation is little developed in the Great Hungarian plain, but the characteristic longhouses are so far missing. Tîrpeşti had so-called pit-dwellings; a longer surface structure survived at Nezviska in the Ukraine but hardly fits the typical model. Settlement locations in the Great Hungarian plain initially followed the Körös pattern but were gradually extended to the edge of the uplands surrounding the plain, and while some riverside occupations in the middle phases were smaller superficially than Körös sites, and probably shortlived, by the late phase small tells developed in the Szakálhát group in the south of the plain and along the middle Tisza. At this stage there is some evidence for a greater range of crops with barley better represented, and a shift in emphasis from ovicaprids to cattle. It has been suggested that expansion of settlement is connected with the emergence of a regional system of economic exchange and interdependence, with cattle acting as a mobile resource exportable to the fringes, which in turn were able to exchange obsidian from sources around Tokaj, and good quality flint from the north-west edge of the plain. Several sites have been investigated with evidence of intensive flint and stone working, such as Boldogkőváralja, Co. Borsod, where amongst finds one pot beside a small rectangular house contained over 500 flint blades.[102] Pottery too was developed for exchange, such as the very finely decorated Bükk pottery, which was widely distributed to the north, west and south; it is often connected with the movement of obsidian (as at Olszanica in southern Poland, and perhaps Vinča to the south). As well as this specialisation and differentiation another difference of the Great Hungarian plain compared to the LBK of central and western Europe is the continued elaboration of ritual paraphernalia and ritual sites. Figurines are rare from north-west Hungary westwards, though they do occur as far away as the Paris basin, whereas elaborately decorated figurines and large face-pots are well known in the plain. Certain caves, such as Baradla near Aggtelek in north-east Hungary were the focus for ritual deposition of artefacts including *spondylus* and pottery.[103] The context of such ritual is to date dimly perceived, but it is plausible that as further south, in the Balkans, ritual was an important element in both social cohesion and social differentiation. Burials where found remained scattered within settlements. Much less

is known of the situation in the east Carpathian zone. Settlement distribu-
tion followed the diverse Criş pattern, taking in both valley bottom as at
Nezviska and high terrace as at Floreşti and Tîrpeşti. Obsidian was present at
Tîrpeşti, and there were fragments of an anthropomorphic figurine.

## The unity of the LBK, its origins and fringe developments

In the light of this evidence much further thought needs to be given to the
unity of the LBK over its whole area. Are the eastern groups really variants or
rather different cultures altogether? A distinction between form and content
can be made. In terms of content the Great Hungarian plain had far greater
specialisation and diversity in the economic sphere, and this seems to be
connected with the wider pattern of social relations in which ritual seems to
figure prominently. In central and western Europe there are hints of social
differentiation too but ritual is not an obvious factor of the archaeological
record in the same way. If social control is a relevant factor, it may there have
been achieved and expressed in other forms of material culture, in production, in house form and settlement layout, and both expressed and concealed
in burial in western areas. The difference may reside partly in the contrast
between the extension of settlement in an area settled for centuries with its
developed neighbours to the south and the conditions of pioneer agricultural
settlement on the loess of central and western Europe. In the latter zone there
are already signs of social differentiation but in the more empty landscape the
consolidation of pre-eminent social position by particular groups would not
have been easy while the option of further colonisation and the establishment of fresh settlements remained available. Indeed the apparently rapid
spread of the LBK, and its replication in so many new areas, might be seen to
stem from just such a process of social change in the zone of primary
settlement rather than directly from population growth. The chronological
coincidence of early Vinča and LBK would then be no accident.

   This raises the question of origins again. There have been two schools of
thought, one that the LBK represents the continued colonisation by new
agricultural population with specific Starčevo–Körös origins, the other that it
represents the acculturation of indigenous populations around the fringes of
the Starčevo–Körös culture.[104] The case for continued colonisation has been
sketched above, with both social relations and indirectly population growth
encouraging migration and relocation. Indigenous groups such as the Szatmár
and Medina groups are ill defined, in both time and space, and the sparse
indigenous presence on the loess of central Europe has been noted repeatedly.
Lithic continuity from the Great Hungarian plain westwards is impressive.
On the other hand a general case for social and economic transformation of
indigenous populations can be made by this date, which would also have
necessitated at last a full indigenous colonisation of the forested loess
landscapes of central and western Europe. One may point to the early and
middle phases of the LBK on the Great Hungarian plain itself to show
essential continuity of settlement with the Körös culture, and to ask whether

substantial external colonisation to the west would not have been accompanied by greater signs of internal settlement change (evident rather in the late phase). There are likewise no good precedents for significant aspects of LBK material and culture in the Körös culture, especially the longhouse and the decorated pottery. Lithic similarity might be explained by functional reorientation. The historical problem of origins is difficult, and exactly mirrors both that seen already in south-east Europe and that to be discussed later in north-west Europe. Resolution of the problem will necessitate not only improvement in the full range of empirical aspects, but also further thought on the relationship between people and material culture, especially in periods of rapid social change. In assessing the present difficulties of supporting either hypothesis it can be ventured that the colonisation hypothesis is the less weak of the two at the moment, but a compromise view may be in order. Development in the zone of primary settlement may be critical on the one hand, but may have produced in turn on the other a reaction among indigenous communities.

A final related theme to be considered is development around the fringes of the LBK, which is also considered from the converse standpoint in the following chapter. A contrast can be drawn between those parts which were perhaps affected by the LBK and those which were not. In north-west France for example it has been suggested that the emergence of massive stone-built chambered tombs in the very early fourth millennium bc was due to the admixture of LBK technology to indigenous burial traditions seen in such coastal midden sites as Téviec and Hoëdic. To the east there was some contact with the Bug–Dniester culture seen in pottery movement from the LBK, and possibly the adoption of animal husbandry. By contrast there is little sign of change on the north European plain in the later fifth millennium bc beyond the LBK. There was a pause in settlement expansion at the limits of the loess. This may reflect the predeliction of the LBK for loess soils in preference to the less favourable sandy and morainic soils to the north, but it may also be a further indication that LBK expansion was not simply a question of the growth and spread of incoming population but may have heavily involved the indigenous population. The pause may also be partly explicable in terms of indigenous resistance where the pressures for social transformation were less acute, possibilities also explored in the following chapter.

### 3.3 Mediterranean beginnings, 6000–4000 bc

*Environment*

The general conditions of post-glacial climatic improvement have already been outlined earlier in this chapter and the previous one. The rise in temperature was not as marked in this area as further north, but it has been considered that an optimum was reached for temperature in the mid fifth millennium bc, on the basis of pollen and isotopic studies. Humidity too may have reached its greatest extent at roughly the same date, on the basis of pollen and sedimentological studies, though local and quite rapid fluctuations are evident as in the case of Châteauneuf-les-Martigues, Bouches-du-Rhône, in southern France. Measuring such local variations however is difficult because of the uneven distribution of research. Palaeobotanists concerned with southern France continue to use the Blytt–Sernander terminology for vegetational change, with the Atlantic replacing the Boreal period in the mid sixth millennium bc. In general the transition marks the final trend towards the full establishment of mixed oak forest, including a greater representation of evergreen species than hitherto. In detail however local variation can be seen, where detailed research is available, between different topographies and especially different altitudes. Sea level continued to rise. Around 5500 bc it is thought to be between −15 and −10 m, by around 4500 bc at −7 to −6, the latter shown by the drowned Cardial site of Leucate, Aude, in southern France. The rising sea level created a moving zone of marsh and lagoon. This zone may have been very rich in marine resources including fish and shellfish, and its inner edge attractive to terrestrial animals for grazing. In the shallow northern Adriatic it may have been of considerable extent, rather like the North Sea in the early post-glacial period referred to in chapter 2.[105]

## The nature of the evidence

It is a truism that further research is likely to alter our view of the Neolithic period in Europe, but it may fairly be claimed, without disrespect to specialists in the area, that the greatest alterations may be expected in western Mediterranean Europe (Fig. 3.24). Traditionally much research has been devoted to the excavation of cave or rock-shelter sites and this has been important for the establishment of chronology, though plant and bone recovery has been far from systematic. The search for open sites has been until recently rather limited, even though the lowlands (mainly coastal) of the area are of restricted extent compared to the situation in eastern and central Europe. Though research in Italy goes back to the nineteenth century, it was not until the mid 1940s that aerial photography began to reveal the wealth of ditched sites in the Tavoliere plain of south-east Italy, not until the mid 1970s that the same method revealed the full extent of such sites and not until the last few years that surface survey began to complement this method, recovering yet more sites. Intensive surface surveys have been few in number, but especially in the more arid parts of the western Mediterranean their results have been dramatic; Calabria in the toe of Italy now has at least 300 Neolithic sites, compared with the handful previously known.[106] Large-scale excavation has not yet been attempted on more than a handful of sites in southern Italy. There has been intensive research in northern Italy and southern France, including on open sites as we shall see, but without here the benefit of systematic preliminary survey. Radiocarbon dating too has been most prolific in southern France.[107] In all these respects Iberia (and North

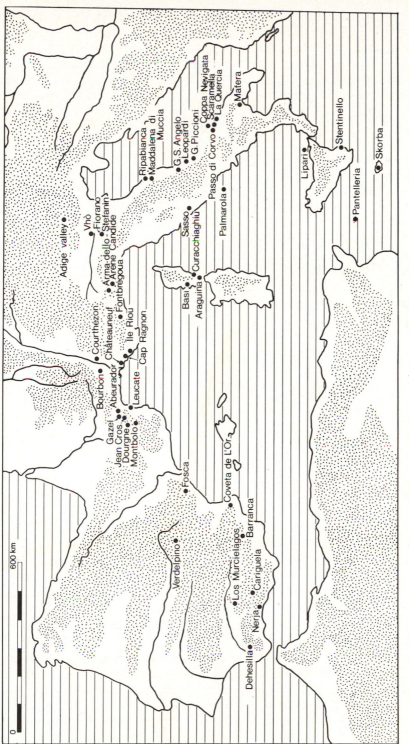

**3.24** Simplified location map of the principal sites mentioned in chapter 3.3

Africa, though this is beyond the limits though not necessarily the interests of this book), is underdeveloped, and despite what has been achieved still awaits the full impact of detailed studies of environment and dating and of survey and extensive excavation. When all these factors are added to the information loss implicit in the known sea level curve, it can readily be seen how our view of these two millennia may presently be distorted.

*Material sequences and chronology*

There are two major patterns in material culture in the two millennia after around 6000 bc, that of continuity of established lithic traditions combined with gradual change in materials and forms, and that of the gradual adoption of pottery. Many of these changes can be ordered locally or regionally on the basis of stratified deposits, and inter-regional differences are increasingly possible due to radiocarbon dating though still subject to the difficulties outlined above.[108]

A classic study of lithic continuity is in south-east France in Provence, where at the rock-shelter site of Châteauneuf-les-Martigues near the coast, the manufacture of scrapers, piercers and notched blades continued unaltered in levels dated to the sixth or fifth millennia, while there is a series of other successive innovations – small flint trapezes (and pottery) replacing the earlier concave-sided type, then rare polished greenstone axes. Unfortunately the absolute chronology of the site is uncertain. The earliest pottery levels were first dated to the sixth and later to the fifth millennium. If the latter series of dates is correct, they emphasise the duration of indigenous traditions. In Languedoc too continuity is observable, as in the Grotte de Gazel, Aude, where the large lithic types continue unchanged, while triangular points of the sixth millennium are replaced by transverse ones at the beginning of the fifth (at the point too where pottery is first represented on the site). Other examples of regional continuity are to hand in northern Italy where, in the Adige valley around Trento for example, sites with pottery, perhaps of the fifth millennium, have lithics including geometric trapezes like those of pre-pottery sites and levels, but also have novel types such as long notched blades and rhomboids. It should be stressed that transition or development is not easily followed everywhere. In central Italy sixth millennium bc sites are still sought, but fifth millennium ones with pottery like Maddalena di Muccia, Marche, have strong indigenous lithic elements, as well as novel blades and polished axes. The lithic situation is perhaps least clear in southern Italy. The south-east coastal site of Coppa Nevigata, with a single disputed late seventh millennium bc date, has a traditional lithic industry associated with pottery. Little explicit information is available from other south-east sites which go more certainly as far back as the sixth millennium, though the lithic assemblages are generally referred to as macrolithic. Continuity is also demonstrable in eastern Spain, as at the Coveta de l'Or, Valencia, in its fifth millennium level with pottery.[109]

Two other developments can be noted. The first is the expansion in use of obsidian. As detailed later in the chapter, obsidian is restricted to four insular sources in the western Mediterranean. It was first regularly used on mainland sites from the sixth and fifth millennia onwards. As already noted therefore lithic continuity did not preclude continued change, including in this example in the sphere of contact and procurement. The other development is the gradual appearance of polished stone axes. Though there is no readily available synthesis of this feature, it seems that these artefacts were not widely used in the sixth millennium, and even on fifth millennium bc sites were neither invariable nor common, in contrast to eastern and central Europe. This cannot be due to technological deficiency, as witnessed by the unusually common polished greenstone axes and rings of the Fiorano group of the Po valley of the late fifth millennium.

Pottery is the other major innovation of these millennia in the western Mediterranean. Its general label is Impressed ware, though the more specialised term Cardial ware is appropriate in the north and west of the area. The general labels however conceal a very considerable diversity of form, decoration and development from region to region, and while the earliest sites with pottery can be dated to the earlier sixth millennium (and controversially to the late seventh) any such general term as 'Neolithic' to mark this stage inevitably also masks considerable variation in the rate with which pottery was taken up over the area as a whole. Recently two major variants have been outlined, the more easterly around the Adriatic and southern Italy with simple bowl, dish and jar forms but including flat bases, and a range of impressed decorative techniques in which shell impressions are rare and probably late, the more westerly – from Liguria, Corsica and Sardinia westwards – with likewise simple bowl and jar forms, but regularly with rounded bases and a dominant reliance on *Cardium* or cockle shell for decoration. This generalisation does little justice to the fine detail. Forms and decorative arrangement on Yugloslav Adriatic sites differ substantially from those in the Tavoliere, while these in their turn are somewhat different from those of the heel of Italy and from the Stentinello style of Sicily and now Calabria (Fig. 3.25). Recent stratigraphic investigations in the south-east of Italy, especially in the ditches of enclosures, have allowed greater awareness of chronological development, with the most elaborate impressed motifs coinciding with the appearance of red-painted pottery approximately around 5000 bc.[110] Corsica provides further contrasts in the earlier to mid sixth millennium. Two sites in the southern part of the island, Basi and Curacchiaghiu, each have distinctively decorated pottery, the former with cardial impressions, and also incisions and red paint, in triangular and chevron motifs, the latter with rare cardial impressions but with more common jabbed impressions and incisions, in horizontal bands.[111] Within southern France differences are also evident, and the Provençal site of Châteauneuf-les-Martigues and the Languedocian site of Gazel have been used to illustrate these. The early phase of Gazel has plastic-, cardial- and comb-decorated globular bowls (c. 5000–4800 bc) but in later layers, cardial decoration is largely supplanted by a great profusion of stroke, incised, stamped and plastic

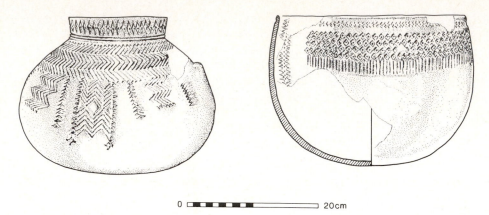

0 ▭▬▭▬▭▬▭ 20cm

**3.25** Impressed ware from Piana di Curinga, Calabria, southern Italy. *After* Ammerman

decoration with dashed, ogival and chevron motifs (around 4600 bc) and then (around 4400–4000 bc) by clumsy and sparser grooved and impressed decoration. In Provence by contrast cardial decoration lasts through the fifth millennium, though in the 'epicardial' phase of the latter part, other techniques are also well used. It may also be emphasised that neither of these sites belongs with certainty to the sixth millennium. The sixth millennium sites Cap Ragnon and Île Riou are in Provence near Châteauneuf. Unfortunately neither has more than a few cardial impressed sherds. The sixth millennium situation in Iberia is also unclear. Two sites with single dates, Verdelpino, Cuenca and Barranca de los Grajos, Cieza, Murcia, have pottery on which cardial decoration is not important, the former with smooth-surfaced vessels, the latter with impressed decoration of other kinds dominant. But the validity of association at the former site between lithics, pottery and date has been doubted. In Andalusia, Nerja and the Cueva de Dehesilla have sixth millennium dates for non-cardial pottery.[112] The Cardial levels of the Coveta de l'Or, Beniarres, Valencia, are dated to the fifth millennium bc, and it may be that many other cardial sites of the eastern Iberian coast are so dated also (Fig. 3.26). The Barcelona and Valencia area also have distinctive regional stylistic differences, and Cardial pottery is rare in southern Spain.

The 'Impressed ware complex' as it has sometimes been called thus turns out to be a very varied phenomenon. Developments in the sixth millennium bc are particularly unclear as we have just seen. Its origins, which are also uncertain, are discussed later. Developments in the fifth millennium bc are perhaps a little clearer, but still rather varied. One is the continued extension of pottery use (and probably manufacture); the bulk of dated cardial sites belong to this millennium. These include sites in all parts of the landscape, from coast to the interior uplands, a range seen in the Aude sites of Leucate, Gazel, L'Abri Jean-Cros and Dourgne.[113] Gazel and Dourgne were occupied for periods before pottery was used at them. Decorative differences between Languedoc and Provence have already been described, and the Languedocian trend to

**3.26** Impressed ware vessel from Coveta de l'Or, Valencia, eastern Spain. Photo: Marti Oliver

plainer pottery is emphasised by the plain assemblage from the cave site of Montbolo, Pyrénées-Orientales, with a single mid fifth millennium date.[114] Pottery use was also extended to the Po valley and environs in the later fifth millennium, as seen in various local groups such as the Gaban of the Adige valley, the Vhò group of south-east Lombardy, the Fiorano group of the Veneto, Emilia and Tuscany, and others, each with individual combinations of bowl and jar forms and a range of impressed, incised and plastic decorative techniques (Fig. 3.27). The Sasso group of central Italy is also closely linked to the Fiorano group. The first pottery on Malta is dated to this phase, impressed pottery from Skorba of the late fifth millennium bc. The main development in southern Italy was of red-painted pottery, from the late sixth millennium, according to recent investigations of ditch stratigraphies in enclosure sites, such as Scaramella and Masseria La Quercia. According to this model, painted pottery in the Tavoliere was part of a general improvement in ceramic products and was accompanied by fine plain *figulina* pottery and impressed pottery of fine fabric also.[115] Painted motifs include bands of chevrons, triangles, lozenges, and circles. This Masseria La Quercia phase was succeeded at some point in the fifth millennium by the Passo di Corvo phase with more varied forms but still red-painted decoration. A little further south around Matera novel, painted pottery was also accompanied by dark pottery with incised decoration applied before firing. Further north, on the eastern side of the Apennines, in central Italy, fifth millennium sites have also a mixture of impressed and red-painted pottery; the earliest known sites from the west side of the Apennines belong to the Sasso group of the very late

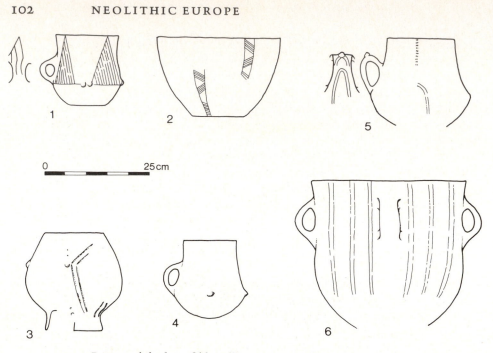

**3.27** Pottery of the later fifth millennium in northern Italy. 1–2 Gaban group; 3–4 Vhò group; 5–6 Fiorano group. *After* Bagolini and Biagi

fifth millennium. On Sicily and Sardinia impressed ware may have persisted for much of the fifth millennium.

The development of Iberian pottery styles is very poorly understood, but one probable change is the addition of red-slipped ware in the late fifth millennium in southern Spain at least. Such ware can be seen as an addition in stratified deposits as at Cariguela del Piñar, Granada and has now been radiocarbon dated at another cave complex, Los Murcielagos, Cordoba.[116]

There does not appear to be a great wealth of other forms of material culture in the western Mediterranean in these two millennia apart from beads in shell and other material. The Spanish sites just mentioned have stone bracelets and these occur too on southern French Cardial sites. There are some simple clay figurines from the Passo di Corvo phase of southern Italy, some at Vhò, one from Arene Candide perhaps of the same date, but nowhere is the plethora of ritual paraphernalia so evident in the Balkans repeated in this area.

## Settlement and the social context of production

It has been stressed earlier that the present evidence in this area is more obviously likely to be misleading than elsewhere, but at face value the evidence at present suggests two separate kinds of development in the western Mediterranean. One is the steady development from the sixth millennium of agriculturally based communities in south-east Italy and eastern Sicily, reliant on mixed farming, with large ditched enclosures encircling groups of hut compounds amongst the range of settlement units. It is possible but far from certain that these communities were the result of direct colonisation from the Balkans or the Aegean. Other development is the gradual adoption of changes by indigenous communities, perhaps when they were not simultaneously adopted in order first ovicaprids, then pottery and finally cereals. The slow rate of change and the seemingly stable nature of indigenous settlement and subsistence practices provide the strongest possible contrast to developments in eastern and central Europe in these two millennia. The contrast within the western Mediterranean itself need not at present be overplayed in the present state of the evidence; this is not to deny aspects of the contrast, but to remind one that the early part of the south-eastern Italian development is itself virtually unknown, which means that the contrast could eventually turn out to be one of rates of development, rather than of kinds.

The south-east enclosure sites provide a convenient starting point. These are centred on the Tavoliere plain, but Stentinello and other sites in eastern Sicily seem to be analogous. Great numbers have now been recorded, though few are published even in plan, and fewer still excavated even on a limited scale. The main elements of these sites appear to be an outer encircling ditch (or ditches) within which there are grouped smaller ditched compounds,

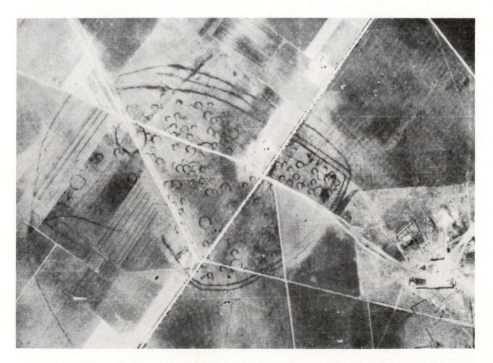

3.28 Aerial view of the enclosure at Passo di Corvo in the Tavoliere plain, southern Italy. Photo: Bradford (Pitt Rivers Museum, Oxford)

**3.29** Recently excavated compound within the Passo di Corvo enclosure, southern Italy. Photo Tinè

roughly circular and 10 m in diameter, with a broad entrance and traces of stone walling on their inner edges, and houses, perhaps rectangular, inside (Figs. 3.28 and 3.29). There is a great range of size of these sites, both in terms of ditch perimeter and numbers of compounds. La Quercia has not less than eight concentric ditches. Passo di Corvo is a maximum of 540 by 870 m, containing over 100 compounds. The triple ditches of this phase appear to overlie earlier ditches. There are two other vast sites in its vicinity, Posta d'Innanzi and Amendola. Other sites with compounds are smaller and lack the encircling ditch; the difference was seen by Bradford in terms of homestead versus village. It remains to be seen however whether there is an element of chronological development in this contrast, with a possible trend to nucleation and aggrandisement of particular sites through time.[117] Survey has also revealed recently even greater numbers of open sites, which must

surely provide other contrasts too, apart from further chronological problems. Unsystematically recorded plant and animal remains include wheat
and barley, and morphologically domesticated cattle, ovicaprids and pigs, but
there is little of statistical worth yet to work on. The soils around what now
seems a very small sample of enclosures and other sites – under 30 – were
examined in detail, and it was found that a high proportion of them close to
the sites were light *crosta* soils (which cover less than 20 per cent of the whole
plain), but also that the sites were rarely sited in the middle of patches of
*crosta* but regularly had alluvial and other heavier soils accessible from them
as well. This locational choice may reflect the balance between cereal
cultivation and animal grazing. It remains to be seen whether this pattern is
repeated over the range of known sites as a whole (Fig. 3.30).

There is thus comparatively little concrete evidence to go on. If it seems
clear that there was a decisive shift to cereals and domesticated animals and
larger settlements in the sixth millennium, the origins and social context of
the change are far from clear, as well as its later development. It has been
normal to ascribe the situation to colonisation from outside, but the model of
ceramic development followed here accentuates differences rather than
possible similarities with the Balkans and the Aegean (and ceramic comparisons further east in the Mediterranean are doubtful and largely anachronistic) though it must be admitted that the ceramic repertoire in western
Thessaly and western Greece was varied and included impressed wares as
well as early monochrome and painted wares. One can at least sketch an
alternative hypothesis in which central importance is given to the local
situation. The coastal site of Coppa Nevigata on the Gulf of Manfredonia
seems to have been reliant at least partially on marine resources, and was
occupied for some time on the evidence of large shell accumulations and
changes in pottery style, though its single date is disputed. It might however
be taken to represent the kind of stable settlement represented elsewhere in
the Mediterranean in the early post-glacial (see chapter 2) and the adoption of
pottery may well be an indication of social importance, as further discussed
below. Changes in Adriatic sea level and in the abundance of coastal
resources however may have encouraged the rapid adoption of new food
staples from across the Adriatic in order initially to maintain the local social
context. The model is not directly deterministic, in the sense that it remains
the local social context not the changing environment which dominates the
suggested changes. Thereafter the social context may have been progressively
altered by the possibilities of greater productivity inherent in agricultural
practice, and the trend to site differentiation, nucleation and larger population accelerated.

Elsewhere in the western Mediterranean, development may have been
different, or at least much slower. Exploitation of native animals can be
documented for much longer, and probably gathering of native plants too, as
well as fishing and the use of shellfish. Ovicaprids may have been introduced
widely in the sixth millennium – from south-east Italy or further east – but
through exchange, barter or theft rather than through colonisation. Cereals

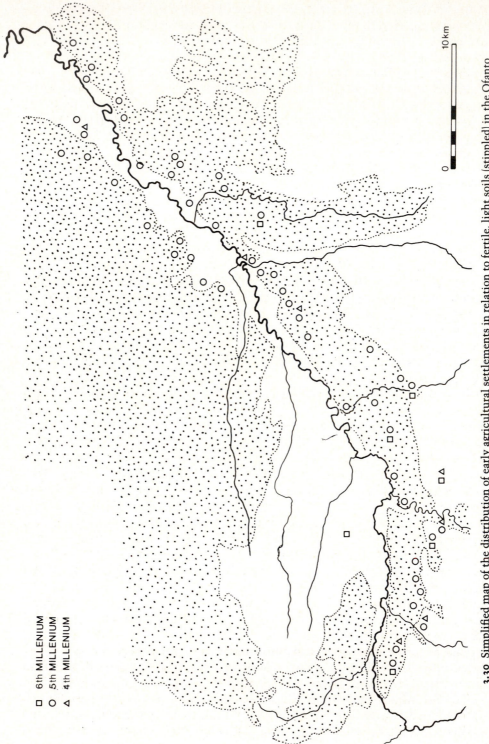

**3.30** Simplified map of the distribution of early agricultural settlements in relation to fertile, light soils (stippled) in the Ofanto valley, southern Tavoliere. *After* Cipollini Sampò

6th MILLENIUM □
5th MILLENIUM ○
4th MILLENIUM △

10 km

may have been spread much more slowly and not fully or widely used till the late fifth millennium and later. There was no necessary or universal link between economic changes and the introduction of pottery, though the social significance of the latter is potentially important. Change of any kind is not visible in certain areas till the late fifth millennium bc, as in the Po valley. This period seems to show a number of significant changes, with the final spread of change and extension of new subsistence practices – witnessed further by the colonisation of Malta – and the beginnings of further change in areas already altered. These generalisations are best supported by a number of selected case studies.

In east central Italy in the Abruzzi and Marche provinces – east of the Apennines – sixth millennium agricultural settlement is so far missing. At face value this suggests at the outset considerable continuity of earlier practices in the region despite developments to the south. The site of Villaggio Leopardi dated to the late fifth millennium in the Abruzzo lowlands is indicative of change. Well placed for cereal cultivation and animal grazing it has cereal remains and pig documented. Other fifth millennium sites however, though with pottery and polished stone, seem to have been oriented more towards animal exploitation, including that of native species. Sites on the border of the lowlands and the Apennines such as the Grotta dei Piccioni and the Grotta Sant' Angelo in Abruzzo have in that order ovicaprids, pig and cattle, as well as red deer remains, while the lowland Marche sites of Maddalena di Muccia and Ripabianca di Monterado again lack cereals and their faunal assemblages are dominated respectively by pig and red deer and by ovicaprids. It is possible to overdraw the contrast and to believe that every early agricultural site must be self-sufficient and show balanced mixed farming, but in this context the continuity of practice with earlier traditions is certainly striking.[118]

In the Po valley and its environs significant change in subsistence practices is not observed till the late fifth millennium.[119] Indeed the economy of the pottery-using Gaban of the Adige valley is little changed at all. The main resources documented are red deer, roe deer and boar, with also ibex, chamois, hare, beaver, dormouse, squirrel, turtle, fish, birds and molluscs. The open sites of the Fiorano group and the Vhò group are the first sizeable significant collection of such sites that we have seen outside southern Italy. They contain various sorts of earth-cut features usually interpreted as 'hut floors', though with no other observable structural elements. These are shallow, with an oval, circular or figure-of-eight plan. An alternative suggestion is that their function was storage. Deeper pits at Vhò itself have been seen as wells. The size of these sites is unclear though it has been characterised as 'often extensive' and Vhò may cover over 20000 m². As well as being large and provided with various structural facilities these sites are interesting for their lowlying situation, in the Fiorano group on the edge of the plain between Modena and Imola and in the case of the Vhò group nearer the Po itself in the centre of the valley. The range of resources used is also striking. Taking the two groups as a whole one finds represented red and roe deer, boar, aurochs, beaver, hare; domesticated cattle (on morphological criteria), ovicaprids and pig; mollusca, turtle and fish; and a few grains of barley and wheat. More detailed investigations at Vhò itself serve to amplify this picture. The site lay in an environment of marsh and forest close to the Po, in which little or no artificial clearance had taken place. The main resources documented at the site were in that order red deer, pig, cattle and roe deer; ovicaprid, hare, tortoise, fish and shellfish, and goose were also found. The pigs were very large and the cattle comparatively small; on morphological criteria the one may have been wild and the other domesticated. The pigs were generally killed off in their second or third year, but this kill pattern is compatible with both hunting and domestication. The ovicaprids were extremely rare and unsuited to the local environment, but presumably domesticated. One wheat grain was recovered in flotation but pollen analysis did not show cereal cultivation; it is possible therefore that cereals like ovicaprids were traded, exchanged or rustled from neighbouring communities rather than locally grown. Even on the Ligurian coast at this time, at Arene Candide native animals were still important resources. The considerable continuity of subsistence practice in northern Italy may testify to a rich and favourable environment but it is clear that changes were being instituted, even if gradually, by the late fifth millennium. One possibility is again the continuing change in the sea level of the Adriatic, which may have had the effect of constraining communities in the Po valley, and encouraging subsistence change in order for existing social formations to be maintained.

In Provence there are perhaps earlier signs of change, though this was nonetheless still gradual.[120] One indication is the greater number of open sites from the sixth and fifth millennia compared to previously, though more cave and shelter sites than open sites are known. However, the permanence and status of an open site of the fifth millennium like Courthézon, Vaucluse, is not clear. The main structures here are circular cobbled floors 5 m in diameter. Continuity of subsistence practice is suggested by the emphasis on fish and molluscs at the early coastal sites of Cap Ragnon and Île Riou, near Marseille, and by the red deer and rabbit bones in other land sites. Change however is suggested by the adoption of ovicaprids. Arguments have already been set out in chapter 2 against the appearance of sheep before the sixth millennium bc in southern France. There are indeed very small percentages of sheep in Late Mesolithic levels at Châteauneuf-les-Martigues preceding larger percentages in early Cardial levels, but given the redating of the site referred to above, the introduction of sheep can still be confined to the sixth millennium. When sheep become established, they exceed cattle, boar and deer in terms of individuals represented, and seem also to replace the previously important rabbit. Cereals are also documented at the site, along with other signs of vegetational interference. The site itself is striking, being a vast rock shelter, and its location near a lagoon between plain and hills may also suggest very varied subsistence practices. Cereals are also documented at the inland site of Fontbrégoua, Var, in the mid to later fifth millennium bc. This site has well-documented plant gathering of the seventh millennium but unfortunately there was subsequently a long hiatus in occupation. It has been suggested that cereal cultivation may have been more important than presently directly recorded, on the basis of finds of rubbing stones, and of sickle flints on open sites, but the picture is again one of stable indigenous communities only gradually adopting and using novel food staples (Fig. 3.31).

Intensive studies in the Aude *département* in Languedoc point further in the same direction.[121] There is again a wide range of locations, and both shelter and open sites, from the submerged coastal site of Leucate, to the inland foothill shelters of Gazel and Jean-Cros, and to the Abri de Dourgne at over 900 m above sea level in the small upper Aude basin surrounded in turn by much higher country. For locational reasons neither of the latter two seems likely to be an all-year site, and sediment analysis at Jean-Cros apparently indicates occupation in either early spring or autumn. Mobility and a network of interdependent sites are thus continuing features of the sixth and fifth millennia, though the fifth millennium Leucate may represent a new kind of open site. Traditional practices can be seen in the fish, molluscs and birds at Leucate, though due to disturbance there is some stratigraphic uncertainty as to their provenance, and in the aurochs, deer, boar, and roe deer found at the other sites, with ibex too at Dourgne along with fur-bearers such as marten, lynx, wild cat, and polecat. There is little published information

**3.31** Deposit of animal bones in a pit, including mandibles of deer and wolf and skulls of badger and marten, from a fifth millennium level at the Grotte de Fontbrégoua, Var, Provence, southern France. Photo: Courtin

yet on plant remains, though seventh millennium plant collecting is documented at La Balma d'Abeurador. Not surprisingly no cereal remains or pollen were found at Jean-Cros, in keeping with its location and transient use. Interest as far as change is concerned is thus centred on the introduction of ovicaprids and the possible domestication of cattle and pig. Sheep are documented first in sixth millennium levels at Gazel and Dourgne, but occur in modest quantities. At these two sites sheep become much more important in the later levels, in the later fifth millennium, though at Gazel they also decline relative to pig subsequent to their high point. Small numbers of cattle and pig may also have been domesticated from the earlier to mid fifth millennium onwards, on the basis of morphological criteria, at which point domesticated goat may have been introduced also. Deer and aurochs were not completely supplanted. At Jean-Cros in the mid fifth millennium sheep comprise some 35 per cent of the recorded fauna but red deer and pig (mostly of large size) together make up 45 per cent. It is important to keep the idea of a network of sites firmly in mind, since some of the resources we are considering could be moved around by people, and the remains found at any one site need not fully document the range of resources being used either locally or regionally. It is important also to enter a caveat here, and to consider the nature of the archaeological sample of settlement in this phase. Sites like Courthézon and Leucate are certainly rare by comparison with the more regularly investigated shelters and caves of the foothills, but their existence may suggest the likely existence of still more like them. It is thus possible to envisage that the archaeological record is seriously biased, and that there could have been faster and more radical change in the lowland plains.

As in other respects, the Iberian evidence is patchy, but it too may point in the direction of continuity. Apart from Portuguese sites discussed in the next chapter, one may cite various sites in eastern and southern Spain which seem to show both continuity and change in subsistence practice, although once again sixth millennium developments – or lack of them – are very poorly documented. The Coveta de l'Or produced wheat and barley which has been dated to the mid fifth millennium. The site itself lies at about 640 m above sea level and there must be a strong possibility that the grain was imported to the site. This then may be indirect testimony to more established cereal cultivation in the coastal lowlands, but it remains striking that such a foothill cave was still being used, especially for herding of sheep and goats with young animals predominantly represented. Grain has also been recorded at Los Murcielagos, along with acorns and domesticated sheep, goat, cattle and pig.[122]

## Social interaction: material culture, exchange and burial

Several references have already been made to the local and regional social context, but other aspects of this than already discussed turn out to be difficult to study at this phase in the western Mediterranean. Burial evidence, communal sites, ritual paraphernalia, to all of which we will return below, are disappointingly scarce, and the most promising line of enquiry may lie in further investigation of the observed patterns of material culture. Although we have stressed the continuity of lithic traditions it may well be significant that new projectile points continued to be adopted, as well as polished axes and, in the specialised case of the Fiorano group, polished stone rings. The hypothesis offered here is that material culture was actively used in the maintenance of group identity. Pottery can also be considered in this sort of context, rather than abstractly as some sort of indicator of 'Neolithic' status or functionally as useful container. It has already been seen that there are very uneven correlations with economic changes, the adoption of sheep for example frequently preceding that of pottery both on a regional and a local level. There are also considerable differences between sites and areas, some with quite prolific use of pottery, others with sparse use. The very varied nature of western Mediterranean pottery has also been emphasised despite certain very generalised similarities in decorative technique. One suggestion has been that pottery should be seen as a status or prestige item in these two millennia.[123] A variation on this promising idea is that it was an innovation variously adopted when group identity was threatened. The favourable climate and environment of the area have been stressed, and may underline the stability of communities in the region. At the same time a range of changes must be recognised. Such use of material culture could have been one of the ways in which change was resisted or absorbed. It would be tempting but perhaps rash to speculate on the possible symbolism of shell decoration itself. There are also cases where such decoration was inlaid or encrusted with coloured matter, which was therefore perhaps at least as important as the source of the impressions. But other elements such as clay spoons in southern France may belong more to the realm of symbolic food sharing or provision than to the realm of practical cutlery. It is striking too that two areas with perhaps the greatest range of forms and decoration can also be suggested to have been subject to considerable environmental and subsistence change. The first example is southern Italy. On the model of ceramic evolution followed here this had the greatest range of forms and decoration, and the fastest rate of change, in the western Mediterranean as a whole. It seems no accident that south-east Italy was probably affected earlier by changing sea level, and that later *figulina* painted and scratched wares developed in a context of potentially numerous population and a hierarchy of settlement types. The suggestion that red-painted wares in Sicily were probably imports from southern Italy would fit the active role in social relations suggested for material culture.[124] Much remains to be understood however, for example whether suggested site nucleation is matched by variation in pottery manufacture, distribution or use. The second example is the Po valley in the late fifth millennium where again it may be no accident that colonisation of the valley, changes in site location and character, and reorientations in the sphere of subsistence were accompanied by the adoption of pottery quite varied in form and decoration.

A gradually increasing concern with group identity could also be seen in the increased range of contacts between different areas. There are seventh millennium examples of long-range movement, as in the case of Mediterranean shells in Mesolithic contexts north of the Alps, but the patterns of obsidian in the sixth and fifth millennia testify to more regular long-range contact. There are four main sources of obsidian in the western Mediterranean, on Sardinia, on Lipari, on Palmarola in the Pontine islands, and on Pantelleria. At none of these sources have the actual workings been closely studied, but analysis of obsidians from archaeological contexts has shown that all four were in use in this phase. Sardinian obsidian was moved at an early date to Corsica (to Basi and Curacchiagiu) and some perhaps later to northern Italy; Lipari and to a lesser extent Pontine obsidian were moved into central and southern Italy; and Pantellerian obsidian was present on Malta around 4000 bc. All the material must have been moved initially by sea. Some may have been procured by people from the site or region where it was used. In Calabria for example it has been observed that on sites on the west coast obsidian comprises a large proportion of the total lithic material, and that on other sites where flint and chert were abundant obsidian was much less used. But some at least may have been moved in a series of direct or indirect exchanges, and therefore have been a high-quality medium through which intercommunal contact was established and maintained. It may again be no accident that the greatest scale of obsidian movement at this phase seems again to have occurred in southern Italy.[125]

While the maintenance of group identity can be thus discussed, internal differentiation is harder to analyse further. Burial evidence – quite apart from its inherent ambiguities – is everywhere sparse, and for the most part consists of single burials with few grave goods within or close to settlements and occupied cave and shelter sites. These are perhaps to be seen in the same sort of context as those discussed in chapter 2 but the general lack of collective burials is something of a contrast (Fig. 3.32). Two examples may suffice. One is the burial of an old man in a pit in the mid fifth millennium southern Corsican site of Araguina–Sennola, whose burial was overlaid by subsequent hearth deposits.[126] There are similar individual burials in shelter sites in both Languedoc and Provence, but these are rare. At Jean-Cros in the Aude there were the scattered remains of an adult, perhaps a woman, and a very young infant. One exception seems to exist in the case of the several burials at La Baume Bourbon at Cabrières, Gard, in a Cardial context, but there are as yet few further details. In southern Italy the range of settlement types may suggest site differentiation on a rather greater scale, but for reasons already explained it is not yet possible to analyse this further.

The gradual nature of change in most of the western Mediterranean remains at present the most striking feature of these two millennia, and the contrast with the other parts of Europe covered in this chapter is notable. Depending of course on one's view of the origins of the south-east Italian communities, all the observed changes can be seen in the context of local rather than external events. The source of the changes and the explanation of their rate are much harder to understand. The favourable environment must

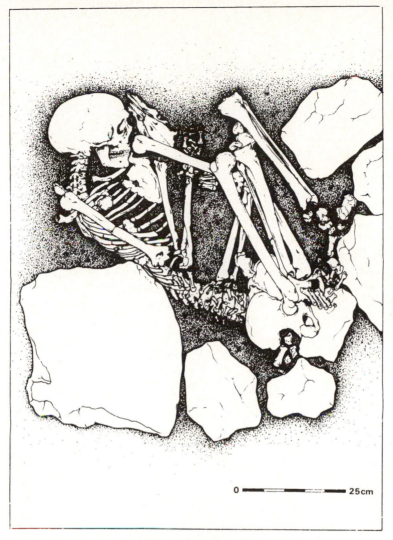

**3.32** Burial of an adult man from a later fifth millennium level in the Grotte de Gazel, Aude, Languedoc, southern France. *After* Guilaine

play a significant part but the final importance must be given to the nature of social relations between and within communities in such an environment. In this perspective the area – despite the imperfections of its evidence and our understanding – may serve to support again the theme underlying the book, that our focus of interest should not be simply the history of agricultural innovations, but the social context in which they were variously adopted, used and modified.

# CHAPTER 4

# INDIGENOUS CHANGE: THE PERIPHERY FROM 6000 TO AFTER 4000 bc

This chapter briefly surveys developments in six widely scattered areas of Europe, in order to continue the examination of indigenous society begun in chapter 2. The examples chosen with one exception lie outside the areas covered in the previous chapter, and the exception is in a remote part of the Balkans (Fig. 4.1). The quality of the evidence as in the early post-glacial period is very varied, but the examples are chosen from amongst the most illuminating studies to illustrate two themes; first, the continued development of native society outside the area affected by the changes discussed in chapter 3, and secondly, the effect that these changes themselves began to have on communities in surrounding areas. Relevant environmental

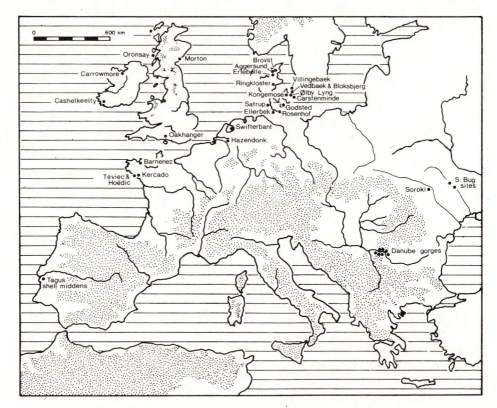

4.1 Simplified location map of the principal sites mentioned in chapter 4

evidence for southern Europe has already been presented, and is given below for the northern examples. Lack of space precludes much discussion of regional material sequences except where vital for chronology, but for the most part these can be followed in references already given.

## The Danube gorges

In the late seventh and early sixth millennium bc according to a rather meagre series of radiocarbon dates there was a group of sites such as Icoana, Razvrata, Ostrovul Banului, and Schela Cladovei in the Danube gorges whose inhabitants seem to have fished intensively, hunted extensively and even controlled the pig population closely, may have used intensively or even cultivated plant resources, and may have used these sites on a permanent or semi-permanent basis (see chapter 2). According to the chronology adopted here, based on novel artefacts such as pottery and on radiocarbon dates, this way of life continued past the middle of the sixth millennium bc to some point in the earlier fifth, while elsewhere in the Balkan river valleys there was the gradual appearance of agriculturally based communities, from whom the inhabitants of the gorges adopted or acquired Starčevo style pottery.

The classic site of the group is Lepenski Vir, on the right bank of the Danube.[1] Of eight stratified levels (though these are not present all over the site), five are assigned to phase I, one to II and two to III. A sparsely represented ninth level has been suggested to represent a proto-Lepenski Vir phase, although it may as well belong to phase I. Phase III has over 200000 sherds of Starčevo-style pottery and other artefacts compatible with that cultural grouping. On typological grounds, the excavator suggests that the pottery belongs to an early phase of the Starčevo culture but criticism of this scheme has already been aired in chapter 3, and the pottery cannot be closely placed, the more so as idiosyncracies of style are recognised in the assemblage. The lithic assemblages of phases I and II were sparse, and chronologically undiagnostic. There was a small number of sherds of monochrome pottery, perhaps some 60 in all, found in 15 houses of phase Ic–Ie. The excavator suggests that these are intrusive, but it is interesting that these were found only in the houses, like the rest of the artefacts in I and II, and in such contexts as between successive house floors. A coherent series of radiocarbon dates for samples from Ia to II runs from around 5400 to 4600 bc; only one date (Bln–652) in Ie may be a little out of phase. The series might even be depressed a little if the oak and elm samples were from large structural timbers as found in house nos. 36 and 37. On this chronology the Starčevo phase would belong to the end of the culture's duration. This evidence seems to preclude any possibility of Lepenski Vir I–II being Pre-Neolithic in a regional chronological sense. The site consists of a series of terraces above the Danube, with around 20 trapezoidal structures set on them, covering about 60 by 30 m in phases I–II (Fig. 4.2). The structures range from 5 to 30 m²; within the rough rows a large central structure is apparent in each level, there being other large structures in Ic and Id as well. (There is also a stratigraphic problem, since

**4.2** North-eastern part of Lepenski Vir I. The individual houses range from phase Ib to Ie. Photo: Srejović

only ten new structures are recognised in Ic, and exact contemporaneity on the slope must be heard to establish.) A miniature structure is also found in both Ic and Id. This layout may continue into phase II though the plan is less complete due to rebuilding in phase III. The structures, their broad ends with a central entrance and facing the river, have plastered floors (in phase I) and seem to have had a wooden tent-like superstructure. The interior is dominated by a rectangular stone-lined hearth pit, set around by slabs in many cases, with a further area at its distal end of stone paving, furnished in many cases with hollowed stones, and large boulders often carved with semi-representational faces, part human, part fish, or with curvilinear designs. In phase Ib, the most complete arrangement is found in the largest structure, no. 54, and it is suggested in Ic that structures nos. 40 and 28 flanking each end of the site were exclusively sanctuaries or shrines. Bones of fish, red deer and dog were found in several structures and can be seen as potential offerings, the more so in view of recurrent finds of red deer antlers and skulls, and red deer shoulder blades. Such other artefacts as were found are restricted to the interior of the structures, but without obvious differentiation from structure to structure. A final notable feature is the disposal of human remains (Fig. 4.3). Parts of the head were found between the structures up to phase Ib; one context in the earliest level consisted of the jawbone of an adult man, stone tools and fishbones. From phase Ib burials were found within the trapezoidal structures, but with decreasing frequency after phase Ic (as far as the burials

**4.3** House no. 65 of Lepenski Vir Ib. The skeleton in the foreground belongs to house no. 36 of Lepenski Vir II. Photo: Srejović

can be accurately phased). Extended burials occur within the hearth area in graves, and partial burial also occurs. A number of burials also seem to be laid across the paving beside the hearth and, if these are not later insertions, must have effectively precluded the use of such structures for other purposes. The burial ritual was on occasion elaborate – thus in structure no. 21 in phase 1d an old man was laid out with the head of an old woman minus lower jaw on his left shoulder, an aurochs skull on his right shoulder, and a deer skull by his right hand with antlers nearby.

Numbers of burials were also found in all levels of the structurally less clear site of Vlasac, though in much reduced numbers in the later compared with the earlier phase, and dated perhaps from the earlier sixth millennium bc to the earlier fifth. Burials also occur in both phases of the site at Padina.[2] Though these lack radiocarbon dates, I suggest that the first is equivalent to the end of the Pre-Neolithic period, and the second, with quantities of Starčevo pottery and artefacts, equivalent to Lepenski Vir I–II. Remains of rectangular hearths survive from the first phase, and trapezoidal structures with hearths and 'altars', terraced into the slope of the second. Other sites lower in the gorges such as Icoana phase II may also belong to the earlier part of the contact phase, though the chronology is uncertain. There is little published information on development of control over resources. It is of interest that the pigs in the succeeding phase III of Lepenski Vir were intermediate in size between supposed wild and domesticated forms, but no age data are available for I–II. Plant remains were not systematically recovered. A site like Lepenski Vir seems permanent, though it is difficult to establish how much was in use at one time. Its status is uncertain too. The emphasis on ritual and burials, some of which may have denied other use of the structures they were in, and the paucity of artefacts, confined to the structures, could all suggest that the site was largely non-domestic, and served as a central ceremonial place for the population of the gorges; settlements might be sought in sites like Vlasac and Padina, though their status too is open to dispute, and in other smaller sites. Despite belonging to the mid sixth millennium and later, and having Starčevo pottery, the sites are best assigned to the same native population, since the ritual, burial and architecture are foreign to the Starčevo culture. One can then suggest that communities in the gorges continued to develop or maintain a settled way of life in this period, but that change beyond the gorges presented increasing stress and threat to their identity which was countered by increased emphasis on ritual and centralised burials. The resolution of the situation can be suggested to lie in Lepenski Vir III. After a short stratigraphic break, different architecture, site layout and burial are found, with pottery abundant, stone axes and even finds of obsidian and *spondylus*. Ovicaprids are also found. The suggestion however that even the physical population changed at this stage must be treated with some caution. The subsistence changes appear to be of degree not of kind, and the change overall may reflect a reorientation of identity rather than the eventual arrival in the gorges of a new farming population.

*The Dniester–southern Bug area*

As agricultural settlement was gradually established in Transylvania and Moldavia in the later sixth millennium, there were communities to the east in the middle stretches of the River Dniester which may have been developing a settled way of life on the basis of indigenous resources. Discussion is centred on ten sites in the region of Soroki, found on the low narrow river terrace.[3] The earliest sites appear to be aceramic; Soroki II has mid sixth millennium bc dates for this phase. The sites do not appear to be large, but include oval semi-subterranean structures interpreted as dwellings. Blades and scrapers are numerous, and there are occasional trapezes. Fishbones, especially of the carp family, were numerous, and Unio shells well represented. Small quantities of animal bones were recovered, with red deer, roe, pig, cattle, fox and wolf represented. Numbers vary, roe being dominant in the lower of two layers at Soroki II, but the samples are small. There is no information on age or sex of the recorded fauna. A morphological distinction between 'wild' and 'domesticated' is however suggested, according to which 12 pig bones (14 per cent of the total) and two cattle bones are seen as domesticated in the lowest layer of Soroki II; 'wild' fauna constitute between 80 and 90 per cent of the assemblage at both Soroki I and II. In the absence of other data, the alternative possibility of sexual dimorphism must be considered, though intensive control of cattle and pigs is an attractive hypothesis. In the succeeding ceramic phase belonging perhaps to the late sixth millennium bc and certainly to the fifth, on the basis of a few radiocarbon dates from two sites and also contact finds of Linear pottery sherds from further west, the proportion of 'wild' fauna by the same criteria diminishes to around 60–50 per cent, with 'domesticated' cattle and pig in roughly equal quantities. Fish continued to be abundant, and impressions of einkorn, emmer and spelt are reported on sherds at Soroki I. It is not reported whether the sherds were local or imported, but it has been implied that both cereals and domesticated animals were merely acquired from agricultural communities to the west. Since plant remains were not systematically recovered, it is difficult to resolve this issue. The case does however raise again some of the possibilities of indigenously developed close control over resources, and the adoption of cereals could be taken as evidence of a further social desire to reinforce settled life. There is however little direct evidence of seasonality at the Soroki sites though surface buildings are found in the ceramic phase. The same possibilities exist in the southern Bug valley. The ceramic phase is lacking, as are radiocarbon dates. A suggested five-phase aceramic typology cannot be wholly supported by stratigraphy but Linear pottery sherds in the suggested fourth or Samcincy phase should presumably indicate a point somewhere in the later fifth millennium bc.[4] The deposits of each phase are rather thin (10–20 cm) and little guide to the date of the group's beginnings. Sites are located on the first terrace edge or on islets, and include one- to two-roomed surface buildings complete with regular hearths. Fish, shells and tortoise shells have been recovered, and the fauna at three sites

Baz'kov Island, Mitkov Island and Mikolina Broyarka was dominated by red deer, with pig and roe, and a few elk and horse. Only 3–7 per cent of the assemblages are suggested as early domesticates, and these are all cattle. The same problems of interpretation recur. Plant remains were not systematically recovered, but perforated tools, querns and flints with gloss suggested to Danilenko the practice of flood-plain and first-terrace cultivation, a plausible enough hypothesis though disputed by Dolukhanov. A final aspect worth consideration is the pottery in both areas. Forms are not elaborate: globular and biconical bowls in the former, deep pointed-base jars and bowls and flat-based jars and bowls in the latter. Decorative techniques include a range of incisions, impressions and roughening, and most seem to be within the range of Criş techniques to the west. The quantities of pottery at these sites are not large. Its presence however is a potentially useful clue to the role of material culture in societies such as these in a state of transition. Pottery may have been adopted not just as functionally useful or as some sort of necessary adjunct to domestication, but as a novel means of expressing identity in a changing social situation.

*Tagus estuary*

Developments in the Mediterranean after around 6000 bc have largely been discussed in chapter 3. One interesting study deserves a separate though very brief mention, for the sake of geographical balance. Several shell middens have been recorded at the confluence of the Tagus and the Muge, at the boundary between fresh and salt water, though only three sites have been examined recently.[5] Radiocarbon dates for Moita do Sebastião fall in the later sixth millennium bc, at Cabeço da Armoreira span the fifth, and at Cabeço da Arruda bracket the fifth and fourth millennia. The resources were wide-ranging – red deer, pig, cattle, fish, birds, marine shells such as cockle (*Cardium edule*), *Scrobicularia plana* and *Neritina fluvialitis*, and land snails – though the relative contribution of each is a difficult problem, further discussed below. The range of resources could have supported semi-permanent or permanent settlement even if there was no close control over particular staples and this group is part of a widespread phenomenon in the Atlantic area at this time of such coastal sites. It is of great interest that older and recent excavations both reveal large numbers of individual burials in the midden at Moita do Sebastião (some 34 in the latter), which in the light of earlier discussion could reinforce its possible role as a semi-permanent base. Pottery is not reported, and flint projectile assemblages were in local geometric styles.

*Denmark*

By the sixth millennium bc developed mixed oak forest was characteristic of much of southern Scandinavia, though as before (chapter 2) the pace of change may have varied from Zealand to Jutland.[6] There are implications for human settlement of new constraints presented by climax forest and its potentially lower exploitable animal and plant biomass, due to less light on the forest floor, less browse, the replacement of hazel stands, the silting up of lakes and marshes and other such factors. The history of shoreline change seems reasonably well established, with the Litorina sea phase of the Baltic current throughout this period, with four major transgressions between 5000 and 3000 bc. The implications are important in terms of land loss, the creation of new coastal zones, and the penetration of marine fauna such as seals into the Baltic. The material sequence also seems reasonably well established; there is considerable continuity from the early post-glacial period, except in projectile styles, now overwhelmingly first rhomboid then trapezoid on broad blades. A notable innovation is pottery, in the form of large S-shaped pointed-base jars and flat oval bowls or lamps; the exact date of its appearance is unclear though on the evidence of sites like the Ertebølle midden it goes back at least to the very early fourth millennium bc. The terminology for the various phases is again varied. One scheme proposes four post-Maglemose phases, Kongemose, Vedbaek, Bloksbjerg and Ertebølle, the latter subdivided, another just two main phases, Kongemose and Ertebølle, subsuming four lithic and artefactual stages whose transition can be set in the mid fifth millennium bc. For the sake of simplicity the latter scheme is adopted here.[7]

In the Kongemose phase, inland sites are known, such as the eponymous site itself by a marsh in central Zealand. Its situation is thus like many early post-glacial sites and, since it is large (about 60 by 20 m) and lacks fish bone or fishing gear, might be seen as a winter site like Holmegaard v. But coastal sites are now recognised such as Villingebaek and Carstenminde and slightly later Vedbaek and Brovst, the first three in north-east Zealand, the latter on the north side of the Limfjord in Jutland.[8] Villingebaek is a large site apparently occupied in summer, whose inhabitants exploited land animals, sea birds and fish. At Brovst which dates to the earlier to mid fifth millennium bc shellfish were also used but these were not important in eastern Zealand at any stage because of the lower salinity of the sea. The site is not extensive (though excavations were limited) and summer occupation is considered possible. This new aspect of settlement must be carefully considered. It is probable that early post-glacial coastal sites existed but have been destroyed by shoreline changes. Taken at face value the evidence suggests that coastal exploitation may have been most frequent in the summer but the sites are relatively few and the seasonality evidence crude. The main change may in fact lie in the visibility of the archaeological record.

In the Ertebølle phase (in the sense here used) it is likely however that there is an increasing emphasis on coastal settlement. Inland exploitation certainly continued, as shown by Aamosen sites on Zealand, Vester Ulslev and Godsted on Lolland, Ringkloster and surface scatters, part of the alleged but now disproved 'Gudenaa culture', in Jutland, and further south by sites such as Satrup and Ellerbek, the latter proposed as the Schleswig-Holstein equivalent of Ertebølle. These sites have been neither extensively explored nor fully published.[9] It is possible that some of them represent specialised sites, such as Ringkloster with its concentration on pig, roe and fur-bearers such as marten, and there is evidence here that hindquarters of pig were regularly removed (or at least were underrepresented at the site).[10] It is also likely that from the later fifth millennium bc at least a certain element of settlement was increasingly restricted to the coast. In the Vedbaek estuary, the C13 content of the bones from the cemetery at Vedbaek Bøgebakken radiocarbon dated to around 4000 bc suggests a largely marine diet.[11] Some sites on the coast may only have been seasonally occupied. There is indirect evidence for seasonal occupation at Ølby Lyng in eastern Zealand for example, in the form of seals and sea birds such as guillemot which are most easily exploited within this part of the year, in autumn or late-winter occupation. Such evidence may be imprecise, and other evidence at the same site raises other possibilities. Underrepresentation of fish head remains suggests the possibility of fish drying, and such simple means of food storage would circumvent the constraints of seasonal resource abundance. Land animals such as deer and pig which are also found at the site could also have been exploited at other seasons. Some coastal sites may have been very specialised, such as the small north Jutish extraction site of Aggersund, whose faunal remains are dominated by swans, presumably winter migrants, to the exclusion of other winter fowl. The swans were perhaps used for their meat and feathers. Other coastal sites may have been more permanent bases, such as the Ertebølle shell midden in the Limfjord (Fig. 4.4). *In toto* the site is large,

4.4 The shell midden at Ertebølle, northern Jutland. Photo: National Museum, Copenhagen

140 m long and from 6 to 20 m broad, but radiocarbon dates suggest a main span of occupation of about 200 years at least. Its size at any point is impossible to reconstruct, though there are apparently no major stabilisation surfaces within it. The evidence of winter and summer birds and the range of pig ages (as seen in their teeth) suggest the possibility of year-round use over this time span, and therefore also the possibility of permanent settlement thoughout the year at any point within it. As at other coastal sites, land animals were exploited as well as marine resources.[12] It is possible as in the early post-glacial period that these animals were closely controlled though age and sex data are meagre for the Kongemose and Ertebølle phases. Two main sizes of adult cattle have been recorded in Ertebølle phase sites but are considered to show sexual dimorphism rather than incipient domestication. Cattle did not apparently survive the Boreal–Atlantic transition on Zealand, perhaps partly due to habitat change but also partly to over-exploitation. The contribution of shellfish to the diet is difficult to estimate. The remains of oysters, the dominant shell, survive better and are more obvious than fish, crab, or even animal bone, but it has been calculated that some 52000 oysters are needed to match the food value of one adult red deer. The total volume of the Ertebølle midden has been suggested as 1500 m³; with a 200 year occupation, there was an average annual deposit of over 7 m³. One cubic metre of oyster shells is suggested to be equivalent to 124 kg of animal meat with a calorie content of 600 per kg; 7 m³ would then provide in round terms half a million calories.[13] Even a single nuclear family (two adults, three children) requiring over 10000 calories a day and living only off shellfish, would not be thus supported for more than two months. However, the contribution of shellfish may be underrepresented, if comparatively few shellfish were brought back to base and many were eaten as meals or snacks at the point of extraction. But even if only a minor resource, shellfish are significant for suggesting that all available resources were in fact increasingly taken up from the mid fifth millennium bc onwards. This raises various possibilities. One is increased pressure on resources. From the representation of land animals at coastal sites, it is hard to believe that the suggested Vedbaek marine diet was typical, or that pressure on resources was sufficient in itself to cause territorial divisions amongst the population. Another possibility is that permanent settlement was increasingly sought socially, perhaps encouraged by constraints in the interior such as habitat and faunal change, and that this was most easily satisfied now on the coast. It is also possible that coastal bases simply replaced the lake and marsh-edge interior sites of the early post-glacial period as the best foci for more or less permanent settlement, but there does at face value appear to have been a significant change. It has been suggested that sedentary settlement would be desirable in itself and communities or groups able to provide the means for it, either by resource control or by choosing areas with a sufficient supply of seasonal resources, would thereby achieve social prominence. The cemetery at Vedbaek Bøgebakken can be interpreted in the light of most of these hypotheses.[14] The settlement lies on the north edge of an estuary on the east

coast of Zealand. Along with Vedbaek Boldbaner it is one of a series of sites in the estuary. There is evidence for exploitation of land animals, fish, sea birds and sea mammals including seal and porpoise. If settlement was restricted to the coast, this would have been a very favourable area, and the cemetery may be connected with such putatively stable settlement. Seventeen graves with 22 bodies were found adjacent to or perhaps in the settlement area. Most graves held single burials of adult men or women (Fig. 4.5). Two were infants. One grave held three burials, probably of a man and a woman as well as an infant, and there were two burials of women with very young infants. The graves themselves were long shallow pits and the bodies were extended. Grave treatment varied though practically all had ochre in them, though it was considered by the excavators that this might be derived from body dye or clothes rather than burial ritual. Grave goods were found with ten burials, though others may have been disturbed. The sample is small but includes adult men with stone and bone tools, red deer antlers, and large stones on top of the body, and other adults perhaps women with many pendants, probably originally sewn on to garments and occasional flint and stone tools and antlers. The quantities of goods are not sufficient to further differentiate any age or sex group (even if one believed that such patterns could yield reliable

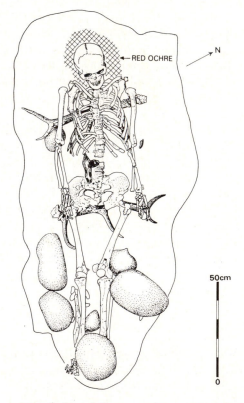

4.5 Burial of an adult man in the cemetery at Vedbaek, Zealand. *After* Albrethsen and Brinch Petersen

information on differentiation in life), but it may be significant that even a young woman as in grave no. 8, tentatively aged at about 18–20 years, was with her infant accorded formal burial along with older men and women and young men. There is another example of female and child (no. 15) and there are two individual infant burials (nos. 18 and 21). It is possible that burial itself was an indication of social prominence given the smallness of the cemetery and such female burials may indicate the possession of inherited rather than achieved status. This obviously makes various assumptions about the likely role of women and also about the original extent of the cemetery. Other scattered burials are known from other sites, and it may eventually turn out that collective burial was far more widespread in this period. In discussing social mechanisms for reinforcing territorial stability and possible social differentiation it is useful to consider again material culture. The striking innovation of the Ertebølle phase in the fourth millennium bc was pottery. This is generally assumed to be learnt from Linear pottery groups to the south (see chapter 3). At a technical level this is plausible, and there are also finds of perforated subtriangular axes (*Breitkeile*) in southern Scandinavia in undoubted Ertebølle–Ellerbek contexts, a type belonging to the earlier fourth millennium bc further south, so that mechanisms of contact must have existed. On the other hand there is no ceramic exchange of the kind seen in so-called Limburg pottery and the individuality of Ertebølle pottery is therefore striking. Its restricted forms are also notable, which surely cannot just be dismissed as merely due to technical inferiority. A hypothesis worth considering is that Ertebølle jars had a specific status role especially on larger base sites, and that if there is a connection between oval bowls and burning oil, such lamps may also have had social rather than merely technical or utilitarian significance.

It is considered that there are no reliably closed finds of ovicaprids or other domesticated animals from Ertebølle contexts, but it has been suggested that cereal pollen in profiles at both Satrup and Rosenhof predates the local TRB horizon and equates with the Ellerbek phase.[15] It may be noted that there has been little or no systematic plant recovery from Ertebølle sites so that this must remain an open question. If there were pressure on resources or territory in the fourth millennium bc in southern Scandinavia it is plausible that new resources of external origin could have been adopted, at the same time as burials and pottery could have been used to reinforce the identity of established groups in both their local and regional setting. The resolution of this situation can be followed in chapter 6.

## British Isles: interior and coast

Though it is not possible to date the event exactly, it is likely that the British Isles were finally separated from the continent by around 6000 bc.[16] Vegetational sequence followed the same sort of pattern as seen in southern Scandinavia with climax mixed oak forest established by the sixth millennium bc. The material sequence shows much continuity from the early post-glacial period, but with the gradual development of more geometric microlith styles and the nonappearance of continental blade-and-trapeze traditions. The nature of the lithics and settlement have been closely studied, but excavated faunal and plant assemblages are all too rare.

Settlement seems to have been expansive, on the basis of the very wide-spread distribution of flint and stone scatters including not just microliths but also heavier tools such as axes. Ireland too was settled from around 7000 bc at the latest, both in the interior as well as on the rivers and coasts of the north-east which have been best explored. Inland settlement is well documented in England and Wales, and the previous pattern of larger lowland sites and smaller and upland sites outlined in chapter 2 seems to have persisted. There is virtually no direct evidence from inland sites for the use of animals. Pollen analysis however has provided substantial evidence for deliberate interference with forest cover, either by felling or fire or both. Such evidence is widespread, for example from Dartmoor, the Yorkshire Pennines and moors and East Anglia. It has been shown that regeneration of the forest after clearance would significantly increase the quantities of browse available to grazing animals, and deliberate clearance would therefore serve to increase the quantity of animals in any one area and thereby to manipulate their behaviour. The clearances cited were obviously large enough to be detected in pollen diagrams, but it has been noted that the optimum size of clearance might have been too small for regular detection in conventional diagrams. Those cited were also episodic or relatively short lived. There are areas however where clearance may have been sustained, as on the southern Pennines over 300 m above sea level. The same may apply to sandy areas in south-east England, on the basis of microlith densities. There is occasional pollen evidence, as at Oakhanger VII, Hampshire, perhaps dated to the early Atlantic period (though the typology of the microliths conflicts with the single late fifth millennium bc radiocarbon date) for an unusually high concentration of ivy pollen in association with small sites. It is possible that ivy was collected as an animal lure or fodder, and since ivy flowers in autumn and early winter, there is a plausible season for this kind of activity. As with animals there is virtually no plant evidence apart from hazelnuts. Clearances would have increased the density of edible plants on the forest floor, and encouraged hazel which would otherwise have had severe competition from the other major forest species. Though proof is lacking, there is every reason to keep firmly in mind Clarke's suggestion of arboriculture and horticulture. Whatever the deficiencies of the inland evidence there is clear evidence for a positive response to climax forest, even though this need not be seen as uniform or ubiquitous. The contrast with Denmark is interesting. Axes and fire were available in both areas, but it has not been suggested to date that the Danish pollen diagrams show the same kind of inland clearance as in the British Isles.

The evidence from the British coasts is more complete, as two well-investigated examples illustrate.[17] Morton on the Fife coast in eastern Scotland is a large site with two concentrations each about 30 m long but probably made up of successive smaller occupations and used over hundreds of years after around 6000 bc. Beneath and amongst the build-up of shells and other midden material there are areas of hearths and stakeholes, possibly the remains of shelters, drying racks and the like. The range of resources is by now familiar – land animals including red and roe deer, pig and aurochs; sea birds including guillemot; marine shells including edible cockle (*Cerastoderma edule* L.), and *Macoma balthica* L.; edible crab (*Cancer pagunus* Bell); and fish especially cod, but including also haddock, turbot, sturgeon and salmonid – though marine mammals are absent. There is little data on age and sex of the animals, but the sheer variety of resources could, as elsewhere in north-west Europe, have supported more or less permanent settlement in the coastal zone. On the small Inner Hebridean island of Oronsay in the west of Scotland there are several shell middens, dating from the fourth millennium bc, which are the best investigated of a group of similar sites in the general area. Careful investigation has shown the exploitation of shellfish (limpets, scallops, crab) and also of deer, seals and fish, especially the saithe (*Pollachius virens* L.). There are some indications of hearths and stakeholes at the base of at least one of the middens. The middens are spaced around the coast of the small island. From its position it might be expected that Oronsay was only used seasonally, and specifically at some point in the summer for specialised exploitation. Study of the growth rate of the earbone or otolith of the saithe however suggests a rather different pattern. Four sites out of a total of six on the island have been analysed. Samples from the otoliths suggest that each was occupied at a slightly different season, Cnoc Sligeach in mid-summer, Cnoc Coig from later summer into the autumn, Priory Midden from after mid-autumn, and Caisteal nan Gillean II over a longer period, both in summer and in later autumn or winter. Despite the many interpretative difficulties, not least again the question of storage, the overall implication is striking, that the island was being exploited for much of the year, except later winter and spring. This sort of evidence does not prove semi-permanent occupation on Oronsay at any single point in the fourth millennium bc but it is certainly compatible with it. The size of group involved is also unclear, the middens themselves being quite small (Cnoc Coig is about 30 m long), and variation in use over time is possible too, since Cnoc Coig for example unlike the others has its other fish bones concentrated at the base of rather than in the matrix of the shell midden. But such evidence seems a further indication of permanent or semi-permanent settlement in what we have called native communities, in this case at a date when elsewhere in the country agricultural activity was beginning (see chapter 6). As in Denmark, this kind of development may eventually have encouraged the native adoption of new food resources, though its stability could have delayed it. The Oronsay case may not be isolated. Evidence from the area of the so-called Larnian culture in north-east Ireland suggests a concentration on rich coastal and inland river resources. In western Brittany too coastal middens such as Téviec and Hoëdic dated around 4000 bc point in the same direction. These sites contain also individual and small collective burials within them, in rudimentary chambers or stone- and antler-lined graves. The earliest Breton chambered tombs are dated to the early fourth millennium bc (such as Barnenez and Kercado) and it was suggested some time ago that native traditions and practices could have played a substantial part in their emergence.[18] There might also be Irish evidence for the use of formal burial in a native context, putatively as elsewhere as a source of social identity and stability in a situation of change and competition for resources. Recent excavations at Carrowmore in Co. Sligo in the so-called passage grave cemetery have produced one early fourth milennium bc radiocarbon date for site IV, one of the low circular kerbed mounds with simple orthostatic passage and polygonal chamber. The context for the date is the stone packing of one of the stones of the central chamber. The other dates from the excavated sites are later in the fourth millennium bc, and whether the construction of the monument is yet reliably dated is unclear. Large quantities of burnt human and animal bone were found in the central chamber. It is possible therefore (though controversial) that the construction and such use of the monument were due to native communities.[19] These are not well investigated in the region but small (undated) shell middens have been recorded in the area of the cemetery, and unopened seashells have been found in the excavated monuments, and the excavator has suggested that the monuments were used as part of an annual round of restricted extent by native communities. Further south in western Ireland there is radiocarbon-dated pollen analytical evidence for cereal cultivation at Cashelkeelty in Co. Kerry in the earlier fourth millennium bc. The cultural context is unclear, but the clearances and cultivation seem to have been abandoned before a second phase in the later fourth millennium bc. So there may be again a case for arguing native involvement in the first phase. As far as is known native communities in the British Isles did not use pottery, but it is possible that the individuality of British and Irish microlith styles was due not simply to physical isolation, but to their role as markers in some way of group identity. The appearance of geographically more restricted styles in the Later Mesolithic such as Horsham points may support this.

## The Dutch coast

The final example carries the discussion of the development of native communities a little further into the process of change, and overlaps with the discussion in chapter 6. As seen in chapter 3 agriculturally based communities were restricted to the favourable loess and comparable soils in north-west Europe in the later fifth millennium bc. On the Dutch coast in the area of the Ijsselmeer polders or reclaimed lands there were at this date native communities living in the freshwater tidal delta of what was later to be the Ijssel valley (Fig. 4.6).[20] Occupation of the later fifth millennium has been excavated on dune sites flanking the river system in the vicinity of Swifterbant in the Nord-Ost Flevoland polder (sites s11–13), and sixth and earlier fifth millennium dates have come from other dunes (sites s21–22). These sites were

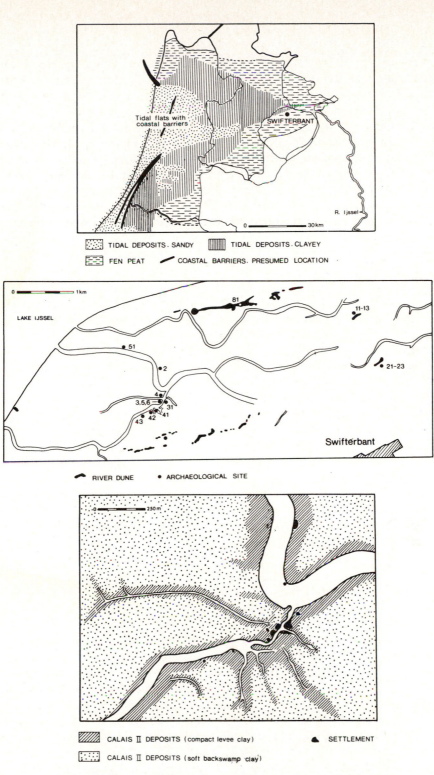

**4.6** Simplified maps of the setting and location of some of the principal sites at Swifterbant, Ijsselmeer, Netherlands. *After* Van der Waals *et al.*

probably seasonal. By the later fifth sea level had risen considerably, coastal barriers began to form and an extensive intercoastal area of lagoon and marsh emerged in which marine and riverine deposits (Calais II in the Dutch sequence) were laid down. The sites were in the inner part of this zone. The occupations are quite small with hearths and stakeholes. Flint assemblages were in the native tradition, but pointed-base S-shaped pottery, roughly decorated, was apparently in use on site S11 (though it might belong to a later phase). It can be compared with Ertebølle pottery and the idea could be seen again as derived from the area of the Linear pottery culture, though the forms and techniques are again strikingly different. Economic evidence is not available, though further south at the sand ridge of Hazendonk in the Rhine–Meuse estuary cereal pollen has been recorded around 4000 bc which may testify to local cultivation unless the pollen is river transported from further afield. Further sites are known in the Swifterbant area dating to the mid fourth millennium bc (sites S2, S3–5). Their location is a little different, for during the Calais II transgression the freshwater tidal delta in the Swifterbant area had further developed, and occupation (though not necessarily absent from the dunes) was concentrated on the natural levées of a system of creeks running into a larger channel. Behind the levées were low-lying marshy backswamps, with willow carr and more open marsh vegetation. The difference between high and low tide would not have been more than 10 cm. Winter flooding was frequent. One site, S2, is on a larger channel, but the majority are on the side creeks close to their confluence with the former. The sites consist of spreads of occupation material, hearths and stakeholes, the latter numerous on S3–5. Subsistence has been studied at this site. A wide range of river and anadromous fish were recorded, as well as birds, red deer, aurochs, elk, horse, beaver, otter and polecat, and domesticated cattle, pig and dog (according to conventional morphological criteria). Both young and old cattle were represented, and were locally slaughtered. Local plants and fruits are well represented, though it is difficult with some to know whether they were actually used as food. Cereal remains were also found, of naked six-row barley (*Hordeum vulgare var. nudum*) and emmer (*Triticum dicoccum*). As well as the grains there are also glume fragments and rachis internodes of the barley. This is considered proof of local threshing and therefore local cultivation, which would indeed be possible in clearances on the levées. However it cannot be accepted without some reservation since glume and rachis internodes could have been part of a partially processed crop transported from elsewhere. Contact with the hinterland is seen in fragments of *Breitkeile* in S3–5, but pottery remains firmly in the style already described. Yet again some of the sites have burials, of all ages and both sexes, the largest number being a minimum of eight on S2. The burials are not closely dated, though one radiocarbon date from S2 is of the mid fourth millennium bc. The environmental situation perhaps makes it unlikely that these sites were permanently inhabited, and seed remains of plants that do not tolerate disturbance could also indicate periodic abandonment at least of individual locations.

There are many indications from the examples selected that both social and economic development in the native communities discussed were different only in degree rather than in kind to those of agriculturally based communities elsewhere in Europe. The repeated signs of more permanent settlement and some degree of inter- and intra-group differentiation are important, and hints of greater control over resources are by no means isolated or easily dismissed. Had the cereal-domesticated animal 'package' never been adopted in prehistoric Europe it may still be argued on the basis of the evidence presented in this and chapter 2 that social development would have been extensive and complex. Nevertheless it was adopted, and at this stage there were two sorts of effect around the periphery of its distribution. In the long run the new resources were adopted virtually everywhere, not so much causing social change from scratch but being used to reinforce or accelerate already established processes of change. In the short term the other effect may have been to cause native resistance to cultural change. This hypothesis can be used to explain developments in the Danube gorges with the proliferation of ritual and burials, and may also explain features in areas as far apart as the Dniester–Bug valleys and southern Scandinavia. It was argued that the emergence of formal collective burial in north-west Europe at this time is no coincidence, and that the adoption of pottery in many (but not in all) areas could have more than technical or functional significance. As has been observed in southern Scandinavia there was a considerable time-lag between the appearance of agricultural communities on the fringes of the north European plain, and the widespread adoption of cereal based agriculture in Denmark in the TRB horizon, despite the possible indications from sites like Rosenhof for a phase of experimentation. Set against the speed of the previous spread of cereal-based agriculture, an explanation for this pause is required. It may lie partly in the subsistence of the Ertebølle culture, but also in the social formations of the area. This view is consistent with the argument running through the book that interest should be centred primarily on the social use of resources rather than on the abstract and mechanistic effect of particular resources on passive recipients.

# CHAPTER 5

# CONSOLIDATION AND DENOUEMENT IN SOUTH-EAST EUROPE

## 5.1 Social development, 4000–3000 bc

### Environment

There is little evidence from south-east Europe to suggest any significant changes in climate in this period, and one may refer again to the discussion at the beginning of chapter 3. The situation results partly from the dearth of suitable data in the area, but where this is available as in northern Greece no radical changes can be seen. Evidence from further north in Europe, discussed in more detail in chapter 6 suggests the possibility of a cold spell at the end of the Atlantic period in the later fourth millennium bc, and of more continental climate in the Sub-Boreal period after around 3000 bc, but these fluctuations were relatively weak and cannot be seen to have imposed major new constraints on contemporary human communities.

### The nature of the evidence

This chapter covers developments in four major areas of south-east Europe: Greece minus the Thracian coast, the central Balkans, the eastern Balkans including the Thracian coast, and an area stretching eastwards from Transylvania through north-east Romania to the River Dniester and ultimately the River Dnieper in the USSR (Fig. 5.1). In total the evidence is impressive in both quantity and quality, and in some respects has a claim to be the best surveyed in this book. Its apogee is undoubtedly the study of settlements in the last two areas listed above where research especially since the war has resulted in the complete or near-complete excavation of several settlements.[1] Notable examples in Bulgaria are the sites of Azmak, Chatalka, Vinitsa, Golyamo Delchevo, Polyanitsa, and Ovčarovo, and in Romania the sites of Hăbăşeşti, Truşeşti and Tîrpeşti. There has also been large-scale investigation of many others notably in Bulgaria, Romania and the USSR. There have been large-scale excavations of cemeteries, such as Cernavodă and Cernica in Romania, and Varna and neighbours in north-east Bulgaria.[2] Indigenous copper metallurgy has been documented including mines with a large productive capacity, such as Aibunar in Bulgaria and Rudna Glava in Yugoslavia.[3] A side-effect of tell excavation especially in Bulgaria has been the refinement of local chronologies. The potential for further interpretative studies is thus enormous and has hardly yet been realised. At the same time

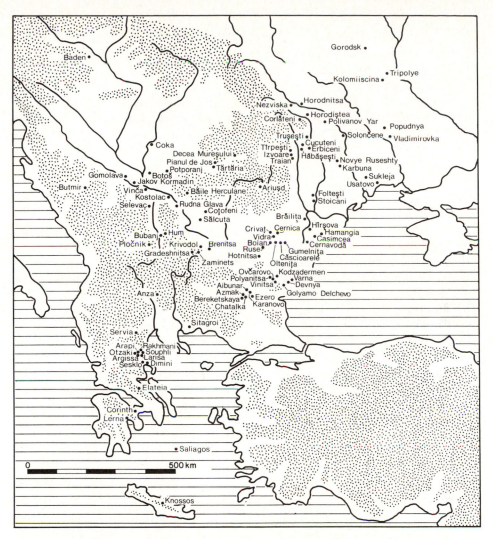

**5.1** Simplified location map of the principal sites mentioned in chapter 5

one must point out imbalances in the evidence, such as the lesser intensity of research in Yugoslavia and Greece, the concentration of excavation on tell settlements at the general expense of open sites in those areas where they occur or may have co-existed, the failure systematically to recover economic evidence, the lack of large series of radiocarbon samples, the lack of published detail about the spatial distribution of artefacts in houses and in settlements, and the sometimes long delay between excavation and publication. In addition the first half of the third millennium bc is not well understood in most of the area, partly through a lack of relevant excavation, and partly, as I will argue, through various theoretical misconceptions.

*Chronology and material sequences, 4000–c. 3000 bc*

The end of the period will be discussed separately at the close of the chapter. Before looking very briefly at the various material sequences, some general remarks on chronology are necessary (Fig. 5.2). Absolute chronology is not well established.[4] The old Vinča–Troy equation which provided a starting point around 3000 BC has fallen to both typological reassessment and the advent of radiocarbon dating. The latter has in turn provided a general picture of cultural development from 4000 bc but unfortunately has not been applied in anything like sufficient quantity. There are large series of dates from only three sites in this period, Sitagroi, Căscioarele in Romania and Azmak. There are radiocarbon dates for only phase A2 of the proposed Gumelniţa sequence, and no more than five from any Vinča site, while dates for the Cucuteni– Tripolye culture are few and largely single, and not yet available for all proposed phases of the Cucuteni sequence. Considerable reliance is therefore still placed on typological schemes of ceramic development. Pottery as before is very varied and the schemes are clearly necessary, and their virtues can be seen in the partly typological reassessment of the Vinča–Troy link based on the Karanovo sequence. Where sufficient sites with good stratigraphy have been investigated, they may be elaborated with some confidence (Fig. 5.3). This is best exemplified by Bulgaria where reliance on the Karanovo sequence has been replaced by regional schemes, each divisible at a simplified level into early, middle and late phases, but with further subdivisions and even subdivisions of these.[5] A site like Golyamo Delchevo with 17 horizons of this period illustrates the potential for such refinement. The key assumption however is that *ceteris paribus* like is of equal date and duration to like, which makes

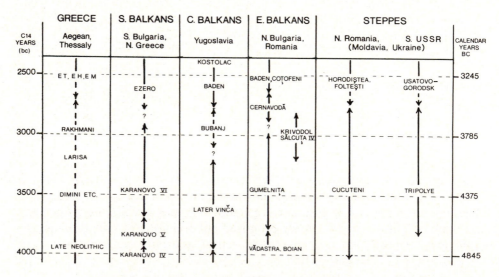

5.2 Simplified outline chronology of the main areas discussed in chapter 5, c. 4000–2500 bc

**5.3** View of the main section at the Karanovo tell, central-southern Bulgaria. The vertical scale is metres. Photo: author

insufficient allowance for regional or temporal variation as well as raising doubts about the objective assessment of similarity. One example is the erroneous comparison of Cucuteni 'violin' figurines with examples at Troy.[6] Many of the other typological schemes lack the solid stratigraphic basis available in Bulgaria, and make generalising extrapolations from eponymous sites to others roundabout as at Vinča. But it has been suggested that the end of the later Vinča sequence is not in fact represented at the type site itself, and the succeeding Bubanj group in southern Yugoslavia is best placed by reference to the sequence in surrounding areas typified by the sites of Sălcuţa and Krivodol.[7] In Greece it has gradually been realised that the Dimini group was an isolated phenomenon and the putatively succeeding Larisa and Rakhmani phases neither have a secure stratigraphic basis in sites like Arapi and Otzaki nor necessarily have universal validity in northern Greece, as already hinted at Servia in Macedonia.[8] The Cucuteni–Tripolye sequence may be better established than its confusing terminology sometimes leads one to consider; broad typological development is backed by stratigraphy at numbers of sites and a differential pace of regional development has been recognised.[9] Some of the many proposed subdivisions of Cucuteni phases may not have separate existence such as pre-Cucuteni I or Cucuteni AI, and even if there is a difference at some sites between phases with bichrome and bichrome plus trichrome pottery, it can be very hard to test at others such as Tîrpeşti, where houses with both belong to the same general stratigraphic horizon but are superimposed; the chronological argument may quickly become circular. One way however in which typological schemes can be checked is by inter-regional exchanges of specific artefacts, especially pots. An example is the Cucuteni A pots at Gumelniţa itself, in the A2–B1 level. In this way many general synchronisms can be built up, especially between the Cucuteni and Gumelniţa sequences.[10]

In Greece the fine-painted pottery of Dimini and related sites in eastern Thessaly, with its spiral and meander motifs, may be placed in the mid fourth millennium bc, on the slender basis of one radiocarbon date from the Sesklo acropolis and one from Argissa. Elsewhere matt-painted and polychrome pottery seems to have continued, and the position of fine dark pottery (Larisa) and crusted pottery (Rakhmani) is uncertain. In the central Balkans later Vinča pottery (or Vinča–Pločnik after a southern Yugoslav tell) continues the early tradition, with increasing regional divergences, with an emphasis maintained on fine black burnished ware and decorative fluting.[11] None of the pottery is painted, in striking contrast to surrounding areas, though paint was used in the area on figurines. Painting in the form of graphite decoration, along with rippling and impression, was used in the Bubanj–Hum Ia phase which seems to succeed Vinča in the Morava basin around Nis. Chapman suggests on the basis of radiocarbon dates that the Vinča culture may have persisted to around 3300 bc; in more-northern Yugoslavia it was succeeded by material akin to the Lengyel, Tiszapolgár and Bodrogkeresztúr cultures, and on that basis may have ended rather sooner (see chapter 6). The stratigraphy of Gomolava in the Sava valley provides one of the best yardsticks in a very confused situation.[12] In Transylvania likewise early Vinča–Turdaş ceramics were replaced by elaborate painted Petreşti styles early in the fourth millennium bc, and in Oltenia perhaps by the mid fourth by the Sălcuţa style with some graphite painting.

A steady rate of change also characterises the eastern Balkans but there was also much more continuity in the cultural complex formed in the area than in the region of the Vinča culture. In the Maritsa (as seen at Karanovo v) and Boian (after the eponymous site on a peninsula in a lake near the Danube) cultures, pottery was decorated by channelling, incision, excision and white paint, and latterly by graphite-painted designs.[13] This technique came to dominate the decorative repertoire of the succeeding complex which may fill much of the fourth millennium bc. It was found over a wide area and has been named principally after Karanovo level vi in central-southern Bulgaria, the tell site of Kodzadermen in north-east Bulgaria, and the Gumelniţa tell (Fig. 5.4) in southern Romania.[14] The complex can now be seen not to be uniform, and further regional subdivisions are important, such as those named after Gradeshnitsa in north-west Bulgaria, Polyanitsa in the middle phase of development in north-east Bulgaria, and the Varna cemetery in the late phase of development on the Black Sea coast.

Further east the eponymous sites are Cucuteni, between the rivers Siret and Prut in Moldavia and Tripolye, far to the north-east near Kiev and the River Dnieper and excavated at the turn of the century.[15] But ceramic

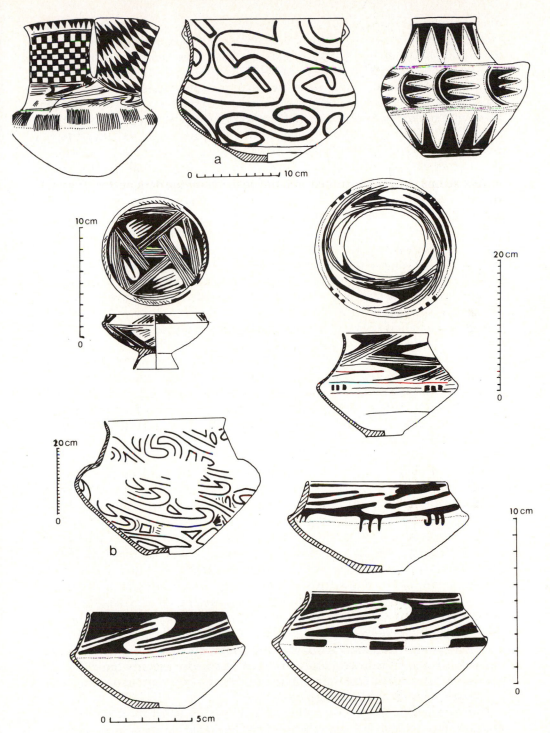

5.4 Gumelniţa graphite-painted and encrusted pottery and imported polychrome Cucuteni pottery (a–b) from Căscioarele, Danube valley, southern Romania. *After* Dumitrescu

development was complicated and regionalised.[16] The basic development is from fine dark ware with a variety of fluted, channelled, stamped and incised decoration in the pre-Cucuteni–Tripolye A phase, to the addition of bichrome and trichrome painting (mainly red, black and white) in the Cucuteni A–Tripolye B1 phase and then to subsequent phases of dark colours and no incision, such as the black or orange motifs of Cucuteni A–B, and B, and red black and brown of Tripolye B2 and C1 west of the River Bug. Decoration is dominated by spiral and curvilinear motifs, and the range of shapes varied, from bowls and pedestalled bowls and stands to large jars. Regionalisation is illustrated by the gradual eastwards spread of the complex starting in Transylvania and Moldavia, and a faster rate of change being maintained in the west. Thus Tripolye A to the east of the Bug was probably contemporary with B1 to the west, and B2 styles east of the Bug were black on orange, not trichrome as to the west. The terminology goes a little way to making amends in the late stages with Tripolye C denoting the northern area around Kiev, and that to the south around the Bug. A further terminological source of confusions is the label Cucuteni C, which is not a ceramic phase but a type of shell-tempered and cord-decorated pottery, first appearing in the Cucuteni A–Tripolye B1 phase.

The origins of all these styles are best sought primarily in their local areas or in interactions with neighbouring areas. The pre-Cucuteni style for example has been seen as in some way a development of combined Linear pottery and Boian traditions, and it is interesting to note that no new population is summoned from far away at this point. But on the other hand the search for specific local or regional antecedents may underplay the striking novelties of this style. Further Cucuteni development may have been influenced by neighbouring painted styles. The spread of the various styles is commonly agreed to be due to a mixture of colonisation and acculturation, as will be discussed below, which is a further indication of the inconsistency of seeking purely external sources of change at earlier and later stages than this.

As before the discussion has ignored till now other material which must be incorporated, though pottery remains the most numerous and probably most changeable category.[17] One can trace further development in figurines for example, with a variety of clay, bone and marble types in the Gumelniţa–Karanovo complex and even large hollow clay figurines. Perhaps the most useful generalisation is that there was a considerable increase in the numbers and kinds of artefacts in the fourth millennium bc, seen for example in the greater quantities of chipped stone implements and the almost ubiquitous use in the eastern Balkans of honey-coloured flint from north-east Bulgaria, or in the appearance of perforated stone tools in the Boian and Maritsa cultures. We will return to the explanation of this artefactual diversity later. For the present it can be illustrated in a little more detail by the further development of metalworking, both of copper and gold.

Later fifth millennium bc copper trinkets were noted in chapter 3. On present evidence they were of relatively restricted distribution, and technologically simple, being worked from native copper or copper smelted from its ores, a simple process where oxide ores are involved and one not requiring temperatures over 700–800°C. In the fourth millennium bc copper artefacts became more widely distributed, technically more advanced and typologically more elaborate. The tradition of the central and eastern Balkans continued, to reach its apogee in the Gumelniţa–Kodzadermen–Karanovo VI complex, and locally worked copper artefacts are found to the east from the pre-Cucuteni III–Tripolye A stage, as well as in northern Greece from the end of Sitagroi phase II. Technically there are a number of possible lines of development but the most likely next stage perhaps is of the melting of smelted metal (and even native copper) for casting where appropriate into one-piece moulds, with final finishing by the earlier techniques of cold and hot forging. Melting of copper requires a temperature of over 1080°C. Simpler techniques characterise the early part of the millennium, but the ability to weld, a difficult skill requiring temperature control, clean surfaces and a flux to prevent surface oxidation, seen for example in pre-Cucuteni III–Tripolye A contexts, illustrates improvement. The first cast objects belong to the horizon of early Gumelniţa and Cucuteni A–Tripolye B1. Such skills were not evenly shared or used. Even in late Vinča contexts smelting did not entirely replace hammering, as seen in hammered malachite ornaments, and it is likely that the Pločnik hoards which include cast hammer-axes, chisels and ingots belong not to the Vinča phase at the site but to the Bubanj–Hum Ia phase. It was asserted that graphite paint needs similarly high temperatures to copper melting for adherence to pottery and that the relevant kiln technology was therefore only available in the eastern Balkans, but it is now seen that graphite paint does not need such high temperatures so that the development of casting need not be so restricted in space.[18] Typological development was from the 'trinket' stage consisting of beads, hooks, awls, bracelets, discs, and the like to heavier cast tools such as flat axes, chisels, axe-hammers and axe-adzes (Fig. 5.5). Several types of the latter two categories are evident but it is not easy to order them chronologically since relatively few are from closed, dateable contexts.

Copper objects varied in abundance from area to area. One constraint was obviously the distribution of copper ores. Thus the Cucuteni–Tripolye area is considered to lack suitable ore deposits for exploitation at this date, and all its copper must have been imported as raw material or finished products. The quantities are fewer than in eastern Balkans, and of 750 objects (excluding Cucuteni B–Tripolye C) some 440 came from the hoard found inside a pot along with many other objects at Karbuna on a tributary of the Dniester, attributable to the later Tripolye A or B1 phase (Fig. 5.6). Analysis indicates that the metal was of Bulgarian origin.[19] Greece also has little indigenous copper and few copper objects at this date. This cannot be the only constraint, since quantities are lower also in the central Balkans in the late Vinča culture, where ores are abundant. And even within the Gumelniţa area, ores are of variable distribution, copper being found in geologically old formations generally in highland zones, and raw material movement is seen in mould fragments from Căscioarele.[20] We will return therefore later to the all-

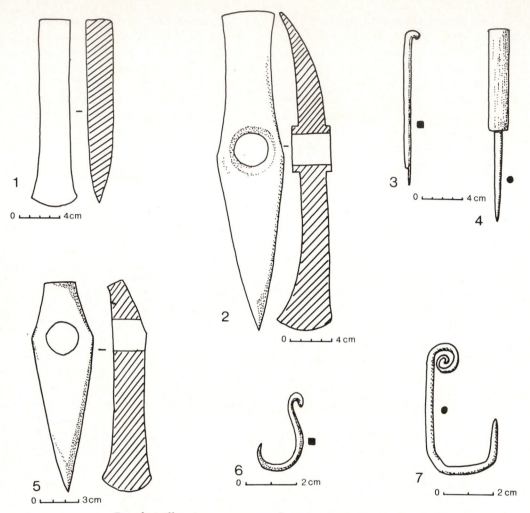

5.5 Fourth millennium copper artefacts in eastern Europe. 1 Ruse, northern Bulgaria; 2 Timisoare, south-west Romania; 3 Yasatepe, central-southern Bulgaria; 4 Kazanluk, central Bulgaria; 5 Slivnitsa, western Bulgaria; 6 Solončene, Ukraine; 7 Azmak, central-southern Bulgaria. *After* Tringham

important social context of the use of metal objects. One complicating factor is the nature of the evidence. Small copper objects oxidise and mould fragments break, and may be archaeologically lost; heavy objects could be 'curated' and also recast. In the eastern Balkans known quantities of objects are relatively small. Yet in striking contrast there are two main mine sites known, Rudna Glava in eastern Serbia and Aibunar in central-southern Bulgaria in the Sredna Gora hills not far from Karanovo, each of which must have produced many tons of copper oxide ore. Each has several shafts dated respectively by late Vinča and Karanovo vi artefacts. At Rudna Glava the narrow sloping seams are up to 20 m or more deep (Fig. 5.7).

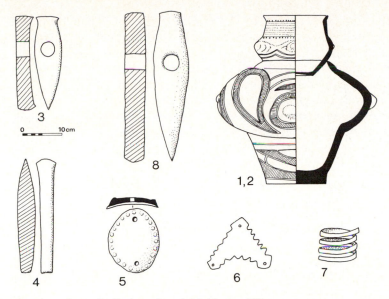

5.6 Artefacts from the Karbuna hoard, Moldavian SSR. 1–2 pottery; 3–7 copper; 8 marble

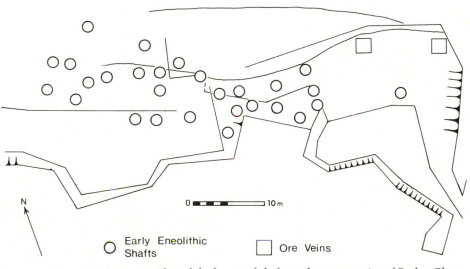

Early Eneolithic Shafts

Ore Veins

5.7 Diagrammatic plan of the layout of shafts at the copper mine of Rudna Glava, eastern Yugoslavia. *After* Jovanović

Worked-gold objects are also known. Before the discovery of the gold-rich Varna cemetery finds were scattered in the Balkans and Greece.[21] The technology is simple, gold being malleable in its pure native form and also easily smelted from ores. Beads and pendants were known before but the Varna discovery has added new dimensions to gold use from a phase late in this period. This can be seen from the point of view of quantities, for example

800, 1000 and 1500 g in three graves, the technical proficiency of three-dimensional objects in beaten gold, and the sheer typological variety. This ranges from trinkets, ornaments, mountings and plaques to sheet figurines, V-insignia, and model astragali, sceptre mounts or tubes, and a solid gold axe, even though humbler forms are most numerous. The source of the gold may lie outside Europe in the eastern Mediterranean and east of the Black Sea. The dazzling inventory of gold finds need not blind us to the equally impressive list of other raw materials used in the cemetery – copper, marble, flint, obsidian, hard stone, bone, clay, *spondylus* and *dentalium* shells for artefacts, and graphite and ochre in their raw state.

## Settlements and their social context

One striking feature virtually throughout the area in the fourth millennium bc is the extent of infilling and expansion of the zones of settlement. The overall impression is of more numerous and more widely spread settlements. External expansion may best be illustrated by the eastwards spread of Cucuteni–Tripolye settlements according to the available chronological schemes. But the process of cultural spread may not be wholly equated with a movement of population, since the indigenous communities of the Dniester–Bug area may also have adopted new forms of material culture at the same time as further transforming their economic base. As we have seen in the last chapter there is a consensus that the Linear pottery and Dniester–Bug cultures though in contact were for the most part independent. From the pre-Cucuteni stage onwards however agricultural settlements are found progressively further eastwards, but in the early Tripolye stage in the USSR settlements were still largely at flood-plain or lower-terrace level in the river valleys with a considerable use of fishing and native animals such as red deer, roe deer, pig and elk, which suggests considerable continuity of practice from an earlier date. Ultimately perhaps the two processes became indistinguishable as settlements spread further east, with a more explicit agricultural base in the later Tripolye settlements and a wider range of locations including especially the edge of the interfluves. Although many sites have stratified deposits there do not result the same sort of tell settlements as in the other areas under discussion. Elsewhere infilling can be seen in the continued colonisation of Aegean islands such as Aegina, Keos, Mykonos, Antiparos and Naxos. The process of expansion in eastern Thessaly already referred to in chapter 3 should continue into the fourth millennium bc but may be modified in fact by the subsequent abandonment of small newly colonised sites. In the Karanovo area there appear to be a number of tells which were occupied mainly in the Karanovo v–vi phase which also suggests infilling. It appears hard to differentiate between the early and later phases of the Vinča culture in this respect since not enough sites have been securely dated, but the whole Vinča phase has been characterised as one of infilling and it is unlikely that the process stopped at 4000 bc or so. On the other hand there are individual sites which were abandoned at the end of the fifth and in the earlier fourth millennium bc, such as respectively Anza and Selevac and perhaps Vinča itself, which should warn that the process was not entirely straight-forward. In western Yugoslavia sites of the Hvar culture on the coast and of the Butmir culture inland in the upper Bosna valley seem to represent further infilling. The whole area of the lower Danube may provide another example of infilling with so many of the sites of this period being new foundations, such as eponymous sites like Boian, Gumelniţa, Kodzadermen, Polyanitsa and Gradeshnitsa or other important sites like Căscioarele or Ruse.[22]

As far as can be seen this feature is not due solely to the relocation of settlements. This was however seen already between the Criş and Dudeşti cultures in this area, and is also visible in the north-west of Bulgaria where settlements shift progressively through the period from lower to upper terraces thence to promontories or other high locations, exemplified in the sites of Brenitsa (Fig. 5.8), Gradeshnitsa and Zaminets respectively.[23] Though few areas have been intensively investigated, the impression one has is of denser settlement with closer spacing between sites and wider boundaries to the zone of settlement. Sites in the Karanovo area, one of the few intensively investigated, lie from 1 to 5 km apart, and spacing of 6 to 7 km has been suggested for Bulgaria as a whole taking into account discontinuities at individual sites.

For the most part settlements are as before nucleated, but there is consider-

**5.8** Overlying houses of the fourth millennium bc at Brenitsa, north-west Bulgaria. Photo: Institute of Archaeology, Sofia

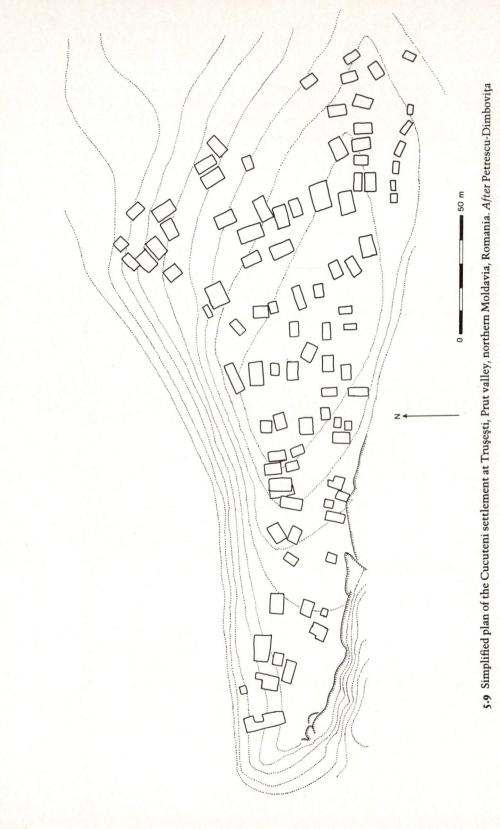

**5.9** Simplified plan of the Cucuteni settlement at Truşeşti, Prut valley, northern Moldavia, Romania. *After* Petrescu-Dimboviţa

able variety in the orderliness of internal layout and the spacing of internal features. A rather loose layout may be seen in both phases of settlement on the island of Căscioarele (with a diameter of about 100 m) in the small lake of Catalui close to the Danube to the south of Bucharest, which has been extensively though not completely excavated. In the upper layer some 16 buildings were recovered, widely spaced and without regular orientation. Similarly in another area, the foothills of Moldavia, the site of Tîrpeşti in both pre-Cucuteni A levels has an irregular layout of larger and smaller buildings; not all the structures assigned to the individual phases may be contemporary. Even Vinča itself might be put in this category, at least for those levels (6–9 m) for which published plans exist.

Another variety of settlement layout appears to be more orderly but not closely nucleated. Examples of this include Hăbăşeşti and Truşeşti (Fig. 5.9) in Moldavia of the Cucuteni A phase. The houses of Hăbăşeşti share a roughly similar alignment and may also lie in rows, though it has equally been suggested that a circular pattern may be discerned around the larger houses such as nos. 1 and 15. The larger site of Truşeşti has some rows within its overall plan, and some three or four foci within which the spacing between individual houses is reduced. The radial layout found in some Tripolye settlements east of the Bug may be included in this category such as Vladimirovka. A third category of layout consists of similar houses and lanes but more densely packed, such as Traian–Dealul Fintinilor in Moldavia, Karanovo or Azmak.[24]

A final category consists of yet more closely arranged buildings. One variant is the acropolis area of Dimini and Sesklo in the fourth millennium bc, where there is a planned fortified centre with a large central building or megaron but including also open space or courtyard space (Fig. 5.10). Another variant is rather different, seen in the recent excavations of the north-east Bulgarian sites of Ovčarovo, Golyamo Delchevo, Polyanitsa (Fig. 5.11) and Vinitsa where within squarish or subrectangular defences (at the first three sites) the whole of the relatively small interiors were filled with buildings set more or less back-to-back and divided only by narrow lanes on the principal axes defined by the entrances. It has been suggested that the close spacing would have necessitated guttering. In the upper of the eight levels at Polyanitsa the settlement expanded keeping its original character but resulting in a more circular plan. The same division of the interior into four sectors can also be seen at Vinitsa but with larger spaces between the houses.

The four categories serve perhaps to outline a continuum of types rather than mutually distinct types. It is hard to see the extent of variation within one area at present. For example though the squarish defended and highly planned sites like Polyanitsa are so far known from the river basin around Shumen in north-east Bulgaria, there is evidence from not far away on the Black Sea coast for other sorts of site, including what may be shortlived 'open' settlements and lake-shore or pile dwellings on Lake Varna such as Ezerovo.[25] The extent of change therefore in settlement layout in the fourth millennium bc in this and other areas is difficult to measure accurately, though the

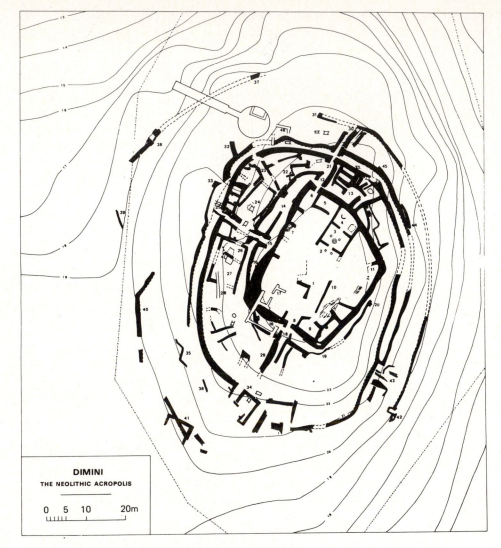

**5.10** Plan of Dimini, Thessaly. *After* Theocharis

Polyanitsa type appears to represent radical innovation. But the possibility remains that all or many of the kinds of site discussed were special within the regional social context by virtue of their nucleation and layout. As before too little is known of other possible types of settlement, but the spacing of sites like Vinitsa, Ovčarovo and Polyanitsa at 10–15 km intervals may suggest a locally special role for each within the local pattern of settlement.

In the eastern Balkans, Greece and the Cucuteni–Tripolye area, though not apparently in the central Balkans, there is an increased emphasis in this period on defined boundaries and even defences, which may further serve to emphasise the special nature of some of these sites. Many Cucuteni–Tripolye

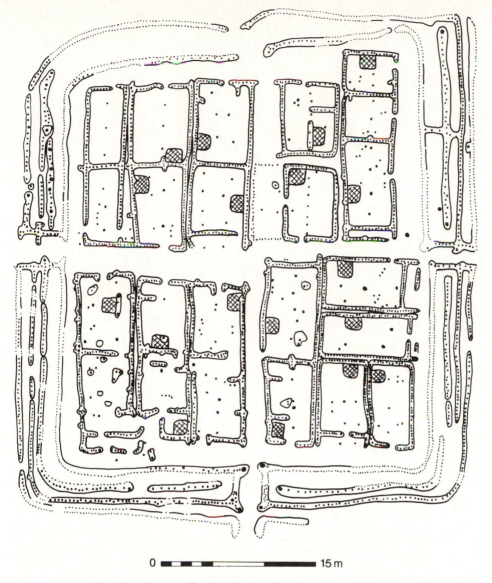

**5.11** Plan of Polyanitsa (first building level), north-east Bulgaria. *After* Todorova

sites are surrounded by a ditch, which may be extended or relocated as at Tîrpeşti or Traian to accommodate expansion of the settlement. Both small and large sites are thus bounded by ditches. On the basis of their dimensions and shapes (usually wide and shallow) it is unlikely that these ditches were actually defensive though this suggestion has often been made. There may be similar demarcations at other sites elsewhere, such as the low narrow bank (only 1–2 m) assigned to the Karanovo v level at Azmak with discontinuous stretches of single and double fence or palisade.[26] Other tells may have more obvious defences such as the ditch, bank and palisade found on one side of Ruse in northern Bulgaria. The most formal defences so far found accompany the most nucleated and planned layouts. Polyanitsa and Ovčarovo have three rows of palisades, at the first interrupted by four, at the latter by two entrances; Golyamo Delchevo has palisades and bank and ditch; Vinitsa one to two palisades cutting off accessible parts of the site. The complexity of the original defences and their development is impressive. At Polyanitsa the primary system consisted of large posts (up to 45 cm in diameter) set in a ditch on whose flanking banks or upcasts were set smaller fences, the whole being interconnected with horizontal beams and clay, earth and rubbish packing. This was added to by earthen banks on part of the circumference, and the entrances were flanked by massive clay, stone-faced towers, and flanked by ditches 2 m deep; remains of jointed beams at the western entrance were interpreted as a drawbridge. It is possible that the defences were actually carried over the entrance itself. At both Dimini and Sesklo in Thessaly, there are substantial stone retaining walls around the acropolis area which may also have been defensive as well as structural supports or symbolic boundaries, and there are some signs at other Thessalian sites of ditches around settlements.

In considering site differentiation further size is a factor of varying importance. In some areas size increase may have reached a peak in the fourth millennium. It has been suggested that a few settlements in Thessaly exceeded 1 ha in extent by the post-Dimini phase and in the central Balkans growth at the exceptionally large (in total area covered) open sites such as Potporanj and Selevac continued into the late Vinča phase, though the preferred site size remained around 1 ha, or 2 ha for sites occupied in both phases.[27] There may also be discernible growth over time in Cucuteni–Tripolye settlements on the evidence of stratified sites, small such as Tîrpeşti or large such as Traian, and on the basis of the largest examples to the east such as Vladimirovka coming from later Tripolye phases (in this case B2). In the eastern Balkans however, features already discussed such as nucleation, layout and boundaries, and others to be discussed below such as shrines, seem to be more important factors in site differentiation than size. It is possible that the largest tells only attained their full extent in the fourth millennium bc but this has not yet been documented. Indeed Polyanitsa is relatively small with space only for around 20 buildings in the lower level (the uncertainty being due to the difficulty of separating building units at the closely packed site).

Further ways of approaching the difficult interpretative questions of site differentiation are to consider the continuity and internal features of individual sites in more detail. The difficulties of recognising stratigraphic hiatus have already been discussed and the evidence is varied in quality, but for parts of the area the hypothesis may be fruitful that the success of certain sites can be measured in a crude sort of way by the depth and continuity of occupation deposits. Simple statistics are available for example for the Karanovo area and averages for parts of Bulgaria have been computed, for

example some 9.1 m for central-southern Bulgaria and its environs, or some
8.9 m for north-east Bulgaria, for total 'Chalcolithic' deposits. Many factors
are likely to be involved, and detailed differences within a given area rather
than wider averages are required. Sufficient detail is probably not available,
but there are potentially interesting correlations. Thus defended sites like
Polyanitsa, Ovčarovo, Golyamo Delchevo and partially defended sites like
Vinitsa do have deep deposits, the latter for example 4.6 m over an estimated
450–500 years; the 17 levels of Golyamo Delchevo are another example
already mentioned. The importance of such sites may therefore perhaps be
seen in the very continuity of their existence as much as in their defences or
other features. The most detailed phasing of Bulgarian settlements available
however, based on artefact typology rather than absolute dating, suggests that
no site was continuously occupied through the fourth millennium bc though
the sites mentioned above and certain tells such as Azmak itself rank highly
in this aspect.[28] Interestingly Karanovo was on this analysis discontinuously
occupied through the period. Other examples of abandonment such as Vinča
and Selevac have been noted; Sitagroi after the end of phase III is another to
note. Much depends on the validity of suggested phasing and the 5.5 m of
Karanovo V and VI seem unduly compressed in time to take just one example.
In the Cucuteni–Tripolye area there were not the same sort of tell formations,
but even within this complex, some sites are differentiated from others by
their greater stratigraphic continuity such as Izvoare, Traian or Cucuteni
itself to the west, or Nezviska, Polivanov Yar or Solončene II a little further
east around the Dniester. There is little point in labouring the argument in
the present state of evidence, but details such as the plaster of one house at
Ovčarovo repainted 47 times may come to be very useful in the future.

There does not appear to be great differentiation among the majority of
buildings within settlements or between settlements in terms of their size or
care of construction, though this has rarely been investigated systematically
on a regional basis. Most sites have surface-built buildings, of regional type in
terms of both construction and internal arrangements. Thus one may contrast the mud-brick buildings of Thessaly with the timber frames and the
carefully laid timber sub-frames of buildings further north, which were
perhaps deliberately charred. The basic social unit housed may have
remained the nuclear family on the evidence of the continued use of single-
roomed buildings and the addition of buildings partitioned into two, with
anterior and main room, as in Karanovo VI. This kind of interpretation
however is crude, and runs into difficulties with Cucuteni–Tripolye houses
which have more-equal divisions into two or occasionally more parts, each of
which may sometimes be provided with its own hearth. Generalisation
should be avoided, since a single small site like Tîrpeşti can show considerable variation, assuming that all internal divisions have equally been
recovered. The example of Polyanitsa is also instructive. The basic unit
seems to be of main room with hearth plus anteroom but one notes also parts
where one hearth may have been shared between two or more rooms. In
Greece the continued possibility of two-storey buildings is another source of

interpretative confusion. Nonetheless those cases with obvious internal differentiation are rare, such as the three larger buildings noted already at Hăbăşeşti, the central megaron buildings at Dimini and Sesklo, the central probably two-storey buildings at Ovčarovo and Radingrad, or the two much larger than normal buildings at Azmak in the Karanovo VI level. Here one was 18.4 by 6.3 m and three-roomed, the other two-roomed measuring 19 by 9 m. To further test the inference that these buildings were in some way special requires more evidence. Evidence of internal and external decoration is present, as at the two buildings cited at Azmak, but does not appear restricted to such cases. Analysis of artefactual contents should be attempted, though it has rarely been applied, which probably makes isolated observations unreliable. Thus the two Azmak buildings contained fine decorated pottery but little in the way of other artefactual remains, and the Ovčarovo building in question apparently contained seed corn and grindstones on its lower floor, and over a hundred pots on its upper. The buildings at Dimini and Hăbăşeşti were not thus distinguished however, and there are indeed scattered indications elsewhere of workshops or store buildings not remarkable for their size, such as the workshops at Hotnitsa, Golyamo Delchevo, Ariuşd and Hîrşova (for bone figurines, everyday stone tools, pottery firing or *spondylus* working respectively) or the house at Karanovo in level VI with over 100 pots.[29] Analysis of whole settlements however is required (including also the range of depositional and post-depositional factors); where this is possible, as at Tîrpeşti in the Cucuteni A phase, there does not appear to be a strong positive correlation between house size and quality or quantity of artefacts.

Other artefacts to consider are those putatively connected with ritual. There appears to be a general increase in the quantity of figurines and associated ritual paraphernalia in this period over most of the area though we so far lack the kind of quantified generalisation offered for earlier periods. Tîrpeşti offers one example, where of 17 houses assigned to the Cucuteni A phase ten contained figurines (or fragments); three of the other houses were incompletely preserved or excavated, while a fourth had pottery with anthropomorphic designs. The figurines consisted of standing, semi-reclining and sitting anthropomorphic figures, and also of animal figures. Another example at an opposite extreme in terms of quantity is Vinča, which in total produced over 2000 figurines, though little detail is available on their context (Fig. 5.12). The most common context where figurines have not been recovered from so-called rubbish deposits seems to be within ordinary buildings. Within the Cucuteni A level at Tîrpeşti, for example, the figurine fragments are recorded somewhat imprecisely as coming from the buildings, though in the previous pre-Cucuteni level, an almost intact figurine was found attached to the kerb of a domed rectangular clay oven, while other figurine fragments came from pits beside the houses along with other 'rubbish'. Data from the eastern Balkans are sparse, since many figurines are from rubbish deposits, though some were from unspecified positions on house floors (Fig. 5.13). A domestic contest is suggested also in the Vinča culture, though data are again scarce. It is possible that other features such as the four-lobed clay platforms

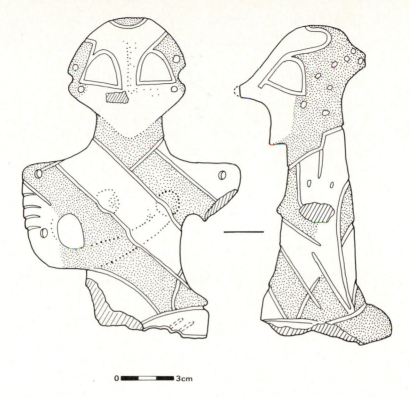

0 ▬▬▬ 3cm

**5.12** Late Vinča figurine from Vinča, with red-painted bands. *After* Tringham

found within Tripolye houses were connected with out-of-the ordinary activities, though there is rare specific evidence for this. A model of the interior of a building from the late Tripolye site of Popudnya in the Bug valley has either a female figure or a female anthropomorphic figurine beside its oven, probably the latter since it is schematised, in strong contrast to the unusually lifelike female figure at a grinder. Other features of the model including designs on the wall and a four-lobed clay platform have led to its interpretation as a shrine rather than a domestic interior.[30] Another way of approaching evidence for ritual, whether or not contextual detail is available, is to look at numbers of relevant artefacts per excavated volume of deposit. Where this has been done, in the Vinča culture, there are indications that the ritual content of some sites far exceeded that of others. The already quoted figure from Vinča itself is exceptional; Vinča and a few other sites like Potporanj appear to stand out as ritual centres. It is likely on this basis as hinted also in aspects of the previous discussion that there is greater differentiation to be observed between settlements than within them.

However a further aspect of the evidence for ritual shows interesting ambiguity in this respect. A restricted number of sites contain buildings whose ritual content has been widely considered sufficient to designate them shrines or cult houses rather than 'domestic' or 'ordinary' interiors with a

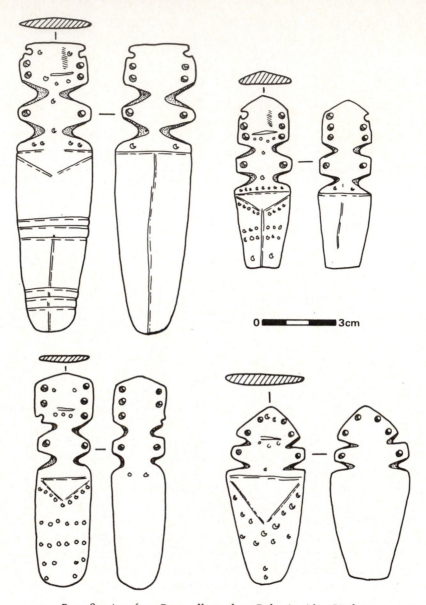

**5.13** Bone figurines from Ruse tell, northern Bulgaria. *After* Gimbutas

ritual component. There is a considerable problem of definition here; one alternative to consider is of a continuum of ritual activity within certain settlements making distinctions of this kind unrealistic, another that all buildings with ritual content within are special whatever the precise quantity preserved. Some examples lack clear contexts, such as the concentration of 34 figurines (including six intact) and fragments of miniature clay chairs and table in an area of 20 m² in the pre-Cucuteni level of Tîrpeşti;

the overlying Cucuteni A building (no. 5) had nothing similar. But this is perhaps not dissimilar in terms of quantities to the ritual objects recovered from a house in the Karanovo VI levels of Ovčarovo, not otherwise distinguished from its neighbours.[31] The Ovčarovo building contained a small decorated model of a house interior beside the oven, and on the floor 1 m away an assemblage of 27 miniature cult objects – three altars, four standing female figurines, three tables, three cylinders, three pots with lids, nine dishes and two other larger pots – though there is little detail available on its exact arrangement (Fig. 5.14). The house had been burnt. There are other buildings considered to be shrines principally through their contents. At Sabatinovka II in the Bug valley a substantial but not large rectangular house in the Tripolye A settlement had largely ritual contents.[32] A central oven had its figurine, besides pottery and bones, and other figurines were arranged beside quernstones and a hearth. At the back of the interior there was a clay chair in one corner, and a long raised platform in the other with some 16 seated female figurines on stools. There were 32 figurines in all. A number of otherwise unremarkable buildings in Vinča settlements had remains of clay bucrania, lifesize and highly stylised, as at Vinča itself, and Jakov Kormadin. In northeast Bulgaria there is a recent discovery at Rozsokhuvatka of a two-storey building with a pottery workshop on the ground floor, and a shrine on the first floor with a clay altar 75 cm high, flanked by figurines, models of buildings and a loom.[33] Pots near the altar were filled with clay beads. The final structural example is rather different, since it is the building itself rather than its contents which is the criterion for the status of shrine. In the late Boian level of Căscioarele, radiocarbon dated to around 4000 bc, a two-roomed building 16 by 10 m had one room richly painted in cream on red with curvilinear and angular designs. One wall had on it a raised clay area further painted with red and cream spirals. From the floor rose remains of two clay pillars, both also elaborately painted with interlocking curvilinear designs. Other features included a crouched burial by one of the posts, a clay bench and remains of much pottery on the floor.[34]

Other examples can be cited where the distinction between house and shrine is even harder to maintain, such as the Tripolye B building at Kolomiiscina in the Dnieper valley south of Kiev with a red-painted platform in its middle with 21 figurines around it, four miniature clay tables or altars, 12 miniature pots but also 31 normal vessels.[35] Many models are subject to similar ambiguity, as seen in the Popudnya example, but some may seem to reinforce the possibility of special cult buildings. The classic example is from Căscioarele, with more fragmentary examples at sites like Ruse and Izvoare. The model at Căscioarele comes from a Gumelniţa level, radiocarbon dated to the mid fourth millennium bc.[36] It was found in a fragmentary state outside a building. The reconstructed model was some 24 cm high, 51 cm long at the base, and consisted of a substructure on which sat four horned buildings interpreted as temples or shrines (Fig. 5.15). The building near it was 10 by 7 m, with a raised bench and several unusual perhaps votive pots. There has been speculation that this was a sanctuary and that the model was originally

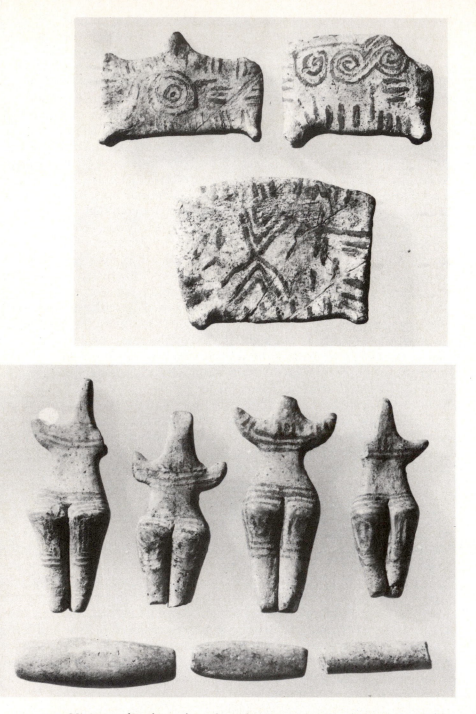

**5.14** Miniature clay objects from the 'cult scene' in level IX, Ovčarovo, north-east Bulgaria. (a) altars or facades; (b) figurines (rear view) and 'drums'. Photo: Institute of Archaeology, Sofia

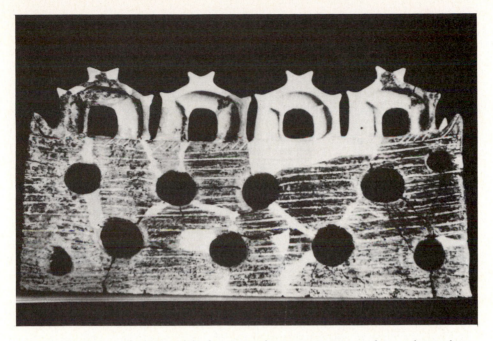

**5.15** Restored clay model of a storeyed structure interpreted as a shrine, from Căscioarele, Danube valley, southern Romania. Photo: Gimbutas

located in it. On the other hand it is striking that no remains of such a vast edifice have been recovered in the many excavations of south-east Europe and certainly not at Căscioarele itself where excavation has been quite extensive. If the model is of a shrine however, it is nonetheless interesting for suggesting something about the wished-for status for deities, assuming that these are what figurines variously represent. Other finds too reinforce the impression of a generally increased emphasis on ritual, such as the assemblage found in a Petreşti context at Pianul de Joş in Transylvania consisting of a triangular clay-coated wooden table with eight differently shaped pots on it and a large storage jar underneath. The Tărtăria and Gradeshnitsa plaques are further cases in point, though it has been pointed out that these examples are the only two out of the wide range of finds with inscribed signs whose context specifically demands a ritual interpretation.[37]

Despite all the uncertainties two issues are raised by these data. The evidence can be taken to support the already canvassed suggestion that in this period certain sites were differentiated from their local and regional neighbours by their greater emphasis on and perhaps therefore greater control over cult. One means of achieving this, through food production, brings us back to the discussion of chapter 3. Still further evidence for this will be reviewed below. The other issue is of social differentiation. If this existed it appears largely to be masked in terms of obvious differences in house size, settlement planning or artefact assemblages within buildings, but the possibility remains to be considered that the control of ritual itself was a focus of competition in society, both within and between separate sites or communities. On this hypothesis the gradual increase in ritual paraphernalia, the specialisation – or at any rate its beginnings – of certain buildings as shrines, and the appearance of potentially arcane ritual activities symbolised in the inscribed signs, could all be taken to imply both increased emphasis on ritual and a more restricted access to its practice and control. There is no decisive answer available. As far as it can be discerned at all the actual content of ritual as derived from subjective interpretation of figurines seems to remain focused on such contrasts as people–nature and female–male and other themes such as birth and fertility. It is possible that this in some way symbolises a general concern with increased conflict at the family level between men and women, and with an increased conflict within and between communities for social leadership and the control of production. Ritual activity would thus have been the means of alleviating social tension, as well as one of its foci, and the relative durability of social arrangements in the various areas of south-east Europe under consideration may testify to its importance in this respect.

The use of material culture could be exploited much further in investigating social differences of the kind examined above, but the data are generally not organised in reports to allow easy reconstruction of their context. The example of Tîrpeşti can be returned to. The differing house contents of the Cucuteni A level can be partially reconstructed. While some of the houses have polished stone tools, copper artefacts and bichrome and trichrome painted pottery there are variations in the extent to which these are represented in others. I do not intend to draw any conclusions from this isolated example but systematic studies of this kind are now called for. Nor should they ignore the greater mass of material found in 'rubbish' deposits and usually subsequently ignored, since it has been shown in ethnographic studies that such material can also be used in the delineation of social roles and differences.[38] For the present attention must be restricted to unusual artefacts which often originated far from the sites in which they are found.

A wide range of artefacts and materials may have been distributed beyond their source, such as pottery (of which more later) obsidian, *spondylus* shell, and copper and copper artefacts. The quantities of obsidian at early Vinča sites were seen to vary widely; at Vinča itself in the late Vinča phase the quantities declined greatly, which may in some way reflect the fortunes of the site as regional centre. *Spondylus* was widely distributed from a source presumed not to lie in the Black Sea but in the Aegean or Adriatic. Interestingly the bulk of *spondylus* in Vinča contexts comes from north of the Sava–Danube line. A *spondylus* workshop has been claimed at Hîrşova on the Black Sea coast of Romania, which would imply movement of the raw material by sea, and *spondylus* objects are found also in the Cucuteni–Tripolye area, as in the Karbuna hoard between the Prut and Dniester.[39]

Much effort in recent years has been concentrated on the study of copper production, distribution and consumption and this will be discussed at greater length here than other materials just mentioned. It is salutory however to remember the wider context of artefact and materials distribution in which the movement of copper took place, and also the relatively small overall numbers of copper artefacts. Like other materials copper is likely to have been important in the societies of south-east Europe. First, it was derived from sources that were, at least in the important case of Rudna Glava, physically remote from contemporary settlements, perhaps over a distance of up to 50 km, and which were probably also seasonally exploited. Deliberate, sustained exploitation is implied. (Gold too was derived from distant sources, but perhaps outside the area and the constancy of the supply and the method of its transport over the Black Sea are both uncertain.) Secondly, it was distributed widely and over considerable distances from its sources as suggested most strikingly by putatively imported copper in the Cucuteni–Tripolye area as far east as the Dnieper. There is however much variation in the apparent abundance of copper artefacts from region to region. The small quantities in Greece and southern Russia are understandable from the point of view of local availability, but this argument does not work for the central Balkans where ores were available but recorded finds relatively few. One must posit therefore a varying regional social context for the use of copper. In the central Balkans, despite early occurrences or perhaps because of them, copper artefacts do not appear to have had the importance they were given in the eastern Balkans. This must be because the artefacts were either of minor functional use, such as hooks and awls, or ornamental or overtly symbolic, such as axe-adzes and hammer-axes. The occurrence of larger quantities of copper in archaeological contexts of the post-Vinča horizon, such as the Pločnik hoard, reinforces the point. On this line of argument the impressive capacity of the Rudna Glava mine may have been used for the sustained export of raw material rather than for widespread use of copper within the Vinča culture itself. It is also unlikely that kiln technology was a constraint in the spread of sophisticated casting technology in the way envisaged when it was considered that only Gumelniţa graphite pottery was fired at temperatures over 1000°C.

The specific role of copper artefacts must be considered in the light of their contexts of discovery, and the evidence for this is unfortunately varied. Five categories are useful to consider, though I am unable to quantify them. Stray finds account for a certain proportion of larger objects. A number of small objects come from definable contexts within settlements, such as the remains of small tools and ornaments associated with seven of the Cucuteni A houses at Tîrpeşti or the small chisel, awls and rings from the Hîrşova workshop. It is noticeable that copper was not used in any of the putative ritual contexts discussed above. From undefined contexts within settlements there comes the full range of small and large objects. There is remarkably little published information on the context of larger, cast objects but settlement finds include such sites as Ruse, Hotnitsa, Vidra, Horodnitsa II, Cucuteni, and Čoka. The example of Pločnik shows quite large assemblages or hoards of both heavy and small copper artefacts. Hoards or collections of small objects also occur, such as the pins at Boian. In those areas where graves are arranged in cemeteries separate from settlements all categories of copper artefacts occur, including in one or two cases large heavy-cast tools or weapons, as at Varna and Devnya on the Bulgarian Black Sea coast. At Devnya, Vinitsa and Golyamo Delchevo copper artefacts occur with both men and women, though in lesser quantities with the latter. The same appears to be the case at Varna. The numbers of objects remain low however, for example the 66 copper objects found at Varna up to 1975 compared with the far more numerous gold, ceramic and shell finds. A final category consists of deliberate deposits or hoards outside settlement contexts, such as the Karbuna hoard in a pot. The nearest well-known settlement to this find is Novye Ruseshty (of the Tripolye A and B1 phases) with small copper objects within the settlement.[40]

It therefore turns out to be rather difficult to analyse the social context of the use of early metallurgical products. Those from settlements do not make it clear whether ownership of these items, produced and distributed at considerable cost in labour and time, was private or communal. Those from graves may suggest the former, though the situation is not straightforward, as will be seen below at Varna as part of an overall assessment of mortuary practice, and the bulk of copper grave goods are anyway small tools or ornaments. Perhaps one should not expect, as suggested above, an equal value to be ascribed to copper everywhere. For producers and distributors, it may have been a means to become involved in prestigious exchange cycles, for communities at a distance from sources of supply it may have been a valuable, durable token of long-range alliance and connections, and it potentially offered particular groups within a community the opportunity to exploit its acquisition socially for more individualistic, competitive concerns.

A final aspect of the evidence reinforces such ambiguities. The skills involved in mining, smelting, melting, casting, finishing, welding and the range of other technical procedures, and those involved too in stone working, pottery manufacture and decoration, and gold working, suggest the existence of specialist crafts, and one might argue for a qualitative change in this respect compared to earlier periods. The social position of such specialists is however hard to recover. Were they full-time specialists? Were they dependent for their livelihood on the community as a whole or sections of it? It is tempting to see craft specialisation as a further differentiation within the community but it has to be set against the past pattern of craft and subsistence activities in which the range of skills may not have been evenly spread through the community. As far as the evidence survives, craft activities are found firmly in the settlement itself – as in the cases already cited from Hîrşova, Karanovo, Hotnitsa, and Ariuşd. Other examples are the two moulds for axe-chisels found in the Gumelniţa building (no. 4) at Căscioarele and the possible crucibles and hammerstones in Cucuteni A contexts at Hăbăşeşti. One case, the storeyed building at Ovčarovo, suggests a less usual context, with pottery working and possible shrine housed in the same building. The capacity of larger settlements to support a greater concern with exotic material products has been noted from an early stage; this might again emphasise the communal aspect. Finally figurines themselves can be considered. Many of them are specialised craft products, involving on occasion not just high ceramic skill but also graphite decoration and copper attachments. If ritual itself can be seen as used for both communal and more individualistic ends, so too perhaps can the crafts associated with its practice.

In chapter 1 note was taken of critical reviews of simplistic attempts to derive social interpretations from burials and it was proposed following this that social arrangements in life cannot be read off in a simple fashion from people's behaviour in dealing with death. This awareness poses a dilemma however since many prehistorians are understandably reluctant to abandon their attempts to understand the implications of burial data. The most promising line of enquiry seems to be to renew attempts to set burial evidence in as wide a social context as possible, though even this need not necessarily avoid interpretative pitfalls of which we are now more aware. In earlier periods in this area, recognised burials (and therefore potentially only a sample of contemporary mortuary practice as a whole) have been located within settlements themselves. They could be seen as another means of emphasising the importance and continuity of both family and community. In this period the same sort of situation seems to continue in many parts of south-east Europe, such as the central Balkans, Greece and the Cucuteni–Tripolye area, and probably also in central-southern Bulgaria (all subject of course to the limitations of past excavations). Within the eastern Balkans however there is a discernible shift in practice, particularly centred on north-east Bulgaria and south-east Romania, where there appear separate cemeteries of the dead. Examples are Ruse, Golyamo Delchevo, Ovčarovo, Vinitsa, Polyanitsa, Devnya and Varna, and in Romania Cernica, Cernavodă and Boian.[41] For the most part these are set close to known settlements, but settlements have not been identified with certainty at Varna and Devnya (though 'pile dwellings' and other sites are known in the vicinity), and not at all at Cernavodă. There are two examples from the Vinča culture area, Gomolava and Zivaniceva Dolja at Botoš though in both cases, while over 20 burials are involved, the record is very incomplete. In the Aegean the small cemetery at Souphli in Thessaly is not closely dated though assigned to the Larisa phase, and collective burials elsewhere are a third millennium bc phenomenon.[42] Cemeteries north of the Black Sea seem for the most part to be similarly dated (apart from indigenous pre-Tripolye examples in the Dnieper valley) and are discussed later. For the most part the graves are more or less simple earth-cut rectangular pits in which the dead were placed with varying quantities of grave goods, and are generally quite closely spaced. Their numbers vary, from around 20 at Devnya to over 300 at Cernavodă, though the upper limit is more regularly around 100 as at Cernica. (Their duration seems to match those of adjacent settlements, where this can be judged.) Both men and women are represented and to a lesser extent adolescents and children.

One general explanation of these cemeteries could be that they are connected with an increased need for communal cohesion and identity, given that they are located in an area in which settlement had expanded, in which population probably had increased and in which there are signs of site differentiation and features such as defence. To some extent this would be compatible with the Gomolava case, though it does not explain why burials were not so used in other areas of settlement expansion. The essentially communal basis of these separately grouped burials could be argued on the strength of a generally weak differentiation between sexes or age sets as seen in treatment of the grave or its artefactual contents. Thus for the most part graves were earth-cut rectangular pits, and the bodies were simply laid in them in extended or contracted position according to regional practice. Grave goods were not obviously differentiated. Thus at Cernavodă most bodies were accompanied by a pot, and many by a figurine and ornaments. In north-east Bulgaria there is the same sort of pattern though practice varied locally. At the three sites of Devnya, Golyamo Delchevo, Vinitsa, pottery was the most common grave good, and men overall were accompanied by slightly more goods than women, but in actual fact at Golyamo Delchevo and Vinitsa there were few goods at all other than pottery, such as ornaments, stone tools and copper artefacts. A small number of graves at each of these three lack burials at all, though they are provided with similar quantities of goods. In these terms, though there is a greater volume of grave goods, there is not more marked internal differentiation at such sites than in the earlier burials.

Differentiation however can be sought in another way. Though the dating is imprecise, it appears that these cemeteries grew gradually over long periods of time. The size of adjacent settlements can in some cases be seen. Where age data are available, they suggest a comparatively young buried population. The 40 or so bodies from Vinitsa for example may therefore constitute a selected sample of all the generations inhabiting the settlement during its occupation. On this interpretation such cemeteries could represent the consolidation of dominant groups within the community, those able for example to acquire copper artefacts and other unusual items. This possibility is extremely difficult to disprove, not least because to compare quantities of say copper in settlement contexts with those in burials would be to assume that it was of comparable importance in both aspects. The cenotaphs too can be taken to show some element of concealment or distortion, which may be connected with internal social differences. This is discussed further below.

Interpretation is also complicated in the case of Varna, which superficially provides the best evidence for differentiation on the basis of the sheer abundance of grave goods in certain graves (Fig. 5.16). The cemetery was discovered by chance and many of the 190 graves in the 6500 m² excavated up to 1982 have been disturbed. Detailed information is more available for 60 or so graves excavated up to 1975. The cemetery lies a little to the north and 12–18 m above Lake Varna. It belongs to the Karanovo VI–Kodzadermen horizon. The graves were on average 2 m long, and from 0.6 to 3.1 m deep, but are simple and earth-cut, with rounded corners. Ochre here accompanies most graves. The first striking feature of the cemetery is that about one-sixth of the

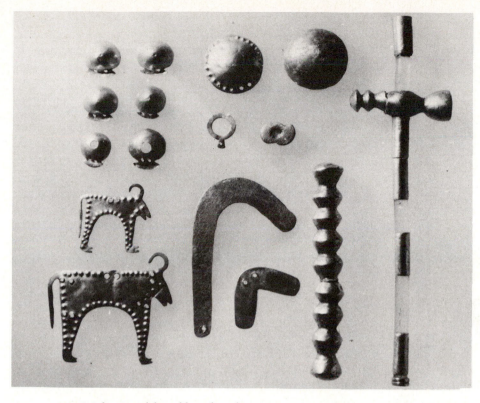

**5.16** Selection of the gold artefacts from grave no. 36 at the Varna cemetery, Black Sea coast, Bulgaria. Photo: Institute of Archaeology, Sofia

graves (31 up to 1982) were not accompanied by a body; differential decay or subsequent removal are not in question. These cenotaphs thus match those at Devnya in the same area, and Golyamo Delchevo and Vinitsa further inland. The majority of the Varna cenotaphs (16 graves to date) have a poor range of grave goods, more or less like those in other cemeteries, with such items as gold rings and copper axes. A few (nine to date) are also reported to have a mixture of disarticulated human and animal bones as well as a few goods. Cranial abnormalities are reported. A third small category (three up to 1982) have simple sun-dried clay masks of the human face, with beaten gold plaques either in the form of facial features, such as the mouth in no. 3, or as decoration on the forehead, cheek, chin, ear and so on. Other goods include thousands of gold beads, gold pins, copper needles, *dentalium* shell beads, bone pins, spindle whorls, graphite- and gold-painted pottery, marble rhytons and flint knives, and figurines. A fourth small category of cenotaphs (also three to date) lacks the masks but has extremely large quantities of gold artefacts beside other artefacts of copper, flint, stone, bone and pottery. No. 1 has 1225 gold objects (weighing 2093 g) in 15 groups, no. 4 320 objects (1518 g) and no. 36 853 (797 g). The gold assemblage of no. 1 includes two gold tubes with perforations matching the size of two copper axes. No. 36 includes a solid gold axe with a gold shaft; two gold bull figurines; 30 gold miniature horns; a gold shaft; gold mask attachments, plates, beads, earrings, V-insignia, a model astragalus and an arm ring, and a copper shaft hole axe, flint tools, a marble dish and four lidded pots. These seem to be arranged as if a body were present; following the orientation in filled graves of head to the east or north-east, no. 4 has at its shoulder a stone axe with a tubular gold shaft, at its head pottery and beads, and a mass of other artefacts at its side. Of the graves with bodies, the majority have extended corpses on their backs, which are probably mostly male. Their inventories are poor, restricted to pottery and flint tools, and occasionally a stone or copper axe. The striking exception is no. 43, a 3 m deep grave. This contains three necklaces, three massive rings on each arm, two rings for each ear, six small rings on the head, large discs, oblong and other plates, beads, and nails – all in gold – as well as copper tools, and pottery. There were over 1011 gold objects (1516 g). Contracted burials on their right side were the last category and were mainly women. Their inventories were poor, some only with pottery.

The accumulation of material is certainly to our eyes overwhelmingly impressive. It would be interesting to be able to compare quantities of similar artefacts in neighbouring settlements, but as pointed out the comparison is likely to be inapt. Certainly the site stands out by comparison with both its immediate neighbour Devnya and other cemeteries and settlements in north-east Bulgaria and south-east Romania, and with any site in south-east Europe and elsewhere. It highlights, as no other site does to the same extent, the theme of social differentiation on a regional basis. It is tempting therefore to infer similarly developed internal differentiation. With the exception of no. 43 however the very large inventories accompany the cenotaphs. It is insufficient to argue that these can be categorised straightforwardly with the male burials on the basis of their goods. An alternative hypothesis is that the cenotaphs really are make-believe burials, at it was suggested that two-storey shrines might be make-believe. The context for such burials might also concern religious belief, or if social meaning is to be extracted, it could suggest that social tension and competition seen in other activities were relieved or masked by devoting the greatest quantities of goods to deities or other non-human beings. The smaller number of cenotaphs in the three other cemeteries discussed is matched by a correspondingly poorer range of grave goods.

In considering why there should be such accumulation of material and such putative social tension within the Varna community, one must take account of its position. Its coastal location could have placed it across several distribution routes, for copper, shell and pottery for example, both around the Black Sea coast, and also at not too great distance from the Danube, and would allow contact with sources of gold if these lay eastwards across the Black Sea. The wealth (if such it is) of the Varna cemetery may be based then on an opportunistic exploitation of a favourable geographical situation, which would also provide unusual opportunities for particular groups within the community. This would go some way to explaining its individuality. But that such opportunities on this hypothesis were taken may provide a further general clue to the competitive nature of social relations in south-east Europe at this time. Interpretive difficulties are not far to seek. It may be dangerous to assume that the cemetery (and others) were restricted to local residents, and the cenotaphs are open to other interpretations. But the kind of explanation sought should attempt as above to take account both of the site's individuality and the wider regional social setting. Though the settlement evidence is here shadowy, Varna can also be used to repeat the argument that a social development of this kind should be related to the social use of resources in the widest sense, not just to say the amount of arable land on the north side of Lake Varna.

Developments in the sphere of agricultural production can also be reviewed in the context of social change, rather than in isolation as in the debate over the causal primacy of agricultural innovation or population increase. The staples of subsistence do not appear to have changed much in this period. It has been suggested that there was a shift in the Vinča culture to use of allegedly higher-yielding bread wheat, but the detailed evidence remains sparse. At Gomolava, where plant remains were scanty, bread wheat was present in levels equated with Vinča C, and absent in levels equated with Vinča C–D. There were greater quantities of einkorn, emmer, barley, millet and oats, peas, lentils and vetch. The presence of millet may represent greater crop diversity on a local basis but like bread wheat had been present in south-east Europe for much longer. Flax at Gomolava might also represent diversity of produce, and the resulting textiles (seen also in corrosion patterns on copper axes in the Varna cemetery) would provide an exchangeable commodity. The exception to crop stability is the apparent trend towards domestication during the fourth millennium bc of wild fruits such as the vine, the olive and the pear. The morphology of grape pips at Sitagroi can be traced in its successive levels towards its cultivated form by levels IV and V, radiocarbon dated to the mid and later third millennium bc. Carbonised figs were also found at Sesklo, Rakhmani and Dimini. There are some very pure cereal samples, as of emmer at Sesklo, but this cannot in itself be seen as a change from earlier practice. The scale of cereal cultivation is more important to consider but it is still difficult to estimate. Clearance was gradually extended, which would allow for increased production.[43] There have been suggestions that ploughs were in operation, which could be used for the same purpose. The evidence is varied, such as suggested antler shares as at Căscioarele, the heavy soils close to some large Vinča settlements and the evidence of stress on cattle long-bones suggesting their use for traction.[44] There are some signs of increased or centralised storage capacity, as in larger earth-sunk pots at Karanovo, or pits in Thessalian settlements of the Larisa phase, or the two-storey building at Ovčarovo whose ground floor is seen as a seed-corn store room, but this sort of evidence is far from being universal. Animal husbandry remains difficult to study due to the dearth of well-excavated assemblages. The overall contrast between the Aegean area and the more northerly Balkans seems to have persisted though in Thessaly ovicaprids numerically declined slightly to the advantage of cattle and pigs. At Gomolava cattle were of first importance, followed by pigs then ovicaprids. It is possible that there were some developments in animal economies. Woollen textiles are claimed to have been in circulation in Bulgaria, on the basis of supposed looms at Ovčarovo and Golyamo Delchevo and of corrosion patterns on copper tools, though doubt must persist whether such textiles were not rather linen. Of the sheep at Sitagroi 61 per cent were immature, suggesting at face value that the bulk of the flock was kept for meat rather than wool. There is a similar trend at Knossos. Bones of fur-bearing animals are reported in some numbers from Dimini, which may show specialised hunting. Crude calculations at Gomolava suggested that the actual numbers of animals in use at any one time may have been rather low, and it is worth remembering other roles that animals may have played. Clay cattle heads with real cow horns (so-called bucrania) are found in the Vinča culture, and at Gomolava there is a pit with a cow skull carefully set at its base. Animals could also have been accumulated as a source of wealth in their own right and a medium for social exchanges, though again the question of scale remains difficult. The suggested development of more mobile animal economies in Thessaly could be seen as part of an increased scale of animal use though the issue is not yet resolved on data from individual sites.

Developments in the Cucuteni–Tripolye area are worth separate consideration. According to available data, cereal agriculture and animal husbandry only became established gradually on the Dniester and eastwards; sheep and goats became the favoured animal in the forest–steppe environment. Given the contribution of native population and remembering the nature of Tripolye settlements this development may suggest again that it was social change that encouraged the full adoption of mixed farming and in this case also perhaps the emergence of large-scale animal husbandry rather than vice versa as has often been envisaged.

A final aspect of society to be considered is the nature of relations at a wider geographical level. One feature of considerable interest is the patterning in the distribution of material objects and their associations. The Childean notion of culture never specified how recurrent such associations should be to qualify as a 'culture', and the notion of 'polythetic' cultures made up of a series up of overlapping traits has since been widely canvassed. It has even been doubted whether distinct groupings occur at all rather than progressive spatial variation from any given starting point of reference.[45] However, though boundaries themselves do not seem particularly sharply defined, as in south-west Romania between the Vinča and Gumelniţa cultures, the distinct nature of the major cultural groupings is hard to deny, even though internal variation, as in the Vinča culture, is also apparent. A further way to appreciate this, other than the brief survey at the beginning of the chapter, is to note a long series of distinctive pottery imports (some of which have been extensively used in chronological correlations). Thus at Gumelniţa itself there were a few distinctive Cucuteni A imports; at Kodzadermen a red-painted pre-

Cucuteni figurine; Thessalian or central Greek grey-coloured vessels at Corinth and Elateia and possibly Corinthian vessels at Saliagos; four-legged rhytons at Corinth found also up the Adriatic; and so on. In the other direction one can cite Macedonian or Thessalian pottery in the Cucuteni A level at Tîrpeşti in Moldavia or the claimed two Thessalian figurines at Gumelniţa.[46] The spatial distribution of the cultural groupings varies, from the very large Vinča area to smaller groupings in Thessaly. It is noticeable too that the late Vinča culture comes to an end before the major groupings in the east Balkans. Set against the patterns of local or regional material culture is a distribution of non-local material, such as the pottery just mentioned or the copper, gold, shell, obsidian, flint and stone already discussed.

Both aspects of the use of material culture demand explanation, and both perhaps can be seen as related to each other. Referring to the discussion in chapter 3 one must see the spatial patterns of material culture as non-random, reflecting on the hypothesis followed there a regional sense of identity, itself perhaps engendered by social difference at local and regional level. The hypothesis of social stress or competition discussed earlier in chapter 3 may also be fruitful here. It is interesting for example that recent research has both defined a more distinctive cultural grouping in north-east Bulgaria than previously admitted and revealed considerable signs of social hierarchy and competition seen in the settlement types and cemeteries of the region. If this sort of social context is to be admitted, the movement of exotic materials and artefacts such as pots, copper and gold could be seen as complementary to the regional need for expressions of identity. It could have provided a reinforcement for social differences within regional groupings, the very exotic nature of non-local products itself being a potent source of legitimation of social differences, just as it was suggested that increased emphasis on ritual and an increasingly arcane ritual content could have reflected and aided social differentiation. The basic interpretative suggestion is to see as many features as possible of the period as in some way linked, so that from the nature of cultural groupings, material culture, settlement types, subsistence, and ritual, one may begin to reconstruct societies which contained a broad range of contradictions and conflicts, as between male and female, family or kin group and the community, the community and its wider regional setting, and finally between regional groupings. Such contradictions seem to have been regularly masked or concealed, but taken together provide a dynamic source of change, which is visible in the mutable nature of the major features of the archaeological record. There is no convenient label with which to characterise such societies, since neither the concept of 'tribe' nor 'chiefdom' in evolutionary anthropological theory seems directly applicable, and it would be misleading to suppose that social relations and transformations were uniform over the area in question. The existence of a horizon of considerable further change in the first half of the third millennium bc, to which we now turn, is further indication of the necessity to seek in this preceding period a plausible interpretation of the social processes which culminated in the changes now to be described.

## 5.2 Transformations, 3000–2500 bc: local or external?

### The nature of the evidence

Approximately within the span between 3000 and 2500 bc there were numerous and widespread changes in many aspects of the archaeological record in eastern Europe, and the way of life described earlier in the chapter can be seen to have altered profoundly in many areas. For the most part, archaeological commentators have agreed in seeing these changes as connected with the movement of new population into the region and the displacement of existing population. Such a view has been reinforced by and is often inextricably mixed up with the linguistic hypothesis that at some stage in European prehistory there must have been a large-scale spread of speakers of Indo-European or some early form of it, and with the view that it is possible and desirable to match the conjectural restricted proto-Indo-European lexicon against the material culture record of this period. The nature of the linguistic hypothesis can be commented on later, but here one must stress again that the archaeological evidence available is far from perfect. Many of the key sites from the Aegean to the Carpathian basin and the Pontic steppes have been excavated on a small scale, and have not been fully published. There has been little systematic recovery of economic data, and virtually no systematic survey of non-tell sites. Chronology is again a major problem. Radiocarbon dating has been unevenly applied and with uneven results. For example the long series from Ezero does not correspond with the stratigraphic sequence, and the series at Sitagroi has suggested a hiatus in occupation over this timespan. Radical material changes offer many possibilities for interpretation, apart from the conventional one of population change, once the active role of material culture in social change generally is admitted. The aim of this section is therefore to first describe the range of changes as objectively as possible, and later to consider alternative interpretations.

### Chronology and material sequences

*Thessaly and southern Greece.* One of the important features of the southeast European region as a whole is that the sequence of material change is different from area to area. The following account is necessarily summary, but to start with Thessaly provides an area where there was continued occupation of tell sites such as Arapi, Otzaki and Argissa. This is not to deny that there were stratigraphic hiatuses at individual sites nor that there have been severe problems in interpreting the stratigraphy of such tells when certain phases are represented by pits alone or are truncated by ditches from later in the third millennium bc.[47] The use of tells however continues in the area as a whole. The suggested sequence follows the results of Milojčić's team's exploration. After the classic Dimini phase, the Larisa phase is notable for varieties of black-polished pottery, as well as brown- and white-painted pottery. It is not represented by closed layers in the tells already mentioned and some doubt could be cast on its validity by the occurrence of black-polished pottery at Servia in Macedonia in undoubtedly pre-Dimini contexts. The succeeding Rakhmani phase marks a return to more elaborately decorated painted pottery, particularly by means of 'crusted paste'. After this comes in conventional terms the Early Bronze Age or early Thessalian phase, and there are indications of continuity in tell occupation and of overlap of ceramic styles. In southern Greece the early Helladic period begins according to radiocarbon dating by around 2500 bc, though direct dates for Thessaly are non-existent. Likewise dates for the Dimini, Larisa and Rakhmani phases are scarce. Continuity of material culture has also been argued in southern Greece over the time-span in question; the essential difference between north and south lies in the greater range and rate of changes after around 2500 bc in southern Greece, with greater site differentiation and related economic and social development.[48]

*Northern Greece and southern Bulgaria.* At Sitagroi in northern Greece phase III with its strong Karanovo VI resemblances ends around or before 3000 bc according to radiocarbon dates. A stratigraphic hiatus was not clearly recognised but the dates for phase IV, around 2500 bc, certainly suggest one, and the dark-faced pottery of phase IV is also new. In the tells of southern Bulgaria three features regularly recur: the destruction or at least burning of final Karanovo VI levels, a succeeding stratigraphic hiatus visible as a humic layer, and considerable artefactual change in the following layer (the 'Early Bronze Age' in conventional terminology). Pottery was now largely dark faced, and where decorated, by means of incision and impression. Dominant new forms were handled jugs and jars and bowls with rather straight sides and inverted rims, as at Ezero (Fig. 5.17). Ritual paraphernalia were now very scarce, with more animal than anthropomorphic figurines. Houses at Ezero include ones with a slightly curved or apsidal end, though the tradition of construction and internal fittings seems otherwise unaltered. Metal forms were restricted to awls and needles, tanged blades, chisels and flat axes (Fig. 5.17). The artefacts from the lowest levels at Ezero were of copper or copper with low quantities of arsenic, but this later increased. A major problem is again chronology. There are very few radiocarbon dates which suggest a continuation of the Karanovo VI complex to the end of the fourth millennium bc, but links with the Gumelniţa and Cucuteni–Tripolye complexes as well as the Sitagroi evidence suggest that a terminus around 3000 bc is reasonable. The Azmak series ends around 3600–3500 bc. There is no necessity either to see every stratigraphic hiatus as strictly contemporary, nor to pay particular attention to burnt layers since both these and hiatuses occur with some frequency within the Karanovo sequence as a whole. The duration of the hiatus is also uncertain. The Ezero series of dates is inconsistent, though the earliest dates go back to around 2700 bc, and only begins anyway with level x, which is only the fourth Early Bronze Age level at the site, whose Chalcolithic layers have not produced dates of their own. Unlike in Greece, it

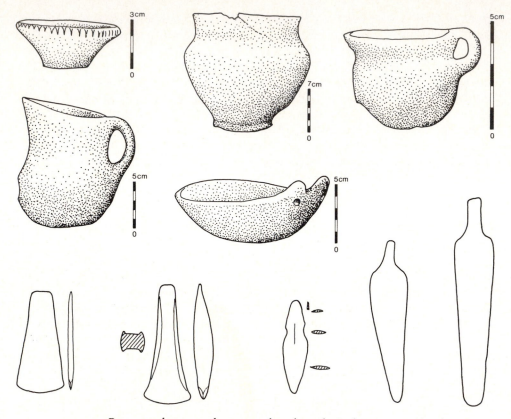

**5.17** Pottery and copper or bronze artefacts from the Early Bronze Age levels at Ezero, central-southern Bulgaria. *After* Georgiev *et al.*

is much more difficult to suggest what material if any should be assigned to this transitional period; suggestions made so far consist of marginal sites or unpublished sites or elements such as stone 'sceptre' heads (schematic models of animal heads) which have a wide chronological range. After the transition it is worth emphasising that many tells were reoccupied.[49]

*Northern Bulgaria and southern Romania.* In this area also there is a general dislocation of the tell settlement pattern at the end of the Karanovo VI–Kodzadermen–Gumelniţa phase. Here dislocation generally takes the form of final abandonment rather than hiatus, though several important sites such as Gumelniţa and Căscioarele themselves have some material from the succeeding phase. Unfortunately this was not found in any significant quantity and seems to have been disturbed. The date of the end of this phase is as usual problematic. No appreciation is possible yet of regional variation. Though hardly yet supported by large series of dates, the sequence could continue as late as 3000 bc or beyond. Some material from the next complex in the eastern part of the area, named after sites at Cernavodă beside the Danube, is found on Gumelniţa sites, and while the Cernavodă complex too as yet lacks radiocarbon dates, it in turn has imported Cucuteni B pottery from further north, as at sites like Olteniţa. As set out below the Cucuteni B horizon has radiocarbon dates around 3000 bc. Cernavodă itself comprises several sites, and it offers the possibility therefore of significant continuity within one location, even though no one site was used continuously from the fourth into the third millennium bc. As well as an early fourth millennium bc Hamangia culture cemetery there is an unpublished Gumelniţa settlement. Some 400 m south is another settlement with 3 m of deposit and up to 14 occupation layers. This is Cernavodă I and has been noted amongst other aspects for its pottery, rather plain bowls and handled jars and jugs, with some finger-nail, shell and cord decoration, and distinctive shell tempering. There are also schematic figurines. This is generally considered to precede (through its connections with the Gumelniţa complex) the neighbouring site of Cernavodă III. This has some 2 m of deposit. Its shell-tempered pottery has more elaborate decoration, with ribbons set below the rim, fluting, incision and long tubular handles. Cord decoration is hardly represented. This in turn is thought to precede but perhaps overlap with Cernavodă II (the numbering reflects the sequence of discovery) again with substantial cultural deposits of 2–3 m. This is again notable for a further distinct ceramic assemblage with impressed motifs dominant. No absolute chronology is available but the Cernavodă sites are generally considered to lie in the period between 3000 and 2500 bc. The relations between the three sites are unclear, and it is not firmly established whether we are dealing with a straightforward chronological succession or a more complicated situation of contemporary material differentiation. In the Black Sea area of north-east Bulgaria the sequence is even less well known due to a dearth of excavated later settlements, relevant examples of which may lie beneath the water of the Varna inlet. A hiatus has been suggested between the Varna and Cernavodă complexes in this area, but its reality remains to be established. Likewise the chronological position of a single ochre-sprinkled crouched inhumation at Devnya with copper, gold, flint and *spondylus* artefacts, which has been suggested to lie in the supposed hiatus, is also far from securely established.[50]

*North-west Bulgaria, western Romania, and Yugoslavia.* As set out earlier in the chapter there are reasons for believing that the Vinča culture ended earlier than other major complexes of the Balkans. It was succeeded by a series of more-regional complexes which may span the later fourth and earlier third millennia bc, and represent a new kind of cultural unity over this area. At Sălcuţa in Oltenia or south-western Romania the uppermost layer of a substantial tell is considered to represent a cultural development beyond the end of the main Gumelniţa complex. The pottery of this Sălcuţa IV horizon includes bowls, small two-handled jars, and jugs with a distinctive handle projecting above the rim. In Yugoslavia another regional complex has been named after the sites near Nis of Bubanj, Novo Selo and Velika Humska Cuka, Hum, both settlements on high terraces or promontories. Unlike the continuity implied in the continued use of the Sălcuţa tell, dislocation of the previous settlement pattern is strongly suggested by these and other sites scattered between Belgrade and Bitolj. Bubanj itself has had only limited excavations but has some 2 m of deposit, divided into four phases; stratigraphically there is no visible interruption to this development. The material from the lowest level, Ia, includes handled bowls with incision, channelling and graphite paint as decoration, and from Ib, plain cups with very high projecting handles. There is no absolute chronology available, and the sequence has been often and variously correlated with neighbouring developments. Contrary to earlier opinion, Ia is generally correlated with Sălcuţa IV, some part of Bodrogkeresztúr (for which see chapter 6) and Cernavodă I. Phase Ib is either placed in this horizon, or more plausibly correlated with distinctive Baden pottery of the Carpathian basin (see chapter 6 also), dated from around 2700 bc. In the latter treatment this involves assuming a hiatus between Ia and Ib. The very existence of numerous schemes underlines the chronological uncertainties involved. In north-west Bulgaria the site of Krivodol is used to represent the period spanning the end of the fourth millennium bc and the beginning of the third, and Krivodol and other sites are regarded as initially parallel to but eventually outliving the Karanovo VI–Kodzadermen complex elsewhere in Bulgaria. Absolute chronology is rare, though there are a few radiocarbon dates of the later fourth millennium bc.

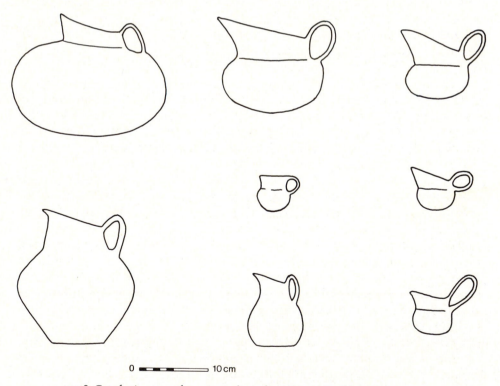

0 ▬▬▬▬▬ 10 cm

5.18 Coţofeni pottery from central-southern Romania. *After* Roman

The correlation with Karanovo VI is made through shared elements like graphite decoration though the distinctive character of this area has already been outlined earlier in the chapter. The view that the Krivodol group lasts longer rests on the appearance of ceramic forms such as plain dark handled jars and squat one-handled askoi or leaning jugs, as seen at Zaminets near Vratsa, which are not represented in the Karanovo VI complex. Sites like Krivodol should therefore reflect some continuity at the period of transition around 3000 bc. The major succeeding complex is that of the Coţofeni culture in western Romania (Fig. 5.18), with Baden material to its west in eastern Hungary and to its south in eastern and central Yugoslavia, to which levels Ib and II at Bubanj may be equivalent. The Baden connection provides a starting point around 2700 bc; unfortunately the only Coţofeni dates so far come from the shelter site of Băile Herculane and do not seem reliable. Most Coţofeni sites are new foundations, apart from stratified shelter sites like the last named, though this too had been abandoned immediately before the Coţofeni horizon. Coţofeni pottery includes bowl, handled jugs and jars, amphorae and askoi, with a wide repertoire of decoration, including incision, relief, encrusting and painting.[51]

*North-east Romania and south-west USSR.* Radiocarbon dates support the gradual evolution of the Cucuteni and Tripolye cultures suggested by numerous scholars.[52] Cucuteni B and the synchronous Tripolye C1 phase are dated around 3000 bc, with some Tripolye C1 sites also dated to around 2800 bc. In the next horizon sites previously occupied were largely abandoned, and new sites occupied, such as Gorodsk far inland near Zitomir in the Ukraine to the west of Kiev and Usatovo near Odessa on the Black Sea coast, also in an area not previously involved in the Cucuteni–Tripolye culture. The horizon is labelled Usatovo–Gorodsk by those who believe it to represent fresh cultural development or Tripolye C2 by those who believe in continuity.[53] Usatovo pottery includes rare painted pottery in the Tripolye tradition alongside coarser plainer pottery decorated with cord impressions. There are schematic flat figurines. Metal forms are partly different, with triangular blades with central midrib, and developed shafthole axes probably cast in two-piece moulds alongside flat axes. Analysed Usatovo implements have low percentages of arsenic (under 2 per cent). Radiocarbon dates start from around 2600 bc. In north-east Romania in this horizon previous sites were also often abandoned and new sites founded, such as the eponymous Horodiş-tea on the Prut in the north and Folteşti near the same river further south above its confluence with the Danube. Both have substantial deposits. The two sites are representative of one complex, though there are differences within it. Folteşti has painted pottery and corded pottery like Usatovo, and Horodiştea some painted pottery and corded ware in the late Cucuteni tradition as well as more numerous grey ware. The absolute chronology is not secure, and direct dates are lacking. While Usatovo–Gorodsk dates provide some indication of position, the two complexes need not be exactly contemporary and it is quite possible that Horodiştea and Folteşti are a little earlier. Corded decoration had been in the Cucuteni–Tripolye tradition since the Cucuteni AB–Tripolye B2 phase.[54]

This brief survey has highlighted not just the usual problems in establishing reliable chronologies but also the extent of differences between and within the areas discussed. This simple observation must be kept in mind when it comes to historical interpretation. On the other hand there are by the middle of the third millennium bc widespread elements of new cultural unity, which must also be explained. It remains therefore only to emphasise the similarity of cultural development in the eastern Aegean and western Anatolia to northern Greece and southern Bulgaria, and to note that ceramic assemblages as far apart as the Carpathian basin and western Anatolia have long been compared.[55]

### Settlement and the social context of production

For the sake of brevity of treatment of this wide area, it will be convenient to treat this aspect thematically. In those areas where a hiatus is claimed or suspected in the cultural sequence it is easy also to assume a hiatus in the settlement record, with accompanying dislocation of previous patterns. There has been a tendency to invoke pastoralism as an economic mode which would fit the observed or claimed lack of settlement data in certain areas. This kind of view should not readily be accepted. The evident hiatus in tell settlement in Bulgaria for example, where humic layers are widely found, need only reflect a temporary abandonment of major tells. The situation could be comparable (though more complete) to that in the Karanovo IV phase in the area around Karanovo, where the eponymous site itself has a rather thin deposit but numbers of open or non-tell sites were founded. When subsistence evidence becomes available again there is little sign in most areas of any radical shift to a more pastoral economy. Indeed many areas under discussion show above all considerable continuity of settlement and economic practice in this period, and others, where a hiatus is likely or possible, show renewal of many previous aspects. In terms of settlement tells remain the most obvious feature in northern parts of Greece, even though individual sites like Sitagroi may have been abandoned for periods of time. Many southern Bulgarian tells were reoccupied and then remained in use for long periods of time. Large sites of around 1 ha now seems to have become the norm in Thessaly. There were ditches around the site of Otzaki in the Larisa and Rakhmani phases, and larger ditches were dug around Argissa in the early Thessalian phase. Likewise there was a stone enclosure wall around the top of the Ezero tell from the first Early Bronze Age level, a feature paralleled at several other sites. The Ezero wall was 1.5 m thick but its original height and therefore function are harder to reconstruct (Fig. 5.19). Continuity can also be seen in north-west Bulgaria in the renewal of Krivodol settlements like Zaminets whose buildings were replaced exactly after two fire destructions, and in the Cucuteni B–Tripolye CI pattern of settlement. But the situation was by no means everywhere static. Continuity of stable settlement, as

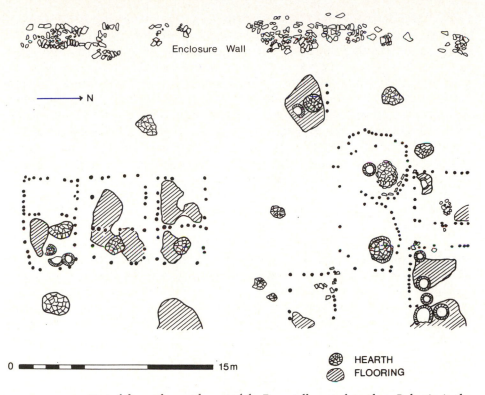

Enclosure Wall

→ N

0 ▮▮▮▮▮▮ 15m

🕸 HEARTH

🗁 FLOORING

**5.19** Part of the settlement layout of the Ezero tell, central-southern Bulgaria, in the Early Bronze Age levels. *After* Georgiev *et al.*

reflected in substantial deposits and house plans, can be argued in the Cernavodă and Bubanj cases, but these involved site abandonment and relocation. Cernavodă itself has already been discussed, and the uncertainty whether this is a feature only of the Gumelniţa–Cernavodă transition or a repeated feature of the Cernavodă phases itself. In other areas again some significant expansion of settlement can be seen. This might be argued in the case of Bubanj from the kind of location that the eponymous site itself shows, on a small hill beside a river, rather like Krivodol locations, but the overall sample is too small. Coţofeni sites however are both numerous and widely spread over the landscape. Coţofeni itself is on a striking promontory. The variety of site sizes and durations would also be consistent with a phase of expansion. In the final Cucuteni–Tripolye phase sites like Horodiştea and Folteşti can be taken to reflect local relocation but essential continuity, whereas a site like Usatavo shows the intake of the coastal area not previously within the culture's distribution.

In nearly all these cases there is little sign of change in the general character of site layout and in the range of differentiation between sites, but some aspects are of interest. Ezero house styles have already been noted, but the change is not accompanied by any obviously greater differentiation of house size or layout within the site. In northern Greece it is suggested that an increase in site size follows the earlier developments at Dimini and Sesklo. In southern Greece there are also indications from the mid third millennium bc onwards at sites like Lerna and Knossos of individual buildings and sites being accorded special importance. In contrast, the Baden–Cotofeni phase to the north can be taken to represent a less obviously differentiated pattern of settlement than seen earlier in the tell pattern, though as pointed out above there remain significant differences between individual Cotofeni sites.

Subsistence and production have generally been less well investigated than the continuity and distribution of settlement. There are very few economic data for large areas such as the Cernavodă and Cotofeni cultures, but it may still be possible to pick out some significant themes and regional variations. Continuity of previous practice is an important feature. In southern Bulgaria for example this is implied in the resumption of tell settlement, but is often rather unsystematically recorded. More rigorous recovery of subsistence data was however achieved at Ezero and showed the continued cultivation of emmer, barley and pulses and the strong possibility of crop rotation, and the husbandry of ovicaprids, pig and cattle, in that order of numerical importance.[56] The bone sample was however very small. Another feature at Ezero was the presence of a few grape pips which may indicate the addition of viticulture. This is suggested more firmly at Sitagroi where morphological changes in grape pips culminate in level iv. Elsewhere in northern Greece continuation of cereals and pulses and animal husbandry is relatively well documented. It has been suggested that settlement growth and nucleation may have affected the organisation of field layout, and that the numerical balance between pigs, cattle and ovicaprids may reflect a more varied use of these animals from season to season in different parts of the landscape. Ovicaprids were still exploited for milk and meat rather than wool which was probably a product more developed in the Early Bronze Age.[57] Further south there are also indications of the cultivation of grape and olive, which were to be resources of increasing importance from the mid third millennium bc onwards. Further north in south-east Europe it is likely that the horse became a more important resource, though it may have been exploited sporadically at least as early as the later Cucuteni and Gumelnita phases.[58] Bone data however are scarce, though those from the four sites at Foltești, Horodiștea, Stoicani and Erbiceni suggest that horse was much less important than cattle, ovicaprids and deer, and also that its numbers varied from site to site. Horses present very difficult problems of interpretation, since distinguishing domestication is problematic, and they could have been exploited equally for meat, traction or transport. It is worth emphasising the very varied figures just mentioned from Moldavia and the absence of horse from Ezero; horse and ass are likewise not documented in Greece till after around 2500 bc. Horse-riding however could have been very important as a mechanism of communication over wide steppe areas.

Two other innovations, the cart and the plough, have been suggested to belong to this horizon along with the necessary animal traction, and to start a 'secondary products revolution'.[59] Direct chronological evidence lies for the most part outside south-east Europe. The suggestion relies in part on Near Eastern pictographic evidence just before 3000 BC, and in part on Baden, TRB and other evidence from central and north-west Europe around 2800–2700 bc, which is detailed in chapter 6. The crucial assumptions are made that the source of these innovations was to the east of Europe, and that the different aspects are part of a more or less unitary phenomenon. A reasonable alternative involves rather more piecemeal development. In the Near East itself plough cultivation may long precede the Uruk period; Halafian settlements on heavy terra rosa soils in the fifth millennium BC for example are good candidates for having developed cultivation techniques. Pointed bone artefacts have been interpreted as plough shares in Gumelniţa contexts. The TRB and other northern and north-western evidence for ploughmarks around 2700 bc may reflect primarily an increase in the building of suitable monuments needed to cover and preserve the marks. Evidence for animal traction in Gumelniţa contexts has been noted earlier in the chapter. It has also been suggested that there are wheel models in Cucuteni A and Gumelniţa A contexts. The objects in questions are small circular clay discs with a central perforation through a raised boss, though their interpretation as wheel models must be open to question. But in the same critical vein one may note that other suggested innovations, milking and wool, thought to follow soon after animal traction, the cart and plough, also have potentially earlier antecedents. Milk could have been a minor product of earlier herds of ovicaprids and cattle. There is some evidence from a later fifth millennium bc Dudeşti context – admittedly from a very small bone sample – for a preponderance of old ovicaprids, which is consistent with wool production. This is not to deny the later, much larger scale development of wool production from after the mid third millennium bc onwards.

The specific evidence between 3000 and 2500 bc already reviewed does not support a picture of radical changes which these innovations might have encouraged, though an exception might be made in the case of wheeled transport. Here the evidence from the Caucasian area is consistent with the Near Eastern evidence for a later fourth millennium BC development, but there need be little actual time-lag in diffusion if the innovation reached south-east and central Europe by the earlier third millennium bc (note the two chronologies being used).[60] After all across the steppes there had been far-flung cultural connections from much earlier, and a ready-made route of diffusion therefore existed well before 3000 bc. But within south-east Europe only Thessaly presented a picture of site nucleation in which wheeled transport would have been critical in reducing the effects of larger communities having to travel further to their fields. For the most part therefore it seems that the main development was of local resources and techniques (though wheeled transport may be an important exception), and that the greatest scale of changes may have been in Greece.

*Sources of authority: prestige goods, ritual and burial*

The social importance of metal objects in the fourth millennium bc has already been described, and the scale of production was seen best in the extent of known mine sites. In the earlier third millennium bc however output seems to have been reduced. A couple of copper axes from Sesklo belong to this transitional phase; the finds at Ezero represent about half the known objects in Bulgaria. Quantities of metal in Usatovo contexts are restrained. One Coţofeni site, Băile Herculane, has evidence of local copper working. Another feature is the change in artefact styles, already noted at Ezero and Usatovo. A further stylistic innovation was the sleeved single-bladed axe, seen for example in a Cernavodă context at Crivaţ near Bucharest. This is a product of closed casting in a two-piece mould and may be an import from the Pontic steppes or beyond. This reflects a progressively closer connection between south-east European and Caucasian traditions of metallurgy, which began only in the Cucuteni AB–Tripolye BII phase, but intensified in the Cucuteni B–Tripolye CI phase. Another expression of this may be the progressively larger additions of arsenic in south-east European objects. Such alloying dates back to the earlier fourth millennium bc in Caucasia. Very low percentages of arsenic are found in late fourth millennium bc artefacts from the Balkans, and the additives may be neither significant nor purposeful. The same is true of artefacts from the first levels of Ezero, but higher quantities are recorded in later levels, and also in a blade from Băile Herculane. This may reflect the beginnings of larger-scale working of sulphide ores, and likewise the reduced scale of output might reflect a working-out of the previously abundant and widespread oxide and carbonate ores. On the other hand, having previously emphasised the social context of early metallurgy, one should continue to consider that now as well. As well as possible changes in supply of ores one must therefore also consider changes in social use. In the artefactual record generally there are perhaps less prestige goods than before in many areas. Copper objects are scarce. Gold is absent though silver is present, as in the ring at Sukleja near Tiraspol inland from Usatovo and of the same period. The finest painted pottery was no longer produced, *spondylus* no longer circulated. A possible innovation in this sphere are the few schematic stone animal heads, thought to be sceptre heads, and of this period, though they are not closely dated. Returning to copper, less may have been produced or at least deposited because social conditions did not require such overt consumption as before.[61]

Ritual paraphernalia are also much less obvious now than in the fourth millennium bc. In Bulgaria the quantities of figurines are substantially reduced, and zoomorphic figurines are more common than anthropomorphic ones, which while represented in other areas as described earlier are also far less common. Associated objects such as lamps, altars, or other models also drop out of the archaeological record, and there are no reports of the buildings and structures which were seen in the fourth millennium bc and interpreted as domestic and other shrines.

There are also interesting changes in the burial record.[62] Some separate cemeteries continue as at Bereketskaya near Stara Zagora in Bulgaria. The inhumations were of people of all ages and both sexes, and bodies were laid in the crouched position. Most graves were single but some had men, women and children. Grave goods were restricted to pottery and occasional ornaments and copper objects. There are occasional cemeteries elsewhere but in rather different contexts. One is at Kephala on Keos in the Cyclades, where there was an early third millennium bc group of small collective burials in cists together with child burials in pithoi and another is at Souphli in Thessaly of the Larisa phase, where cremations and inhumations in pots are found. These represent the first collective, separate cemeteries in Greece. There is also a concentration of 62 crouched burials at Brăilița in a Cernavodă II context but this is in an area which earlier had had a well-established tradition of cemeteries. In many areas burial is much less conspicious than in the fourth millennium bc. Little is known of burial practice in the Sălcuța–Krivodol–Bubanj complex, or the Coțofeni culture. At Ezero and similar sites in Bulgaria burials were restricted to child burials in pots beneath houses.

A third aspect often discussed is the appearance of burials beneath and within round tumuli. The burials are usually inhumations of individuals though there may be more than one burial per tumulus, set in a simple pit, often but not always sprinkled with red ochre, and generally with few if any grave goods. There are several hundred such tumuli in south-east Europe excluding Greece, and they extend from the Pontic steppes to the Carpathian basin. Many probably belong to the third millennium, but – crucially – to the second half not to the period of transition. Thus the often-quoted examples of Stoicani, and Erbiceni and Corlăteni overlie respectively Foltești–Usatovo occupation and Horodiștea–Foltești occupation, while Valea Lupului near Iași has a sterile layer between late Cucuteni B occupation and the tumulus. The impressive barrows of the Usatovo complex are also radiocarbon dated no earlier than after the mid third millennium bc. There are no firm dates yet from barrows in Bulgaria. Some tumuli might date to the period in question, but the tradition of such burial dates from only much the same period in the steppes and Caucasia. At Casimcea near Tulcea in the Danube delta an ochre-sprinkled skeleton under a large tumulus is accompanied by amongst other objects a stone zoomorphic head, which might be dated to this period, though this is far from certain. There are also individual flat ochre burials with few goods in a Cernavodă I context at Brăilița and in a Horodiștea–Foltești context at Tîrpești, amongst other examples, but these lack tumuli over them. The number of such early candidates is therefore strictly limited, and supposed steppe influence may easily be greatly exaggerated in the transitional period itself. Ochre had long been used in burial, as seen even in chapter 2, and it seems highly tendentious to classify the Transylvanian cemetery of Decea Mureșului, which may date to the Cucuteni AB or B phase, as showing early steppic influences mainly on the basis of ochre-covered burials. An interesting feature however of many tumuli, even though they may be post-2500 bc, is the accompanying stone stele with schematic figures,

perhaps male, holding or wearing in their belts hafted axes. These extend
from Bulgaria into the Ukraine. They can be taken to reinforce the emphasis
given to individuals by tumulus burials, and this in its turn may be a useful
clue to the nature of social change during the transition between 3000 and
2500 bc. In the same way Globular amphorae burials found as far east as
Romania probably postdate the transitional period (on the chronology
advanced in more detail in chapter 6). These consist of small numbers of
inhumations in stone cists with grave goods including distinctive decorated
pottery, bone ornaments and polished flint axes. As discussed further below
they also may be a clue to the outcome of social transformation within the
transitional period itself.

## Patterns of material culture

By 3000 bc established distributions of material culture were changing
widely, though at different rates in different areas, a process which has been
outlined above. By 2700–2500 bc new patterns of distribution of material
culture can be discerned, and the first important feature to be noted is the
reemergence of several large such blocs. The labels of Baden, Coțofeni,
Bubanj, Ezero, Usatovo, early Helladic and Thessalian reflect this, and do not
just denote different present-day national boundaries. At the same time there
are elements which link these different areas on a far wider scale than seen in
the fourth millennium bc, and it is worthwhile to further emphasise these.
On one axis there are very wide ceramic similarities especially in dark-
coloured pottery in the form of handled jugs and jars, and of open dishes
which extend from the Carpathian basin to Greece and Bulgaria and beyond
to western Anatolia. On another axis connections with the steppes to the east
are intensified. These connections were of long standing, first in Linear
pottery–Bug–Dniester contacts, then implicit in the spread of the Cucuteni–
Tripolye complex, and occasionally more explicit as in the case of the shell-
tempered often cord-decorated Cucuteni 'c' pottery which goes back to the
late Cucuteni A phase and is believed to derive from some point east or north
of the Cucuteni–Tripolye complex. These connections are realigned in the
Usatovo–Gorodsk complex, and burial practice and metallurgy after 2500 bc
in south-east Europe seem to owe increasing amounts to steppe traditions. A
third axis from around 2500 bc onwards is reflected in Globular amphorae
burials, whose wider distribution reaches central and the fringe of northern
Europe.[63] The distances over which connections and similarities in material
culture can be discerned – if necessarily somewhat subjectively – are far
greater on all three axes than in the fourth millennium bc or earlier. Indeed
the third is novel altogether, and the first at least as striking as that
commonly assumed at the beginning of the Neolithic period.

*Interpretations: population change or social transformation*

The explanation of cultural discontinuity or radical cultural change at this period in the prehistory of eastern Europe has mostly been sought in terms of population change and replacement, either partial or complete. The assumption is often made that radical cultural change is not compatible with the continuation of an established population and that the inference of new population from changes in material culture is relatively straightforward. The hypothesis gains further popularity because it is readily linked to another hypothesis, albeit linguistic rather than archaeological, which states that at some historical point speakers of an ancestral and undifferentiated version of Indo-European spread from a homeland or area of restricted origin. Further linguistic hypotheses are that this must have happened before around 2000 BC when Hittite provides an indication of already differentiated Indo-European language, and that a lexicon of ancestral or proto-Indo-European words can be reconstructed, which includes most importantly terms connected with metallurgy and wheeled transport. The assumption is also made, though rarely explicitly, that a specific language is restricted to a specific human group defined in another way by its material culture. Cautious formulations of the homeland hypothesis suggest that a broad period between 4000 and 2500 BC is reasonable for the existence of the proto-Indo-European homeland, and many formulations imply that geographically the supposed homeland is located somewhere east of the Carpathians, out on the steppes, and possibly far east, though others are far less explicit.

When the linguistic and archaeological hypotheses are put together, the one seems to reinforce the other. Populations beyond the Cucuteni–Tripolye complex are identified with the proto-Indo-Europeans, and changes from the later fourth millennium bc onwards are seen to result from either the direct results of westwards movement by proto-Indo-European population or the indirect results of secondary population shifts and readjustment in the face of primary movement. Subsidiary explanations involve actual hiatus of occupation in the face of such pressures, or alternatively some measure of population mixing and subsequent restabilisation. While the pages of the literature do for the most part resound to the thunder of horses' hooves and the twang of new human accents it is important to emphasise that many varied interpretations are available on the detailed course of events. Thus Gimbutas has suggested three 'waves' of Indo-European advance, the first responsible for the end of the Gumelniţa–Karanovo VI–Vinča complexes bringing copper–arsenic alloying, tumulus burial and 'royal' graves from the Black Sea to eastern Hungary. The longer survival of Cucuteni culture is attributed to its better-defended settlements, and after the lesser shocks and subsequent population mixing the final wave is seen as 'a massive invasion that wiped out the Baden culture of central Europe and led to the extermination of the Old European strongholds in the Aegean'. Others have elaborated the 'knock-on' effects and blurred the distinction between waves. Thus Garašanin has suggested a general picture of gradual infiltration by steppe groups, as far back as the Cucuteni AB or B phases, as alleged in the Decea Mureşului cemetery in Transylvania, and envisages numerous successive phases or waves of infiltration. The theme of gradually increasing contact is also developed amongst others by Comşa, who has dated 'les premières signes des troubles' to the late fourth millennium bc and has envisaged the retreat of advanced Neolithic communities 'devant la pression incessante des communautés de la steppe, cherchant asile dans les endroits écartés, les collines boisées'. Discussion of the formation of the Coţofeni culture has involved Pontic pressure, but also internal reaction and new formation such as that of Cernavodă III which is seen as having had a 'shock' effect on other areas.[64] Some Bulgarian opinion favours population change and disruption at this point connected with both the steppes and Anatolia, though with some measure of internal change. The concept of hiatus is gaining ground, though it has not been explicitly explained in human terms. Internal continuity and change has been stressed by others though the Indo-European hypothesis has not been explicitly denied.[65] Continuity has been argued in Greece particularly by Renfrew, against the common view of Indo-European immigration at the start of the Early Bronze Age; for example two waves have recently been proposed, one equated with the Larisa phase, the other with Early Helladic–Thessalian.[66] In all these various accounts relatively little attention is given to the explanation of the supposed Indo-European expansion. Perhaps the most explicit view has been that of Gimbutas who has suggested that the motive for expansion lay in the increase in domesticated horse numbers and the consequent need for greater supplies of grazing.

Such are the main trends of the conventional approach to this period of transition. The intention here however is briefly to present a radical alternative which takes account of difficulties in the linguistic hypotheses, and the very varied archaeological situation, and further develops the picture of changing social relations. In the author's opinion the Indo-European expansion cannot be tied down to the required chronological horizon and indeed may be an illusion altogether, while the observed changes in the area – varied from region to region – are best seen as the outcome of internal social processes in the preceding period, leading to more overtly expressed social differences and a changed ideology, in which long-range contacts as a source of alliance and legitimation of position became increasingly important.

Criticism of the Indo-European homeland and dispersal hypotheses can be prefaced by the observation that there is no universal correspondence in ethnography between language groups and groups defined by their material culture. Clarke's elegant model of the overlap between groups as defined by culture, physical anthropology or genetic characteristics, political affiliation and language can be amply documented, though there may indeed be some cases where the correspondence is exact. Language is part of the complex question of individual and group identity, and many studies show how individuals can leave one group and assume the identity of another, be it within or across a language boundary as well. The notion of the Indo-European dispersal cannot be closely dated on purely linguistic grounds. A cautious evaluation of the reconstructed lexicon with cross-reference to archaeology can only suggest the long period 4000–2500 BC which can imply that the supposed dispersal could have taken place well before the period of transition under discussion.[67] The proto-Indo-European lexicon cannot tell us in detail what kinds of metallurgy or what kinds of wheeled vehicle it denoted, and is little use therefore as a precise chronometer. The notion of the homeland itself is a projection from the reconstructed lexicon and makes the further assumptions that there was no significant variation in vocabulary and that this implies a restricted geographical area of use. The first assumption sets up a circular argument, since any possible early variation is by definition excluded from the common proto-Indo-European stock. The second seems to rely on the equation of language group with specific human group, although the notion of homeland in itself does little to specify the size of the homeland. It makes no allowance for the borrowing and assimilation of new words for new things across wide areas, either in a rapid process of more or less simultaneous diffusion or more gradually with a greater time-lag between areas. As more than one critical linguist has pointed out, innovations like coffee and tobacco in modern Europe were gradually assimilated and are now marked by vocabulary variation around a common root (e.g. coffee, *café*, *Kaffee*; tobacco, *tabac*, *Tabak*) which has nothing to do with the origins of modern European languages today, or a proto-European pulling deeply on his favourite weed or contemplating his favourite drink. Other linguists have long been aware of these problems, particularly of confusing the ancestral form or forms of IE with the reconstructed version of common IE, and sophisticated alternative approaches based on the study of morphological complexity, or semantic development in daughter languages, seem to have done little to overcome the fundamental chronological and geographical problems. Other scholars have therefore entertained the notion of very much earlier Indo-European dispersal, ultimately back into the early post-glacial period and there seems little reason why it should not go further back still.[68]

Though this question poses severe hazards for the non-specialist like this author, it does seem that its inherent difficulties should leave one free to formulate alternative hypotheses based on internal processes and in human terms. The terms offered here consist principally of a resolution of the conflicts and contradictions inferred in the previous period and of a resulting change in social formation and ideology, but it is likely that the process of change was not completed by 2500 bc, or rather that change continued thereafter to be further consolidated. The previously great emphasis on communal ritual now disappears in many areas, which must be significant. The previous tradition of metallurgy also goes, to be replaced by another with novel and perhaps more arcane technology and forms. This also suggests a significant change in the social context, specifically a reduced need for the production and exchange of prestige goods or alternatively an attempt to create less accessible kinds of prestige goods. Cemetery burial partly ceases to be important, and could reflect a lapse or change in the need to reflect communal identity; where dateable many burials of the period or shortly after it seem to emphasise more individual personages or groups. This is finally reinforced by such features as the relief-decorated grave stelae. But the process is far from uniform, as the Bulgarian and Greek data suggested especially. Long-range contact can be seen in metallurgy and other artefacts, novel burial traditions and in the very widespread ceramic similarities cross-cutting the maintenance of regional boundaries. If it is correct to see more overt social difference, these features in their turn can be seen not as features explicable in terms of population movement but as the expression of external reference points for the new social order, of sources of political alliance over very wide areas, of new forms of legitimation of social difference contrasted with the earlier period in which difference was concealed. This suggested use of the external is not entirely novel, and the social use of material culture is argued throughout the book. Long-range contact is well documented in the previous period, and finds one of its most spectacular expressions in the Varna cemetery gold. In this phase however it seems to have become more import-ant still. Any interpretation of this kind must also take into account variation from region to region, but it is better equipped to do this than the alternatives already described and discussed. Rather than explain for example the con-tinuation of the Cucuteni–Tripolye culture through its better defensive works, one may posit different internal social process. Thus in the Cucuteni–Tripolye area and also in southern Bulgaria the system of regional centres lasted longer, but in Thessaly the development was towards increased site differentiation and perhaps changes in the organisation of production, while in the Coţofeni–Baden area the old regional centres disappeared altogether. The subsequent development of society in southern Greece and the Aegean, set apart from other areas as the label 'civilisation' attempts to denote, likewise need not be referred to the strength of the Indo-European gene pool in the area. Such interpretation can also avoid deterministic explanations such as the need for horse grazing, when the evidence for horses is plainly so varied, and the economy of many regions clearly not geared to large-scale pastoralism of this kind. A deterministic role for 'secondary products' is also avoided, though a greater emphasis on animal products, were it to be well documented, could indeed fit a changed social picture of increased production and acquisition of storable, mobile resources.

Problems remain also. There is little obvious shift in the internal structure of settlements towards overt expression of social difference, apart from the stone enclosures of sites like Ezero. To some extent the suggested resolution of contradictions and change of ideology rest on negative features of the archaeological record, and overt differentiation in contrast to long-range contact is not abundantly documented. Another sort of problem is that it remains very difficult to do more than sketch the historical conditions of such a series of changes as a replacement for Indo-European events and repercussions (though these themselves are largely unexplained). Interpreta-tions of the kind offered here offer a more plausible context for the changes under discussion, without yet explaining why they happened when they did. But perhaps I protest too much. Given the present nature of the evidence it may be satisfactory after all to have outlined gradual shifts in the social formations of the area from as far back as the sixth millennium bc, and to show that each successive formation can be at least partially understood by reference to its predecessor. Here the essential factor should lie in the ultimate instability of the previous period, located in the conflict between communal and more individual interests, not necessarily those of individuals as such but of smaller groups than the community as a whole. There is again no ready label for the state of society either in the fourth millennium bc or the first half of the third millennium bc. Those such as 'tribe' and 'chief' are too anachronistic and ethnocentric. But the lack of vocabulary is no barrier to the need to rethink the conventional interpretations of the end of our period.

CHAPTER 6

# THE CENTRAL AND WESTERN EUROPEAN MOSAIC

## Introduction: the nature of the evidence

This chapter covers a very wide area, from the Great Hungarian plain in the east to Ireland in the west, and from Hungary and the Alpine foreland northwards to southern Scandinavia, and it discusses the period from the end of the Linear pottery culture to the Corded ware horizon (Fig. 6.1). In order to do so three divisions of the time-span have been made, rather than of the area, though many regional differences will become apparent. The nature of the evidence is extremely varied. Detailed reliable chronologies are everywhere problematic in the absence of long stratigraphies. One example is the evident importance of a site like Jevišovice in southern Moravia which despite being dug long ago still provides crucial evidence for cultural transformations in the region in the earlier third millennium bc. Settlement excavation is varied in scope and quality – limited on the Great Hungarian plain; extensive on the loess; intensive in the waterlogged sites of the Alpine foreland which are however perhaps only part of the full range of local settlement; and so on. Cemeteries and monuments holding burials have long been an object of interest, shown for example by the publication of the eponymous Lengyel site at the end of the last century, but have suffered from isolation from other aspects of the evidence.[1]

## Environment

Direct evidence for the environment is perhaps more forthcoming in this large area than in eastern Europe, with an abundance of pollen-preserving deposits long studied and the potential of land snails, waterlogged wood and tree-ring studies, insects and buried soils more recently recognised. The period covers the late Atlantic and early Sub-Boreal periods in the Blytt–Sernander terminology; the transition is dated in most studies in north-west Europe to the later fourth millennium bc. Vegetationally these are periods of climax forest, though not without regional variation and some effect from indigenous communities. Overall the climate may have been as warm and wet as in the Atlantic period, though there have been suggestions of cooler conditions from the later fourth millennium bc. These are based on Alpine glacier activity, and on the decline or retreat of elm, ivy, mistletoe and holly in Denmark. There are suggestions of drier conditions too, the classical view being of increased continentality from the Atlantic–Sub-Boreal transition. Very varied recent research does not indicate decisive change, though short-

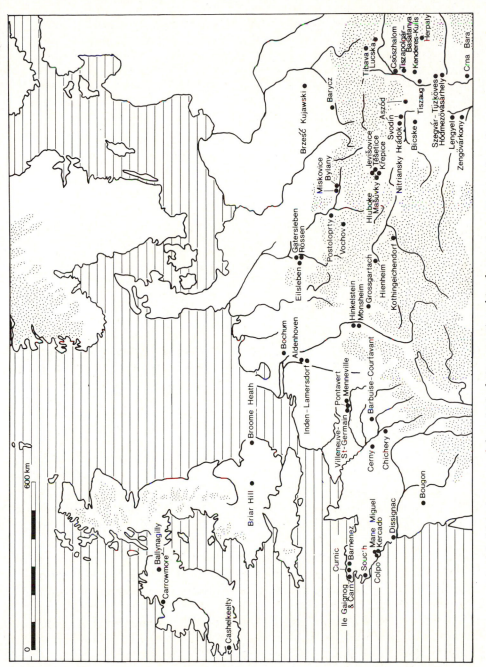

6.1 Simplified location map of the principal sites mentioned in chapter 6.1, c. 4000–35/3400 bc

term fluctuations are possible. The contribution of insect and tree-ring studies lies in the future. In this setting many soils may have been still at the peak of their post-glacial fertility, though there have been suggestions in north-west England for example of natural soil-leaching. Finally sea levels continued to fluctuate under the combined effects of continued ice melt, isostatic recovery and tectonic downwarping as in southern Britain and the Netherlands. The most detailed sequence has been worked out in the Netherlands. Transgression could mean considerable land loss, as in the fens of East Anglia in the earlier third millennium bc, and has resulted in parts in a probably high loss of settlement evidence.[2]

## 6.1 Post-LBK developments: a new diversity, 4000–3500/3400 bc

### Chronology and material sequences

Long vertical stratigraphies are everywhere extremely rare though their lack has been compensated for by short vertical or horizontal stratigraphy, detailed typological studies and to some extent by a rather limited application of radiocarbon dating. Overall the general course of post-Linear pottery developments seems clear though many points of detail remain unresolved (Fig. 6.2). The trend of material culture through the span of the Linear pottery culture was towards regional differentiation, and this continues in the first half millennium after it. Three major regions can be distinguished, again on the main criterion of pottery. In the Great Hungarian plain the Tisza culture succeeds the later Alföld Linear pottery culture, and is typified by a high proportion of elaborately decorated figurines, anthropomorphic and theriomorphic pots, face pots, altars and clay rattles. This decorative elaboration extended also to house exteriors and interiors, as at Hódmezövásárhely–Kökénydomb. Stratified deposits up to 2 m deep provide a basis for periodisation, and sites like Csöszhalom and Herpaly for further late regional differentiation in decorative styles, but none of the sites in question have been either extensively excavated or well published. Succeeding this complex in the same area comes the Tiszapolgár culture, falling in the middle part of the fourth millennium bc, though the point of transition is not exactly established because on the one hand radiocarbon dates are few, and on the other Tiszapolgár sites are generally smaller, more scattered and with thin habitation levels. A good example of the kind of relationship observed is the intersection of a Herpaly pit by a Tiszapolgár grave at the eponymous cemetery of Tiszapolgár–Basatanya. Tiszapolgár pottery consists of undecorated biconical pots and pedestalled bowls, and is essentially uniform over the area. Figurines too are absent, but copper, sparsely represented in the Tisza culture, is more abundant in the form of ornaments and heavier perforated hammer-axes and adzes, and gold pendants are also found.[3]

To the north, from northern Hungary into Slovakia and Moravia on the Pannonian plain and to the west of the Danube, there was an interestingly similar process, in the development of the Lengyel culture, after the

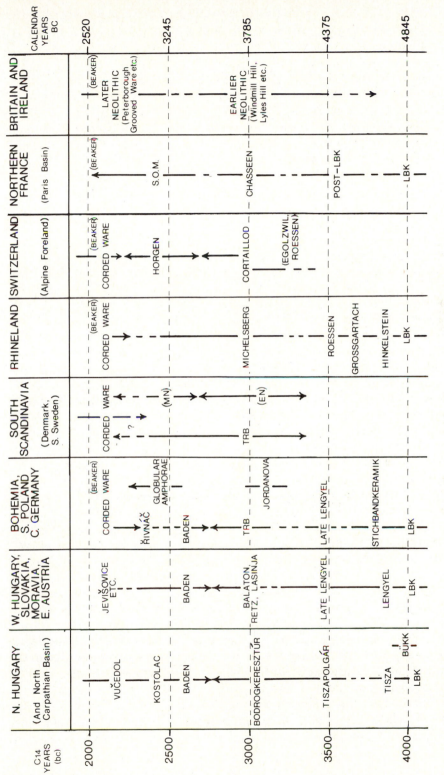

6.2 Simplified outline chronology of the main areas discussed in chapter 6, c. 4000–2200 bc

eponymous site in Tolna county in western Hungary. Characteristic forms were bowls, biconical pots and pedestalled bowls, with typical red, yellow and white painted or encrusted decoration, whose variations have been ordered chronologically into a sequence starting with polychrome painting which developed into combined incised and painted decoration, proceeding thence to white painting, and finally, perhaps around 3500 bc to an abandonment of decoration altogether, as in the Tiszapolgár pottery.

Vertical stratigraphic support is rare, and it is a measure of wider uncertainty that the recent chronological schemes have varied between four and five phases, and in the number of pre- and proto-phases. Radiocarbon dates remain few and further study is required of regional rather than purely temporal variation as well as of key sites such as the settlement and cemetery of Zengövárkony. Spindle-whorls, figurines and house-models seem to continue more southerly traditions.[4]

Over a wide area from Bohemia and southern Poland into central Germany the latest Linear pottery is succeeded by *Stichbandkeramik* or Stroke-ornamented pottery, with bowls and pearshaped bowls evolved from the earlier traditions and decorated with double linear patterns of distinct jabs rather than continuous lines. This pottery is also present in Moravia till succeeded by Lengyel styles. A five-stage development has been proposed on the basis of associations and typology and followed in essentials in the *Saalegebiet*, though supporting stratigraphic and radiocarbon evidence is still required from most areas. In south-east Poland there was an area of overlap between *Stichbandkeramik* and Lengyel traditions. These styles were interestingly again succeeded by a phase of plainer pottery, the so-called late or unpainted Lengyel horizon, found over much the same area and dating perhaps approximately to the mid fourth millennium bc.[5] In the Rhineland and western Germany there was a slightly different sequence. Equivalent to the *Stichbandkeramik* is Hinkelstein pottery, after a cemetery in Kr. Worms, which in turn was succeeded by increasingly elaborately decorated Gross-gartach and Rössen pottery; the sequence has only comparatively recently been established, indicating the poverty of opportunities for reliable stratigraphic observation. In central Germany near Halle the cemetery of Rössen, Kr. Merseburg probably indicates an analogous variation to the Rhineland, though this is at the eastern limits of the distribution and Rössen pottery is poorly dated over the area of its distribution (Fig. 6.3). It may be coeval with plain Gatersleben pottery, with tripartite pots, pedestalled bowls and necked bowls, reminding one that not all variation need be chronological. Indeed Gatersleben pottery has a more restricted distribution, and tends to come from graves. Stone artefacts in this complex now include perforated adzes and hammer-axes, perhaps in imitation of perforated copper artefacts further east. Copper as well as figurines and other ritual paraphernalia are generally absent from the complex.[6]

In the Paris basin of northern France there was a different sequence, as far as it can be reliably established at all on the basis of limited excavations. The general pattern may be for Linear pottery to have persisted longer than

**6.3** Rössen pottery and perforated stone axe from central Germany. *After* Behrens

elsewhere (*Rubané récent*) to be succeeded by a variety of regionalised decorated styles in the earlier or mid fourth millennium bc, first grouped under the general heading of the Cerny group or culture but increasingly viewed as a series of regional and chronological variations. Intensive investigations in the Aisne valley are part of this process, in which a Villeneuve–St Germain group is seen to replace the *Rubané récent*. Radiocarbon dates are few and scattered with evident overlap between the two horizons. Varied ceramic styles (Carn, Souc'h, Colpo) in Brittany may be part of the same process of post-Rubané differentiation. It has also been suggested that the earliest pottery styles of the British Isles can be derived from the post-Linear pottery horizon. Plain pottery of the Lyles Hill style was radiocarbon dated at Ballynagilly, Co. Tyrone, to the earlier fourth millennium bc and by the mid fourth millennium there are dates for Grimston bowl pottery at Briar Hill, Northampton, and Broome Heath, Norfolk. It is not yet clear whether decorated pottery can be dated quite so early (see next section) though this has been suggested likely. Characteristic narrow flake flint industries with distinctive leaf-shaped arrowheads are associated with this early pottery; perforated stone tools, shoe-last adzes, figurines and copper are lacking.[7]

*Settlement and the social context of production, 4000–3500/3400 bc*

Tisza settlement on the Great Hungarian plain followed the trend started in the Szakálhát–Lebö group of the late fifth millennium bc in which settlement became progressively nucleated in the settled areas.[8] Fewer sites appear to be known but those that have been identified are very large, up to 500 by 500 m such as Hódmezővásárhely–Kökénydomb and Szegvár–Tüzköves, and some forming true (though low) tells such as Szeghalom–Kovácshalom. In the Tiszapolgár phase some tells were still occupied, as at Herpaly itself where

Tiszapolgár sherds were found in the upper level. But for the most part settlement seems to have reverted to a more dispersed pattern, with smaller sites of diameter 50–100 m and thin occupation levels, but including rectangular houses, such as Crna Bara, Tibava, and Kenderes–Kulis. It must be emphasised again that there has been little systematic excavation. In both phases settlement was river-oriented. According to the results of unsystematic sampling and recovery cattle were the dominant domesticate in the Tisza phase, while aurochs were prominent especially in the eastern part, and the range of sizes and morphological characteristics may reflect local domestication. In the Tiszapolgár phase cattle remain dominant, and represent almost entirely domestic stock. Horse bones in graves are a striking innovation but their numbers are low. It has been suggested that the appearance of harpoons in the Tisza culture can be equated with a decline in net fishing and hence of fish as a major source of protein. Cereal cultivation is poorly documented but probable. It has been suggested that settlement form and distribution and the economy should be seen as linked, with the export of cattle from socially important nucleated centres in the river valleys and lowlands being important in the Tisza phase. Wider aspects of regional interaction are considered below.

The range, distribution and density of Lengyel settlements have not been closely studied as an integrated whole though it appears that some sites at least in the southern part were large and sited on the upper parts of valley sides and on hilltops. There is also a notable series of enclosure sites currently undergoing more intensive investigation, and both these features strongly suggest expansion of the primary LBK pattern and development towards nucleation or a hierarchy of sites, as is possible also in the Tisza culture. The process may have started in the late LBK phase since an enclosure ditch, at present incompletely published but including at least one terminal or gateway, is assigned to the immediately pre-Lengyel phase at Bicske in western Hungary. At Svodín in Slovakia systematic excavations have revealed two successive early Lengyel enclosure systems, the first with an external ditch up to 3.5 m deep and two internal palisades, the second with two external ditches up to 5 m deep and three internal palisade and fence systems. Both are roughly oval. The second with a maximum diameter of about 160 m encloses the first. Both presumably had four opposed entrances though in fact it has been only possible so far to excavate three in each. Settlement traces are not represented inside the ditches, but outside in the area excavated to the west there are numerous timber long-houses of characteristic Lengyel type (with fewer internal postholes than in the LBK) and accompanying pits. If the whole area around were to be excavated, it seems likely that a very large settlement would be represented. In addition there were numerous graves distributed amongst the settlement area. The internal chronology of the settlement area is far from clear, but the whole site belongs to the early Lengyel phase.[9]

Further north-west in southern Moravia at the site of Hluboké Mašůvky a ditch up to 2.8 m deep and 4.5 m wide encloses an area of some 6 ha with a maximum diameter of 350 m. The ditch has several interruptions and is backed by two internal palisades and gateways. At Křepice an elliptical enclosure (50–60 m across the shorter axis) was formed by a ditch and three internal palisades, and occupation material was found both inside and outside the enclosed area. At Těšetice–Kyjovice too a circular enclosure was only part of a larger site (Fig. 6.4). A circular ditch 55–60 m in diameter was broken by four opposed entrances and two internal palisades, the innermost less continuous than its pair. The V-shaped ditch itself was up to 6 m wide and 3.5 m deep. There is *Stichbandkeramik* pottery on the site but the monument belongs to the early Lengyel phase. Settlement traces were not found inside the enclosure but extended beyond it, and include a further length of palisade some 40 m distant. The large numbers of anthropomorphic and animal figurines, mainly from the ditch of the enclosure, could support the interpretation that this was a high-status site, with settlement attached and with importance as ritual centre.[10] This notion requires testing against the range of other settlements. These include large sites like Lengyel, Zengö-várkony, and Aszód, which all have large cemeteries attached and lie in varied positions in the landscape, the first on a hill some distance from the nearest river valley.[11] Comprehensive mapping and analysis however is required to back up this impression of considerable change in Transdanubia and the Pannonian plain. Another uncertainty concerns the later Lengyel

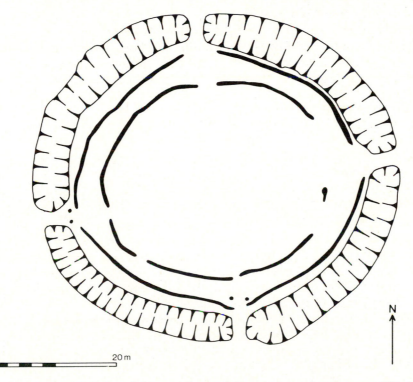

0        20 m

N

**6.4** Simplified plan of the central part of the early Lengyel enclosure at Těšetice–Kyjovice, southern Moravia, Czechoslovakia. *After* Podborský

phase. The large enclosures seem to be absent, and the best-known sites seem to be smaller and less concentrated, as in and around Nitra.[12] This problem is returned to below.

Further north, the impression is of greater continuity with the LBK. In Bohemia the *Stichbandkeramik* pattern remains riverine with in fact some contraction of settlement and fewer apparent scattered sites. Much the same features were observed in the central German *Saalegebiet*, and in the south-east Polish area of mixed *Stichbandkeramik* and earlier Lengyel traditions similar continuity was also found by Kruk in his settlement survey, with some slight increase in the size and density of sites, and use of uplands flanking the valleys.[13] Two sites discussed in chapter 3 may exemplify this continuity. At Bylany in Bohemia there were far fewer *Stichbandkeramik* remains in the main LBK area excavated, but these include large trapezoidal long-houses with fewer internal posts and bowed sides, and one 25 m stretch of large closely spaced postholes with a funnel-like entrance. However a little to the west near the adjacent village of Miskovice there is a cemetery of this phase, a double-ditched enclosure, and further indications of settlement in the form of pits. Excavation has not yet been extensive in this part of the vast site. At Hienheim in Bavaria the *Stichbandkeramik* houses are more scattered than those of the LBK phase, but include at least six and possibly eight houses, of considerable size and trapezoidal plan.[14] The best preserved, no. 15, is about 20 m long and 4–7.5 m broad. Various possibilities arise from such sites. While there may be continuity with the Linear pottery culture, there may also be contraction and nucleation of settlement (seen also in some areas in the overall pattern of settlement). Other kinds of sites such as the enclosures of Vochov in Bohemia or Kothingeichendorf in Bavaria could reinforce a picture of some change from the Linear pottery culture, though both sites also have LBK material on them as well. Vochov has two ditched enclosures, 36 and 49 m in diameter, the inner backed by three palisades. Kothingeichendorf has twin ditches about 70 m in diameter with four opposed entrances and discontinuous traces of an outer stockade, and other long stretches of double and triple ditch. It must also be said that, despite a few late LBK enclosures as at Eilsleben, Kr. Wansleben with a single 3 m deep ditch, there was not in this broad area the same kind of site differentiation seen in the southern Lengyel area.[15]

The change in house type persisted into the late Lengyel horizon, one of the few examples at Bylany for instance (no. 500) being 19 by 9 m with an apsidal narrow end. Another well-known example comes from house no. 15 at Postoloprty in Bohemia, notable for its length (33 m) and the four internal features interpreted as hearths, though this has been doubted.[16] Other examples come from Brześć Kujawski in southern Poland on the edge of the Vistula valley.[17] This is a large site with many superimposed house plans and a recent study has sought to isolate the basic unit of the site, which may consist of trapezoidal longhouse and its flanking borrow pits, and other associated pits and graves at a distance of up to 20 m from the house. The house illustrated here (Fig. 6.5) may belong in fact either to the end of this

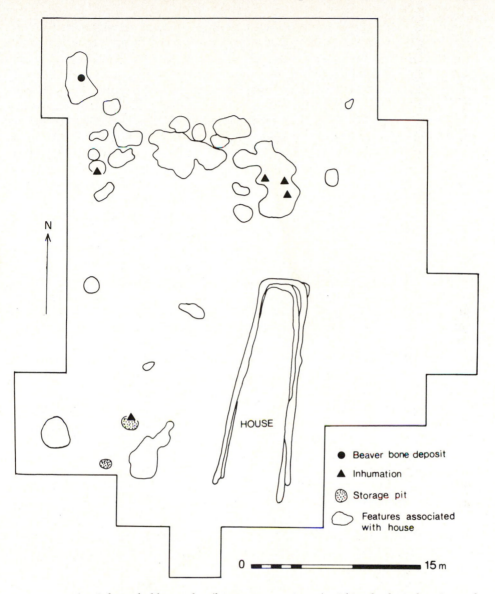

N

HOUSE

● Beaver bone deposit

▲ Inhumation

⊕ Storage pit

◯ Features associated
with house

0 ▬▬▬▬▬▬▬▬▬▬▬ 15 m

**6.5** A household complex (house no. 42, site III) within the large late Lengyel settlement at Brześć Kujawski, central Poland. *After* Bogucki and Grygiel

phase or the beginning of the next. Kruk's study of southern Polish settlement suggests some change in the late Lengyel phase. While settlement remained basically valley-oriented, there are some slight signs of nucleation seen in slightly larger sites, of an overall broader distribution of settlement, and of more upland use.

The same trends are not visible in central Germany but may be more accentuated in the Rhineland though identical problems of fewer and smaller sites have made the horizon difficult to study. The distribution of Rössen settlement, while overlapping that of the LBK, for the most part seems to be extended slightly beyond it, with sites slightly higher up the valleys in areas of relief and also to a slightly lesser extent on loess soils and also at the other extreme lower into the main valleys and perhaps also beyond the northern margin of the loess on to more sandy soils.[18] On the Aldenhoven plateau one Rössen site has been excavated close to the Merzbach, and consisted of at least nine trapezoidal houses spread in four foci over 120 by 60 m, with further traces beyond (Fig. 6.6). There are lengths of shallow ditch and palisade to the north and south of the site though these do not form an enclosure. The trapezoidal houses with additional external buttressing posts, fewer internal posts and well-defined front portion range in length from 9 to 30 m, five being from 18 to 30 m, and four from 9 to 12 m. At nearby Inden–Lamersdorf several similar houses were more closely grouped and delimited on one side by a strong palisade. Here again there may be a trend towards settlement nucleation, contrasting with the dispersed homesteads of the LBK phase, though periodisation of the sites has not been attempted in the same detail. Other larger Rössen houses, apparently isolated, have been recorded in the Rhineland, as at Bochum–Hiltrop, where an example 50 m long adjoins

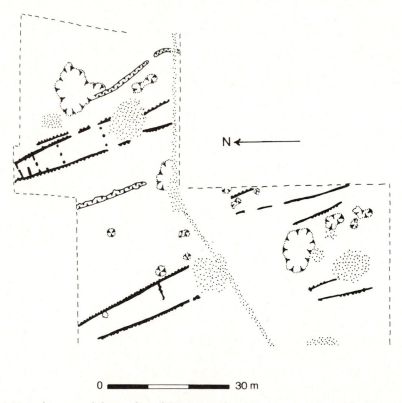

N ←

0 ■■■■■■■■■ 30 m

**6.6** Main features of the nucleated Rössen settlement at Langweiler, Aldenhoven Plateau, near Köln. *After* Jurgens

two adjacent palisaded or fenced enclosures. These again could reflect different units of settlement. There is also a small number of Grossgartach and Rössen enclosures, such as Langweiler XII with ditch and internal palisade and perhaps Bochum–Harpen, and Monsheim on a much larger scale, though the existence of ditched enclosures of the late LBK (see chapter 3) precludes these from being an original development in this phase.[19] The Paris basin has yielded fragments which may parallel the processes more visible in the Rhineland, such as Cerny itself with its valley-edge setting or Pontavert in the Aisne with trapezoidal houses and stout palisade, and the extension of settlement southwards beyond the Loire. Study of early settlement in Brittany has been extremely limited, restricted to the coastal distribution of megalithic monuments and the occasional occupation traces which they cover (e.g. at Dissignac near the mouth of the Loire), and rare and poorly preserved open settlements such as Curnic-en-Guisseny on loess soil on the north coast.[20]

Over this whole area from Moravia to the Paris basin subsistence data are disappointingly scarce, and few sites have been systematically investigated for plant remains or bones, and many areas of the loess do not have well-preserved bone. Thus at Heinheim only 104 bones were recovered in association with *Stichbandkeramik* features, though they do show the same range of species as before: cattle, pig and ovicaprids and some 'wild' animals. A relative increase in pigs is reported in the late Lengyel phase. Unusual preservation of animal bone was found in recent excavations at Brześć Kujawski (spanning the mid to later fourth millennium bc), and revealed an increased importance for pig and sheep alongside cattle, as well as substantial use of fish, birds and game. There was also increased representation of cereal remains compared with the LBK phase.[21] Cereal cultivation is likely to have continued everywhere, and is represented in a new area on the northern coast and hinterland of Brittany. The range of crops used may be the same as in the LBK, though any statement of this kind could be radically changed by future research. In the Rhineland for example it seems that barley was now consistently cultivated along with wheat, unlike in the LBK phase, and spelt and bread wheat as well as emmer and einkorn are now represented; on the other hand pulses were not recorded at the Aldenhoven settlement, though found on several LBK sites.[22] Such changes could be connected with a wider zone of settlement, in which it could be argued that animals would have played a larger role than in the LBK garden system, but this brings us back to the social context of production, and without evidence comparable even to the unsystematically recovered Hungarian data it is difficult to even outline that context. It has been usual to see expansion of the zones of settlement as directly related to population increase but without further comment; if the relationship is valid such increase should yield information about the nature of social relations – presumably therefore expansive and competitive – and settlement spread along with increasing differentiation of types of site could indicate the same sort of social context. From this perspective population increase could be seen as an effect rather than as a cause of social change.[23]

The discussion below develops these possibilities in considering a wider range of evidence.

Finally the case of the British Isles deserves brief separate mention. Arguments for indigenous development have already been presented in chapter 4, and here the alternative possibility of population movement from the changing post-LBK situation on the adjacent continent should be mooted. In this putative pioneering phase of the earlier fourth millennium bc, settlement appears to have been dispersed and isolated, on the basis of occasional 'pre-elm decline' disturbances of forest cover recorded in pollen analyses and of very rare settlement traces such as the few pits and hearths at Ballynagilly, Co. Tyrone. It is possible that some megalithic monuments as at Carrowmore, Co. Sligo, belong to this horizon. Subsistence data are scanty. The pollen evidence suggests small forest clearings. Cereal pollen has been identified as early as the earlier fourth millennium bc at Cashelkeelty, Co. Kerry, south-west Ireland, but this is not common in profiles at this date. The poor dispersal of cereal pollen is a hindrance to investigating this early stage. Since identified foci of early activity are not confined to fertile lowland soils, a broad range of resources may have been exploited. Shellfish in the Carrowmore tombs and the Oronsay middens (*contra* chapter 4) could belong here. Evidence for animal exploitation is unfortunately lacking. By 3500 bc sites of other kinds start to appear, such as the lowland open sites of Broome Heath, Norfolk, and the ditched enclosure at Briar Hill, Northampton, in the Nene Valley, and this fully established settlement is considered in the discussion of the next phase.[24]

## Social relations: ritual and burial, 4000–3500/3400 bc

When a wider range of evidence is considered the contrasts already hinted at between regions are further accentuated, and a variety of contradictions within each region may be visible. This is not a period of social uniformity across the wide area studied, and indeed the area provides a further fascinating case study in the uneven nature of social evolution. To start with the Great Hungarian plain as a link between the Balkans and the rest of temperate Europe, in the Tisza phase there was considerable elaboration not just of decorated pottery but of ritual paraphernalia as well. The exuberant decoration was extended to buildings as well, some of which are seen as containing shrines; one example at Hódmezövásárhely–Kökénydomb had an unusual setting of stone axes with their cutting edges upward set in the floor of its interior. There was considerable centralisation of settlement. Artefacts were exchanged or moved in some quantities (discussed further below) and regional interaction could also have involved the large-scale domestication and export of cattle to surrounding areas. Burials were still made (as in much of the Balkans) within the settlements or abandoned parts of them, with few grave goods deposited (pots, shells, rings and a little copper), but with some male–female differentiation. This aspect might be reflected in the more prominent role of male figurines. One interpretation of the situation has focused on the economic factor of cattle export and regional exchange but a still wider perspective and some comparison with the Balkans could be considered.[25] Centralised settlement and ritual elaboration can be matched in the later Vinča culture, its contemporary to the south (see chapter 5), and some mutual influence is possible. As in that case too, many of the above features suggest a social situation of considerable tension and competition, both at a local and a regional level, which several of them may have sought to conceal. The economic factor can indeed be reintroduced here, for it may have provided greater opportunities for group or community differentiation than were usually available.

By contrast with the later Vinča culture however resolution of these putative contradictions came sooner. In the Tiszapolgár phase settlement reverted to smaller units in a more dispersed pattern. Ritual paraphernalia disappeared, with the figurines strikingly absent for the first time; plain pottery was rather uniform over the whole area. The further striking change comes in the burial record. Some burials continued within settlements but cemeteries separate from settlements appeared, most strikingly at Tiszapolgár–Basatanya, where at least 59 graves (others have been lost) belong to the Tiszapolgár phase (Fig. 6.7), but in several other cases as well ranging from a few graves only at Lucska to over 40 at Tibava. The potential distance between settlement and cemetery may vary from a few metres as at Tibava, to 2 km as at Tiszaug but the evidence is of doubtful reliability. No Tiszapolgár settlement was identified at Tiszapolgár–Basatanya itself, though the site includes settlement traces of the LBK and Baden phases. At Tiszapolgár the burials, which included men, women and children, were set in simple rectangular graves, arranged in rows, on a west–east orientation, with men on their right sides and women on their left. Perhaps two graves lacked bodies, and all but one or two had grave goods with them. The range of these goods was wide and included pottery, clay, bone and antler artefacts, flint, obsidian and stone, copper ornaments, and shell and limestone beads. A further interesting association was that of pig mandibles (of wild and domesticated boar and domesticated sows) and tusks, found exclusively with male burials; only two male burials lacked such mandibles. Further differences within the buried population as measured by grave goods were not very marked; both men and women received the same sort of ornaments (including copper), and tools, though men only had weapons such as stone hammer-axes and arrowheads, and non-adults were less well furnished. It is important to realise that the burial rite is not uniform through the area of the culture, and new examples continue to come to light, as most recently at Vel'ke Raskovče or Tiszavalk–Teteşti. Some graves have horse bones which are seen as a long-range, high-status novelty, accessible only to elite groups, and the nature of the resolution has been interpreted in terms of increased social hierarchy.[26] If so, the stresses suggested in the Tisza phase may have been solved by the emergence of dominant local groups able to command access to prestige goods and needing to bolster their newly achieved position by new rites and ideology. If this sort of hypothesis is followed, it is of great

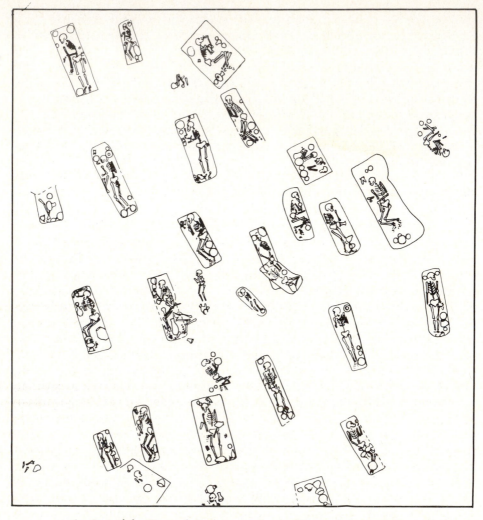

**6.7** Part of the Tiszapolgár phase cemetery at Tiszapolgár–Basatanya in the Great Hungarian plain. *After* Bognár-Kutzián

interest to note that this is the earliest resolution of this kind in the Balkans and east-central Europe, though it has been suggested that the Vinča social system began to encounter stress and decline from about this date and in its turn changed profoundly before those of the eastern Balkans.[27] Such an interpretation is not without difficulties or alternatives. It remains dangerous to 'read off' social change directly from the burial record. Despite the appearance of objects which can be seen as prestige goods such as shafthole copper hammer-axes and adzes (and perhaps also local working on the basis of a copper ingot in grave 59 at Tiszapolgár–Basatanya), these are represented in the burial record of the Lucska (and perhaps Deszk) group only; gold ornaments are restricted to the Tibava cemetery. Separate cemeteries and prestige goods could be seen to reinforce a measure of decentralisation and local autonomy as much as the emergence at this stage of clear local hierarchies. But there remains a sense in which individual or group position seems now a far greater matter of concern than before. The old ritual ideology was abandoned; prestige copper objects were circulated and even locally manufactured; men adopted animal tokens or totems; burials were laid out at Tiszapolgár–Basatanya in careful rows, which whether chronologically successive or perhaps related to different groups or families, seems to show more conscious concern with group membership. These developments are in fact one of the best illustrations of one of the underlying themes of the book, that the nature of prehistoric social evolution in Europe is not easily predictable, and that social evolution did not run along the same path at the same rate in all areas.

The Lengyel culture immediately provides a useful contrast and comparison. In the earlier phase there is a wealth of elaborately decorated pottery and ritual paraphernalia, and there are preliminary indications from sites such as Těšetice that figurines may be most concentrated at large sites which in several cases incorporate a variety of impressive enclosures. These various elements can be seen as due to both centralisation and an increase in social tension and conflict accompanying it. At the same time separate cemeteries appear in the southern part of the Lengyel area, as at Lengyel, Zengővárkony, Aszód, and also Svodín in Slovakia; in most of Slovakia however and further north much smaller numbers of burials seem the rule, and more closely integrated with settlements. Such graves are numerous. There is an estimate of some 90 at Lengyel, and there were nearly 400 and 200 at Zengővárkony and Aszód respectively, the former spread out over a large area some 300 by 200 m and arranged in clusters. Single inhumation was dominant, and men, women and children are represented. A wide range of grave goods were deposited including pottery, ornaments (including occasional copper) and also perforated stone hammer-axes, though little detailed attention has yet been paid to the variations in Lengyel rites and grave associations. At Zengővárkony, only 47 graves had preserved skeletal material; within this sample some differentiation between men and women has been observed with men more often having tools alone as grave goods than women, women more often having ornaments alone than men, but both sexes share assemblages of both tools and ornaments.[28] It may be suggested that in the southern Lengyel area there was a more Balkan-like situation, with a series of unresolved contradictions between hierarchy and communal ideology, seen in the range of settlement types, the emergence of prestige goods, the elaboration of ritual sites and paraphernalia, and the symbolism of exclusion in enclosures and separate cemeteries, but without yet at this stage any clear resolution or reordering of these different strands in society. It remains to be established whether in the later Lengyel phase there was significant change. The enclosures as we have seen at Svodín and elsewhere seem to be earlier rather than later. The shift to plain pottery in Slovakia has been equated chronologically with the appearance of Tiszapolgár pottery and might be taken also to have similar portent for social change, though the unpainted horizon has been doubted in western Hungary. Small scattered sites may be more the rule, as in and around Nitra in Slovakia, but we lack sufficient other evidence to compare the situation properly with the Tiszapolgár culture.

Further north in the remaining Lengyel area and the *Stichbandkeramik* area there is less obvious change from the LBK settlement pattern and range of site types. Shafthole adzes and hammer-axes in the *Stichbandkeramik* culture can be seen as an elaboration of existing types resulting in more distinctive and, in terms of labour, more costly, prestige objects. Cemeteries continued in the Rhineland, as at Hinkelstein, Kr. Worms itself (reminding one that the existence of cemeteries has to be seen in context), and in central Germany. The recent discovery of a large *Stichbandkeramik* cemetery at Miskovice near Bylany in Bohemia is another case in point. For the most part burial rite and the range of grave goods are much as before, and the distribution of figurines and other occasional cult objects does not show any obvious spatial clustering.[29] In southern Poland in the Cracow district there are middle Lengyel (Pleszow group) salt pans comprising ditches and sumps at the site of Barycz, and there are other sites around rock-salt sources at Wieliczka and Bochnia.[30] The production of salt may have been for local purposes, but it is possible that it too was part of a flow of goods of which artefacts are more obvious survivors, just as cattle were suggested to be an invisible export in the Tisza phase of the Great Hungarian plain. There may be a little more perceptible change in the middle of the fourth millennium bc (as far as the chronology allows one to say). In Little Poland the white-painted group of the Sandomierz area (though poorly dated) has figurines and copper ornaments in its range of material culture, though still only small groups of graves as at Zlota. Further down the Vistula, the Brześć Kujawski later Lengyel group (if not dated a little later) also acquired copper, deposited as ornaments as in the graves at Brześć Kujawski itself. Here at site IV there were 39 burials as well as 51 longhouses, but the cemetery is not really self-contained nor separate, and analysis of the smaller site III suggests that burials were still made in relation to individual longhouses. In central Germany the inventories of inhumation graves at Rössen itself were richer and more varied than in the LBK, with men having axes, adzes and arrow-heads and women having bracelets as distinctive goods. If the spatially more restricted but plain Gatersleben pottery style is contemporary with Rössen material in central Germany, there is further interesting differentiation which might have significance in this direction. But this is again difficult to study without coherent settlement excavations; at Rössen itself for example it is the cemetery of 90–100 graves which has been investigated though a settlement nearby is known. In the Rhineland Rössen burials are rare, and the cemetery tradition thus fades after the Grossgartach phase.

In the Paris basin there may be a similar development, with the small cemetery of seven burials at Chichèry having one radiocarbon date of the earlier mid fourth millennium bc but later examples being not yet apparent.[31] Ditched enclosures may be represented in the post-LBK horizon as at Bar-

**6.8** View of the restored facade of the Barnenez cairn, Finistère, Brittany. Photo: author

buise–Courtavant in the Yonne and Berry-au-Bac in the Aisne. In Brittany and the British Isles the only well-documented aspect of society marks a new development, but one which is not at this stage easy to study for the lack of evidence for other aspects. In Brittany at the sites of Barnenez (Fig. 6.8), Mané Miguel, Île Gaignog, and Kercado, south of the Loire at Bougon, and in Co. Sligo at Carrowmore there are stone-built barrows or cairns incorporating passages and chambers which may have held burials, whose construction may be radiocarbon dated to the early fourth millennium bc.[32] Caution is appropriate since several French dates are derived from old samples, the date for Carrowmore site IV is derived from a sample underneath one of the stones of the central cist or chamber, and no site has a large series of dates. But in the French case at least the fact that there are other sites dated to little later, such as Île Carn and Colpo in the mid fourth millennium bc, does support the validity of the early dates. A similar series can be argued for the British Isles though the dating evidence is sparser. Barnenez is a vast trapezoidal stone cairn 70 m long reconstructed as rising in a series of irregular steps and incorporating 11 round chambers built either out of dry-stone walling or with large upright stones; it is probable that its eastern half with five chambers is primary. Île Gaignog IIIc is also trapezoidal with four circular chambers. The huge earthen and stone mound covering cists at Mané Miguel (if this early – another date is late fourth) and the circular mound with square chamber and kerb at Kercado provide further variation. The circular cairn of Carrowmore 4 has already been described in chapter 4. The central chamber and passage here contained 11 kg of cremated human bone, and there were a further 11.5 kg in two quadrants of the mound, perhaps disturbed or thrown out, and it is generally assumed that the Breton monuments held inhumations since disappeared in acid soil conditions (and see next section). The combination of imposing free-standing architecture and burial must have had powerful symbolic importance. Their significance may lie mostly in a further separation of burial from settlement, analogous to the Tiszapolgár and Lengyel developments in central Europe or the elaboration of Rössen inventories in central Germany, and in this case the long debate about origins matters far less than the regional context. Origins canvassed include Mesolithic traditions, these in combination with LBK technology, the symbolic representation of the LBK tradition houses, and similar developments in Iberia, but it is the role the monuments played which is important.[33] With so little evidence for this early stage it is impossible to choose between alternative suggestions such as symbolic foci of communal identity, actual territorial markers with the dead as ancestors to reinforce claims to resources and social position, or a means of masking communal fission.[34]

Just as there was elsewhere a further break-up of Linear pottery ceramic uniformity in the earlier fourth millennium bc, so in Brittany and the British Isles the meagre evidence suggests distinctive pottery styles. It is not yet clear however whether this was due to indigenous acculturation, the social conditions of colonisation, or the further use of material culture by either natives or colonists as a means of reinforcing a new identity.

## 6.2 Regional variations on the theme of social difference, 35/3400–2600/2500 bc

*Chronology and material sequences, 35/3400–26/2500 bc*

In general the same comments as before can be made about the chronology of this area in the next period to be covered, in that good stratigraphies are no commoner and many sites lack adequate radiocarbon dating (Fig. 6.9). There are however some grounds for optimism. First, radiocarbon dates are relatively more numerous here, as can be seen in a number of date lists for various regions; lists which do include some sites with series of dates.[35] Secondly, settlement was extended into areas which offer now the opportunity to achieve dendrochronologies through waterlogged wood from occupation sites, notably on the north Alpine foreland. The potential has been apparent in Switzerland for 20 years and has gradually been realised. At the same time other regional dendrochronologies are coming into existence on the basis of wood recovered from river valleys and bogs, as in the Rhine, northern and central Ireland and south-west England, such that in westcentral Europe the dendrochronology extends back to 4057 BC, with three further 'floating sequences' extending as far back as 8518 bp.[36]

On the Great Hungarian plain and its fringes the Bodrogkeresztúr culture

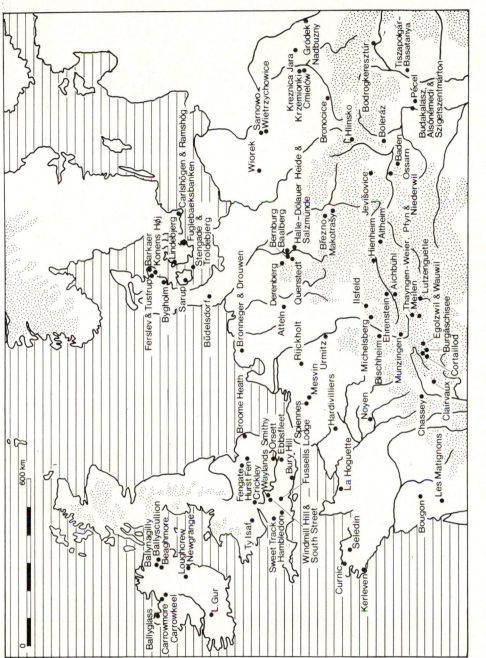

6.9 Simplified location map of the principal sites mentioned in chapter 6.2, c. 35/3400–26/2500 bc

succeeds the Tiszapolgár culture. The replacement is gradual and the relationship is stratigraphically documented. The cemetery at Tiszapolgár–Basatanya illustrates these features, among other sites. Bodrogkeresztúr material continues Tiszapolgár traditions with plain grave pottery, a continued absence of figurines, and copper and gold objects, but settlement pottery with impression, incision and white encrustation is an innovation. At an uncertain point due to the paucity of radiocarbon dates, but perhaps around 2700 bc, Bodrogkeresztúr is succeeded by the Baden culture.[37] This culture or complex is variously known, after eponymous sites such as Baden and Pécel in Hungary or Ossarn in Austria, or the character of its ceramic decoration as the Radial decorated pottery or Channelled ware culture, and extends beyond the plain to northern Yugoslavia, north-east Austria, most of Czechoslovakia, and southern Poland. The most complete of several stratigraphic cases is perhaps Jevišovice in Moravia where in layer CI putative early Baden material overlies developed TRB (see below) material; it is indicative of the uncertainties involved that this site is an early twentieth-century excavation in far from ideal circumstances. Another proposed early site is Boleráz in western Slovakia though there is no general consensus about fine periodisation. Later Baden periods are described in the next section. Baden pottery includes a wide range of bowls, cups and jugs, the latter with high protruding ribbon handles; channelled decoration is dominant with also incision, impression, ribbons and even encrustation. Copper is much rarer than before, with small axes, awls, wire and tube ornaments; the Vörs diadem is notable. A few flat figurines and anthropomorphic pots are known.[38]

To the north the Lengyel sequence ends with the plain pottery Ludanice phase in Czechoslovakia, and seems to be succeeded in Bohemia by the Jordanowa group, which is also found in Silesia and central Germany, though its position and status are not fully clear. This in turn may overlap the beginning of the TRB culture (*Trichterrandbecher* or funnel-necked beaker) which extends from Czechoslovakia and Poland through Germany to the Netherlands and southern Scandinavia, a distribution often broken down into five areas, north, west, south, east, and south-east. Each area has its own chronology which to a certain extent is independent of the rest of the complex.[39] The duration of the TRB is also varied from region to region, being replaced by Baden in the south-eastern area, while being complemented from the mid third millennium bc onwards in the eastern and southern areas by the Globular amphorae culture and from a little later in all areas by the Corded ware culture. The northern chronology however has been dominant and influential, with its proposed early phase of plain bowls, followed by successive decorative styles. Stratigraphic proof of the sequence has been difficult to provide, and the pottery from individual sites has long been subject to being placed in local typological sequences, with individual sites representing phases from ENC onwards. Some awareness has been shown of possible spatial (rather than temporal) variation but as in many other schemes the passage of time has been seen as the main cause of ceramic and other artefactual variation.[40] The application of radiocarbon dating has not supported the fine detail of the scheme since there is considerable overlap between phases, though the overall trend of the scheme is supported. The stratified pottery from the ditches of the enclosure at Sarup on Fyn also provides support for the MN I–II sequence but this is perhaps the first real stratigraphic test so far published despite various refinements of the scheme.[41] Differences between settlements and graves have not been extensively investigated. The Danish scheme has been influential particularly on Czech and Dutch workers. The western *Tiefstichkeramik* for example is seen to start late and run parallel to the Danish MN I–V phases, though the scheme is supported stratigraphically only (and this not wholly satisfactorily) by the fill of *hunebed* D21 at Bronneger. A recent synthesis even rejects an early or pre-Drouwen phase proposed on the basis of finds outside the peristalith of *hunebed* Drouwen D20 even though there are palynological indications of agricultural activity in the northern Netherlands by around 3000 bc.[42]

TRB pottery includes a wide range of bowls, carinated bowls, jars, flasks and amphorae, with handled jugs in the southern, eastern and south-eastern groups, and pedestalled bowls in the Salzmünde group (Fig. 6.10) from the alleged middle phase of the southern group.[43] Decoration is sparse in pro-

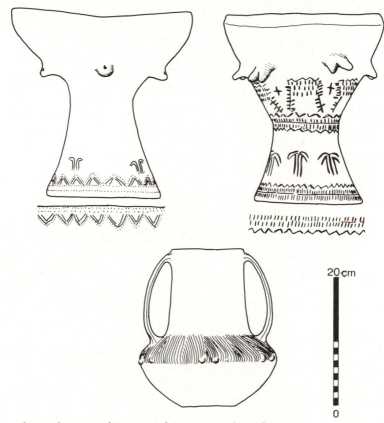

**6.10** Salzmünde pottery from central Germany. *After* Behrens

posed early phases but more abundant from ENC onwards (and the basis for the definition of some local variation it must be admitted) and on *Tiefstich-keramik*, and also from the Wiorek and Salzmünde phases onwards (Fig. 6.11). There was a wide range of heavy stone implements including chipped and polished flint axes, polygonal perforated 'battle-axes' and perforated and unperforated maceheads with knobbed ends (Fig. 6.12). Copper was locally worked in the south-eastern group (as at the settlements of Ćmielów and Gródek Nadbużny, of the late fourth and early third millennia bc), and axes, chisels, awls and ornaments were produced. Copper artefacts are known from the eastern and southern groups, especially simple ornaments, but were perhaps not locally manufactured. Copper was also distributed but not locally worked in the northern and western areas, as in the Bygholm ENC hoard of flat axes and ornaments, or the Buinen spiral ornament.[44]

In the Rhineland several regional styles are proposed to fill a late Rössen horizon such as Bischheim, Aichbühl, Bischoffingen, Wauwil and Schwieberdingen in the later fourth millennium bc though none is closely dated. Some at least overlap (such as Bischheim pottery) with the

**6.11** TRB pottery (ENC and early MN) from Denmark. Photo: National Museum, Copenhagen

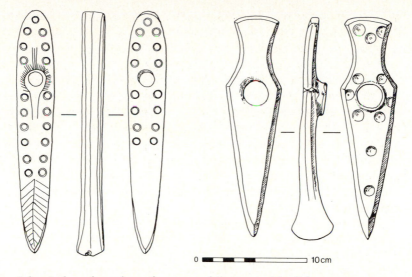

0 ▬▬▬▬▬▬▬▬▬ 10 cm

**6.12** Salzmünde perforated axes from central Germany. *After* Behrens

Michelsberg culture radiocarbon dated from the later fourth to the mid third millennium in the Rhineland and Belgium.[45] In this there is a wide range of cups, bowls, carinated bowls, 'tulip-beakers', jars and so on, elaborately typologised recently, and the basis for some regional differentiation. Five phases of development are proposed but while there is apparently stratigraphic support for the MK I–II succession at Ilsfeld, Kr. Heilbronn there are many other cases of assemblages composed of material from allegedly separate phases. Flint and stone axes are known but not perforated forms or battle-axes, and there is no copper. The Michelsberg culture was contemporary with others to the south, such as the Altheim culture in southern Germany, the Pfyn culture of north-east Switzerland and environs or the Cortaillod culture of western Switzerland. The Pfyn culture has distinctive if undistinguished mainly flat-based pottery, with jars and handled jugs predominant, mostly plain except for surface rustication. There are perforated stone battle-axes, and copper was locally worked, perhaps from eastern Alpine raw material, to produce awls, daggers and flat axes.[46] Internal periodisation has proved problematic despite stratified sites such as Thayngen–Weier. Varied success is evident in Switzerland. For example the Lutzenguetle group in the Alpine Rhine valley is not well dated, the supposedly primary Egolzwil group with flat-based pottery and Wauwil assocations might only be a regional variation and an earlier periodisation of Cortaillod pottery into early and late has been amalgamated into a classic phase, with a wide range of bowls, carinated bowls and jars including birchbark decoration, followed by a more poorly defined evolved stage.[47] On the other hand dendrochronology allows great precision; the Cortaillod site of Seeberg, Burgäschisee-Süd falls between the two Pfyn settlements of Thayngen–Weier. A caveat on dendrochronology may be pertinent. The event thus dated is the death of a tree (as in radiocarbon dating) rather than the span of its use and re-use in settlement, and there is evidence from Niederwil to suggest that felling phases and settlement phases were not rigidly parallel.[48]

In northern France the post-LBK traditions are succeeded by the northern Chasseen culture in the later fourth millennium which is also found in newly settled areas of east-central France.[49] There is a wide range of plain bowl pottery, with decoration confined to 'vase supports'. The recent sequence from Compiègne is rare. Pottery from sites such as Vallon des Vaux in newly settled parts of the Jura belongs more to the Cortaillod tradition. There is further variation in Breton coastal styles and bowl styles in central-western France. Flint and stone axes are found in all these areas, but perforated forms are lacking, as well as copper. In the British Isles there is much further ceramic variation. Decorated bowl styles are radiocarbon dated from the later fourth millennium bc in southern England and other decorated styles from northern and western Scotland respectively are probably as old. Some functional variation has been recognised. Of the range of Irish styles only the coarsely impressed Carrowkeel bowls were deposited in the chambers of passage graves. There has been great caution in chronological orderings after an early suggestion that decorated styles succeeded plain ones in southern England and only the Ebbsfleet decorated bowl style is seen as a clear innovation, in the earlier third millennium bc. Other material includes abundant flint and stone axes, and distinctive leaf-shaped flint arrowheads.[50]

### Settlement and subsistence, 3500/3400–2600/2500 bc

Within the framework thus created there is a rich and varied range of settlement evidence and, though the data are regionally patchy, some of the insights offered must count amongst the best covered in this book. In the Bodrogkeresztúr culture the kind of settlement documented follows that of the Tiszapolgár culture, with small dispersed and not very longlived sites recorded, though few have been systematically investigated, such as Tarnabod. There is some sign of relative depopulation or less visible settlement in the central part of the plain. A more radical change is evident in the Baden culture, from perhaps around 2700 bc onwards, though the rate of transition is not well documented. Settlement was extended greatly both within areas such as the Great Hungarian plain and into surrounding hilly areas. The more upland sites are provided with enclosures or defences consisting of palisade, ditch or bank. A recent spectacular example is the site of Hlinsko near Lipnik in the upper Morava valley, where there were impressive fortifications on a small hilltop spur, consisting of first a palisade, ditch and entrance gate and then of stone- and wood-revetted rampart and ditch. The latest occupation dates from the end of the 'classical' Baden phase. Huts were recorded in the interior and the special nature of the site is reinforced by evidence for craft production (stone, textiles and pottery), exchange and ritual. The textile evidence at this site is in the form of many spindlewhorls, loomweights and also seeds of flax, but elsewhere, as on the Great Hungarian plain, there is a marked increase in numbers of sheep (which are also included in the Hlinsko fauna though in small numbers). This may indicate a greater importance for wool. Horses appear in limited numbers. It has been suggested that milk was another 'secondary animal product' which achieved new importance in this horizon seen indirectly in the form of handled drinking cups and mugs. Cattle were important in a second aspect, as providers of traction. There are paired cattle burials in the Baden cemeteries at Budakalasz and Alsónémedi and small clay models of four-wheeled vehicles, one at Budakalasz, buried in a separate grave in the cemetery, and another from a grave at Szigetszentmárton (Fig. 6.13).

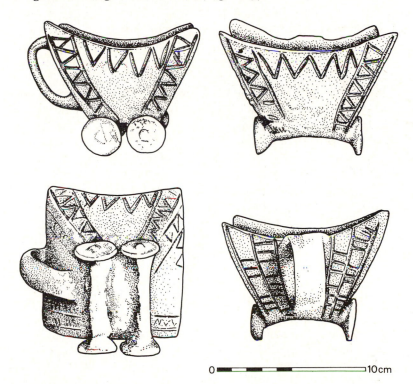

**6.13** Wagon model or cup from the Baden grave at Szigetszentmárton, near Budapest, northern Hungary. *After* Kalicz

The plough has been linked with wheeled transport as part of a traction complex derived from the Near East but there is no direct evidence for it in the Baden area.[51] The notion of a unified technological and economic complex raises several issues. First, there is the question of the nature of the evidence. There is a danger in relying on pictographic evidence from the 'civilised' Near East as a reliable *terminus post quem*. There is a pottery handle from Kreznica Jara in Poland in what appears to be the form of a pair of yoked animals; the context is TRB C–Wiorek – potentially earlier than Baden or the Near Eastern pictographs. The earliest ploughmarks under barrows in Denmark are now dated to ENC, and so potentially substantially before around 2700 bc. However a pot from Bronocice from a late TRB context estimated at around 2700–2500 bc has decoration plausibly in the form of a wagon.[52] Possible evidence for traction in the Gumelniţa culture has already been noted in chapter 5. Secondly, one must choose between seeing an intrusive technological complex with attendant social changes, and a changed social situation with a more widely distributed population, a more differentiated range of sites and also specialised products in which possibly external technological changes were acceptable and widely adopted. It is possible to suggest a much more regionally oriented economy over wide areas than was apparent before, but there are local antecedents for this, as in the Tisza phase of the Great Hungarian plain. At the same time it is unwise to deny the real possibility of long-range contacts in this horizon, as the evidence reviewed at the end of chapter 5 concerning the Balkans and the steppes indicates.

Further north in the area of the TRB and Michelsberg cultures the nature of the evidence is varied. The content of settlements is nearly everywhere poorly defined, and after the long phase of impressive longhouses house plans are very rare. There are a few examples from southern Poland, and one from beneath barrow 6 at Halle–Dölauer Heide in central Germany. In the northern TRB area there may be elongated longhouses at Stengade on Langeland unless these are like the supposed longhouses at Barkaer in Jutland now thought to be barrows. Rectangular Michelsberg house foundations at Ehrenstein, Kr. Ulm in the upper Rhine and the Aichbühl and Riedschachen settlements on the Federsee may indicate a change in house construction with greater use of sleeper beams, resulting in generally greater archaeological invisibility. Another example quoted from earlier periods, the Aldenhoven plateau, has no definable Michelsberg structures though there are some traces of Michelsberg occupation; Hienheim too merely has scattered pits in this phase.[53]

By contrast the total range and location of settlements has been in parts well studied. The general trend was an extension of settlement, in the already settled areas higher out of the valleys which were the earlier focus of settlement, and in newly colonised parts of the north European plain and southern Scandinavia on to a varied range of locations and soils in the diverse morainic landscape. (One must note also some areas of apparent abandonment, as in parts of central Germany.) The extension of agricultural settlement into central Sweden and southern Norway is part of the same process.[54] The phenomenon has been particularly well studied in southern Poland, as before, with larger numbers of sites higher up the valley sides on the edge of the interfluves, with larger sites particularly shifting to the latter location (Figs. 6.14 and 6.15). The chronology is not well studied yet, though it is suggested that the shift occurs from the beginning of the TRB onwards. The large site of Bronocice is a recently excavated example, covering over 50 ha (though with several phases), by far the largest site in the Nidzica valley, a

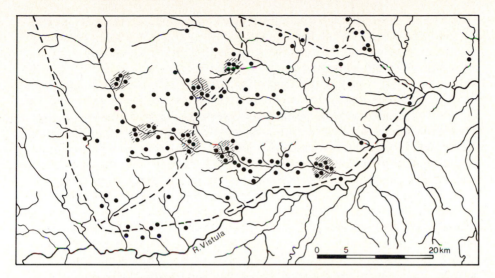

**6.14** Simplified map of the distribution of TRB settlement in southern Poland. (Dotted lines define subregions.) Compare Fig. 3.23. *After* Kruk

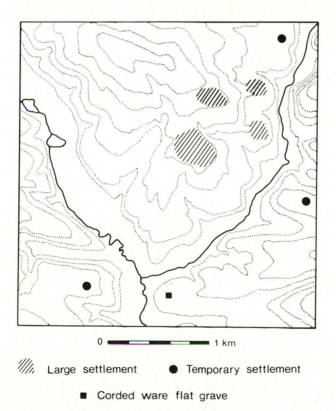

0 ▬▬▬▬ 1 km

//// Large settlement ● Temporary settlement

■ Corded ware flat grave

**6.15** TRB settlement location in the upper Szreniawa river basin near Szczepanowice, southern Poland. *After* Kruk

tributary of the upper Vistula. Cultivation marks in sandy soils beneath a barrow at Sarnowo, on the Kujavian interfluve, far up the river Zgtowiaczka, are another indication.[55] The process can be seen in the Rhineland too though one may note that some major sites such as Urmitz remained low-lying. The size of large sites is not well established, and very little of Bronocice for example has been excavated. In Denmark it does seem that there are more MN than EN settlements and eponymous sites of the MN phases such as Troldebjerg, Klintebakke or Blandebjerg are substantial open settlements.[56] There is also a number of large enclosure sites in the area.[57] These are most common in the Rhineland and include a wide variety of sizes, with palisade and continuous or interrupted ditches. Urmitz, a semicircular enclosure abutting the Rhine, has twin interrupted ditches and palisades, and is truly vast, enclosing over 100 ha. Occupation remains seem scarce within it, but were more numerous at the upland enclosures of Michelsberg and Munzingen. Sarup on Fyn has two phases of twin interrupted ditches, each backed by a palisade, the earlier with an elaborate system of entrances and palisade bastions by the ditch interruptions. Settlement traces are rare inside the first, but commoner inside the second. Büdelsdorf in Schleswig-Holstein is another example dating from the early MN with up to five interrupted ditches and two sets of internal palisade and double post-fence, as well as internal occupation traces. In central Germany the plateau enclosure at Halle–Dölauer Heide is very big, covering some 600 by 400 m with in parts up to six ditches and internal palisades (Fig. 6.16). The ditches here are continuous and on average 2 m deep. There is some internal occupation, though investigation has not been large scale. Other southern TRB examples are Derenburg and Wallendorf–Hutberg. Quenstedt too may belong to this horizon, since it underlies a Bernburg settlement. It consists of an elaborate concentric pattern of palisades (from about 40 to 100 m diameter) with some interruptions, more formal entrances and a palisade bastion. Other examples include Makotřasy in central Bohemia with a long arc-shaped ditch and a 300 by 300 m² enclosure and lengths of ditch at Bronocice and other sites. Altheim itself is an elaborate small enclosure with close-set ditches.

The functions of these sites probably varied. The enclosure at Spiennes in Belgium could be connected with control of the flint mines; Dölauer Heide and others certainly seem defensive. Some are self-contained, while others are part of wider or larger settlements. Many of them may not have been practical defences (to the modern eye at least) and the feature of interrupted ditches could well be seen as a symbolic barrier, though often backed by strong palisades as at Sarup and Büdelsdorf. It is important now to investigate the wider social context in which symbolic exclusion was important. It is interesting too to note that many of these examples can be dated to the early third millennium bc, by radiocarbon dates and cultural associations, suggesting something of a horizon in which site differentiation became fully developed. Other social developments of this horizon are discussed below.

Site differentiation is in part connected with a wider use of the landscape, though over this whole area subsistence data are disappointingly scarce.

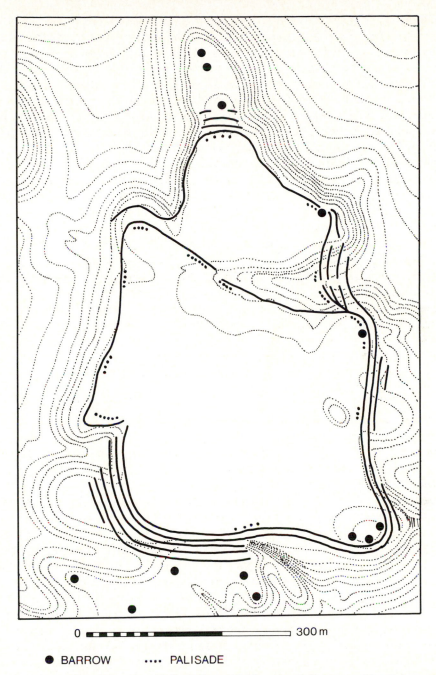

0 ▰▰▰▰▰▰▰▰▰▰▰ 300 m

● BARROW    ••••  PALISADE

**6.16** The enclosure at Halle–Dölauer Heide, central Germany. *After* Behrens and Schröter

Enough have been recovered to suggest the continuation of mixed farming but little further detail. Some of the data noted earlier from Brześć Kujawski are dated to the later fourth millennium bc. Pollen analysis in Denmark, thus in newly colonised areas, suggests rather small clearances initially with more noticeable clearance coinciding with the start of the MN phase around 2700–2500 bc. This fits well the generally small size of early settlements, as seen recently in studies in both east-central Jutland and north-west Zealand, and the more diverse pattern of settlements including enclosures in the MN phase in both areas. The other striking piece of evidence is the first direct evidence for the ard or light plough, probably a crook-ard, in the form of several cases or ard-marks preserved in sandy soil under barrows, one in Poland at Sarnowo probably in the Wiorek phase, and the others in Denmark, again mostly from beginning of the MN phase, such as Fuglebaeksbanken, but some also from the ENC phase. Ploughs have been seen as part of the traction side of the secondary products complex but the issue of survival of the evidence is raised again.[58] These dates coincide with an increase in the building of monuments such as passage graves, without which the marks would be lost. The appearance of a single complex must be controversial, but there is no reason to doubt that colonisation of the interfluves and of the north European plain either led to technological innovation or a more prominent role for existing technology, since the plough would have enabled extensive cultivation to compensate for the poorer returns of less fertile and less well-watered soils, on a scale far exceeding that possible with hoe or digging stick.

The quality of settlement preservation in parts of the north Alpine foreland between Lake Leman and the Bodensee is amongst the best in Europe (and the quality was heralded early since discoveries go back to the 1850s). The preservation is due to waterlogging of sites placed originally on lake edges and subsequently flooded or on the edge of marsh or bog and subsequently covered with peat. Elsewhere, as in the Aare valley, a tributary of the Rhine, preservation is less distinguished, and there has been a natural tendency to neglect 'land' sites, though this imbalance is being redressed. One should not exaggerate the state of preservation. Some bogs nowadays are being drained and wood therefore decays, and a mass of tightly superimposed and distorted house floors presents considerable problems for the excavator. But here in many well-known sites such as Pfyn, Niederwil, Thayngen–Weier, Seeberg Burgäschisee-Süd, or Egolzwil III, V and others around the Wauwilermoos, there is direct evidence not just for the shape and size of small rectangular houses (mostly under 10 m long) or the layout of structural posts, but for upright timbers themselves, floors, hearths, and perhaps walls and roofs, walkways and areas between houses, palisades around, and a generally close-set settlement layout.[59] Added to this is often a wealth of organic debris as well as the more usual cultural remains, which include such spectacular finds as sheep or goat droppings, the puparia of house flies, and elm branches probably gathered as fodder, at such sites as Egolzwil III, Egolzwil IV and Thayngen–Weier respectively (Figs. 6.17 and 6.18).

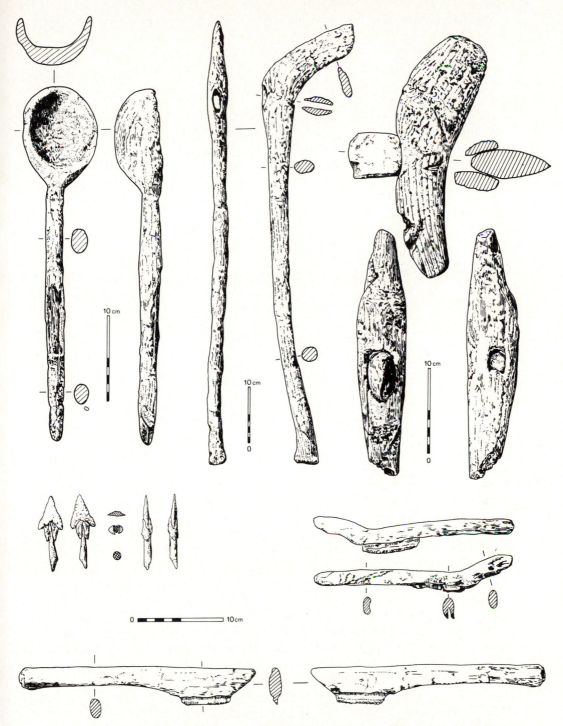

**6.17** Artefacts wholly or partly of wood, from the settlement at Seeberg, Burgä-schisee-Süd, Canton Bern, Switzerland. *After* Müller-Beck

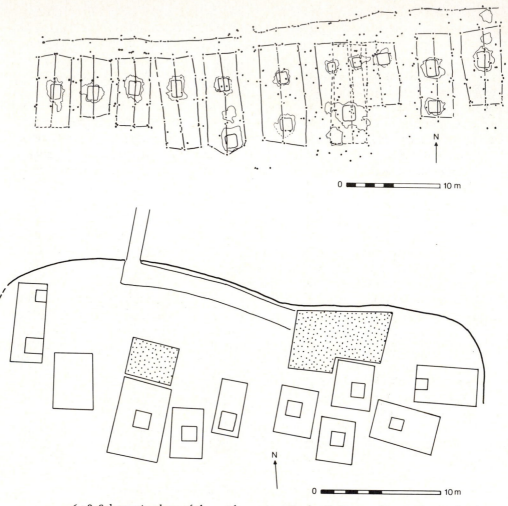

**6.18** Schematic plans of the settlements at Egolzwil, Canton Luzern, Switzerland. (**a**) Egolzwil iva (**b**) Egolzwil ivd. *After* Vogt

Three main zones of settlement can be identified, indicating a wide range of locations – the hinterland of the upper Rhine and along and around its tributary the River Aare; the major glacial lakes such as the Bodensee, the Zürichsee, and Lac Neuchâtel; and the morainic landscape of the Alpine foreland proper broken by frequent small lakes and marshes. Settlements have also been found in the Alpine Rhine valley and in locations such as the head of the Thunersee, and occasionally up to 1000 m above sea level. It will be remembered that in the previous phase settlement was confined to the upper Rhine and environs, and the subsequent infilling, in which there is as yet no discernible difference in time between the areas outlined, is one of the more notable examples of the wider central-western European phenomenon. There is a range of site sizes, with a contrast evident between larger, more low-lying sites such as Niederwil, Pfyn and Thayngen–Weier in the Thurgau and those on the foreland itself such as the various sites around the Burg-äschisee or the Wauwilermoos (the Egolzwil sites) in the Ober Aargau. At least some sites on the large glacial lakes such as Zürich–Kleiner Hafner on the Zürichsee or those on Lac Neuchâtel or the Bielersee such as Twann were probably also larger than the latter group though complete or extensive excavation has rarely been achieved. The contrast is also to be seen in site layout, with a contrast again between the nucleated rows of terraced houses set within a strong palisade at Niederwil and the short single rows of houses at Seeberg, Burgäschisee-Süd or Egolzwil v. Other detailed differences await further examination (and full publication). Is, for example, the concentration of finds in the successive houses nos. 7 and 7a at Egolzwil v, suggestive of some sort of special role for the buildings despite their normal size, a pattern to be found elsewhere?

Most sites in all sorts of locations are assumed to have been occupied all the year round, and in fact this can be more reliably demonstrated (assuming that resources were locally obtained) at some of these Swiss sites than virtually anywhere else in Europe, the evidence coming from both the Burgäschisee and Wauwilermoos sites and the Zürichsee. At Meilen–Rohrenhaab for example spring is indicated by newborn cattle, mid-summer by red deer calf, and perhaps by a roe deer skull fragment with antler attached, autumn by a 4–5 month old red deer, and winter by swan, thought to be a seasonal visitor between December and January. Another remarkable piece of evidence comes from the analysis of the pollen in goat droppings at Egolzwil III, which indicated that the animals were grazed locally throughout pollen production seasons. Alpine valley sites, as well as those at high altitude are more likely to have been seasonally occupied, though there is insufficient evidence to test this. The duration of sites may offer more discrimination, since the glacial lake and Thurgau sites appear to have more extensive stratigraphies than the morainic lake and marsh sites but the question is complex. While dendro-chronology indicates only 12–15 years for the span of Egolzwil v, this may only document timber felling not occupation, which was long enough for the replacement of at least two houses. The same method indicates a duration of 30–70 years for both Thurgau, Zürichsee and foreland sites, and radiocarbon dates though clearly less precise do indicate a longer duration at Niederwil, Thayngen–Weier and Seeberg, Burgäschisee-Süd. In terms of regional con-trast, the question of site density should be considered too. The Burgäschisee and Wauwilermoos have what appears to be a succession of smaller sites. A further difference which may underline a contrast between the foreland proper and lower-lying sites is the greater extent of potential arable land around the latter.[60]

A still unexplained feature of all these sites is their precise location at the edge of the water or on damp ground. No individual variable that has been considered such as climate, defence, soil, ease of communication or direct economic advantage from fishing or lakeside grazing, seems wholly adequate to explain the locational regularity since they would all have been satisfied by dry-land settlement close to water or marsh, and explanation may lie in a combination of factors. The location raises other puzzles. The general subsistence picture is of mixed farming, perhaps with cereal and other plant cultivation dominant since pollen analysis indicates rather small clearings, supplemented by other plant and animal resources. Cattle and pig are generally more numerous than ovicaprids; there is evidence at many sites for high numbers of adult cows, which suggests the possibility of milking as well as breeding stock. Yet the lakeside position in many cases precludes a central location in available arable land, and fishing is very badly documented, despite the quality of preservation and careful excavation. The constraint of winter temperature is likely to have been more severe than many other lower parts of Europe, and animals may have had to be stalled in winter and provided with fodder. The cases of elm fodder, ovicaprid droppings and house fly puparia can be cited in support of these practices. Water could then have solved the problem of fodder transport.

Despite reasonable preservation, bone assemblages are not without problems. Low overall numbers at Seeberg Burgäschisee-Süd or Egolzwil v for example, or the relatively high proportion of 'wild' animals at those sites, raise the question of whether the bone left on a site is representative of even the local economy. And despite the preservation of a wide range of plants, including some notable caches such as the 3–4 l of clubwheat at Egolzwil–Schötz II, the scale of production is no easier to analyse, and storage facilities archaeologically visible are limited to pottery and other containers in houses. The potential differences between the areas indicated raise also the question of more regional economy and of interdependence between different sites. The pattern could be one of local self-sufficiency but there are some possible indications of a more complex situation. Hypothetically seasonal sites connected with animal grazing are one strand, and a limited exploitation of fur-bearing animals is another. The low numbers of bone generally and of domestic species in particular at sites like Seeberg Burgäschisee-Süd could indicate a movement of animals on the hoof between sites, in this case hypothetically from smaller to larger sites. The discovery of a string of copper beads at Burgäschisee-Süd which had been in use for some time might be seen as part of the workings of a regional economy, but of course a direct connection between the beads and the sphere of subsistence and production is debatable.[61] But given that copper production was localised in the Pfyn area, some explanation has to be sought for the movement of distinctive ornaments in a rare material to a small, distant foreland settlement.

Newly investigated lakeside settlements in eastern France such as Clairvaux are beginning to offer the same range of evidence as Swiss sites, and are also part of the same process of settlement extension and infilling, which is visible in the valleys of the Paris basin, in central-western France and even in the interior of Brittany. Chasseen sites like those of the TRB or Michelsberg cultures have poorly defined houses, but often are larger than their post-LBK predecessors and are regularly sited more on the interfluve edge or on high locations than before. There are again a number of enclosure sites, with interrupted ditches, as in the Aisne valley, at Noyen in the Seine valley or L'Étoile in an upland setting above the Somme. Recent investigations in central-western France have greatly increased the number of ditched enclosures known particularly on the interfluves of the Sèvre and Charente river systems. Though excavations have so far been relatively limited, radiocarbon dates from sites like Les Matignons do again indicate the earlier third millennium bc as the horizon of expansion and enclosure.[62]

Britain and Ireland present a varied range of evidence. The content of settlements has been poorly defined though many sites have been identified especially through flint scatters and a number of them excavated. Hurst Fen on the Suffolk fen-edge and Broome Heath, Norfolk, in the Waveney valley, are examples of open sites with pits and other features but no clearly defined structures. It is possible however that the patterns of pits at Hurst Fen could define rectangular buildings. Such have been recorded at a number of sites such as Ballynagilly, Co. Tyrone, Ballyglass, Co. Mayo and Fengate on the western edge of the fens in Cambridgeshire ranging from 6 by 6 m, to 13 by 6 m. The locations of all these five sites indicate the wide range of settlement which is apparently evident throughout Britain from the beginning of the phase of established settlement from around 3500 bc. Such eclecticism is supported by pollen analysis showing upland clearance in some areas, though in others it was limited, as around the stone-axe source in the Langdales in Cumbria. While numerous sites therefore both lowland and upland are known, and settlement was also extended by 3000 bc or soon after to the northern isles, the density of settlement is less clear. Fengate suggests that the basic unit of settlement may have been the dispersed homestead, for here much wider excavation of later prehistoric remains failed to reveal other contemporary structures, apart from a burial some 120 m from the house. But though dispersed settlement may not have been sparse, as the well-preserved series of houses at Lough Gur, Co. Limerick, may suggest. There are other indications of this in the environmental evidence (discussed below) and in the Somerset Levels in the form of wooden trackways which crossed the wet fen (subsequently fen-wood) surface from before 3000 bc (Fig. 6.19). The successive replacement of trackways as they fell into disuse, and the associated environmental evidence for a widespread range of activity in and around the Levels, as well as the evident interest in the grazing and other resources, all serve to show that few lowland areas were neglected.[63]

The most obvious sign of site differentiation consists of a series of over 40 enclosures in southern and central England, in a range of locations from valley to chalk upland. As in other areas already considered they vary also in size (from 3 to over 20 acres) and form, with circular and semicircular examples, and with from one to five rings of ditches and banks known, as well as less common evidence for internal palisades and gateways, subsidiary outer ditches and subsidiary enclosures. Outstanding recent excavations include Hambledon Hill, Dorset, Crickley Hill, Gloucestershire, and Orsett, Essex. At Hambledon shallow inner ditches have a more substantial outer ditch at some distance with further outworks beyond. Though the ditches are

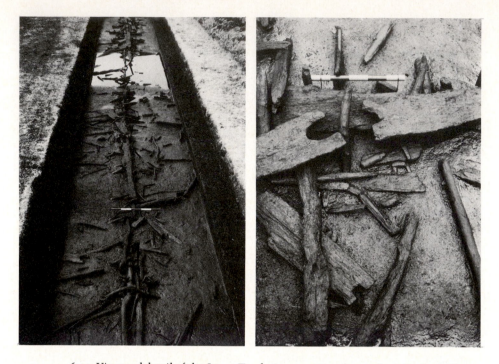

**6.19** View and detail of the Sweet Track, Somerset Levels, southern England. Photo: Somerset Levels Project

interrupted there is evidence for a more continuous bank behind, perhaps with a palisade on its crest. A subsidiary small enclosure has a more continuous ditch with evidence for a wattle breastwork on the bank inside (Fig. 6.20). Crickley has a stone rampart behind two interrupted ditches and the succeeding continuous ditch. There is evidence of attack by archers using leaf-shaped arrowheads. These two sites are in upland locations while Orsett is on the main gravel terrace of the lower Thames. Its semicircular circuit may be genuinely incomplete. Despite severe truncation of the original surface there is evidence for a palisade inside twin interrupted ditches and there is a third, inner ditch. All three sites have evidence for internal occupation, though at Hambledon the contents of pits in the main interior differ from those of the subsidiary enclosure in being more specialised and selected. Primary deposits of human remains in the inner two ditches also suggest differentiation within the site. Other sites such as Windmill Hill, Wiltshire, have animal-bone deposits in their ditches which have been interpreted as non-domestic, and the feature of interrupted ditches backed by more solid barriers is recurrent, again it may be suggested part of the symbolism of exclusion. This has been reinforced by the recent realisation that there are small enclosures often with continuous or near-continuous ditches, known from air photographs and assigned to later prehistory, which date in fact to this period, as at Hambledon Hill or Bury Hill, Sussex.

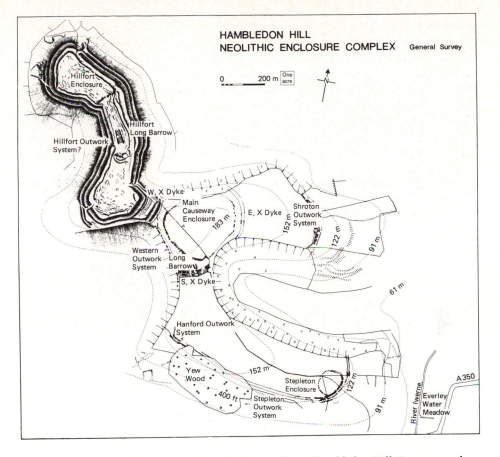

**6.20** Main features of the enclosure complex at Hambledon Hill, Dorset, southern England. Plan: Mercer

Radiocarbon-dated enclosures fall into the later fourth as well as the earlier third millennia bc, but recently the majority of dates suggest the latter period as the main horizon of construction, providing a further indication of the importance of developments by this stage, half a millennium or so after the second phase of agricultural expansion in western Europe.[64]

Subsistence data are disappointingly scarce in Britain though mixed farming is documented. Cattle (including oxen), pig and ovicaprids are known, in that order of importance. Meat may have been the chief product, though an assemblage with mature cows at Hambledon has been taken to reflect a dairy economy. Wheat and barley have been found as impressions on pottery and carbonised, but legumes have not been recorded before the late third millennium bc perhaps due to sampling deficiencies. Barley rather than wheat was used in the northern isles. Study of cereal impressions on local and imported pottery at Windmill Hill suggests that wheats were favoured for heavier and barley for lighter soils. Criss-cross ard-marks have been preserved under the

South Street long barrow, Wiltshire, with a radiocarbon-dated *terminus ante quem* of around 2800 bc (Fig. 6.21). The ard in question may have been substantial since the marks are deeply scored into the chalk subsoil, and it is unclear whether this was due to regular ploughing or initial break-up of the ground. The date compares with those from Denmark and Poland, but the question of the preservation of evidence must be considered again. There are wooden implements beside the Sweet Track in the Somerset Levels before 3000 bc which could be seen as plough components, so that the supposed horizon of the introduction of the plough must again be cautiously treated. Nonetheless it may again fit a picture of extended settlement and continued site differentiation as on the continent, which other environmental evidence helps to fill out. Studies of buried soils show various kinds of soil working and disturbance, some deep as at South Street, others shallower. Study of chalk soils suggests that they may originally have been deeper in many areas, and

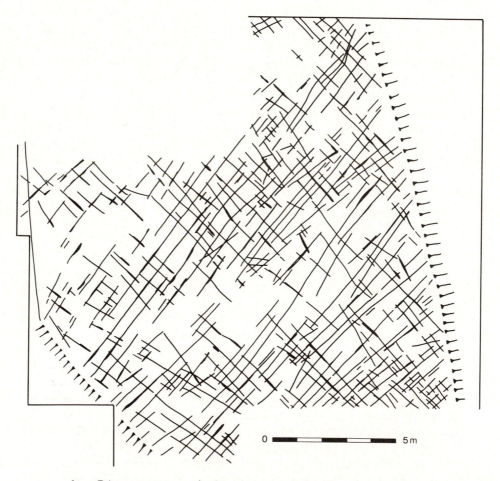

0 ▬▬▬▬▬▬ 5m

**6.21** Criss-cross pattern of ard-marks in the chalk subsoil beneath South Street long barrow, Wiltshire, southern England. *After* Evans

there is evidence for soil erosion from the early third millennium bc. Soil disturbance can also be seen in other areas, through the study of the chemical composition of lake silts.

Pollen analysis is feasible in many areas due to acid soils and peat deposits. The technique is not without problems of interpretation. The pollen of some species travels far beyond their local area, others (such as cereals) hardly at all, and more than one sampling point is desirable. But closely spaced vertical samples and radiocarbon dates can provide a detailed insight into vegetational changes, as in the three northern Irish sites of Ballynagilly and Beaghmore, Co. Tyrone, and Ballyscullion, Co. Antrim where pre-elm decline clearance already referred to is followed by a phase of more extensive clearance with cereal pollen, then a phase with more pastoral indicators, and finally woodland regeneration after up to four radiocarbon centuries of activity. The beginning and end of the process have been even more closely studied at Hockham Mere, Norfolk where two temporary reductions in tree pollen precede the major clearance, and may represent pioneer settlement, woodland grazing and garden horticulture, while later scrub regeneration may show some shifting cultivation before reclearance and final regeneration. The status of the elm decline is still disputed. On the whole the British evidence does not support the model of shifting agriculture as the main means of cultivation, since pollen analysis indicates large sustained clearings, but it may have been locally practised. Stable agriculture implies fixed plots, and there is some evidence of stake fences under long barrows, as well as small lynchets in the same context and possibly elsewhere. A further indication of the scale of activity comes from pollen 'transects' in the Somerset Levels, which do not suggest equal activity everywhere. But a suggested contraction of settlement and widespread forest regeneration towards the mid third millennium bc may be further indication of the preceding onslaught on the forest.[65]

The pollen data can be complemented from two other sources. Analysis of buried snail faunas provides some insight into the environment of calcareous regions such as the chalk where pollen analysis is difficult. A picture of early clearance emerges in this part of the environment too. Tree-ring studies in the Somerset Levels are another fruitful source of information. They show not only the very varied nature of forest use which included probably deliberate hazel coppicing from the early third millennium bc but also provide some insight into its composition. Wood in the Sweet Track comes from both primary and secondary woodland, suggesting local variations in the intensity of clearance. Also there is some evidence for stockpiling of wood at places where more planks than usual have been recovered. This begins to offer insights into the social background of the trackway with at the least considerable communal cooperation implied and possibly centralised leadership.[66]

On the whole however it is difficult to evaluate the scale of production or the use of cereal and animal produce. There are clear signs of site differentiation, and possibly an important role for animals as part of ritual in important enclosures. It is possible too that as suggested elsewhere in this section there was a development towards a more regionally based economy with considerable regional interaction, as well as a phase in the earlier third millennium bc of increased production and enclosure. These trends however cannot be studied solely through the settlement and subsistence evidence, and wider aspects of the record must now be examined.

### Ritual, burial, exchange and material culture, 3500/3400–2600/2500 bc

Turning back to east-central Europe, it can be seen that the Bodrogkeresztúr phase in the Great Hungarian plain was largely a continuation of the preceding Tiszapolgár period. The same burial tradition continued, with ritual paraphernalia absent, and still plain grave pottery. There are some signs of change however which could indicate a need to reinforce the newly established possibly more hierarchical social order. There is a greater weight of copper deposited in graves, and proportionately more now deposited with men than women in the Tiszapolgár–Basatanya cemetery, including now copper implements and weapons as well as ornaments. Here there are other interesting changes in associated grave goods. Pig mandibles are now rare, and of five examples four were found in women's graves. Variations in grave orientation may be locally based and indicate local differentiation. In the succeeding Baden phase there is further more profound social change. The range and differentiation of settlement alters considerably, and new subsistence products and transport technology may have been part of a much wider regional economy which would have offered a more clearly established social elite further means of social control and of competition with peers. If wagons and milk drinking were the result of far-flung influences, their very external nature may have offered new forms of prestige and legitimation of social position for those able to command them. There is a dual symbolism of wagon models serving as both handled drinking vessels and objects of separate veneration in burial. Ox-burials may also symbolise the ability to destroy new forms of wealth, since an ox-pair is specialised in function and expensive to maintain, especially in an increasingly infilled landscape. The reappearance of figurines could suggest also changes in the social order, perhaps connected with new forms of ideology. The distribution of similar material culture especially pottery shows a much wider orbit than before in the region, and 'parallels' and 'influences' extend through south-east Europe to the Aegean and Anatolia. There is little need to involve population movement, rather the wider pattern seems to reflect again the wider sphere of social contact and the importance of the external in the new social order.[67]

Two elements however perhaps changed little. There was less use of copper than before, which may partly reflect interrupted supplies from south-east Europe and a gradual diminution in the available quantity of oxide ores after a millennium or more of exploitation and before the more difficult sulphide ores were tackled. Cemetery burial was maintained, as at Budakalász and Alsónémedi, with abundant grave goods, some cremation as well as inhumation and variable grave orientations. In sum considerable change is implied. Its explanation is not easy in view of our restricted knowledge of the Bodrogkeresztúr phase and it may be dangerous – yet again – to see renewed signs of tension and conflict in the Bodrogkereztúr burial evidence which finds new resolution in the more open differentiation of the Baden phase. The transition may mark the moment when the plain rejoined the Balkan social order after a long period of separate and in many ways precocious develop-ment. A final point to stress is the importance again of the external as part of new, more explicitly differentiated social order, as has already been suggested for contemporary south-east Europe and will in turn be suggested for central and western Europe, but later, in the next horizon considered.

Further north study of settlement suggested increased site differentiation by the earlier third millennium bc in the large area of the TRB culture, and a range of other evidence can be produced to fill out a picture of increasing social competitiveness. The symbolic nature of elements of enclosures has already been noted, but the symbolism is vague, perhaps deliberately, since it is not wholly clear who or what group fits the role of other, to be excluded – either separate communities or different groups within a community. Such ambiguity may mask a process of transition to more differentiated society, as other TRB evidence hints at. Cemetery burial continues in parts as in the Jordanowa group, or in the small groups of up to ten burials known in Baalberge contexts (such as the two at Quenstedt, of an old woman with two pots and of a mature man with a pot and an arrowhead) and up to 23 at Salzmünde itself, including small collective burials of up to five people. Two graves covered by the later barrow (no. 6) at Halle–Dölauer Heide are further examples, the one a disturbed stone packing grave with two arrowheads and no body, the other a wooden coffin with a child's head and part of its vertebrae, with no goods.[68] The trapezoidal ditched enclosure 30 by 9 m also under the barrow may belong to a post-Salzmünde horizon. In the eastern TRB area such modes were supplemented or replaced by the appearance of a variety of barrows, such as the long triangular mounds of Kujavia in central Poland – as in the example of Sarnowo already noted in another context – or the more rectangular mounds of the north European plain with massive stone kerbs and cists.[69] Their chronological development is not well understood though the Kujavian barrows at least go back to the later fourth millennium bc. These have two significant features. Though often of considerable length (up to 100 m and more) the earthen mound covers individual or small collective burials only (Fig. 6.22). It is possible that these were socially prominent, or alternatively that they are a sample of a much bigger popula-tion – or perhaps the ambiguity is again deliberate. Secondly, their location seems to represent a further separation of burial from settlements, even though the precise relationship between the two is poorly understood in many areas, especially where settlement survey is underdeveloped. Could this reflect again an original ambiguity, a denial of social reality, and the provision of an invented fixed point in the range of expanding settlement and changing social relations? The range of other explanations already considered

**6.22** Long mounds at Wietrzychowice, pow. Wloclawek, central Poland, after excavation. (**a**) no. 2; (**b**) no. 3. Photo: Archaeological and Ethnographic Museum, Lodz

will be remembered. The distribution of these monuments is limited, and further south in the southern and south-eastern TRB one is restricted to examples like the linear enclosures at Březno near Louny in Bohemia. These are narrow (3–4 m) and bounded by palisades, one over 140 m with three burials along its length, the other parallel to this, some 25 m long with two burials inside.[70]

Perforated battle-axes in this part of the TRB distribution can be seen as prestige objects, and they are sometimes many-faceted and even decorated as in Salzmünde contexts, though most do not have closely defined contexts in settlements and rarely appear in graves. Copper objects are likely to have the same significance as new prestige items, and copper ornaments were evidently common enough to be deposited in graves. Though there are some indications of local working these artefacts suggest a considerable volume of exchange. This is also to be seen in large-scale exploitation of Polish flint sources, mainly from the Upper Vistula region.[71] These include chocolate-coloured flint from the Swietokrzyskie mountains, banded flint from Krzemionki, grey-speckled flint from Świechiechów, and banded chert from the Krakow area. These sources were used in various products including blades, especially from the Świechiechów, and axes, especially from Krzemionki. The scale of production must have been considerable judging by the extent of mine shafts and extraction pits at the latter site. Between 700 and 1000 shafts are known, some as much as 11 m deep in search of the best seams of flint. It is notable that the mines lay some 10 km from recognised settlements. Mined flint from various sources has been found in pits at Ćmielów radiocarbon dated to the early third millennium bc. Some of these products were widely distributed, Krzemionki flint being found up to 700 km from its source, with a steady fall-off in numbers with distance. Such movement and patterns are subject to a wide range of possible interpretations. A prosaic one is connected to the extension of settlement and increased clearance, and a greater need for woodworking tools. The number of pristine finds however suggests that axes too can be seen as valued artefacts whose distribution was not solely for functional purposes, though symbolic value may have been added by sharing the form of utilitarian tools. The spatial pattern of distribution is compatible with originally random movement by a number of short stages, which in turn is compatible with gift exchange as known from the ethnographic record, though it may be stressed that the same spatial pattern can result from different processes.[72] The problem is therefore complex, but at the risk of over-simplicity, it can be suggested that an increased flow of exchanges between communities, to cement alliances and so on, plausibly fits the context of extending settlement already outlined. At the same time such a flow perhaps offered individuals or groups opportunities for personal rather than communal acquisition of status and prestige.

In the western area the chronology of rectangular megalithic *hunebedden* or *Riesensteingräber* is insecure, though there is a consensus that these are late and coeval with *Tiefstichkeramik*, and in the north of the central German *Saalegebiet* at any rate preceded or overlapped by Baalberge and

Salzmünde graves with megalithic elements in them.[73] Though varied these monuments generally have an elongated rectangular plan with the chamber, which may or may not be as long as the kerb, approached laterally. Overall lengths of 50 m are not unusual, and some reach 90 m. There are examples with double passage and chambers, and also terminal rather than lateral entrances. There is no clear evidence that form varied consistently with time despite archaeological efforts at producing sequences, though there may be some evidence that monuments were a little larger by Dutch phase D if the present ceramic sequence were to be accepted. Contents have often been disturbed and bone badly preserved. Recent salvage excavations at Atteln, Kr. Paderborn in Westfalen indicate that bones were originally present, perhaps not in large quantities. As often elsewhere the western group megaliths are spaced out around the landscape, in the northern Netherlands characteristically in slightly elevated positions. There is an interesting, marked distribution just north of the loess in central Germany. Their social significance is hard to study because of their condition and the deficiences of the settlement record, but it is interesting to note that capstones and endstones regularly weigh some 5–10 metric tons, occasionally 20 or more. It has been suggested that 15–20 men are required to pull one ton weight, so even a modest 5-tonner would require 75–100 men working cooperatively, though frozen ground would reduce friction considerably. Animal traction would also reduce man-hours, though there are no good experimental figures. It is tempting to relate the advent of traction (seen in the plough evidence) to the proposed late chronology for *hunebedden*, and to suggest a horizon in which settlement was extended, clearance increased, stone clearance increased, and also in which monuments played an important part as actual or notional fixed points in the landscape. The interpretational dilemma persists here, whether the monuments reflect the communal or the more individual, or indeed the individual in the guise of the communal, providing a hint of further contradiction and conflict. Other features of the area such as the battle-axes and copper artefacts may support the latter sort of interpretation.

The Danish chronology offers similar possibilities of considerable development around 2700–2600 bc, at the start of the MN, and the evidence is wide-ranging and has been well studied.[74] In the EN there was a variety of burial modes including flat graves, round and long *dysse* or megalithic monuments, and long earthen barrows covering graves at one end. Some flat graves were flanked by axial pits, which are interpreted as the remains of tent-like mortuary structures, as at Konens Høj in Jutland. This contained a single inhumation. Others of its type may have been covered by earthen mounds as at Lindebjerg on Zealand which suggests a possible developmental sequence in mortuary ritual, some but not all sites being important enough for mound construction. Few grave goods were deposited, chiefly pottery in small quantities. The supposed longhouses at Barkaer on Jutland have recently been reinterpreted as long mounds in the same tradition, house compartments being seen now as constructional compartments. In the MN the nature of burial monuments changes and the so-called passage grave becomes

**6.23** Passage grave at Flintinge Byskov, Lolland, Denmark. Photo: National Museum, Copenhagen

dominant, with polygonal chamber and capstone approached by a passage and set in a circular, often kerbed mound (Fig. 6.23). Fuglesbaeksbanken on Zealand, already mentioned in connection with the ard-marks which it covers, can serve as one example.

The complexities of human bone assemblages in passage graves of this kind have been recently studied in the south-east Swedish sites Carlshögen and Ramshög, part of a group of eight or possibly more monuments apparently associated with contemporary domestic settlement sites.[75] Large quantities of bone of both men and women and children were successively inhumed in the chambers and there arranged in piles. The piles however do not represent differing numbers of complete bodies, but a bewildering variety of non-natural anatomical assemblages, such as at Carlshögen ribs and vertebrae set on femura or skulls on top of long bones, and differing bone categories dominating in differing bone piles. As well as the large-scale collective deposition of bones another feature to note is the deposition of grave goods or rather associated artefacts. These chiefly take the form of broken pottery in the outer passage and entrance. The quantities may vary considerably, in the southern Swedish case for example, from 40 sherds at some sites to about 50000 at one or two sites of major or prolonged importance. The greatest quantities of such pottery were deposited in the early stages of the MN in

Denmark. In one or two cases it has been possible to trace this ritual or mortuary activity a little further, in Danish cases such as Tustrup and Ferslev where there are small rectangular structures ('cult-houses') close to passage graves, which contained further deposits of broken pottery.[76] These can be taken as further indication of ritual elaboration at this stage. These two examples are dated to MN ib, though radiocarbon dated to around 2500 bc.

Perforated maceheads and battle-axes, and imported copper items are potential status items and are documented as early as the EN. The source of the perforated artefacts is not known, but there was certainly local production of flint axes from the cretaceous region of northern Jutland where shafts and galleries are again known as at Hov. Sources on Rügen were also exploited, and it seems that the products of the latter were distributed mainly in the south and south-east, while the Danish products circulated in Denmark and to the north.[77]

Some of these elements can be pulled together. In the early phase of agricultural colonisation or agricultural transition (see chapter 4) settlement was dispersed with a wide range of locations. Clearances were small. There were no large collective burials, and some burials were considerably enhanced by the construction of large stone or earth coverings. There were some prestige goods in circulation. A study of the distribution of prestige goods and burials in relation to categories of contemporary land value suggests that social display was concentrated in the areas with greater arable potential.[78] According to the Becker chronology pottery types were at first rather uniform and plain, but by ENC more richly decorated and to some extent locally varied. Growth and settlement extension is more obviously seen from the MN phase with the pollen-documented *landnam*, plough agriculture, greater numbers of sites, and perhaps also some larger open settlement sites. The first enclosures are recorded, as at Sarup, with occupation and defence or practical enclosure evident, but also some signs in pit contents of enhanced ritual activity and a symbolic element in enclosure as well. Numbers of burial monuments increased, while their variety perhaps decreased. Large collective burials were made, with considerable attention paid to anatomical selection and rearrangement, and some sites were perhaps repeatedly used as pottery deposits indicate. There were specialised cult-houses connected with this activity. Plough-marks under passage graves could also be seen as symbolic rather than purely accidental remains of previous cultivation (though clearly monument construction was easier on open ground). Pottery itself may have been more locally varied than before.

The evidence for change is thus considerable and this provides better opportunities for interpretation than in many areas outside east-central Europe. From the beginning it is hard to see communities as egalitarian since there are indications of differences both between and within them. This can be related either to the nature of colonising communities or to the preceding social situation in the Ertebølle–Ellerbek phase, though interestingly in that case there could be a potential decrease in social hierarchy. From the MN there is increased site differentiation and ritual activity. It is likely that differences between and within communities were increased, but it is of the greatest interest that in comparison with the Baden phase of east-central Europe these differences were not as explicit. The extent of ritual activity itself may be a clue to social division and conflict, and the emphasis on collective burial a formal denial of changed and changing social reality, while the elaborate anatomical treatments of burial deposits have been seen as perhaps reflecting on another level a society deeply concerned with personal categorisation and position. Extended settlement may itself be as much a symptom of changing social relations as a cause, since the pressure to increase clearance, shift settlements and take on the more labour-intensive requirements of plough agriculture and draught animals may stem as much from emergent leadership and social differentiation, in which increased production was important for the maintenance or enhancement of social position, as from supposedly independent pressures of population or a decline in resources. In this view the symbolism of ard-marks under passage graves could have served as a further underlying contradiction of the superimposed constructions.

Passage graves may have another symbolic aspect, a reference to the external, which could provide an analogy rather than a contrast to Baden developments. Much ink has been spilled in the past on the question of origins of barrow and megalithic traditions. The discussion here has largely avoided the question, preferring to present the chronological evidence for each region independently, and to sidestep the tangled issues of megalithic chickens and eggs. This is not to deny however the possibilities of long-range contact between different regions, nor their place in social relations. Long-range resemblances have most usually been seen as evidence for movement of population and the archaeology of the period comes to resemble a catalogue of ethnic displacements. This hypothesis is largely rejected here, on the grounds that the extension of settlement already documented suggests infilling of already settled areas and colonisation of adjacent areas, not long-range movement. One could also argue for independent development of the northern long mound tradition, with a background of Mesolithic cemeteries and LBK tradition longhouses. And yet the echoes of the same idea in western France and the British Isles in the earlier and mid fourth millennium are difficult to dismiss, and some elements as will be seen below such as triangular mounds and mortuary structures have good parallels in the British Isles. The exact resemblances are not however impressive in this early phase, but with MN passage graves there is perhaps a more obvious parallel with British, Irish and Breton passage graves. This need not portend the setting out of colonising flotillas around the Atlantic and North Sea coasts, but could better be seen in the context of changing southern Scandinavian society. Movement of individuals is not difficult to envisage, and we have already seen the ethnographic evidence that this is not barred by the existence of cultural boundaries. The resemblance in form could then be seen as the result of direct knowledge of other contemporary areas, and the imitation as a use of the external in various ways, for internal purposes, such as to seek legitimation for social position by reference to long-range alliance or to bury social division by reference to a wider community of ideas or ancestry. The use of the external is limited in this case however, as pottery styles and other artefacts do not share the same resemblances; the distinctive forms of the western TRB group megaliths are also to be noted again.

The Rhineland and northern Alpine foreland offer further contrasts. Formal Michelsberg burials seem absent though there are deposits of human bone in the ditches of some enclosures. It is possible that this absence is in some way connected with the rather greater number of enclosures known within the Michelsberg distribution than elsewhere, enclosures serving to both unify and differentiate. There is no discernible development in the earlier third millennium bc despite the proposed elaborate sequence. Exchange was most visibly based on the movement of flint axes, blades and other products. There is a large series of mines in the cretaceous regions of southern Belgium and southern Limburg, such as Spiennes, Mesvin-sans-Pareil, Obourg or Rijckholt–St Geertruid. The numbers of shafts are again impressive, those at Spiennes in places penetrating loessic overburden before reaching the chalk and going up to 16 m deep in all. The crushed miner of Obourg is a reminder of the dangers of radiating galleries in unstable chalk with intrusive sand cones. It has been suggested that at Spiennes a development can be traced from open pits to deeper shafts but this is contradicted by recent research on both sites of the river Trouille, with open trenches well away from the surface outcrop supposedly worked first, and conversely shafts close to the outcrop.[79] The grey flint thus mined is quite distinctive (perhaps less so than the Polish examples already cited) and it has been claimed that it is found on Michelsberg sites well up the Rhine.

The range of Swiss evidence is perhaps disappointing after the quality of other data so far reviewed. There are some groups of Cortaillod burials on land sites and one in the Pfyn culture. Investigations at Egolzwil IV for example produced four burials underlying or in the settlement which are thought to have belonged to Egolzwil V whose fence was some 40 m distant. There are no other clear indications of the development of a special role for separate burials as seen elsewhere. The Burgäschisee-Süd copper beads have already been mentioned, and can be used to reinforce a further contrast between the copper-importing and -working Pfyn culture and the more rarely copper-importing Cortaillod culture, though both were in similar environments and were in close contact, and the latter is little further from eastern Alpine sources of metal than the former. Organic remains preserved include linen textiles originally with elaborate designs, which may have been an exchanged commodity, but the frustrating situation remains that perhaps the best settlement evidence available for study lacks a wider range of other evidence to aid interpretation of social development.

The converse is frustratingly true of western France. Direct settlement evidence from the coast or later the interior is disappointingly sparse. There are later fourth millennium bc dates from Curnic. Attention has been focused on the range of megalithic monuments, which continue in earlier traditions of long and round mound or cairn construction. There are signs of regional styles of monument development by the earlier third millennium bc such as the square compartmentalised Kerleven type of southern Finistère. The special nature of several of these monuments is reinforced by internal decoration pecked out in curvilinear abstract and semi-representational designs on the orthostats of chamber and passage. The great disappointment of the Breton tombs is the generally sparse preservation of bone. There are signs that human bone was indeed deposited, but it is not possible to tell in what quantities. In Normandy the chambers of the long cairn at La Hoguette, Fontenay-le-Marmion, Calvados contained collective deposits of men women and children, while its neighbour La Hogue may have had fewer, so that it is impossible to predict whether the Breton mounds were used for the deposition of individuals or groups, though the replication of chambers suggests the latter.[80] Small quantities of pottery and stone axes are usually found in the monuments, but there is also a larger series of fine jadeite and other stone polished axes and rings, and callais beads and pendants from the Carnac long mounds. Some of the jadeite axes are up to 46 cm long and are very finely polished. It is possible that the jadeite is of western Alpine origin but it may well be from a local Breton source. A range of other hard rocks were used for axes. In the early stage of tomb construction local types were used but later the inland source of dolerite 'A' at Sélèdin, Côtes-du-Nord, with radiocarbon dates beginning in the later fourth millennium bc, came to provide up to 40 per cent of known axes in Brittany as well as significant quantities elsewhere. The main technique of extraction at Sélèdin was by detaching large blocks by percussion followed by their working down by other forms of hammering. There is little evidence for polishing on the site.[81]

The evidence is similarly fragmented in central-western France and the Paris basin. In the latter area the range of evidence seems to be rather similar to that of the Michelsberg culture but less intensively researched. The range of enclosures and settlements has already been discussed. Burials are few, and the megalithic monuments of the region seem to belong to the following horizon. There was certainly flint production on some scale, as mines at for example Hardivilliers, Oise testify, and stone axes were certainly imported from Brittany but there has not been sufficient study for the processes to be examined in detail or related to other evidence. Central-western France may have a rather wider range of evidence like the TRB complex, but its study so far is not closely integrated. Megalithic monuments of various types are distributed through the area but generally with a denser distribution to the north of the valleys with enclosures, and while long mounds and passage graves as at Bougon may start in the fourth millennium, the chronology of the type *angevin à portique* is uncertain. Axes were locally produced on flint and imported from Brittany.

The evidence from the British Isles is rather fuller. The contents of some ditches at some enclosures are unusual and are generally considered to have ritual significance. Thus the heaps of partially articulated animal bone in the middle and inner ditches at Windmill Hill have been seen as the remains of feasts rather than ordinary domestic consumption and at Hambledon Hill too (see Fig. 6.20) there is a contrast between the more fragmented bone of the subsidiary Stepleton enclosure and the less fragmented bone of the main inner ditch, a difference also interpreted in terms of normal and special use. In the main inner ditch at Hambledon Hill there is a primary deposit of occupation debris which seems to have been deposited deliberately in a narrow central linear spread, perhaps originally in containers. The primary deposits include also human remains. In at least one case these consist of a truncated body, but most commonly represented are skulls, spaced at intervals on the bottom of the ditch. Some 70 have been recovered from the 20 per cent sample excavated of the inner ditch, giving a likely total for the site far in excess of that known from any southern barrow. The ritual evidence varies from site to site, and it is noteworthy that at Hambledon there is evidence for substantial inner banks, maintenance of the ditches after the primary deposits in the form of recutting as well as more normal silting and deposition of rubbish. Some of the heavily eroded pits in the interior may also be unusual, since they contain concentrated selections of artefacts such as axes or objects such as red deer antlers. It may be pointed out that too little is known of the range of rubbish deposition on settlement sites generally, though it is claimed that some sites such as Goodland, Co. Antrim, dating from the earlier third millennium, stand out for the unusual nature of sherd-filled pits.[82] Overall there are good indications that some enclosures at any rate were important centres of ritual, even if this was not their only function; indeed the socially most important sites may come to be defined as those where the greatest range of functions coincide.

The importance of the dead for the living is reinforced by earthen and megalithic monuments. It is fortunate that some evidence survives for non-barrow burial, as in part of the TRB area. There is a single burial from Pangbourne, Berkshire, and a quadruple burial in an irregular-shaped pit some 120 m distant from the isolated house at Fengate, and it is likely that a large proportion of the population received no more formal burial than this. Others – again of an unknown proportion – may have been deposited in communal exposure areas (it has been suggested that some enclosures may have served this purpose) since many of the bodies placed in barrows were disarticulated, and those from the primary monument at Wayland's Smithy, Oxfordshire, may have been gnawed by rodents prior to deposition in the mound. The probability of selection is reinforced by the generally small numbers of bodies in southern barrows, not exceeding 50 or 60. It is also reinforced by the realisation that in the case of many earthen barrows, the construction of the mound was the final act in a long sequence of events beginning with in some cases the deposition of bodies in small mortuary structures, which were only later covered by a mound with timber revetment and monumental timber facade, as for example at Nutbane, Hampshire. So only certain burial places may have been selected for final aggrandisement, though in the case of megalithic or stone barrows – at least in the south – such a choice may have been made from the beginning. The range of forms of monument, even in southern England to say nothing of the British Isles as a whole, is impressive, and includes rectangular and trapezoidal long mounds, oval and round mounds in the non-megalithic tradition and long mounds with a variety of terminal and lateral chambers in the megalithic tradition. Two examples must suffice.[83] Fussell's Lodge, is a long trapezoidal earthen mound contained within a stout timber revetment and flanked by two quarry ditches covering at its eastern end remains of some 50 individuals arranged in piles between and over three pits. The burials were either covered or flanked by a flint cairn or possibly a wooden superstructure. The burials may have been followed by the timber revetment, and this in turn infilled by the mound. West Kennet, Wiltshire, in the vicinity of Windmill Hill, is another long earthen and chalk mound with flanking ditches, but with terminal megalithic facade, passage and transepted chambers. Primary burials in each of the five chambers totalled at least 50. Mound and chambers coexisted, and there are no visible means by which access to the chambers could be restricted. The collective burials of both monuments contained people of all ages and both sexes, though it may be noted that some monuments in the south covered individuals. At Fussell's Lodge the burials were disarticulated and show considerable arrangement and careful selection. In West Kennet too there has been much rearrangement of the skeletons, which are largely disarticulated. Particularly noticeable is the artificial ordering of longbones and skulls, but the treatment extends to the placing of fingerbones in the cracks of the chamber walls. There are also fewer skulls than the minimum number of individuals represented which has led to the suggestion that, as well as either simultaneous or successive deposition of already exposed skeletons, there may also have been deliberate removals of bones at some stage after deposition in the monument. It may also be noted that the range of possible practices, from direct burial to excarnation and post-deposition removal, varies from site to site and area to area.

The role of these monuments can be considered along with others already discussed. Most recent interpretations of the English tombs agree in ascribing an important social role beyond the sepulchral or religious.[84] They can be divided into more general explanations such as Renfrew's territorial and group markers, and more specific such as the symbol of differentiated society based on the small numbers represented or the deliberate masking of differentiated society through the assertion of the collective and denial of the individual and differences between individuals. One difficulty in choosing between these sorts of explanations lies in the tendency to treat the burial evidence in isolation. Given that the interpretation of burial evidence is fraught with problems either sort of explanation may seem plausible in its own right, and the assumption of balanced or differentiated social relations is then external. The physical placing of the monuments in the landscape in relation to settlement must be considered, but it is not well understood in detail. In general monuments in southern England are in upland rather than lowland locations, as on the Wessex and Sussex chalk and the Cotswolds, but largely absent from the upper Thames and East Anglia, though there is a small lowland Medway group in Kent. If then such monuments were territorial markers, why were they placed away from the most fertile areas, though certainly in areas as the environmental evidence shows which were cleared, sporadically cultivated and grazed? Do these represent marginal areas where pressure and competition between communities were most acutely felt? Or if the monuments were part of the ideology of more differentiated society, were they deliberately placed on the fringes of settlement as a further masking of social reality in some way? One example where settlement and monument coincide is Hambledon Hill, where a short barrow lies between the inner ditch and crossworks. Disappointingly the barrow has largely been destroyed by ploughing, though traces of human bone were recovered in its vicinity. Human bone in the Windmill Hill ditches can also be considered in relation to West Kennet long barrow. Closer at hand there is the Windmill Hill or Horslip long barrow, which probably lacked burials and may have been built originally with a low mound. There is then here the possibility that the monument was built to deceive, to look old, to artificially create legitimation, for instance of access to land or of social position, for its builders. Some other southern English evidence is relevant. There has been a long debate about the nature of stones on the outsides of long cairns in the Cotswold and Severn area. This 'extra-revetment' material in some cases may be the result of the natural decay of dry-stone walling, but in others it may again be a deliberate falsification, an attempt to create instant antiquity. One example, Ty Isaf in Powys, south Wales, seems to combine both artificial extra-revetment material and a combination of circular and long-barrow form, which appear contemporary rather than successive.[85] This evidence does not provide any neat solutions to the issues raised, but it does reinforce the impression that the burial monuments were a significant part of communal politics. The assumption has always been that they are local monuments, but the presence may be noted of dry-stone walling in West Kennet which is partly composed of oolitic limestone from a source some 30 km to the west.

There is little space to detail the range of monuments and burial practices in other parts of the British Isles. Virtually all the types known to belong to the Neolithic period are likely to date back to the fourth millennium bc, including passage graves. The pattern is of variation repeated and renewed from area to area, and within a given area, to suit local needs, so that no area has yet yielded a reliable typological sequence. A recent attempt to devise one in the Orkneys is based on the notion that the simpler tomb forms were earlier than the more elaborate, but the supporting radiocarbon dates are in several cases from secondary not primary contexts. Likewise in Ireland court cairns and passage graves appear not to succeed each other but to be contemporary. There are several cases documented of multi-period tombs, in which monuments were progressively enlarged and altered in form. Cremation was more widely practised than in the south of England, especially in northern England and Ireland. In court cairns rather few cremated remains are recorded, and they seem not to have been made in situ, while in other monuments such as the major Irish passage graves, or Quanterness on the

Orkneys, rather large numbers of individuals are presented, perhaps reaching into hundreds over the span of their use. The latter was thought to have provided burial for the whole population of its local area. But contrasts abound. The basal layer in the main chamber investigated at Quanterness contained three individual inhumations only. One of the most interesting contrasts exists in Ireland, between the widely distributed and numerous court cairns and the more nucleated passage graves, with the major cemeteries of the Boyne, Loughcrew, Carrowkeel and Carrowmore spaced at intervals from 25 to 70 km in a transect across the country. These have been seen as successive types, and to reflect a change from egalitarian to chiefdom society but, if as the radiocarbon evidence suggests they were contemporary, then they could be seen to have functioned at different levels, the court cairn more locally, and the great passage grave cemeteries having significance over a far wider area. It may then be no coincidence that architecture and associated ritual were heightened in the latter, with monumental facades, architectural extravagance or arcane ritual as in the Newgrange roof-box, decorative art both on the inside as well as the outside of orthostats and kerbstones, major tombs and 'satellites', elaborate decorated stone basins in the chambers to hold some of the cremated remains deposited, and only one pottery style – Carrowkeel ware – used inside the monuments (Fig. 6.24).[86]

6.24 The entrance stone at Newgrange cairn, Boyne valley, Eire. Photo: Commissioners of Public Works, Dublin

The wider connections of such cemeteries can be variously interpreted, such that on the one hand they reflect a means of resolving inter-communal competition or conflict, or on the other reflect the existence of considerable local hierarchy, and regional dominance by particular groups. If the latter, there is perhaps here another interesting case of the external or wide-ranging as a source of legitimation of power.

Such a notion requires further testing. The petrological study of stone axes other than flint in the British Isles is the most extensive and best published of its kind so far in Europe, and may offer some further insights, though leaving many questions unanswered.[87] Over 20 main stone groups have been indentified for the Neolithic period as a whole as sources of axes and other stone implements and in most cases the location of the source can be fairly precisely fixed on the ground. In some cases too the prehistoric workings can be traced, as in the case of the volcanic tuffs which needed flaking, as in the Lake District with group VI or in north Wales with group VII. It is difficult precisely to date their history but several sources were being exploited from the late fourth millennium bc, such as VI, and in Cornwall I, IV, XVI, and XVII; groups VII and IX in northern Ireland were in use by the earlier third millennium if not earlier. The range of groups used only in this earlier period was small, such as XVI and XVII, and the pattern of distribution one of steady fall-off in numbers with distance from source. Two groups, I and VI, have the greatest concentration of their products at over 100 km from their source. It is however difficult to relate the concentration of group VI products in east Yorkshire and Lincolnshire or of group I in East Anglia to the rest of the archaeological evidence, as by far the majority of the finds are strays. There is also a chronological problem, since there are indications that both sources were exploited for much of the third millennium. Interpretation is also incomplete without consideration of flint products. Flint mines and other sources are well documented, as in Sussex and Wessex, and were being exploited from the later fourth millennium bc. But while here the process of production is quite well understood, that of distribution is not, since the flints are rarely visually distinctive, and a programme of chemical trace-analysis has not yet come to fruition. Both flint and stone axes were probably widely used as functional tools, as marks on the preserved wood of the Sweet Track testify, and some part of the patterns of distribution could be explained in terms of functional demand and supply. There is a certain degree of mutual avoidance by the stone sources but the flint distribution is not yet integrated in this picture. The scale of production and the range of distribution – such as group VI axes into southern England, as at Windmill Hill – demand also non-utilitarian explanations. The distribution of very finely finished jadeite axes over the country, most probably from a non-British source, and also the handful of Breton dolerite A axes indicate the reality of the long-range exchange of prestige objects. This may have varied, and the contrast between the patterns of groups XVI and XVII, and I and VI could be seen as the difference between localised exchange and more organised and controlled distribution. The archaeological contexts of consumption remain however frustratingly rare. Flint axes are deposited whole in settlements, but were re-used as a source of quality flint; stone axes often erode badly. Neither are deposited in burials, though they recur in some numbers at enclosure sites. One of the most vivid clues is the presence beside the Sweet Track of a chipped flint axe and a jadeite axe, both in mint condition, in a context which suggests deliberate deposition not accidental loss. It is also difficult reliably to derive sociological information from the kinds of distribution, though it is tempting to see the patterns of groups I and VI as the result of more differentiated society. Perhaps also a contrast can be seen in the various levels of exchange, since one transaction could have served both to cement communal alliances and to enhance individual prestige. Perhaps the most significant aspect of all is the evident frequency of exchange, even though its nature is hard to pin down, which suggests that communities were extremely conscious of their mutual relations, even if these were ambiguous. This is reinforced by the realisation that even pottery was probably exchanged over considerable distances in south-west England, though it is not certain whether for its own sake or its contents, and that flint arrowheads too may have been exchanged as high-quality products.[88]

Other patterns of material culture can be brought into account. Styles of enclosure, barrow and pottery fall into broad regional zones though these are not coincident. Flint working was more uniform. As far as the chronology allows us to say, these differences were already established in the later fourth millennium bc, and could therefore be contrasted with the more uniform material culture of the early LBK. Material differentiation may be accentuated in the earlier third millennium bc, if the majority of enclosures can be thus dated and if Ebbsfleet pottery is then added to the decorated repertoire. Regional identity could be seen as increasingly important, though again there is an ambiguity in the overlapping distributions of different aspects. The change is not as apparently abrupt as in the northern TRB area but the earlier third millennium bc is again highlighted as a horizon of significant social change. It fits one of the themes of the book that subsequent developments over the wide area under consideration were nonetheless highly varied.

## 6.3 Change and continuity, 26/2500–2200 bc

*Chronology and material sequences 26/2500–23/2200 bc*

The final phase to be covered (Fig. 6.25) presents difficult problems of interpretation. Over many parts of the area settlement evidence has been sparse, and ritual and burial evidence dominant. Material change, with patterns of long-range unity as well as regional differentiation, has too often been seen as the result of population movement. Detailed chronology is no less doubtful, with vertical stratigraphies rare outside Hungary and Czechoslovakia or the Alpine foreland. Radiocarbon dates have occasionally been sought systematically, as in the Dutch and Danish Corded ware–Single grave complex and are accumulating for other areas, though a mere dozen

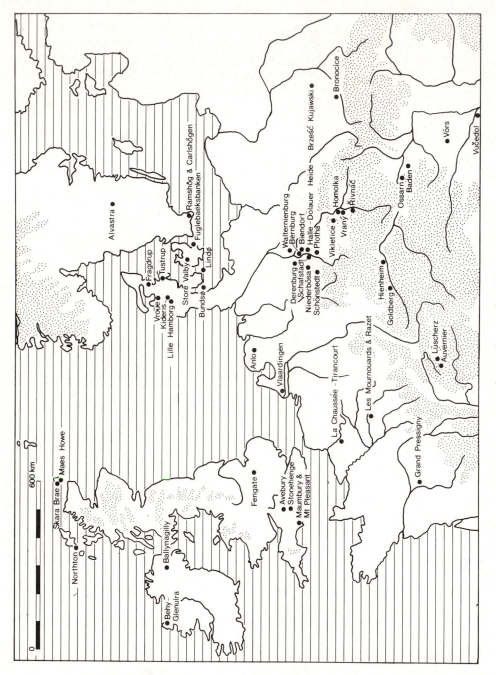

6.25  Simplified location map of the principal sites discussed in chapter 6.3, c. 26/2500–2200 bc

were quoted for four combined phases of the Baden culture in a recent survey. Where stratigraphy, radiocarbon dating and dendrochronology can be combined, as in Switzerland, there is a conflict with typology based on the claimed results from wider areas. Thus the supposedly early style of Corded ware from western Switzerland, as at Auvernier-la Saunerie, is on the basis of dendrochronology later than the supposedly mature style from Zürich–Presshaus in the north.[89] The later stages of the Baden sequence are not clearly established though various schemes have been proposed. A general trend seems to be towards more regional ceramic styles. In the eastern part of its distribution the site of Kostolac in north-east Yugoslavia represents development or variation probably in the mid third millennium bc, and this phase is in turn succeeded at some point late in the millennium by the more strikingly different Vučedol phase, the eponymous site being beside the Danube in northern Yugoslavia with underlying Baden layers. Vučedol pots include necked bowls and jars, and the tall, handled bowl is no longer represented. This sequence is seen in several stratigraphies, as at Gomolava. The later phases in Slovakia and Moravia are represented by local variants, the latter again by the site of Jevišovice. In Bohemia the Řivnáč phase is the equivalent late Baden phase or derivative, with a wide range of jars, amphorae jugs and bowls. The eponymous site was dug in the last century.[90]

The TRB continued to develop, marked by fresh phases in its respective five areas. Baden 'influence', as in the pottery at Bronocice, is posited in the south-east area, and a highly interesting development in the southern area is the apparently contemporary differentiation seen in the Walternienburg and Bernburg pottery styles probably dating to the mid third millennium bc. These developments are variably overlapped by two other novel complexes, that of Globular amphorae and Corded ware. Globular amphorae material comes from a wide area embracing the Elbe, Oder and Vistula rivers (with extensions further east), though not in continuous distribution, and from a range of settlements and burials. Characteristic artefacts are large handled amphorae often richly decorated, with other bowls and jars, and flint flat axes and chisels. Rather few radiocarbon dates indicate a position straddling the mid third millennium. The material overlaps with Řivnáč in Bohemia, and its beginnings may be variable in different parts of Poland.[91]

It overlaps also on the basis of radiocarbon dates and associations with the Corded ware or Single grave complex, which however seems to have begun at the earliest a little after the mid third millennium bc. This was more widely distributed, though again not continuously, stretching from Poland and Moravia (with a few extensions in Slovakia and northern Hungary) to the Rhine and the Netherlands and from the Alpine foreland to southern Scandinavia. The middle Elbe area with over 1000 finds has the densest regional distribution (Fig. 6.26). The most common sites are burial sites, indeed the great majority of those in the previous example, with flat graves, barrows and re-used megaliths, but there are also settlement sites known, and others may be poorly recognised.[92] Characteristic artefacts, at least from graves, include beakers and amphorae and perforated stone battle-axes, but

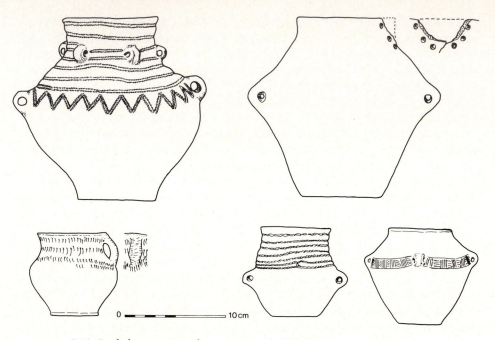

**6.26** Corded ware pottery from graves at the Schalkenburg, Quenstedt, Kr. Hettsdedt, central Germany. *After* Behrens and Schröter

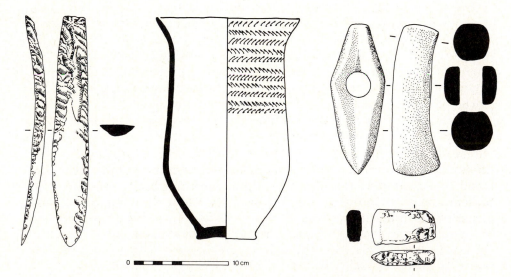

**6.27** Corded ware culture (Protruding foot beaker) artefacts from tumulus Galg-wandenveen 3, Eext, Drenthe, Netherlands. *After* Lanting and Van der Waals

assemblages include also other bowls and jugs, flint axes and arrowheads, and a range of shell and bone ornaments. Copper is hardly ever found (though sparsely represented in Globular amphorae contexts). A number of regional groups can be distinguished: thus graves on the Danish islands and Jutland rarely include amphorae. But it is widely believed also that beakers with corded neck decoration, A-type battle-axes and amphorae with incised and impressed decoration in metopic panels can be included in an early, rather uniform horizon.[93] There is radiocarbon and stratigraphic support for such a position for these beakers and battle-axes from the Netherlands, and Denmark (Fig. 6.27), but the same evidence does not exclude other types being as early, and the situation may be different in other areas. Internal development has been best studied in these two areas again, through the grave sequence which was recognised in the last century, through associated battle-axes and pottery, and more recently by radiocarbon dating, which has tended to blur the divisions between typological stages.[94] The sequence continues beyond the period covered by this book. The radiocarbon evidence suggests that the earliest beginnings are around 2400 bc, on the basis of a handful of Dutch results, with the bulk of dates from there and elsewhere coming from around 2300 bc onwards. After an earlier stage of research in which external origins were sought, the consensus of opinion now sees origins within the TRB orbit.[95] These are discussed below. A final important issue is the extent of overlap with the later TRB in the northern area. The conventional view has been that the Single grave sequence overlapped with the later TRB sequence (MN III–v). The basis for this was slender since the chief point of contact for the two sequences was via a Pitted ware arrowhead in a Single grave barrow at Fragdrup in northern Jutland; the TRB and Pitted ware correlation was more easily accessible. It has now been proposed that only the so-called Under-grave or early Single grave phase can be correlated with MN v, on the basis of a later Under-grave barrow overlying MN v occupation at Lille Hamborg in Jutland. This in its turn places complete reliance on the universal validity of the proposed grave sequence, which can be doubted. Radiocarbon dates certainly suggested greater overlap than with MN v alone (remembering also that MN III–v may not be chronologically distinct).[96]

In the conventional scheme the Pitted ware culture is represented in Jutland in MN III–IV, by a range of settlement sites with coarse pitted and combed pottery with short necks and pointed bases and triangular arrowheads (Fig. 6.28). Similar sites extend into the northern and eastern Baltic, and could be seen as part of a cultural tradition stretching back to the late fifth millennium bc.[97] On the western fringes of the TRB culture the coastal and estuarine Vlaardingen culture of the western Netherlands has plain flat-based pottery from a range of settlement sites. It too seems to overlap with both the TRB and Corded ware cultures, and can be seen as a continuation of the tradition seen earlier at Swifterbant and Hazendonk. To the west and south of the TRB there are similarly diverse developments. The Michelsberg culture is replaced in the middle Rhine by Corded ware, in the upper Rhine by Goldberg

**6.28** Pitted ware culture artefacts. Photo: Statens Historiska Museet, Stockholm

III material, and in the Federsee area by the Horgen culture a little earlier, since this replaces the Cortaillod culture in Switzerland from before the mid third millennium bc. Its flat-based straight-sided pottery is crudely decorated. In western Switzerland the Lüscherz group has coarse round-based pottery. Horgen pottery is reminiscent of Seine–Oise–Marne pottery, which succeeds the Chasseen in northern France and the Michelsberg in Belgium, probably in the mid third millennium bc. SOM material is best known from chalk-cut and megalithic burials, but some settlements are known. Finally across the Channel the Peterborough ceramic tradition continues, with a variety of other decorated round-based bowl styles in Ireland, and Scotland, while from around 2400 bc in England and Scotland the widely distributed Grooved ware style appears seemingly rapidly, with flat-based bucket-shaped pots richly decorated with cordons, grooves and impressions.

*Settlements and the social context of production*

The range of settlement types in the mature Baden culture continued as before, with sites widely distributed across the landscape and including

defended enclosures. It is possible that this development was accentuated by
the later third millennium bc, and the previous introduction of wheeled
transport, the importance given to pairs of cattle in graves, the likely
intensification of sheep husbandry and textile products, the reappearance of
horse bones in limited numbers, all point to the competitive social milieu in
which this may have taken place. While there are many open, lowland Řivnáč
sites, attention has been directed to the generally smaller enclosed hilltops.
Homolka near Stehelčeves in Bohemia consists of two probably successive
defensive systems surrounding a number of terraced houses on a small hill,
the second lying some 10–15 m beyond the first. The main element was
palisades and funnel-like palisaded entrances, but there are also stretches of
ditch. The outer line has not been continuously traced and could be
unfinished. The site as a whole is considered to have been shortlived and like
many others is considered to have ended in a great fire. Vraný near Slaný is
another *Höhensiedlung* with interior occupation inside a two-phase defence
enclosing 0.75 ha (Fig. 6.29). The second phase consists only of a palisade but
the first has a palisade fronted by a broad ditch and a projecting funnel-like
entrance. Further south Vučedol itself lies beside the Danube on a series of
small hills. Defences consisted of two ditches and palisade. These started in
the Baden phase of the site, the focus of the site being a triangular area 31 by
28 by 21 m, but were widened in the Vučedol phase proper. The central area

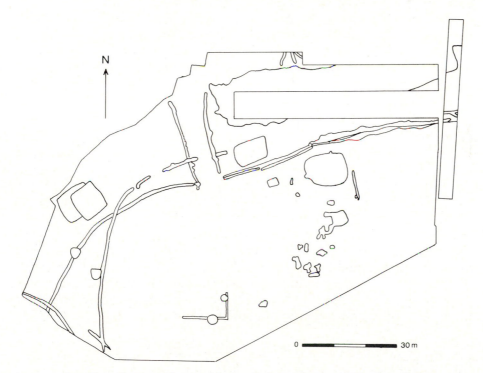

**6.29** Two-phase enclosure of the Baden culture at Vraný, Bohemia. *After*
Pleslová-Štiková

held one or two large houses in most phases, with a copperworking area in the first Vučedol layer.[98]

Further north one of the major themes to be followed is the continued extension of settlement, a process traced from the beginning of the fourth millennium bc. This can be seen again in the southern Polish survey. Late TRB or Baden related sites are found on the interfluve edge like earlier TRB sites, though in slightly greater numbers within the valleys themselves. Corded ware graves however are found further on to the interfluves still. The same sort of process is probably reflected in the numerous graves and monuments of the SOM culture on the chalk uplands of northern France, and there are some signs of small settlements accompanying them. SOM valley sites however remain rare, even in the well-investigated Aisne. The wide-spread appearance of Corded ware burial monuments on the heathlands of western and central Jutland can also without prejudice to the interpretation of the Corded ware culture be seen as part of the same process of continued intake of land. In some parts Corded ware barrows augment earlier monuments, as at Vroue in northern Jutland; in others they seem to represent new land use. The process is not universal or at least cannot be traced everywhere. Much Globular amphorae settlement consists of rather small, valley-oriented sites. While settlements themselves are rare Corded ware occupation in much of central Europe also seems to have an agricultural basis at least partly within the valley systems which had long been the focus of settlement. Where pollen evidence is available as in Denmark there are signs of a fresh impetus to clearance, which is consistent with a picture of extended settlement.[99]

It is clear that in many areas settlements have been difficult to recover or not recognised for what they are. It has been claimed for example in southern Sweden that there are many more potential Corded ware settlements than is appreciated because identical pottery to grave assemblages is wrongly sought on occupation sites. Some areas do however show continued signs of site differentiation, though the evidence is often varied. In the middle Elbe region of central Germany Globular amphorae settlements are small, rather peripheral, and poorly researched. Corded ware settlements are few, but the graves suggest a much wider pattern of settlement. More direct evidence for Bernburg occupation exists. At Quenstedt an extensive series of Bernburg pits overlies the palisade system described above, and at Halle–Dölauer Heide there is a Bernburg palisade enclosure of about 1.5 ha at the northern tip of the Langer Berg, containing dense pits and postholes, some of which extend beyond. Further south at Hienheim in Bavaria there are traces of Cham occupation (with bucket pottery analogous to Horgen wares) radiocarbon dated to just after the mid third millennium bc. Only some 20 scattered pits were recorded in the excavated area, the main feature being part of a substantial double-ditched enclosure up to 58 m in diameter though with rather shallow ditches. The Corded ware culture is also represented on the site, but only by a single burial within a distinctive palisade ditch 5 m in diameter. In southern Poland, Bronocice in the 'Baden-like' phase remains a very large site, and includes two separate stretches of ditch, up to 4 m and 7 m wide respectively though no deeper than 2 m.[100]

The Danish evidence may present a rather fuller picture, on the assumption of a significant overlap between the MN and Corded ware sequences. Major features are a wide range of settlement types, and a perhaps regionally organised economy. Eponymous sites of the later TRB sequence like Bundsø, Lindø and Store Valby are large sites, with well-developed cereal agriculture.[101] Corded ware barrows on the heathlands may reflect a more developed pastoral element, perhaps seasonal or mobile, though several cover traces of criss-cross ploughing, and pollen evidence from the northern Netherlands, as at Anlo in Drenthe shows increased cereal pollen at this stage as well as the creation of more open grassland or heathland.[102] A third element is the Pitted ware settlements of the north Jutish and Zealand seaboard and beyond. These were certainly in contact with TRB settlements, and may have been involved in the movement of flint, as well as swine grazing, fur trapping and sealing. It is possible that sealing was first intensified in the third millennium. Sites of this kind may have provided specialised products to a broader, differentiated regional economy. Much further north in the Baltic, in north-east Sweden, small-scale agriculture was practised in the later third millennium bc only when sealing and similar activities were already well established.[103] Vlaardingen sites in the Netherlands might have made a similar contribution to the local TRB economy. Solid wooden wheels have been dated to the late third millennium bc in both the northern Netherlands and Denmark indicating the further spread of wheeled transport beyond east-central Europe (Fig. 6.30).[104] Transport of this kind was perhaps a further element in a more differentiated economy.

Separate consideration must be given to the Corded ware culture. For a long time the traditional view was of incoming nomadic pastoralists, though this has been much modified by evidence for cereal agriculture, plough cultivation, clearance and wheeled transport connected with the culture. Nonetheless at least in some areas material differentiation could be connected in part with economic differentiation, and the creation of more sharply defined but symbiotic roles in the regional economy (rather than with extraneous ethnic identity). Continued social competition, in subsistence and production as much as in other spheres discussed below, may have encouraged such a trend, with different groups seeking separate niches in a more crowded landscape. In central Germany Corded ware settlement, though marked mainly by graves, represents the first major intake of the interfluves and large non-loess areas. Further north the pattern of permanent settlement in the Pitted ware culture indicates that this is no peripheral element but a flourishing population in its own right, and the permanent, fortified site of Alvastra in central-southern Sweden is a further indication of development in the area.[105]

In the Alpine foreland of Switzerland there is continuity in the kind of lakeside or bogside settlement seen earlier, sites of this nature continuing right into the Corded ware phase and indeed into the second millennium bc, but an interesting series of changes can be detected or suspected. It is possible

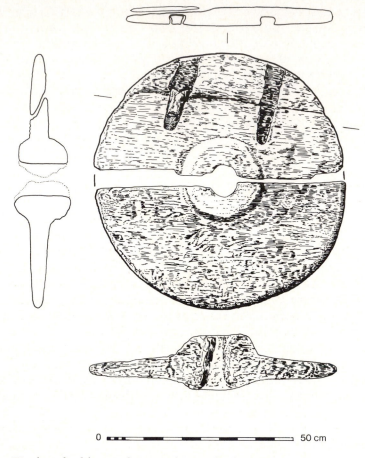

6.30 Wooden wheel from Kideris, northern Jutland. *After* Rostholm

that some sites were longer lived than earlier, on the basis of dendrochronological evidence from the Zürichsee and the Jura Lakes. The smaller moraine
lakes and bogs also tended to be abandoned or less used than before, Horgen
occupation in the Burgäschisee and Wauwilermoos sites being minimal. This
may reflect the emergence of rather larger sites. Pollen evidence from
Yverdon on Lac Neuchâtel and several Zürichsee sites indicates increasingly
large clearances in the later third millennium. Cereals remain abundant and
there are several finds of large quantities of cereals, legumes and other plants.
Peas are recorded in the Zürichsee first in the later third millennium (though
earlier on the Jura lakes) and beans and lentils may be a new crop in this
period, showing a new interest in legumes and possibly thus in crop rotation
and more intensive production. The treatment of different species of
domestic animals becomes more differentiated and perhaps thus more
organised, with greater numbers of adult cattle for example in Zürichsee sites
than previously and a larger kill of young pig. The increase in importance of
pig at many Horgen sites is notable but less easy to interpret. Ovicaprids

become more important in the Corded ware phase, and at Meilen–Rohren-haab on the Zürichsee over 60 per cent of preserved remains are of adults, suggesting that wool was now a major product. Though flax is well represented in floral samples, preserved textiles from this period seem increasingly to be woollen rather than linen. A lack of uniformity in age and sex patterns between sites may also indicate movement of animals. There is evidence for the exploitation of fur-bearing animals, in the form of high concentrations of fox bones at Auvernier–Brise Lames on Lac Neuchâtel. Disc wheels have also been recently dated to this horizon in Switzerland; wheeled transport would again be a plausible part of a more differentiated economy.[106]

In Britain and Ireland the rather diverse and wide-ranging evidence allows appreciation of a varied situation.[107] In some regions as in the north and west of Scotland there was essentially continuity with the previous situation, with small scattered but perhaps quite dense settlements prevailing on the Orkneys and Shetlands. Occupation at Skara Brae begins around 2400 bc, and the site was to include several nucleated stone-built houses with perhaps no little social importance, but the type may not be greatly changed from before. Settlements now appear in the Hebrides like Northton on Harris. Elsewhere the middle of the millennium may have been widely marked by a contraction of settlement and in the south the cessation of enclosure construction, followed by renewal of activity seen in fresh and larger clearances in the pollen diagrams. The example of Ballynagilly in northern Ireland illustrates this trend, with renewed clearance and 'Sandhills' occupation towards the end of the third millennium bc. Settlement was also extended into upland areas like the Pennines and low-lying heaths previously avoided.

In some areas recovery may have led to further intensification of production. At Behy–Glenulra in Co. Mayo in the west of Ireland an extensive field system has been recognised to pre-date blanket peat dating from around 2000 bc (Fig. 6.31). It incorporates a small settlement dated around 2500 bc and three other enclosures and a court cairn, but is itself not yet more closely dated. It consists of a minimum area of 1500 by 700 m divided by continuous parallel curving stone walls set 150–200 m apart, partially subdivided by cross walls forming fields up to 7 ha in extent. The size of the fields suggests that they were laid out for animal husbandry. Many other similar examples of land division are known from the area, and at nearby Belderg Beg probably at a similar date in the later third millennium bc less-regular walls were associated with both plough-marks and ridges of soil artificially raised, probably by a spade. The phenomenon can be variously interpreted. It may be solely due to the accidents of survival that here are the earliest permanent land divisions known in prehistoric Europe. The division of land could show an increased concern with territory among small agricultural communities of the kind already discussed in northern and western Scotland. But it can also be seen as an attempt to regularise and increase production, in the case of Behy–Glenulra perhaps as the excavator suggests, to provide secure winter grazing, or at Belderg Beg to facilitate crop rotation. It may not be coincidence that the first British evidence for legumes comes from the south of Wales at this date.

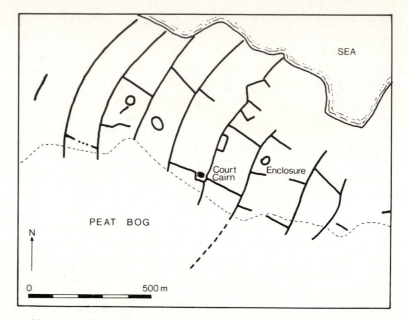

SEA

Court
Cairn

Enclosure

PEAT BOG

N

0          500 m

**6.31** Field system defined by stone walls and overlain by blanket peat, Behy–Glenulra, Co. Mayo, Eire. *After* Caulfield

Amongst all the other uncertainties, the social context of production remains dimly perceived, though one possibility here as elsewhere is that increased production was not merely to feed extra mouths but part of a changing, more competitive and intensive social milieu. The possibility exists also in other parts of Britain such as the chalk downland of southern England which was largely open grassland by this stage, and which perhaps supported an increasingly specialised pastoral economy. Pastoral specialisation is also seen at the end of the millennium on the East Anglian fen edge at Fengate, where small paddocks were defined by ditched boundaries, probably as part of the winter management or movement of cattle. No local cereal cultivation is recorded. Though too few sites have been adequately investigated, such putative specialisation can best be seen again as part of a regional rather than purely local economy.

*Other aspects of social relations: burial, ritual and material culture, 2600/2500–2300/2200 bc*

A danger in relying on the settlement and economic evidence is that despite the regional varieties observed an overall uniform view of society may result. This may be misleading since emergent regional economies may rather have been embedded in or been part of alternative social formations and transformations. One may suggest three main areas in which different social situations developed – east-central Europe in the orbit of the Baden culture; the TRB and Corded ware orbit from the Danube to southern Scandinavia and as far west as the Rhine; and northern France and Britain and Ireland outside the Corded ware phenomenon. Each of these will be examined briefly.

The Baden situation seems to have continued without great change. Burial practice was not strict, and there is considerable variety in the large cemeteries in terms of body position, grave goods and their placing, and so on. What this implies in terms of social ranking is unclear. It may be suspected here as on many occasions before that burial practice in fact to a larger extent masks social reality. As further south, copper seems to have been in short supply at this period, appearing mainly in the form of ornaments, awls, or small axes. The overall range of grave goods is not striking. The copper diadem found around the head of an adult in a small group of graves of Vörs is outstanding. The model cart burial and the cattle burials described earlier are also notable. They are restricted in number and the possession of wheeled transport in life may likewise have been very restricted. The later burial record is more fragmentary. Řivnáč burials for example have only been found sporadically, and at Homolka there were occasional cremations and pieces of human bone within the enclosure. The 'catacomb' burials at Vučedol have often attracted attention, with burials placed in earth-cut chambers beneath the large houses, one containing infants and young children, another a man and woman with large quantities of pottery and animal bones. It was suggested that the uniformity of Baden pottery styles and their long-discussed resemblances to styles as far south as the Aegean could be connected not only with innovations such as wheeled transport putatively coming from that southerly direction but also with the use of the external as a source of unity and authority. This uniformity persists for a while but as described above is gradually replaced by more regionalised styles. This may mirror the inferred increased restlessness and competitiveness of the later third millennium bc in east-central Europe. Evidence for ritual does not figure prominently in the record but is certainly a final feature worth consideration. Ossarn in Austria for example, one of the original eponymous sites of the Baden culture, is a high-lying site with some 30 pits, whose unusual contents suggest some sort of ritual practice. These held mainly complete pots, but also burnt grain and human bone. Some small Baden figurines and face pots have been found, and there are also various items of ritual paraphernalia at Vučedol in the form of small stands, horned tables and legged bird-like models in clay. If this reflects increasingly arcane ritual controlled by socially dominant sites, it reinforces the picture in this part of Europe of established social differentiation by the later third millennium bc.

A rather different and more rapidly changing situation may be suggested in the next main area under discussion, in west-central Europe, which offers rather more contrasts and contradictions, though it does not appear that these were fully resolved by the end of the period covered here, between the collective and the individual, the unified and the differentiated, the regional and the local. For example in the middle Elbe Walternienburg–Bernburg group of the mid third millennium bc burial practices become rather more varied than before in the area, ranging from individual graves (Walter-

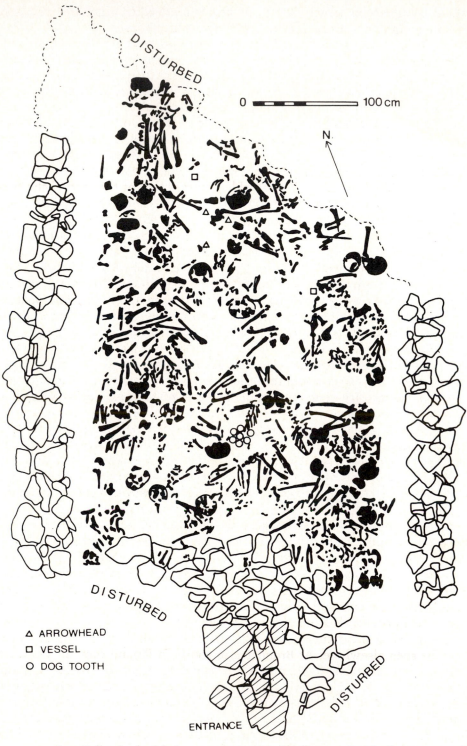

DISTURBED

0 ⊏⊐⊏⊐⊏⊐ 100 cm

N.

DISTURBED

△ ARROWHEAD
□ VESSEL
○ DOG TOOTH

DISTURBED

DISTURBED

ENTRANCE

**6.32** Collective burials in stone structure at Nordhausen, Kr. Nordhausen, central Germany. Walternienburg–Bernburg phase. *After* Behrens

nienburg itself being a group of 20 such) to megalithic constructions. A notable addition are the large collective burials housed in rectangular low-walled structures, probably originally roofed or tented, such as Derenburg, Schönstedt or Niederbösa (Fig. 6.32).[108] Derenburg measures some 3.8 by 9.7 m in the interior. It contained the disarticulated partly burnt remains of some 70 people, of whom only 32 were estimated to be over 20 years old. This can be compared with the rather similar figures of 28 out of 64 and 50 out of 93 at Schönstedt and Niederbösa respectively. Both men and women are more or less evenly represented among the adults though proportionately more older men were found than older women. As always the collective emphasis in the burial mode is hard to interpret, as it may have satisfied either communal or more individual interests. It is notable however that at this period the two ceramic styles become sharply differentiated and seem for the most part to be found on separate sites, though still it is considered in contemporary use. Walternienburg pottery is also associated with very elaborate perforated battle-axes with expanded blades. *Tiefstich* pottery may also have been current for much of the period in the north of this area. Differentiation can also be seen in the area in the Globular amphorae assemblages and burials which must also overlap with Walternienburg–Bernburg assemblages (though as described above of much wider distribution), which contain distinctive pottery, flat flint axes with squared sides and a little copper in the form of ornaments and small tools. The crouched inhumation burials were put in this area in earth-cut graves (elsewhere often in stone cists), either individually or with two or three others, and occasionally more. Grave goods were abundant with up to ten pots per grave, though more usually with three or four, accompanied by one to three flint axes, and animal bones including pig and boar jaw bones. There are also burials which include two or more cattle with the human remains, as at Biendorf, Kr. Bernburg, and separate cattle burials altogether, usually paired as at Plotha, Kr. Weissenfels (Fig. 6.33).[109] In this complex there is thus less emphasis on the collective, and more striking is its differentiation from contemporary and spatially overlapping neighbours. It is difficult to see in this differentiation a simple correlation with separate human groups if these are to be defined as each having distinctive physical, linguistic and cultural characteristics. It is plausible to see in this development the further use of material culture as a source of group identity, and such groups could be seen as ethnic in that rather different sense. The increased need for such self-definition, now in spatially overlapping patterns as opposed to the earlier pattern of contiguous distributions, is a possible further indication of stress in society.

From the nature of the evidence generalisation is difficult but similar signs can be seen elsewhere. At Bronocice in southern Poland there is a curious multiple burial belonging to just after the mid third millennium bc with the partial remains of 17 humans placed at the base of a circular pit, with pottery, burnt clay and animal bones above them.[110] There were 13 children, and two young men and two young women. The oldest man was placed at the centre of the pit, the women on its edge. Further north in the middle Vistula area there

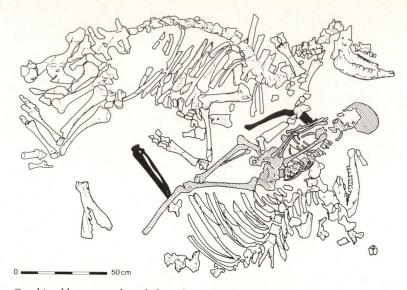

0 ▬▬▬▬▬▬ 50 cm

**6.33** Combined human and cattle burial at Mittelhausen, Kr. Sangerhausen, central Germany. Globular amphorae culture. *After* Behrens

is a wide variety of Globular amphorae burials in cists either earth-sunk, or barrow-covered or even in existing barrows. Cattle burials occur again, at Brześć Kujawski for example actually forming a small separate cemetery. Three graves have two cattle each and two have individual cattle, one of these incorporating also a child burial and the other a dog skeleton. Globular amphorae material also occurs in a restricted area within Bronocice.

In southern Scandinavia chronological difficulties bar any easy interpretations of the evidence. We have already seen that many if not most passage graves were constructed when MN ɪb and MN ɪɪ pottery was available and there are radiocarbon dates of around 2700–2600 bc for this horizon. Some dates however are a little later and this phase of collective emphasis in burial may thus continue into the beginning of the period covered here. As discussed above there is also some reason to believe that MN ɪb is not necessarily wholly distinct chronologically, and thus a small series of 'culthouses' with MN ɪb pottery but with radiocarbon dates firmly in the middle of the third millennium are of considerable interest, and may represent a further elaboration of passage grave practices.[111] In one example at Tustrup in north-east Jutland a stone-walled rectangular structure with one open end had interior dimensions of 5 by 5.5 m, with an original birch bark and turf roof. A stone setting in the interior has been seen to mark a grave but no bones have been recovered, and the notable feature is some 26 decorated pots and clay spoons. These are in the same style as pottery in three megalithic monuments dispersed on the arc of a semicircle about 50 m distant. One is a small polygonal dolmen, another a small round passage grave, and the third a substantial oval passage grave with a lateral as well as a main chamber. Such culthouses may have been an important focus for continued ritual at passage graves, which in some cases resulted in the deposition of thousands of sherds in the passages and entrances of the monuments. At Ramshög in south-east Sweden the total was some 7000–8000 sherds though the figures in Denmark are much lower. At Fuglebaeksbanken, described above, just under 1000 sherds were recovered, covering the range of styles from MN ib to MN v but with a peak in MN iii.

Another late elaboration in the MN tradition are stone packing graves in west and central Jutland.[112] At Vroue these have MN iv and v pottery and are radiocarbon dated to around 2300–2200 bc. The simple earth-cut graves are arranged side by side and are commonly disposed in long lines. At Vroue Hede, in one part there are about 20 between a *langdysse* on one side and a *runddysse* and a passage grave on the other; at another a line of nine lead up to a passage grave. Unfortunately bone preservation is minimal, and grave goods few. This development is not certainly pre-Corded ware, but the more individual emphasis reflected in it is a further possible indication of change within the MN tradition, and a possible clue that the ideology of the collective was being abandoned.

This last possibility is more clearly seen in the Corded ware horizon. Notable general features of the complex are its more pronounced emphasis on the individual in burial practice, the selection of a restricted range of prestige objects, and the very wide area over which common elements were distributed. As has been discussed, the complex is unlikely to be chronologically separate from previous cultures and groups. Though this is controversial in Denmark it is well enough documented elsewhere and one must be careful therefore to avoid discussion of the complex in isolation. Out of a great mass of burial evidence four examples must suffice. At Halle–Dölauer Heide in the middle Elbe area there are 17 Corded ware burials in 11 investigated round mounds. The individual burials, poorly preserved but seemingly of all ages and both sexes, were placed in earth-cut graves or stone cists. Up to four were found under a single mound. The earthen mounds were up to 25 m in diameter and 2 m high. Bodies were generally aligned on a west–east axis with different positions for each sex, males on their right with the skull to the west and females *vice versa*. The cist in mound 3 has a male burial (probably not of the earliest Corded ware type) with beaker, amphora or sandstone axe and a flint axe, and two long flint blades. Another burial contains the unusual total of eight pots, and two have small copper beads. The characteristic battle-axes were not found. One of two cists in mound 6 was formed of large wall- and roof-slabs to form an interior 3.2 by 1.3 m and 1.5 m high, and was marked by two further uprights at one end and an approaching trench. It held the remains of a burial, probably of a man, but no finds, and its attribution to the Corded ware culture is not altogether certain. There are two radiocarbon dates of around 2100 and around 2000 bc. The cist is notable for the pecked decoration on seven of the wall stones, in linear hatched and zigzag motifs, in two cases further highlighted by white colouring. At Quenstedt there were no mounds observed over some 22 Corded ware graves arranged in four small groups at distances of 15–50 m, some cutting the Bernburg pits already

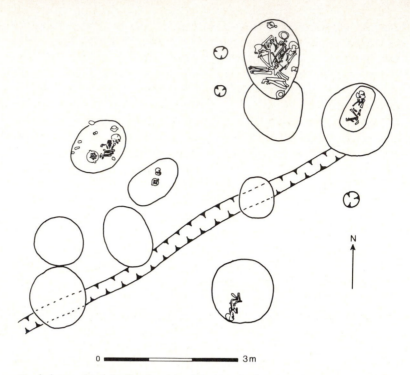

0 ▰▰▰▰▰▰▱▱▱▱ 3m

**6.34** Corded ware burials, Bernburg (and Bronze Age) pits, and part of the TRB or earlier palisade system at the Schalkenburg, Quenstedt, Kr. Hettstedt, central Germany. *After* Behrens and Schröter

described (Fig. 6.34). The graves were simple rectangular or oval earth-cut pits. There were 18 single burial and four double burials, and two graves empty except for goods. Out of 24 people 14 were infant or juvenile. Grave goods were either beakers, or beakers and amphorae, and other ornaments, and small artefacts including a little copper and in two double graves there was also a faceted perforated battle-axe, probably with males. Bodies were mainly laid west–east but with some variation, and there was again a strong distinction between right- and left-sided placings.[113]

Some Corded ware burials have been found in larger concentrations.[114] There is an example in the same area of 70 burials at Schafstadt and the largest example of all at Vikletice in Bohemia with 164 Corded ware graves. One hundred and thirty-eight graves held grave goods. There is again right- and left-side discrimination, and the full range of grave goods, which were mainly not of the earliest Corded ware types and extremely varied in association. Cluster analysis suggests a minimum of eight types of association, though these may not all be contemporary. Some were linked to sex, and in the earlier phase a small group of adult women had decorated amphorae, little jugs or cups and flint blades, and a small group of men had smaller-sized decorated amphorae, beakers, flint blades, and battle-axes or maceheads or stone axes. In northern Jutland close to Vroue there is a series of barrows at Molgård and

Koldkur, up to 23 m in diameter and 3.5 m high which have yielded Corded ware burials. Of those investigated 11 held one single grave, 13 two and 2 held three single graves. The graves themselves had again a mainly west–east orientation though with some variation, but unfortunately skeletal traces were recovered in only 14. The position of the graves relative to the ground surface varied and fits the classic sequence of Under-grave, Ground-grave and Over-grave, the majority here belonging to the middle type. Pots were here rather rare as grave goods (and there were no amphorae), battle-axes and flints being dominant. The typology of battle-axes here quite satisfactorily matches the grave typology. No. 9 at Molgård had one under-grave and three over-graves, the former with remains of a body on its right side with its head to the west, a battle-axe of type E2, a flint blade and a flint chisel. There was also in this probably male grave a flint axe at the base of the grave, and other flints in the grave fill. Two of the over-graves had no goods, but one held amber beads and two more developed battle-axes. Many other examples have been recorded in Denmark, elsewhere in southern Scandinavia with distinctive boat-shaped battle-axes, and in the Netherlands again with distinctive orientations and other features.[115]

Corded ware burials also occur to a certain extent in earlier burial monuments. The mound no. 6 at Halle–Dölauer Heide is one sort of case, where a pre-existing monument was enlarged in this horizon. More typical further north is the example of the passage grave at Hagebrogård in northern Jutland, again not far from Vroue. This was constructed early in the MN sequence (perhaps even with the MN 1a pottery style rather than the usual MN 1b). The upper layers of the chamber however contain two battle-axes. There are other examples from Jutland, and from the islands. Many monuments however were not so affected or disturbed, and the earlier chamber deposits at Carlshögen in southern Sweden for example survived intact through to the local Late Neolithic period, in the early second millennium bc. Even on the minimal view of TRB–Corded ware contact, physical overlap is allowed in the MN v phase, and rather longer overlap has been suggested here. The evidence of the earlier monuments is thus very important, for it may suggest a rather different situation to that seen in the case of Walternienburg–Bernburg and Globular amphorae assemblages further south. There the possibility of distinct self-defining human groups was explored, but no suggestion was made of functional or hierarchical differences between such groups. In the Danish case however such possibilities do arise, especially since Corded ware burials occur in the monuments of the indigenous tradition. If the chronological overlap is genuine, the users of both sorts of material assemblages may have been of essentially the same population, but those with Corded ware material may have been seeking to redefine their position in relation to the rest of society. The material differentiation could then be seen as an expression of social hierarchy beyond increased competition between groups. In terms of burial practice the individual rather than the collective is now emphasised, though the connection with earlier monuments is important, and the occurrence of individual graves in sequences in mounds and the

occurrence of mounds in concentrations or cemeteries (rather than in isolation) indicates that the individual had significance only in relation to a group
even if this did not now reflect the whole community. It may then be possible
to suggest real changes in the distribution of power and authority within
society, at least in this area, and in the ways this was expressed. Considering
the burial sequences, a relevant factor to take account of may be the transfer
of power and authority from generation to generation. It is at this point that
the interests of individual families, kin groups or other special interest groups
may have been under most threat, and required the greatest display by the
living to justify or enhance their achieved position.[116] The very frequency
with which individual burials were repeated could then indicate the state of
social competition.

This picture can be supported by consideration of the restricted number of
prestige goods in use in Corded ware assemblages. The nature of the prestige
goods varied. Copper was again in short supply and hardly significant. Pottery
can only have had ascribed rather than innate value, though battle-axes in
terms of the labour required to make them and the distances over which the
raw material may have travelled may have been rather more potent symbols
of social distinction. Their real significance however lies more in the context
of their use, since similar artefacts had been in use since the fourth millennium bc. The burial context and the restricted assemblages are for the most
part novel. Battle-axes (though more important numerically outside central
Germany) are also now firmly associated with adult men. They are in many
areas relatively uncommon; thus in the former area of the western TRB
group, only 60 or so have been recorded. Their distribution at an apparent
spacing of about 10 km in this area is again consistent with the notion of the
emergence of local hierarchies. The relatively rapid succession of battle-axe
types compared to the earlier rate of change is surely significant too, and
novelty seems to have gained increased importance in its own right. This may
be the best context in which to see the import of flint daggers of Grand
Pressigny flint into the area of the western Corded ware culture, especially in
the lower Rhine area, where they are thought to have been in use for a
relatively short period, equivalent to the Ground-grave phase. Grand Pressigny itself is south of the Loire in France, the source of distinctive honey-
coloured flint used for the production of long blades, which in Corded ware
contexts are fashioned into chipped and polished 'daggers'. Its products were
thus distributed over hundreds of kilometres in preference to locally available flint sources.[117]

Despite the various regional differences in burial practice and artefact
assemblages, a third significantly novel feature of the Corded ware culture is
its broad distribution. Indeed it almost marks a return to the scale of cultural
similarity seen right at the beginning in the Linear pottery culture. The
regional differences cannot however be ignored, even if the consensus of
opinion suggests that they were a secondary development following a primary *Einheitshorizont*. Unfortunately closed finds of this supposed horizon
are extremely rare. There are finds of early beakers and battle-axes in the

Netherlands, and of battle-axes in Denmark, but both lack amphorae. Closed finds of this kind are missing in the middle Elbe region. In Switzerland as we have seen there is the possibility that material typologically early by reference to central and northern Europe was there late. A possible context for this inversion is the deliberate use of 'old' types to reinforce the symbolic nature of prestige objects. This picks up themes discussed as far back as the early post-glacial period. It is also obviously difficult to test the notion of an *Einheitshorizont* without much better dating evidence. But even the less dramatic concept of considerable inter-regional similarity is significant. I suggest that this similarity is not to be explained primarily in terms of population movement, immigration or displacement. First of all, the physical anthropological evidence does not bear any such simple interpretation, and it seems likely that there were too many factors influencing genetic change for any supposed immigration reliably to be identified. The pattern is rather of continuous physical changes in the observed populations (and in several areas bone hardly survives well enough to be examined).[118] Secondly, there is too much continuity with previous settlement and many cultural practices for the hypothesis of immigration to be necessary. Thirdly, the argument for immigration rests essentially on material change and differentiation, and this can have other explanations, particularly as population movement can hardly be sought to correspond with every previous ceramic change, and the preceding horizon in the mid third millennium is also marked in many areas by just such a process of material differentiation.

It remains then to frame alternative explanations. These are best sought in terms of the use of material culture in relation to the emergence of local social hierarchies. Just as in eastern Europe, as we have seen in chapter 5, a period of increased stress and contradiction in society is followed by one of more open hierarchy, accompanied by a considerable increase in the number of long-range cultural features. These can be taken to reflect the creation of long-range alliances and the enhanced use of the external and non-local as a source of legitimation for local social differences, rather than the arrival of new population from an unknown source. This possibility would be reinforced if the claimed *Einheitshorizont* can be substantiated. But precisely because the situation may involve a mixture of long-range and local factors, it is important to recognise that the Corded ware phenomenon may have been very varied in different areas. Within the Vikletice cemetery itself anyway cluster analysis identified some seven or eight sets of associations which cannot all be attributed to change over time. The Swiss context may have been radically different to the Danish, and so on. It is also important in the light of this variety not to overplay the argument for developing social hierarchy. Indeed some authors have considered hierarchy to be little developed in some parts of the Corded ware distribution, or even in some sense reduced, as suggested for part of Denmark.[119]

A final feature of the Corded ware complex of considerable interest is its western limit, since it is not represented much west of the Rhine. In the Paris basin and in the British Isles there is a continued emphasis, at least in part, on elaborate and large collective works, and nothing like the Corded ware phenomenon, though some features within the British Isles do show increased material differentiation and regional link-up. There is a variety of Seine–Oise–Marne burial monuments in the Paris basin, with chalk-cut *hypogées* and megalithic 'gallery graves' being the dominant types. These occur in considerable density overall and far on to the interfluves, and there are also some notable local concentrations, as at Razet, Coizard, Marne (Fig. 6.35). Collective burials have been recorded, where left undisturbed, especially in the *hypogées*. Grave goods are undistinguished, though beads and pendants are abundant, and bone, flint and pottery also represented. The numbers of burials vary from a few to perhaps over 60. Two rather modest *hypogées* at Les Mournouards, Le-Mesnil-sur-Oger, Marne, each contained about 60 inhumations. No. 2 had a chamber only 3 by 3 by 1 m, with the bones in disorder. No. 3 had a small antechamber, and a chamber 5 by 3 by 1 m, with bodies in both parts arranged head to toe, and with some evidence for special treatment of skulls. There are also tombs with perhaps only two or three bodies. All ages and both sexes are represented. The state of bodies or rather skeletons within the chambers has been recorded in only modest detail but it seems that for the most part bodies were placed more or less complete in *hypogées*, but more disarticulated in *allées couvertes*. There are signs of internal ordering of remains in the chambers too, for instance rows of bodies, or vertical or horizontal separation by stones. There is a little evidence too for localisation of certain categories, such as infants, and possibly some for other

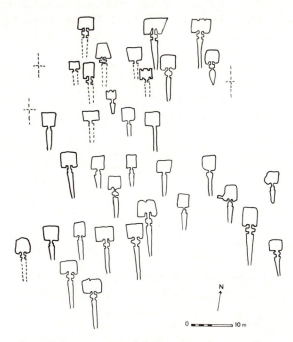

**6.35** Plans of the cemetery of chalk-cut tombs at Razet, Coizard, Marne, northern France. *After* Bailloud

age or sex groups, though the relevant studies cannot now be checked. A few tombs have engraved, perhaps anthropomorphic symbols, generally in the passage area of the monument. The recent excavation of a northerly subterranean *allée couverte* at La Chaussée–Tirancourt, near Amiens, Somme, is exceptional, since the 9 m long monument contained the remains of over 300 individuals. Of further interest was the fact that these were deposited in several phases and in quite separate internal boxes, each with up to a few dozen people and one at least with mainly children's bones.[120] The whole corpus of evidence is in need of review, but one may see in it signs of the separation of burial practice from settlements, of collective aspects mixed with internal categorisation and ordering, such as we have seen already in other areas. Such evidence could be taken to suggest communities in a state of transition, without yet the changes established which have been suggested in the Corded ware area east of the Rhine.

There are some three features of major interest in the British Isles in this period, and if one is to risk such generalisations they may perhaps suggest a situation somewhere between the two just described above. First, the earlier causewayed enclosures were no longer constructed, though they remained in some use with their ditches largely silted up, but are replaced by the 'henge' tradition of enclosures. These are ditched and banked enclosures of rather varied form and size, and the single label is probably insufficient. The ditch is generally but not invariably internal, and there is sometimes an extra external ditch. There are generally one or two opposed entrances. There are internal features such as timber and stone settings in some henges and also pits in an early phase at Stonehenge and shafts at Maumbury Rings, Dorchester, Dorset. The very largest henges such as Durrington Walls, Avebury, and Mount Pleasant in Wessex were probably constructed just after the period considered here. It is generally considered that these were non-domestic ceremonial or ritual sites. It is also worth noting that sites of this general kind occur now from the south of England right up into the Orkneys in the north of Scotland, so that the previously regional monument distributions are now far exceeded. These monuments may also suggest a state of social transition. Considerable labour was mobilised for their construction, and the practice of ritual at them can be documented in the form of deposited artefacts and animal bones, especially of pig. The collective aspect may however be offset by the perhaps more centralised organisation of necessary labour, and by the indications that ritual was controlled. Internal ditches for example may have separated spectators from activities within. There are other large monuments which belong to this horizon, such as the cursus monuments formed of parallel banks with external ditches and often but not invariably closed terminals or ends. The most massive example, in Dorset, is over 10 km long and was probably constructed in at least two phases. There are long barrows at either end, and it is possible that it dates back to at least the mid third millennium bc and is in some way also connected with the cult of the dead as well as the practice of public ritual. The smallest cursus monuments are less than 300 m long. The Dorset example lies on rolling chalk country, but most others are in river valleys, and are found as far north as northern England. Some stone circles were probably also constructed by the end of this phase independently of henges. These too can vary enormously in size and form. Many in fact are not circles but laid out carefully in other shapes such as ellipses. There have been claims of sophisticated geometry and a regular unit of measurement used in their layout, and of a scientific astronomical use for the observation and prediction of the rising, setting and eclipse of the sun, moon and certain first-order stars. But these claims are controversial and it is likely that if regular orientations can be substantiated they can only be classed as the fruits of ritual rather than scientific observation. This may be a further sign of unequal access to arcane ritual practice. Older burial monuments were also re-used or accessible in this period, and there has been the suggestion for the Orkneys at least for continued construction such as of Maes Howe, though the radiocarbon evidence is equivocal since samples are not derived from primary contexts. There are also at least some individual burials in small round mounds belonging to this phase.[121]

The other two features concern material culture. The emergence of the Grooved ware ceramic tradition represents greater material differentiation than before, since it occurs in the same areas and often in the same sites as the Peterborough tradition. At the same time Grooved ware reflects in its findspots a much broader distribution than seen before since variants of it are spread from the Orkneys to southern England (though not in Ireland). Thirdly, there is now a greater variety of unusual artefacts in association with Grooved ware, such as flint knives, arrowheads and axes, bone pins, and stone and antler perforated maceheads. There is a fine collection of unusual carved stone objects at the already mentioned site of Skara Brae on the Orkneys, for example. Grooved ware itself does not appear in burial contexts though maceheads and other objects do, as at Duggleby Howe in eastern Yorkshire.[122] It is possible too that in Ireland local copper working was already under way. The earliest definite associations of Irish copper artefacts are with beakers, in the horizon after that considered here, but the production of thick-butted flat axes, which are generally agreed to be typologically the earliest Irish type, could well go earlier still, since finds are strays or unassociated hoards. If such early copper working were to be accepted, its origins are nonetheless unclear. It is not impossible that by comparison with Iberia and eastern Europe it was a largely independent development, or it may have been derived from other metalworking areas of the third millennium bc in central-western Europe. Copper working in Ireland need not perhaps receive undue emphasis, but it is a further interesting illustration of the process whereby material culture was increasingly used in novel and different forms. The British situation itself need not be seen as uniform, and every allowance can be made for regional variation in the significance of these developments, but taken as a whole it presents a contrast to both the Corded ware and the north French situations, in the former of which it was suggested that there was more open hierarchy expressed combined with long-range link-up between elites, and in the latter some elaboration of 'archaic' collective burial with nonetheless signs of internal categorisation. Britain and Ireland show an elaboration of 'archaic' collective public activity, but combined with regional link-up and also some differentiation expressed in material culture. It has also been suggested that such public collective activity expresses a collective ideology which in actual fact served to mask real social difference by this period in Britain.[123] The various interpretative possibilities and the various regional contrasts when central-western Europe is considered as a whole lie at the heart of the matter. There are on the one hand regularities in the observable patterns, thus repeated contrasts between uniformity and differentiation in material culture or between collective and more individual monuments and ritual, and an overall trend to the establishment of greater social difference within and between communities, but on the other hand variation is everywhere visible, both between and within regions and cultural complexes. The evidence resolutely resists being forced into neat linear schemes of social evolution. This must be seen as supporting the view that we are essentially concerned with the working-out of internal social change, not the effects of external environment, climate or economy, and that the locus of change lies in the web of social relations which were relevant at local no less than regional levels.

# CHAPTER 7

# PATHS OF CHANGE IN THE MEDITERRANEAN REGIONS, 4000–BEFORE 2000 bc

## Environment

As for earlier periods the distribution of environmental evidence if uneven, and the most intensive research has probably been concentrated in southern France. Continued sea-level rise previously described led to further lagoon formation, and at the mouth of the Rhône at least to the creation of an alluvial plain which was exploited from the later fourth millennium bc onwards. But the rate of rise was probably slowing and it is considered that by the mid third millennium bc sea level was little below its present state. The Atlantic period continued in southern France to 3000–2500 bc, succeeded thereafter by the Sub-Boreal, though it remains to be seen whether such terms can be retained as research becomes more detailed. Vegetationally, developed forest continued to be important, with a still large deciduous component. Forest animals are also represented in fourth and third millennia assemblages from lowland south-east Spain. Increasing clearance however was made in lowland French areas, and one effect of this may have been to increase the evergreen forest components such as holm oak (*Quercus ilex*). There is far greater uncertainty over temperature and humidity in these millennia, and the various lines of evidence are frequently contradictory. However isotopic studies of shells in both southern France and northern Italy suggest cooler conditions after around 3500 bc, though perhaps with some relative rewarming after around 2500 bc. Humidity is even less well understood. The long-term trend in southern France seems to be towards greater dryness from around 4000 bc onwards, but different fluctuations are suggested by different sorts of study. Southern Spanish evidence is also compatible with drier conditions in the third millennium, though the evidence from pollen, sediments and soils is rather meagre. The future need is for more detailed research combined with some awareness of regional systems of weather, since aridity may have been more acute further south.[1]

## The nature of the evidence

Many of the remarks made in chapter 3 are also relevant to the area in this period (Fig. 7.1). The recovery of sites has been haphazard, and open sites without upstanding features have been particularly neglected until recent systematic surveys and also in southern France the advent of more extensive earth-moving operations than the uprooting of old vineyards. Excavation has

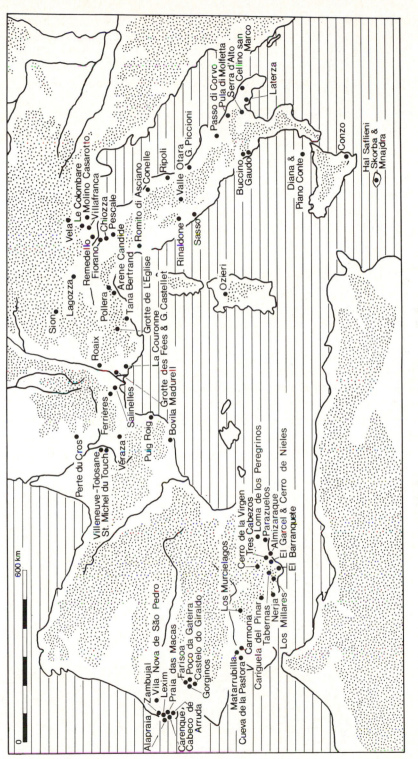

7.1 Simplified location map of the principal sites mentioned in chapter 7

often been limited in extent, and methods of recovery unsystematic. Radio-carbon dates remain most abundant in southern France. There are traditions of research on more visible features and monuments of these two millennia which go back into the nineteenth century in nearly all the major regions concerned. For example, by the end of the nineteenth century such sites as the lakeside village of Lagozza, the enclosed settlement and tombs of Los Millares, and many other megalithic tombs, had already been investigated. In part such traditions are some compensation for the dearth of systematic research, but in other ways are now a barrier to the full understanding of monuments and other features in their wider setting, since early excavation itself was unsystematic and badly recorded. The early investigation of Los Millares provides a case in point. As was stressed in chapter 3, perhaps here more than anywhere else in Europe future research is likely to radically change current perspectives and understanding.

## Material sequences and chronology, c. 4000–c. 2700/2500 bc

In southern Italy as elsewhere continued cultural change has for the most part been monitored through the further development of fine-ware pottery (Fig. 7.2). Four stages have been suggested on the basis of recent investigations and their incorporation with older results. The Passo di Corvo phase described above may last into the fourth millennium but the earlier part of the millennium is thought to be taken up with two Scaloria phases (lower and upper), in which painted pottery was well represented, and in the upper phase

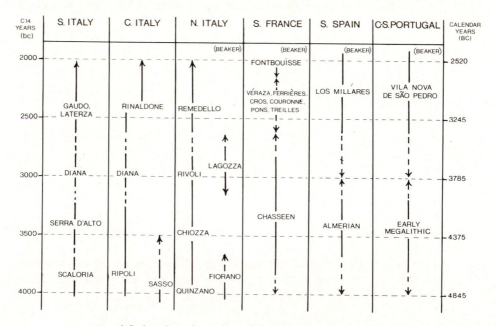

7.2 Simplified outline chronology of the main areas discussed in chapter 7, c. 4000–2200 bc

characterised by a range of garland, flame and meander motifs. At some point in the mid fourth millennium these styles were replaced by that of Serra d'Alto, after an open settlement, which is found all over southern Italy (Fig. 7.3). This style has well-made necked jars and bowls with flat bases with distinctive painted decoration in all sorts of motifs and elaborate scroll handles of often exaggerated proportions. This in turn is replaced by the Diana style, named after a stratified open site on the Lipari islands, with plain well-made red bowls and jars, some bowls still having long horizontal tubular handles.[2]

**7.3** Trichrome (1–2) and Serra d'Alto (3) pottery from southern Italy. Not to scale. *After* Whitehouse

In east-central Italy fourth millennium sites are characterised by a mixture of dark burnished wares and *figulina* with painted decoration, as at Ripoli. There was also a continuation of Fiorano–Sasso styles, and later the occurrence of Diana-style pottery. In west-central Italy the Sasso style continues in places to the mid fourth millennium. Plain and painted *figulina* also occur, and later Diana pottery. In northern Italy the fourth millennium is filled by the development of the so-called square-mouthed pottery. The first phase identified has been named Finale–Quinzano after Arene Candide at Finale on the Ligurian coast and Quinzano in the Veneto. It seems to begin at the start of the fourth millennium, succeeding the Fiorano style. Coarse wares vary locally but the fine pottery including square-mouthed beakers and jars is rather uniform, with black burnished fabrics and incised linear decoration. Imported southern painted *figulina* also occurs. In the succeeding Rivoli–Chiozza phase the dominant fine-ware forms are square-mouthed bowls and deep bowls with rounded rims, with scratched incised or cut-out spiral and meander decoration. In the Rivoli–Castelnovo phase, probably within the fourth millennium, deep quadrilobate bowls are characteristic with incised or burnished and incised decoration. This occurs in Emilia and the Veneto. Further west in the Po valley and Liguria a different fine-ware tradition emerged by around 3000 bc, named after the preserved waterside or marsh site of Lagozza, with distinctive black burnished carinated bowls, shallow open bowls, globular jars and buckets, with decoration restricted to incision on the rim of shallow bowls.

Pottery is not the only category of note however. Flint industries for the most part are now blade based and lack 'epipalaeolithic' characteristics. Polished stone axes are more common. Obsidian also occurs more frequently.

Transverse arrowheads in Lagozza assemblages contrast with tanged forms in the Square-mouthed pottery sequence. There are some clay stamps or seals and figurines also in the latter. The first copper also occurs in the late fourth and earlier third millennium bc, in the form of copper slag in Diana levels on Lipari, and a fragment of worked copper in Rivoli–Castelnovo levels at Rivoli itself. There is a suggestion that local ores were being used, though this has not been tested.[3]

In southern France Epicardial pottery styles are succeeded by the Chasseen (named after the Camp de Chassey which however is in east-central France and does not itself begin as early) which lasts through the fourth millennium into the early third, apparently little changed. It appears to emerge from a rather varied Epicardial background around 3800 bc and is fully established by around 3600 bc. The style is characterised by well made, highly burnished pots, the main shapes of which are shallow bowls, globular necked jars and baggy jars. Decoration is mainly plastic, in the form of buttons, lugs, perforated cordons and multiple perforated vertical tubes or 'pan-pipes'. There is also some incised decoration. Brimmed plates and pedestalled cups or 'vase-supports' also occur more rarely, and have incised decoration. The style is not wholly uniform, and a number of differences exist between Languedoc and Provence (though on a lesser scale than before), such as the greater decoration of vessels in Languedoc and the restriction of vase supports largely to that area. Fabrics seem to be mainly local, and no imported painted pottery has been found. There are also distinctive flint blade assemblages, with a range of transverse, leaf and tanged points. Obsidian is more common, though still rare. Axes and chisels are also more common. Stone bracelets and balls, and indented clay stamps or plaques are also noteworthy.[4]

Iberian chronology is notoriously difficult. The *sepulcros de fosa* of north-east Spain have been assigned to the fourth and earlier third millennia, and there is now one date of the early third millennium from rare occupation traces at the burial site of Bovila Madurell near Barcelona. Such pit graves contain mostly plain pottery: jars, bowls and carinated bowls, with tubular handles and occasional lugs or buttons. The range of forms is not unlike the southern Chasseen. Other material items include a wealth of polished axes, trapezoidal flint arrowheads, and bone and shell beads. One obsidian core is known from a burial at Ripollet. Pottery and stone plaques of southern type also occur in the region, in large megalithic cists such as Puig Roig, Torrent, Gerona; the chronology of these is uncertain but they could begin in this period. In southern Spain absolute chronology suffers from a lack of radiocarbon dates and relative chronology from the dearth of well-excavated and published stratified sequences. The phase is generally labelled Almerian and its major defining feature is polished pottery. Settlements such as El Garcel and Tres Cabezos have a wide range of forms, from simple bowls, carinated bowls and necked jars to flat-based, straight-sided bowls and necked jars with pointed bases. There is a single mid third millenium date from recent excavations at El Garcel. One part of the stratified occupation at the Nerja Cave near Málaga with similar pottery, including also some incised decoration, is dated to the late fourth millennium; an earlier level has much the same pottery. Settlements also have a range of blade assemblages, including sickle flints, and polished axes and gouges, and stone bracelets. Copper slag also occurs at El Garcel though since the site was excavated in the last century by L. Siret there is little certainty as to its precise context. Copper slag also occurs, along with awls and needles, at Parazuelos, Mazarron, Murcia, a site which has been assigned to a late Almerian phase. The various burial monuments assigned to this phase (as described below) have a striking range of associated material items. Pottery, shell bracelets, flint blades, polished axes, and pointed-base and other flint arrowheads are in common with settlements, but there are also stone plaques, typically with fringing or covering incised geometric decoration, schematic bone or stone figurines often in violin form, small bone plaques or pendants with segmented decoration and bone pins with segmented cylindrical heads.

In Portugal rather few settlements are known contrasted with a wealth of burial monuments. Pottery at the first phase of Vila Nova de São Pedro which may belong to the early third millennium includes Almerian types, and also copas or straight-sided bowls with furrowed decoration. There was some copper working. Similar pottery occurs in some of the monuments assigned to this period, though some such as Poço da Gateira I in the Alentejo, which appears to be early, have simple plain bowl forms only. Others such as the large tombs of Savory's suggested 'Pavian horizon', which might lie in the latter part of this period have Almerian forms but a range of impressed, incised and encrusted decoration. In suggested or probable early tombs there are simple trapezoidal arrowheads and polished or flaked axes. Suggested later tombs have a wider range of piercing arrowheads with more covering retouch, and with flat or concave bases. Plaques, figurines and pinheads similar to those already described also occur, as well as a few slate 'croziers' or halberds. Rock-cut monuments of the Tagus area also have a great range of limestone objects. Large quantities were recorded from four sites at Carenque and Bautas including a model hoe and sickle, lunulae, 'pine cones', plaques, beads, as well as bone figurines or amulets, pins and plano-convex cigar-shaped objects. No. 2 at Carenque has a thermoluminescent date of the early fourth millennium BC, for which the equivalent radiocarbon date should be around 3200 bc. Savory suggested that the wealth of such objects including in another example Alapraia a lifesize sandal sole, marked a phase of replacement of earlier slate plaques, in the late fourth or early third millennium bc. The Carenque tombs however have such plaques, and more dates are needed before such a scheme is validated.[5]

*Settlement and the social context of production: Italy and southern France, 4000–2700/2500 bc*

In this period the contrast between southern Italy and other neighbouring areas is somewhat reduced, since after around 4000 bc there is a long phase of consolidation and the full establishment of agriculturally based subsistence.

However the situation in southern Italy is as before poorly understood. One view – by no means universally held – is that ditched and other settlements continued in the fourth millennium bc as before, and if there was a trend towards site nucleation as has been suggested it is likely that it reached its peak in this millennium, but this is at this stage speculation. A greater contrast with earlier millennia exists in central Italy, where the mid fourth millennium bc Abruzzi site of Valle Ottara concerned with hunting and herding in the foothills stands out more sharply against other sites concerned with mixed farming. It is of course possible that this was only a seasonal site. In northern Italy there was throughout the fourth millennium a range of sites from open settlements on the plain, and on marsh and lake edges, to continued cave occupations, with the open sites apparently more numerous than in the later fifth millennium. Change may have been very slow in parts, since even at Rivoli in the Adige valley in the Rivoli–Castelnovo phase, red deer were recovered in more or less equal proportions to pig and cattle. In the earlier Finale–Quinzano phase small possibly seasonal sites are still represented, as at Molino Casarotto, Fimon, near Vincenza where there was a series of small occupation foci along the shore of a lake (Fig. 7.4). In one focus fully

7.4 Detail of wooden platform and hearth at the lakeside settlement of Molino Casarotto, Fimon, northern Italy. Photo: Barfield

excavated structures included a cluster about 18 m broad of rectangular wooden floors or platforms, with underlying vertical piles and overlying hearths. It was not clear whether these were roofed. Food remains included mussel shells, pike and freshwater turtle; red deer and boar or pig; a few sheep and cattle; wild vegetables, including water chestnuts, and a few wheat grains. In later phases as well as open sites in low areas there were numbers of sites on elevated locations, as at Rivoli, Pescale and Castelnovo which may suggest a fuller landscape and more differentiated sites, but the extent of excavation at these is so far limited. There seems to be continuity in the range of sites in the Lagozza phase, with stratigraphic continuity at the waterside site of Isolino, and continuity of type in the site of Lagozza itself. There is now a range of cultivated plants including wheat, barley, lentils and flax, but while spindle-whorls, loom weights and pots interpreted as milk-boilers or cheese-strainers are found, animal bones were not found at Lagozza itself, perhaps due to peat conditions. However, at Arene Candide on the Ligurian coast in Lagozza levels sheep dominate the faunal assemblage in which very few 'wild' animals are represented.[6]

Southern France in the long Chasseen phase shows similar signs of consolidation and establishment of permanent change. First, there are more Chasseen than Cardial sites recorded, and the difference chiefly lies in the greater number of open sites, even making allowance as previously noted for the often haphazard circumstances of discovery. In Provence, figures of 80 versus 28 were quoted some years ago, and Provence is considered to have less signs of Chasseen activity than Languedoc. Open sites range in size from 700 to 50000 m², with two exceptional sites near Toulouse in the Haute Garonne valley, St Michel-du-Touch and Villeneuve–Tolosane, at 200000 and 300000 m² respectively. Structures however are not well understood, and few house plans are known. Recurrent features are hearths, pit hearths and cobbled areas or platforms. The latter two categories are generally rather small, with diameters little over 2 m. A mixture of hearth and platform but between 3 and 11 m in length and between 1.5 and 2.5 m in width, was recorded in large quantities, closely spaced, at the two large sites just mentioned. Regarded by some as 'hut-floors' or *fonds de cabane*, they might be part of the internal fittings of houses otherwise built in an archaeologically less visible manner (Fig. 7.5). It has been suggested that the variation in site sizes could be due to a continued strong element of mobility in the settlement pattern but this is equally compatible with a fuller landscape with a more differentiated settlement pattern, and settlement units of unequal status and importance. The character of the partially investigated large site of St Michel-du-Touch supports this view. Radiocarbon dates suggest a long duration through the second half of the fourth millennium bc and the first half of the third. The site lies on a low but steep-sided promontory at the confluence of the Touch and Garonne. Some 130 hut-floors as previously described lie scattered across the area investigated which is dissected laterally by a series of at least five interrupted ditches, several metres wide but less than 1 m deep. At the innermost part of the promontory there were two palisade trenches roughly parallel and about 50 m apart; their posts were set 2 m deep into the subsoil. Relationships between hut-floors and ditches show that the number of features in use at any one time was less than the surviving total, but even making allowance for this the site must have been large at any one moment, and presumably permanently occupied though there seems little proof of this. The site may have expanded through time as one of the palisade trenches was dated to the fourth millennium, though the number of dates from the site is admittedly insufficient. One can also begin to place the site in its local setting, since other sites in the valley are known at distances of from 6 to 10 km, including Villeneuve-Tolosane. These have been only incompletely investigated, but the possibility of sites like St Michel-du-Touch being in some sense regional centres looks strong.[7]

**7.5** Cobbled features at the Chasseen site of Villeneuve-Tolosane, Haute Garonne, southern France. Photo: Vaquer

Another aspect of Chasseen settlement is the expansion of agricultural activity not only in the lowlands and large valleys but also in relatively remote inland valleys, such as the upper Verdon valley in Provence or the Grands Causses of Languedoc. At the Grotte de l'Église in the Verdon valley for example the inhabitants of a network of small caves not only collected acorns and exploited red deer, boar, ibex, and rabbit, but also had access to wheats, barleys and legumes, and exploited large numbers of cattle and ovicaprids. Fish remains or fishing equipment occur in these sites, and indeed throughout the rest of the Chasseen settlement pattern, including a handful of coastal sites. Cereal remains are evidently more common and more numerous than in fifth millennium contexts. Cattle and ovicaprids were the most important animals, and even when the latter were more numerous, as in the coastal areas and inland of Provence, the former probably provided more meat. Unfortunately there is insufficient data to consider herds in any detail, by means of age, sex or butchery data, and it is therefore not possible yet to look at differences between sites and regions, with a view to investigating the scale of production. One hint however may lie in the observation that there was more local domestication going on in the southern Massif Central than on the plains of Languedoc. This could be related not only to the colonisation of the interior but also to the existence of a regional economy in which communities on the periphery sought to provide desired products such as cattle in return for other goods from the more populous centre, such as fine pottery, stone bracelets and obsidian. The movement of these will be discussed below, but it is worth noting in this context that some finds of obsidian were far inland, at least in Provence.

*The wider social context: Italy and southern France, 4000–2700/2500 bc*

These aspects of the archaeological record can be set in a wider context by considering others such as burial, ritual, movement of goods and patterns of material culture. At a very general level society in these areas can be seen to have changed compared to previous millennia and will be contrasted later in the chapter with the situation in the mid and later third millennium bc. The evidence however for this period itself remains tantalisingly incomplete so that it is hard to follow the nature of change in detail. One generalisation however that may be offered is that, just as agricultural settlement was consolidated and extended in this period, so too social differentiation was accentuated. Indeed the former could profitably be seen as an expression of the latter (rather than vice versa), though there was no uniformity of process between the areas considered.

In southern Italy one noticeable change is the appearance of more regular burials from the Serra d'Alto phase onwards. At the eponymous site itself these occur in pits under house floors, and at the site of Pula di Molfetta about 50 graves occur in oval pits bounded by stones (though only ten yielded skeletal remains). The beginnings of rock-cut tombs in southern Italy are probably also to be set in the late Serra d'Alto phase, or the succeeding Diana phase. Oven-shaped rock-cut tombs (the *tombe a forno*) often of quite modest dimensions, were widely used in the mid and later third millennium bc in the area. They have a round or oval chamber (sometimes two and occasionally three) and were entered by a descending shaft, or occasionally by a sloping passage. They regularly contain collective burials with associated grave goods. The type however can be seen to go back at least to the late fourth or earlier third millennium. There are even two possible candidates with alleged primary associations with Impressed ware, but a better one is the modest *tomba a forno* at Serra d'Alto itself, with a chamber 2 m in diameter and shaft. One skeleton lay in the chamber and one in the shaft. Associated plain pottery is considered to be late Serra d'Alto in type.[8] It is thus obviously tempting to see in this kind of burial construction some more explicit signs of social differentiation by this time. Another feature of considerable interest in this context is the use of caves for unusual deposits such as pottery on stalagmites and clay female heads, as well as wall painting.

Attention is demanded also by material culture. The quantities of obsidian in fourth millennium contexts seem greater than in sixth or fifth, though this is hard to quantify from the relatively few analysed samples. The sources on both Lipari and Sardinia were important. The production and distribution of fine pottery were also obviously important, though this is hard to study at other than a general level so far. The movement of plain and painted *figulina* into central and northern Italy has already been noted. Serra d'Alto pottery is also found as far afield as Sicily, Malta and Yugoslavia (at Obre), and Ripoli pottery has been found on Sardinia.[9] There is some evidence from northern Italy that the main ceramic contacts predated the main obsidian contacts, and it is possible therefore that one sort of distribution replaced the other. But Diana pottery too was extremely widespread, and the contrast may only reflect the state of excavated evidence at present. The real difficulty lies in understanding the nature of fine pottery production and distribution. There was probably some sort of reciprocal flow of goods within the Italian peninsula, since jadeite axes, thought to be from the western Alpine source and of fourth millennium date, extend far down the peninsula; there are probably also more local sources. The appearance of copper working on Lipari is suggestive of the further development of prestige items, but the evidence is too slight to support this notion further. Widely spread fine wares could also be seen not only as a medium of exchange but also as a cultural feature linking broad areas. It is noticeable that the distribution of the Serra d'Alto and Diana styles is broader than the previous painted styles in southern Italy. What this kind of link-up may imply is not clear, but one possibility is that it is again connected with social differentiation and regular communication between hypothetical local elites. Far more study of local variation and local coarse wares is required.

Many of these features recur in northern Italy (the evidence from the central part of the peninsula is too patchy to be brought in here) but with a major difference in that there is greater evidence for change within the period.[10] The first noticeable change is again that of more frequent burials in Square-mouthed pottery contexts. Both children and adults of both sexes are found, the adults with pottery and other grave goods. One kind of burial context is the resurgence of cave burials. There are some 30 in this phase at Arene Candide, and 42 at Pollera. A new development is that of separate burial or cemetery areas in or beside open sites, such as Quinzano. There was also evidently some kind of inhumation cemetery near Molino Casarotto which was suggested earlier to be a rather smaller site, and perhaps only seasonally occupied. There are perhaps 19 burials in the Rivoli–Chiozza phase at Chiozza itself, though their dating is uncertain. It is tempting to associate this development with the fuller landscape already outlined, and to see in the burials a social use of the dead for defining access to territory and resources in each local setting. We simply do not know whether this is connected with internal social differentiation as well, though there are hints in the occurrence of ritual and prestige items in Square-mouthed pottery contexts. There are the pottery imports already mentioned, and the bulk of obsidian in northern Italy comes from the middle and later phases of the Square-mouthed pottery sequence (Fig. 7.6). One site, Pescale, has some 80 per cent of the obsidian from the entire region. There are imports from the other direction too, such as the shoe-last adze – of trans-Alpine type – from a grave at Vela near Trente in the Adige valley, and possibly *spondylus*, as here and also at Arene Candide, but this may equally well have an Adriatic or Tyrrhenian Sea origin. There is thus some circulation of prestige goods, and within northern Italy itself rather uniform fine wares contrast with more localised coarse wares, which may again be an indication of communication between local elites. There is at least here another striking example of regional ceramic 'link-up'. Another feature is that of figurines and stamps or seals which occur in limited numbers, and on the Balkan analogy could suggest differential access to or control of ritual. These features moreover do

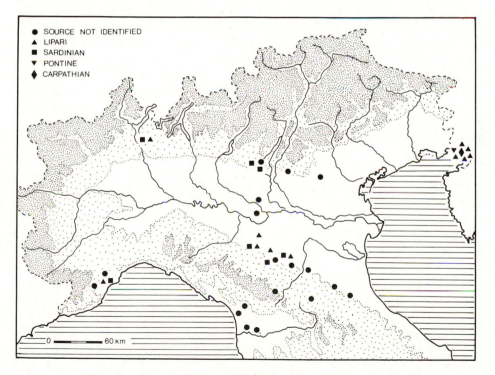

7.6 The distribution of imported obsidian in northern Italy. *After* Barfield

not remain everywhere static. In the Rivoli–Castelnovo phase, restricted to Emilia and the Veneto and probably overlapping the Lagozza phase, pottery has more restrained decoration; there is a local style at Pescale. There is an import of trans-Alpine Aichbühl or Munschofen pottery at Rivoli, and the copper finds already described belong to this phase. In the area of the Lagozza tradition however there are new ceramic and lithic forms, and no burials have been found at or near the main sites. Both pottery and flint innovations can be linked in a general way with the already-existing Chasseen tradition. It is as though a still wider regional link-up was achieved, and this might in this context imply further internal differentiation. The burial record is as always puzzling, but its apparent disappearance could be connected with an attempt now to mask local differences in favour of longer-range contacts and alliances, if it is right to see a situation of potentially increased internal differentiation.

Fine pottery in southern France was again very uniform from at least around 3600 bc, though there are differences between Provence and Languedoc as already stated. The only movements of prestige or unusual items which can be documented are the obsidian in Provence and the Rhône valley and the westwards movement of jadeite from the western Alpine area as far as Languedoc, but the distribution of stone *billes* and bracelets may belong also in this sphere, as also that of the finely decorated vase supports of Languedoc. Most fine pottery however appears to be of rather local manufacture. There are few regular burials in Chasseen contexts though there is a danger that this generalisation reflects only past excavation practice. It is also considered unlikely that megalithic tombs in Languedoc were constructed as early as the Chasseen period though in view of earlier opinion and of the difficulties of dating construction from surviving contents this must remain a possibility. Most of the certain Chasseen burials occur only in ones or twos, in pits or cists without elaborate accompanying structures or rites. St Michel-du-Touch by contrast contained a large and unusual burial, of parts of the skull and longbones of two individuals in a cobble-filled pit over 7 by 4 m and 0.8 m deep. These were accompanied by flint blades, stone palettes, a sandstone plaque, beads, and 12 complete pots including two vase supports. Another burial at the site, but without a defined context, was of a woman with two pots and four hedgehog jaws.[11] The final aspect of considerable interest is the way in which the pre-existing southern Chasseen tradition was linked in the later or late fourth millennium bc with surrounding areas. There is on the one hand the often noted ceramic (and to some extent lithic) continuum between the Chasseen, Lagozza and Cortaillod areas, and on the other the strong resemblances of the southern Chasseen to the northern Chasseen of east-central France and the Paris basin. Both aspects demand explanation. One possibility may again be suggested that this represents at least in part the progressively wider linking of local emergent or entrenched elites. As in the other cases one may also suggest that this kind of material culture was an expression of communal ideology which masked differences between and within local communities, in spite of the suggested actuality of greater internal differentiation. With this perspective the emphasis in explaining continued social change can as elsewhere be placed firmly on the web of local and regional social relations, rather than on any abstracted feature such as the full or fuller establishment of mixed farming which can be seen as much an expression as a cause of change.

*Settlement and the social context of production: Iberia, c. 4000–2500 bc*

The settlement record as well as the chronology is very defective in this phase, and little systematic survey or excavation has yet been undertaken. Generalisations based on this record are therefore more than usually liable to be misguided. In southern and eastern Spain however one trend that is likely to be accentuated by future research rather than reversed is the apparent increase in open-air settlements, though caves like Nerja, Cariguela and Los Murcielagos remain in occupation. Indeed it may be that the arid south-eastern lowlands were first colonised for agriculture at this time. There are numbers of sites with pits and possible structures, which were investigated long ago or more recently and not yet fully published, such as El Garcel, Tres Cabezos, Tabernas or Carmona. El Garcel is sited on a low hill with numbers of round or oval hut-floors, partly earth-cut, and also in pits. Recent excavations showed metalworking traces including ovens. Tabernas has a similar setting and round structures. Some sort of encircling wall at El Garcel may have been contemporary with this occupation. The sizes of these sites are not known. The few details known would at any rate be compatible with a fuller landscape with a greater range of settlement types, and perhaps the emergence of selected sites with special importance. What scale of production was achieved is not known, though it can be noted that even without systematic recovery finds of carbonised grain and also of olive and vine were made at El Garcel, possibly suggesting here as in southern France the full establishment of mixed farming. One pit at Nerja contained 30 l of carbonised plant remains, dominated by naked barley with also wheat, probably emmer, and some acorns and olives. Large quantities of limpet and pecten were also found at this site.

Settlements in Portugal are even more shadowy. Vila Nova de São Pedro has two phases, the first open, the second enclosed. There are no radiocarbon dates. Its hilltop setting is again notable. There were numerous querns and rubbers, and finds of wheat, barley, beans, flax and olives, sheep, cattle and pig; the context of horse bones is uncertain. Other hilltop sites have been suggested to belong to pre-Millaran–VNSP horizons, such as Aboboreira, Carenque and Lexim but the thermoluminescent dates from Carenque and Lexim begin around 3000 BC and equivalent radiocarbon dates should fall in the mid third millennium bc. Likewise inland in the Alentejo the walled hilltop settlement of Castelo do Giraldo has a similar TL date around 3000 BC. One may also note continued use of Tagus shell middens suggested by the single late fourth millennium date from the upper level at Cabeço da Arruda. In north-east Spain there is virtually no settlement evidence clearly recorded at all, in curious contrast to the relatively numerous *sepulcros de fosa* known from gravel digging and other activity in the valleys of the regions, though some occupation traces are at least now reported from Bovila Madurell. For development in this part of the Mediterranean one could perhaps turn to southern France, except that there is no certainty that similar events took place in both areas.[12]

### Burial, ritual and regional communications: Iberia, c. 4000–2500 bc

The other evidence is dominated by burial sites and monuments, the abundant fruits of recording and excavation by the Siret brothers in the nineteenth century, Heleno in the 1930s and others on a lesser scale since. There may have been a high rate of recovery of monuments, since the main distributions have been little altered by fieldwork since the 1940s. Even though rather few reports were published by earlier excavators themselves, the corpus volumes of the Leisners covering Andalucia and south-east Spain and parts of central and southern Portugal have made much of the structural and material evidence available. Three major problems however remain. The first is chronology. Leaving aside a small number of what are considered to be anomalous dates, there are only 20 dates, from 12 megalithic sites, and over 350 monuments may belong to the fourth and third millennia bc in Almería alone. Secondly, the contents of tombs may be tolerably well known in the form of lists of material items, but their arrangement is not well documented, and the recording of human remains is inconsistent. In some areas human remains are scarce, perhaps due to local soil conditions, as in the Alentejan area of Reguengos de Monsaraz. In others such as the limestone area around Carenque to the west of Lisbon preservation has been good, but at the already-cited Carenque II for example the Leisners can only record that Heleno found many skulls in good condition. The third problem is the relation of burials and monuments to the rest of the landscape. In the absence of sufficient settlements the possible significance of dispersed patterns of tomb distribution – for example in the area of Reguengos de Monsaraz – is quite unclear.[13]

The Leisners have suggested evolutionary schemes for both southern Spain and Portugal, based partly on tomb typology and partly on associated finds, and with modifications these have been widely followed.[14] The earliest suggested burials in the sequence in southern Spain are single, double or collective inhumations in large circular pits in the south-east. These contain polished axes, shell bracelets, arrowheads and blades, plaques and a little pottery. Similar finds have been recorded with multiple burials in caves of the Valencia and Murcia areas, but details of the people seem remarkably scarce. There are also polygonal cists with similar contents which are thought to represent subsequent development. At some point emerges the above-ground monument, with a short passage and covering cairn. In the south-east these are circular with dry-stone walling or vertically placed slabs or orthostats, while in Granada and the Guadalquivir valley (and to a lesser extent in the south-east) there is a variety of rectangular or polygonal chambers with short passages, with perhaps larger passages, and longer chambers, also in the form of a 'V', developing subsequently, perhaps in the earlier third millennium bc. Finds include the axes, arrowheads, plaques, figurines and pottery already described.

In Portugal the suggested sequence also begins with a simple form, a series of rectangular stone cists set in the ground, with individual burials and goods of transverse arrowheads and polished axes, Larger rectangular cists with collective burials may be later. From this series is thought to develop a wide range of megalithic monuments incorporating passage, chamber and mound and holding collective burials. The southern cists now have an elongated trapezoidal form and may have a short passage; finds include hollow-based arrowheads and stone plaques. Inland in Alentejo there is a development of freestanding monuments with polygonal chambers, passage and round mounds (Figs. 7.7 and 7.8). Goods include axes, knives, transverse arrowheads and plain pottery of bowl or carinated bowl form. Two examples dated by thermoluminescence to the mid fifth millennium BC are Poço da Gateira 1 and Anta dos Gorginos 11 which belong to a group around Reguengos de Monsaraz near Evora.[15] The mound at Gateira was estimated to have a diameter of about 10 m while the chamber and passage were 3.5 m and 1.5 m long respectively; the mound at Gorginos was destroyed, while the chamber size was a little smaller. Human bones were found in a fragmentary state but the number of people represented is not certain. Estimates vary, based on the assignation of either one or two flint points per individual, giving totals of a dozen or over 20 respectively. At Gorginos the whole of the chamber was not uncovered (because of an olive tree!); the portion investigated contained only sherds, flint fragments and a slate fragment. The passage held two pots and a hoe and an axe, perhaps from an in situ burial. It may be noted that the TL dates are from the pots in both cases, and do not date the construction of the

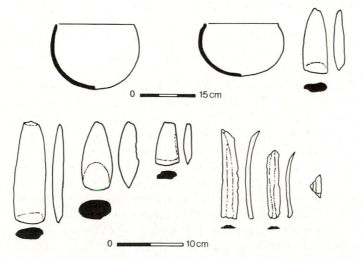

**7.7** Artefacts from the megalithic tomb of Poço da Gateira, Evora district, Alentejo, Portugal. *After* Leisner and Leisner

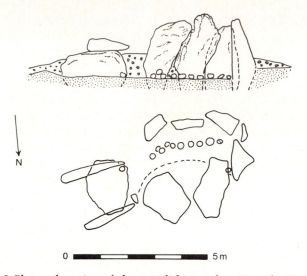

**7.8** Plan and section of the megalithic tomb at Poço da Gateira, Evora district, Alentejo, Portugal. *After* Leisner and Leisner

monuments. There are also similar finds in simple monuments with circular chambers and passages constructed with dry-stone walling. There is a considerable range of forms in the Alentejo especially, which includes monuments with larger dimensions. This size increase may be a chronological development, if contents such as stone plaques, concave-based flint arrowheads, segmented bone pinheads, Almerian-type idols and slate and flint halberds can be considered certainly later than the finds from the previously mentioned example. In one large tomb in the Reguengos district, Anta Grande di Olival da Pega, there were fragments of over 60 plaques, both undecorated and engraved with geometric motifs. Unfortunately bone remains were scanty. There are also very few dates to support suggested developments. Three other sites with TL dates fall in the late fourth and mid third millennia BC, which in radiocarbon chronology would be at the end or after the period covered here.

Another type which may span the fourth and third millennia bc is the rock-cut tomb. Simple forms with passage and chamber are found in central-southern Portugal and also in southern Spain, but there is also a version more restricted to the Tagus estuary with an additional manhole entrance, sometimes with covering slab, into the chamber. Numbers of these sites have goods of Almerian pottery and plaques. Burials which range from a few to many may originally have been set upright against the walls. It has been suggested that these monuments became more elaborate in the later fourth–early third millennia bc, with for example expanded ante-chambers, and the horizon of elaborate limestone objects described above. There is again little direct support for this sequence. Carenque II near Lisbon is one of a group of three only a few metres apart. Cut into limestone it has a circular chamber 4 m in diameter and 2 m high, with a manhole in the top. The chamber is connected through an oval opening with the antechamber and the entrance passage which is 5 m long. The unpublished burials seem to have been numerous, as were the accompanying goods, which included schist plaques as well as a range of limestone objects including horns, cylinders and *lunulae*. The single TL date was of the early fourth millennium BC.

It is easy to be drawn into the temptations of constructing endless developmental schemes, but with chronology in its present parlous state it is more useful to emphasise certain general features of the overall development. There is in both southern Spain and central-southern Portugal an increased social emphasis on burial, seen in the attention given to the dead themselves, the effort put into monuments, and the increasingly specialised artefacts. Part of the process of artefact differentiation and the emergence of prestige items is the development of copper metallurgy. Settlement finds have already been mentioned, and there are rare finds also from tombs; one possibly early example – on the basis of other goods such as plain Almerian pottery – is the rock-cut tomb of the Loma de los Peregrinos, Alguazas in Murcia in eastern Spain, which contained several copper awls. Copper ores are widely distributed in Iberia, and there is no good reason to suppose other than that the development of metallurgy was a local process.[16] It is also interesting that certain specialised objects such as plaques, pinheads and figurines have a broad distribution across the south of the peninsula, which must in some way have served to link up or bring closer areas previously more isolated. It may not then be fanciful to suggest that all these features were, like aspects of the settlement record, the result of increased social differentiation in a more populous landscape. Regional link-up in particular could be the result of communication and alliance between local elites, a further possible example therefore of the use of the external for local purposes which was explored in both the previous chapters. This argument is weakened of course by our present ignorance of the production and distribution of items like plaques. In this suggested scenario there is no need to envisage steady or linear evolution. With reference particularly to developmental schemes for burial monuments, it is potentially misleading to seek chronological order without some understanding of the social situation. It may turn out that elaborate tombs and elaborate goods were in contemporary use with more simple ones. The point then is to try to understand the social context in which such variation occurred.

Little will be said here about northern Spain and Portugal. There are conflicting views about the development of simple passage graves in northern inland Portugal, since these have been argued to be both earlier than and derived from Alentejan types.[17] The *sepulcros de fosa* of north-east Spain have small numbers of burials but a range of goods, and are sometimes found in concentrations as at Bovila Madurell. They may overlap in date with big rectangular, megalithic cists in the area but their chronology too is uncertain.

*Italy and southern France: mid to late third millennium bc*

*Chronology and material sequences.* The range of material which belongs to this period in southern Italy is poorly defined, especially in the Tavoliere, the previous centre for regional sequences.

Settlement material has not been much recognised here, though this is beginning to be redressed. Fine pottery is found however in a scatter of rock-cut tombs which are assigned to this period; such as Laterza near Taranto or Cellino San Marco near Brindisi. These have a range of bowl and jar forms, some with developed single handles, and geometric incised and impressed decoration. The Laterza tombs contain also a range of flintwork (blades and tanged arrowheads) small stone axes, simple beads, perforated stone pendants, perforated bone points, and copper blades. Further south in Sicily the settlement record is much fuller. The suggested sequence is defined largely through pottery, which is very varied, both chronologically and regionally. For example a phase suggested to be before the mid third millennium includes red- and black-painted jars at Conzo in east Sicily, and incised, impressed and encrusted pottery at San Cono, Piano Notaro and other sites of wider distribution. In the middle of the millennium there is added the southern Serraferlicchio style including globular necked forms with exuberant painted decoration in brown-on-red, and also the Lipari Piano Conte style, while in the later third the dominant style is called Chiusazzo–Malpasso, with plain jars, cups and biconical forms. A few copper artefacts are now found. The contents of the Campanian group of rock-cut tombs (with extensions into the central Apennines), named after the site of Gaudo near Paestum, are better known than those in the south-east of the peninsula, but the group is of limited geographical extent. Dominant here is a range of globular necked and handled jugs or bottles, some asymmetrical, with also handled cups, some linked in pairs by a bridging handle. Some of these have incised and impressed decoration (Fig. 7.9). These are also tanged flint arrowheads and unifacially retouched flint knives or daggers, as well as a few copper daggers and pins. Most of the triangular daggers have central midrib and rivets, but the form with projecting tang with a single rivet also occurs. There are also flat copper axes.

In the rest of central Italy there are numbers of settlements known, with

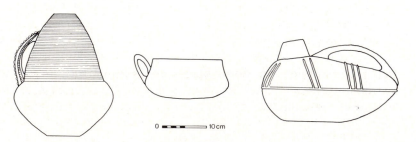

**7.9** Gaudo pottery from central-southern Italy. Scale approximate. *After* Barker

rather varied domestic pottery. Stratified sites like Romito di Asciano in Tuscany or Grotta dei Piccioni in Abruzzi show gradual change only. Forms in the eastern group of sites named after Conelle in Marche include dishes, bowls, jugs and asymmetrical bottles, with dotted decoration infilled with white paste. Fine pottery found in burials is much more uniform. The typical form at the classic site of Rinaldone in Lazio is a plain globular jar with tall neck and lugs on the belly. Other tomb finds include tanged flint arrowheads and fine bifacially worked flint knives or daggers, perforated stone battle-axes with simple cutting edge but knobbed butt, copper triangular daggers mostly with midribs and rivets, and copper flat axes (Fig. 7.10). There are other larger quantities of copper from this group of tombs.

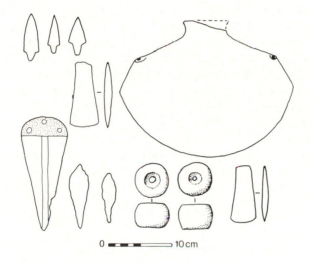

0 ▬▬▬▬ 10 cm

**7.10** Rinaldone pottery and copper and stone artefacts from central Italy. Scale approximate. *After* Barker

In northern Italy settlements are also scarce. In the Po valley the site of Le Colombare near Verona has bowls with bands of incised and dotted decoration, while in Liguria as at Arene Candide rather similar pottery is also found. Again there are richer inventories from burials. At the classic cemetery of Remedello near Brescia pottery includes handled closed bowls and carinated bowls, with bands of incised decoration. Fine flintwork includes tanged and round-based arrowheads and daggers, and there are polished stone axes. Obsidian is not found. Copper artefacts include two varieties of dagger, with midribs, but one with straight heel and rivets and the other with projecting tang with simple rivet. Some blades are asymmetrical and may have been hafted as halberds. There are also copper awls, rings and trapezoidal flat axes with slightly expanded cutting edges and some with low flanges. There is also a substantial silver hammer-headed pin from Remedello and a sheet-silver pectoral or *lunula* from a single burial at Villafranca. In Liguria too burial contents are richer than in occupation sites. Cave burials have yielded a great range of beads and pendants made variously of shell, slate, haematite and copper, as well as copper awls and flint tanged arrowheads and microliths.

In southern France the Chasseen sequence ends in most areas around 2700–2600 bc, though it seems to continue longer in parts of Provence. Many settlement sites are known in contrast to northern Italy. A more regionalised pattern of material culture now emerges, especially if pottery is used as the criterion. Separate styles of cordoned jars and bowls have been identified in western Herault around St Pons, in Aveyron and Lozère on the Grands Causses (groupe de Treilles), in Aude and Roussillon and westwards and southwards named after the site of Véraza, and further afield in the Lot after the site of Perte du Cros. In Hérault, Gard and Ardèche there is the larger Ferrières group, with simple bowl forms but varied incised and plastic decoration, and in the Rhône delta there is a small group named after the settlement of La Couronne which again has bowls and large jars. Flint assemblages are varied, but there seems to be a general preference for piercing leaf-shaped arrowheads, and transverse forms no longer occur. Polished stone axes also continue and there is increased production of flint from certain sources, but Italian-style daggers do not occur. Copper artefacts are found however in the Grands Causses in the form of beads, daggers and flat axes, though hardly elsewhere in pre-Fontbouisse contexts (or before around 2200 bc). There are also many bead forms, notably the winged type, both from occupation sites such as Sargel in the Grands Causses and from the numerous megalithic and other tombs of the area as a whole.[18]

*Settlement and the social context: Italy and southern France,*
*mid to later third millennium bc*

The character and distribution of settlement present a number of puzzling contrasts in this phase, but it is possible to suggest that various discontinuities and changes are connected to continuing social transformations rather than radical alterations in environmental conditions. In the Tavoliere plain relevant settlement sites of the mid and later third millennium bc have not been recognised. This lack of observation has generally been taken at face value and explanations framed either in terms of increased aridity or warlike population incursions. More recently there has been a suggestion that there is an archaeological failure to recognise the relevant domestic pottery.[19] Another possibility is that there were changes in depositional conditions (as has already been observed in other parts of Europe in previous chapters) making sites archaeologically less visible. The aridity argument is weak unless specific local evidence can be produced, since there is evidence for settlement continuity elsewhere in the southern peninsula in the second millennium, and as already outlined in Sicily in the third, as well as central Italy. In the latter area there is continuity at various cave sites on either side of the Apennines, and other evidence such as the foundation of the large ditched site at Conelle in Marche.[20] The argument for the incursion of warlike pastoralists in the peninsula as a whole founders also on the central

Italian evidence, and on the inability of its proponents to suggest a plausible point or area of origin. Another possibility altogether should be considered, namely that in the area of the previously most developed settlement hierarchy there was a radical social transformation which led to the break-up of established patterns of population distribution and organisation of production. This could be envisaged in terms of fragmentation of the settlement pattern, either due to the inability of putative elites to maintain cohesion or due to a trend to more individualised production, which might or might not involve a shift towards a greater importance for animal husbandry. Other evidence such as burial and material culture, to which we will return later, seems ambiguous, since central Italy where the same transformations are not proposed has a rather similar range of tombs, copper artefacts and so on. Here too, and in Sicily, economic evidence is poor in detail, though continuity of previous practice is again proposed for central Italy. But turning to northern Italy we again meet the situation of apparent dislocation of established settlement pattern combined with extensive changes in other aspects, which may again favour the sort of transformation proposed for the south. The same uncertainties about domestic material and depositional factors are met. There is a little evidence from Le Colombare where stone-footed rectangular structures cluster on a low hilltop but otherwise the record is scarce.[21]

In southern France where research has been more sustained a greater number of occupation sites is known. There are three interesting changes. One is the abandonment of previous Chasseen nucleations, at least in Languedoc, where the number of Ferrières cave or shelter sites greatly outweighs that of open sites. Secondly, in Languedoc there appears to be an increase in site numbers overall, and finally site distribution is rather wider than in the Chasseen period, with significantly more sites in upland locations, as on the limestone plateaus of the Grands Causses, where there now also appear large numbers of megaliths and other tombs as if to reinforce the importance of these areas. Sites with evidence of mixed farming have been partially investigated, such as the open plateau site of Beaussement, Chauzon, Ardèche, where sheep and cattle were the most important animals in a rather small faunal assemblage, and it has been suggested also that agricultural production was biased towards animal husbandry. One explanation offered is again in terms of changes in rainfall regimes marking the beginning of the Sub-Boreal period. It is proposed that these led to a progressive abandonment of coastal areas and an increased use of the limestone uplands, especially for sheep rearing, allowing the emergence of highly ranked kin groups or elites.[22] This kind of explanation seems again unsatisfactory. Upland exploitation must itself be predicated on reasonable rainfall; the pattern in neighbouring Provence remains largely unaltered till around 2300 bc; and the Rhône delta has lowland settlements and monuments. La Couronne itself is a large site on a low plateau near the sea. Structures include lengths of stone walling but the exact reconstruction of houses or otherwise seems problematic. The inhabitants had sheep and cattle, and used fish, shellfish and some game; querns and sickle flints are so far the only evidence of cereal use. It seems more plausible to retain the social content of the explanation but to make it primary. In various ways the consolidation of social differences may have led to the break-up of previous settlement concentrations, new forms of organisation of production and accompanying developments in burial and ritual to reinforce them. Indeed, without seeking to argue for exact uniformity of process in the whole area under consideration, one may still propose that the better-investigated southern French case offers the opportunity to support the kind of transformational hypothesis already offered for several parts of the Mediterranean area; the nature of settlement changes in southern France is of particular interest when considering the Po valley and the Tavoliere.

Lack of uniformity is evident where one surveys the evidence for burial and ritual, and patterns of material culture. The use of rock-cut tombs is not a new development in this phase in southern Italy, but the scale of use seems to increase, and there may also have been a shift to more collective burial (unless this is simply the result of more frequent depositions). The four at Laterza are of simple form with sloping short passages and chambers, beehive in section and roughly hemispherical in ground plan. One held around a hundred inhumations, as well as abundant goods of the kind already described. There are also a few above-ground megalithic chambers, as at Melendugno near Otranto, or Albarosa near Bari, here with a stone cairn which may belong to this period. The eponymous Gaudo site is a group of about 40 rock-cut tombs, some with collective burials and rich grave goods. One often cited had 25 inhumations, 32 pots and seven flint daggers and the full range of material has already been described above. The tombs themselves are of simple form with single or double chambers and vertical shafts. There are two other notable groups of tombs, at Mirabello Eclano and Buccino, both with some more elaborate tombs more abundantly furnished with grave goods than the rest. The significance of these tombs is as always hard to assess. The nine Buccino tombs were used for the deposition of men, women, juveniles and children (in all at least 135 individuals). Burials were made successively and earlier deposits cleared aside or out, which only allows study of the final pattern of deposition. Anthropological study suggested two groups within the population but each was distributed both in tombs with more grave goods and those with less. Radiocarbon dates span the later third millennium bc, but even if a short span of use were to be suggested, it is likely that only a portion of the total local or regional population is represented here. This may be of greater significance than the material variation in abundance of grave goods, for the kind of reasons already discussed in chapter 6. The character of the grave goods – rather than their absolute numbers – is also important. There is fine-ware pottery and high-quality flintwork, some of which may be non-local, and there is also a small quantity of copper daggers and blades, as well as pins or awls. The nearest ones are in the Rinaldone area to the north. It is possible therefore that selective burial and artefacts of unusual quality and source both mark further social differentiation in the area, supporting the view of transformation already hinted at.[23]

Rinaldone burials are simpler. Pit graves, caves and *tombe a forno* are used. These are found in smaller groups, the number of burials deposited are fewer (with children generally absent) and grave goods restricted for the most part to pottery and flint. On these grounds less differentiation in the area has been suggested. However selective burial is again evident, and burials are again seemingly separate from settlements. The flintwork includes fine arrow-heads and daggers, some of the latter perhaps non-local. There are stone battle-axes and maces, and copper axes and blades. There are also many other finds of copper axes in the area, not from burials, though not found at great distances from the copper sources. Both selective burial and artefact differen-tiation are therefore represented in this area too, though the overt form of graves is less distinctive.[24]

Remedello in the Po valley is itself with some 120 burials the largest cemetery of flat pit graves of several known in the area, and it may originally have been larger.[25] It appears that there were two main spatial groups of burials, some 15 m apart, and in one part of one group there were regular parallel rows of burials. There were many burials crouched on the left side. Some were disarticulated and may be reburials. Men, women and children are represented. There is a wide range of grave goods. Children had no more than flint knives. Adults had tanged arrowheads, flint daggers, stone axes, copper daggers, axes, awls, and a bangle, and there was one silver hammer-headed pin. The overall quantities of goods however are not vast. Thus in the undisturbed adult graves the largest category was flint arrowheads of which there were 24, but 11 of these were in one grave. Both men and women had flint and copper daggers. There are different local varieties of copper dagger represented, probably made from local Alpine sources. The flint daggers are also thought to have been made from Alpine foreland sources. There is also one Rinaldone type of stone battle-axe, and the silver pin is generally considered analogous to Corded ware forms in central Europe. There is also a silver pectoral or lunate sheet with dotted decoration, from a grave at Villafranca, which is usually compared to a similar one in a Baden context at Velvary in Czechoslovakia. There is conversely a Remedello-style tanged copper dagger from Provence, and other finds of flint and copper daggers in Switzerland are also potential Remedello exports. The duration of the Remedello cemetery is unclear, and it cannot be assumed that it served purely local residents. Selective burial separate from settlement is again an important feature, and artefact differentiation is again striking, with some explicit signs of long-distance movement of high-quality artefacts. Indeed the ability to control long-distance exchange networks may have been one of the distinguishing characteristics of dominant groups in this suggested phase of social differentiation. There is no need in the present state of evidence to invoke the incursion of external warrior pastoralists or Aegean metal prospectors.[26]

Two other developments are interesting. The first is that at least in northern Italy (and probably the whole peninsula) obsidian seems to be no longer found, which may represent a search for novel and exclusive material and products. The second is the series of statue-menhirs or anthropomorphic stelae, especially in the Upper Adige valley and other Alpine valleys to the west. These are variously decorated with belts, collars or neck rings, triangular daggers and axes. These are obviously hard to date, but the re-used decorated slab in a Beaker cist grave at Sion, Petit Chasseur in the Upper Rhône of the Swiss Valais certainly suggests that some may be of the later third millennium bc (Fig. 7.11).[27] Their valley locations may emphasise the importance of long-distance contact in this phase, and in themselves they are new symbols of authority, with explicit use of novel dagger and axe forms. Further understanding however must rest on a fuller appreciation of the settlement record, as well as on the analysis of other cemeteries and burials in the area.

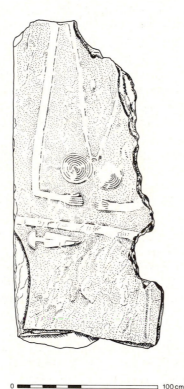

0 ▬▬▬▬▬▬▬▬▬▬▬ 100 cm

**7.11** Decorated stone slab from Sion, Valais, Switzerland. *After* Gallay

Further variety is striking as one moves westwards. There is first of all a number of cave burials north of Milan and in Liguria around Arene Candide, such as Tana Bertrand, which were used for small deposits of collective inhumations.[28] These have large quantities of artefacts deposited but these are largely beads and ornaments. Copper is found, not as daggers, but as awls and beads. In Provence and Languedoc in southern France there are large numbers of megalithic and other tombs.[29] These are widely distributed, from the Rhône delta to the uplands, but their density varies widely. In the *département* of Var for example there are some 45 known monuments which contrasts with an estimated 500 in Lot, and several hundred in Aveyron, Hérault and Gard; rather few are found at the southern end of the distribution in Ariège and Hautes-Pyrénées. There are lowland monuments, as in the coastal area of Provence, the Rhône delta and the plain of the Aude, but the bulk of known sites is in the uplands. There is a very wide variety of form of megalithic monuments, as well as caves and cists used for burials also. In Provence there are roughly round mounds with rectilinear or occasionally circular chambers, as well as rock-cut tombs, or *hypogées*, in the lower Rhône area. The best known of these are south of Arles, such as the unexcavated Grotte des Fées, 23 by 3 m, with descending steps and side chambers at the entrance, or the Grotte du Castellet, rock-cut but with megalithic capstone, and holding some 100 skeletons when excavated in the 1870s. The more recently excavated example at Roaix in the Vaucluse has two levels of deposits of bone, radiocarbon dated to the very late third millennium bc. The earlier level however may begin in the period covered here, since it contains many bodies in anatomical confusion and many goods such as arrowheads, pots and beads, which may represent successive deposits. The plain of the Aude also has large monuments of elongated subrectangular plan and with some subdivision of chambers.

In the uplands there are generally simpler monuments, usually with small chambers and round or oval mounds if present or known. Some in Hérault and Gard have an antechamber formed by the subdivision of the passage, while numbers of those further inland have no recognisable passage at all. The contents of the upland burials seem much less well known though both bodies and grave goods are recorded. Overall the rarity of well-recorded excavations make the evaluation of this phenomenon very difficult. One feature may again be selective formal disposal of certain people, and another is the separation of burial from settlements. The great numbers in the uplands can be taken to testify to the uptake of grazing and other resources there rather than a wholesale shift out of the lowlands. The importance of upland territory in a wider regional economy may then be part of the explanation of the phenomenon of southern French megaliths. Grave goods are on occasion abundant, but none are highly distinctive as in northern Italy, though there are special forms of beads, such as the winged type. There are also numbers of decorated statue-menhirs in Languedoc and Provence, though without weapons.[30] Rare funerary contexts and the re-use of two at the later Fontbouisse site of Lébous suggest that some at least belong to the period covered here, and as in northern Italy they could be seen to represent new forms of authority. There is full evidence for artefact differentiation, in the form of copper working in the Grands Causses of the Aveyron and Lozère *départements*, especially at the site of Sargel. Not only beads but also axes and daggers were produced.[31] In the lower Rhône there was also an increased interest in flint extraction. Sites are known with shafts sunk up to 6 m deep in Vaucluse, and there are also galleries in Gard at Salinelles.[32] Finally it is worth remembering the more regional patterns of material culture outlined above compared with the preceding Chasseen phase. These too may support the notion of the emergence of locally dominant groups and greater social differentiation but it is also important to consider the possibility (as in central and northern Europe in the later third millennium bc discussed in chapter 6) of social 'devolution' in the sense of a breakdown of large-scale regional groupings and an increase in competition between smaller and more autonomous groupings.

### Southern Iberia, mid to later third millennium bc

*Chronology and material sequences.* There is rather different development in the southern Iberian sequence as presently known. The sequence itself however is far from well established. It has been based in the past largely on the typology of tomb types and tomb contents rather than on vertical stratigraphy or radiocarbon dates. There has been a tendency also to underplay possible regional differences through the emphasis on the Almerian and Tagus area sequences. The situation appears to be beginning to change but there is so far insufficient published new information for a different scheme to be presented.

Los Millares in Almería, inland from the coast, is a large site consisting of settlement, bastioned walls, cemetery of passage graves and outlying forts, and has been the key to the south-eastern sequence in past schemes.[33] Indeed the concept of a Millaran culture has also been extended to the southern half of Portugal as well in view of several similarities between the two regions and also the intervening ones. Los Millares was examined in the late nineteenth century by Siret and his assistant Flores, who investigated many tombs, a small part of the settlement and part of the outlying forts. This was largely carried out by Flores and synthesised by Siret who was living elsewhere. It was never fully or properly published, though records and material survived to be studied and synthesised in their turn by the Leisners in their creation of a relative chronology of the site. This scheme published some 75 tombs but only two could be located on the ground. Further work was achieved in the 1950s by Almagro and Arribas who re-excavated 21 tombs and excavated part of the settlement including its wall. There are now two radiocarbon dates, one from a secondary context of the wall, and one from tomb 19. Further recent excavation at the site has revealed the presence of additional bastioned walls and more outlying forts. The Leisners' scheme has in turn been challenged, but it is useful to set it out briefly here, if only to introduce the range of material under consideration (Fig. 7.12). Two periods were identified, the first also subdivided. The general trend proposed was an increase in the complexity of tomb typology with time and a decrease in the richness of the associated artefacts. The essential bases for the scheme were the location of period I tombs nearer the settlement (which did not figure in the scheme) and the greater association of beakers with period II tombs (though they did also occur in supposed period I examples). Period I tombs included round corbelled

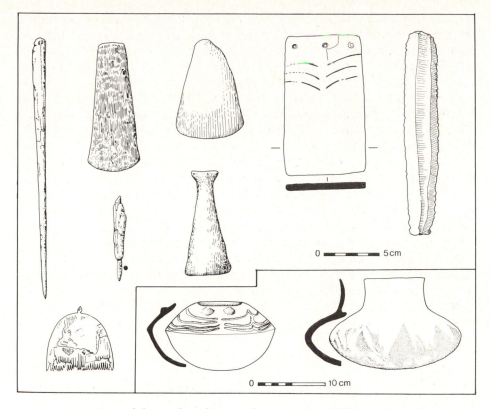

**7.12** Some of the artefacts from tomb no. 40 at Los Millares, Almería, south-east Spain. *After* Leisner and Leisner

tombs with false vaulted roofs, segmented entrance passages, no side chambers, rare portholes, and forecourts and enclosures with 'baetyls' (explained below); their contents included copper axes, chisels and awls; large flint blades and sickles; rhomboid, leaf-shaped, tanged and hollow-based flint arrowheads; *Symbolkeramik* or rather simple forms decorated with incised motifs sometimes in the form of 'eyes'; a little simple painted pottery; occasional beaker pottery; stone and bone vessels; stone and ivory round idols; other ivory objects such as combs, pommels and a sandal; beads of jet, amethyst, amber, callaïs and ostrich shell; and baetyls or waisted stone pillars up to about 50 cm high. Period II tombs were built in dry-stone with corbelled vaulting and had side chambers off both the main chambers and passages, which were generally undivided; goods included copper tanged daggers and saws, decorated bone phalanges, and beakers, and did not include stone axes or elaborately decorated pottery. The quantity and range of other goods were much reduced.

It is likely however that the scheme is inadequate. Several period II tombs are as close to the settlement as those of period I. Beaker pottery, which must come from a phase of use of the cemetery after that considered here, is found in both supposed periods, and in significant quantities also close to the settlement. The typology of the tombs themselves is complex, and side chambers for example do occur with period I tombs. Alternative explanations for differences in tomb types and abundance of goods are explored below. Here we can only lament the present lack of internal subdivision of the material. Other more recently excavated stratified settlements will perhaps however yield the required sequences, such as Tabernas, El Barranquete, El Malagon and El Tarajal. Tabernas, Barranquete and Tarajal, and also Almizaraque, have radiocarbon dates of the later third millennium bc, and the site of Cerro de la Virgen, Orce in inland Granada has a beaker phase dated to the early second millennium bc.[34] Some preliminary points may be stressed despite the lack of present synthesis. We need not expect other sites to mirror the situation at Los Millares. Secondly, it appears that the 'Millaran' phase continued into the early second millennium bc without significant discontinuity, and this account is aimed at the pre-beaker part of a continuum. Thirdly, though the quantities of dates are increasing, the beginnings of the Millaran phase are still unclear, and our ignorance of this is still a major obstacle to explanation of developments.

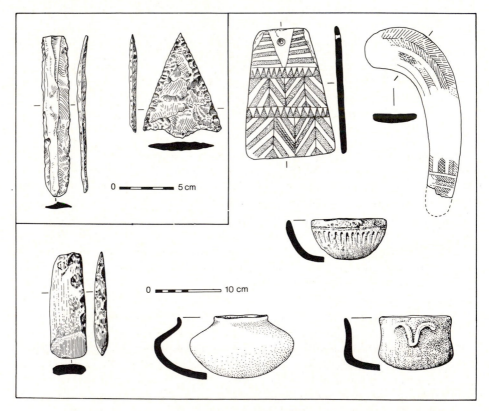

**7.13** Some of the artefacts from the tomb of Anta Grande da Comenda da Igreja, Alentejo, Portugal. *After* Leisner and Leisner

There are similar difficulties in the southern half of Portugal. There are at least two major schemes for third millennium bc development but neither is well supported by stratigraphy or radiocarbon dates, though the classic site of Vila Nova de São Pedro does itself have some stratigraphic development, from a pre-enclosure to an enclosure phase.[35] Material assigned to this phase includes fine lustrous pottery with channelled decoration; long flint blades and triangular concave-based flint arrowheads; polished stone axes; little clay plaques and small anthropomorphic figurines with schematic limbs; vase-headed bone pins; and copper daggers, flat axes, sickles and awls (Fig. 7.13). The lack of dates, and also the inconsistencies between available dates and suggested schemes, has already been noted earlier in the chapter for this area and remains pertinent now. The danger of using tomb contents or particular categories of artefacts as the basis for general schemes is also evident in this area. For example pottery in the sequence at Zambujal can be seen to change rather more rapidly than metal or lithic types.[36] Continuity of development into the early second millennium bc is also likely in southern Portugal as in south-east Spain, on the basis of beaker pottery at Vila Nova de São Pedro and Zambujal. As in the south-east, the beginnings of 'Vilanovan' features remain unclear. It is worth emphasising finally too the need for detailed regional schemes. Rather than merely two large regions, at least six smaller regions can be emphasised each with some distinctive features in its range of artefacts and monuments.[37] Continued link-up between regions is an important aspect of this phase, but the background of more local sequences still badly needs elucidation.

*Southern Iberia: settlements and the social context, mid to later third millennium bc*

The settlement record too is fragmentary. Attention has been focused on a small number of enclosed sites, themselves for the most part incompletely excavated and published. The number, distribution and character of the other sites is not known, partly due to lack of systematic survey and excavation, perhaps partly also due to the masking effects of alluviation in the lower parts of river valleys. Recovery of plant and animal remains has been unsystematic, though the use of wheat, barley, beans, peas and olives, and of sheep and goat, cattle and pig is documented.[38] Nor do we know how arid the environment was at this phase or what effect this may have had on settlement types and locations. Nonetheless there are the known classic sites to consider, and their very existence and character may lead to other inferences about a developed landscape, which recent research is beginning also to support. Los Millares for example (Figs. 7.14 and 7.15) is a strong candidate for being seen as a regional centre. It lies inland at the back of the Almerian coastal plain, and sits high on a plateau above the confluence of two rivers. The settlement seems to lie within a bastioned stone wall about 2 m thick which runs across the base of the triangular-shaped promontory. The wall has not been traced over the full width of the plateau. Recent excavations have found traces of

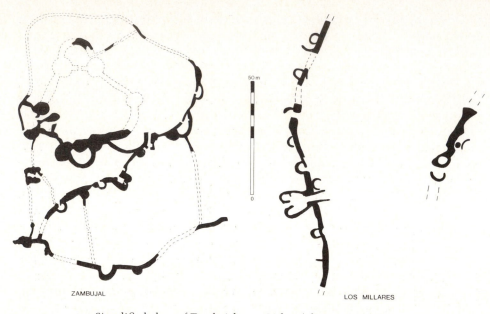

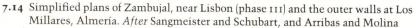

ZAMBUJAL                                         LOS MILLARES

**7.14** Simplified plans of Zambujal, near Lisbon (phase III) and the outer walls at Los Millares, Almería. *After* Sangmeister and Schubart, and Arribas and Molina

two other walls, within it. The settlement may be extensive, since the wall defines an area over 400 m long, but its duration and complexity are unknown, apart from Siret's observation of rectangular buildings nearer the apex than circular buildings explored by Almagro and Arribas. Outside this area there are other features of interest. Siret observed what he took to be a simple conduit or artificial water course of stone and earth running towards the settlement from outside. There were also four outlying forts or small circular walled enclosures on the next ridge of the plateau. The most elaborate of these was about 30 m in diameter and had a double stone wall with projecting bastions and an inner enclosure or tower. Recent investigations have revealed the presence of up to six more such forts, on the ridges surrounding the bastioned walls.

In the area between the settlement wall and the forts there was the largest concentration of tombs known in southern Iberia. The exact number is not known, due to Siret's lack of publication and also the subsequent destruction of the site, but the minimum figure is around 80 and the real total could exceed 100, within 1 km of the settlement. The more recently explored site of El Barranquete is useful for putting Los Millares in perspective, since the settlement is low-lying and has also a group of tombs nearby. Tombs and settlements known from surface finds are also recorded in the lower Aguas valley some 70 km north-east of Los Millares. Indeed the suggestion has been made of lower valley flood-water farming in this period, though direct evidence is elusive.[39] The nature of the settlements at Tabernas and Almizaraque is unclear, though both may have been enclosed and contained a

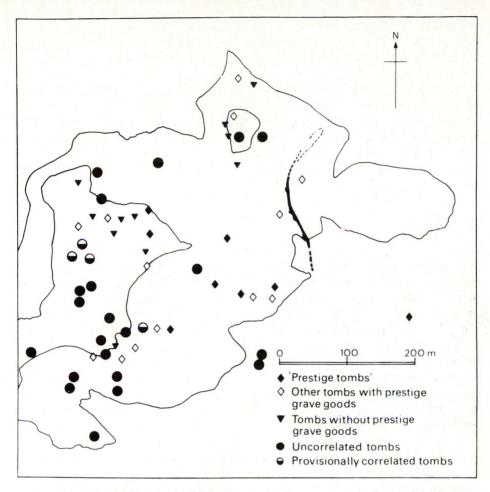

**7.15** Simplified layout of the passage grave cemetery at Los Millares. *After* Chapman

concentration of buildings. Their locations are also interesting, Tabernas being rather like Los Millares at the back of the coastal plain, and Almizaraque – along with other similar sites such as Tres Cabezos and Campos, the latter with a definite bastioned wall – lying in the lower part of the Almanzora valley in the basin around Vera. Though its main occupation lies after the period covered here, the site of Orce also suggests a greater penetration of the upland interior than seen before, but this possibility remains to be fully explored.[40]

Scattered tombs and settlements are known across southern Iberia. The other example to be discussed in more detail is the lower Tagus area. Here there are other sites, such as Vila Nova de São Pedro and Zambujal, which may have been of more than purely local importance, as well as some others which may help to put them into perspective. Vila Nova de São Pedro lies on a ridge on the north side of the Tagus valley near Santarém.[41] Its first open phase has already been mentioned. Several different campaigns of excavation go back to the 1930s but have never been fully published. The enclosed phase consists of an inner squarish wall with several projecting bastions and a single narrow entrance. The interior is roughly 25 by 25 m. At a distance varying from 25 to 60 m out from this is an outer, roughly oval wall with similar semicircular bastions, and there is mention too of indications of a third outermost enclosing wall. There are occupation traces within the innermost enclosure and between this and the second wall. These include buildings and metalworking areas but there is little information on their layout from the small scale of excavation. Though the site has many finds of high-quality arrowheads, copper artefacts and also schist plaques and limestone idols, there is no concentration of tombs in its immediate area. Around Zambujal however there is some clustering of tombs of various types which may partly match the Los Millares case.

Zambujal itself (see Fig. 7.14) is some 11 km from the coast on a steep promontory above a small river.[42] There appear to be three main features to the site. About 120 m from the end of the promontory are traces of an outermost stone wall with at least one semicircular bastion. More diagonally at a distance from 60 to 100 m from the end of the promontory there is a second more elaborate wall which has been more extensively explored. The wall here is up to 3 m thick and has at least four semicircular bastions and two narrow entrances. At points as close as 5 m to this is the third wall. At its thickest this is up to 17 m across and incorporates also semicircular bastions, two circular towers, a large semicircular enclosure and a narrow entrance over 10 m long. This third wall may have been connected to the second wall, and in turn may have in fact been part of a roughly circular enclosure on the apex of the promontory, roughly 40 m in diameter. All three elements have evidence for modification and rebuilding (the excavators suggest five major phases), and there is Beaker pottery from the final phase or the abandonment of the inner enclosures. Published radiocarbon dates begin around 2300 bc but do not appear to relate to the earliest parts of the sequence. The inner wall may have been most modified. It is suggested that at first it was only 1 m thick though 4 m high, and merely cut off the promontory. There is evidence too for early occupation of the inner interior including buildings. Finds from early stages included fine pattern-burnished pottery; cylindrical idols; bone boxes, pins and comb; flint arrowheads, and copper chisels, awls, axe and knife. These are all compatible with a high-status site. Another settlement in the area is the unenclosed small hilltop occupation of Penedo de Lexim, thought to be contemporary with Zambujal and with a single TL date in the early third millennium BC.[43] In the area around Lisbon there are other hilltop and cave occupations known, including the Serra das Bautas at Carenque, with a similar TL date. (Both dates however have large standard deviations.) The Lisbon area is notable also for another concentration of tombs, and one may predict the eventual discovery of another major enclosed site.

*Southern Iberia: burial, ritual and material culture,*
*mid to later third millennium bc*

Many earlier tombs may have remained in use in this period over the area under discussion. The general consensus seems to be that the main novelty of this period was the development of tombs with a round chamber, either orthostatic or dry-stone; a passage often segmented by slabs or perforated slabs; sometimes side chambers and forecourts; and generally round covering mounds or cairns. These are often referred to as *tholoi*, in explicit reference (at least originally) to collective tombs in the eastern Mediterranean, a hypothesis we will return to below. These tombs are thought to be late developments partly because of their contents and partly because of their refined construction and frequent complexity. Surviving contents may of course be a misleading guide to the initial construction of such monuments, and complexity of form and construction need not necessarily increase steadily with time. There is a danger too in relating all the tombs in a case like Los Millares to the period of the settlement (itself anyway poorly known). Despite these caveats however there is some justification for believing in a late date for the kind of passage grave just described since there are eight radiocarbon dates from five tombs which fall in the later third millennium bc – Los Millares and El Barranquete in Almeria and Anta dos Tassos, Farisoa and Praia das Maçãs in Portugal.[44] The small number of dates needs little comment by this stage of the book, and the context of the sample at Los Millares is unknown, while the two samples at El Barranquete are associated with a central pillar – a strictly secondary context.

The tombs are in fact quite regionalised in type. At Los Millares as we have already seen there is some variation in details. Some chambers are orthostatic, others wholly made of dry-stone walling. Passages are usually divided into segments, from two to four with three being most common, by slabs which have large portholes in them and which in turn seem to have had at least in some instances their own sealing slabs, but there are also undivided passages. Some tombs have side chambers and enclosures outside the entrance which held baetyls. A feature of many is the corbelled dry-stone roof vaulting. Some had a central pillar which may have helped to support the roof vault, though in other cases this is considered only to be a ritual stele. There are reports of red painting on gypsum plaster from the interior of some (in the Leisners' early period), and others again have developed forecourts outside. The mounds are rather modest, being less than 20 m in diameter, and the chambers too are usually less than 4 m in diameter. Other tombs of this same general kind can be found both elsewhere in south-east Spain and further west in southern Iberia, but there are notable regional traits such as trench construction, long passages and megalithic capstones in the Seville region, as at Cueva de la Pastora or the Dolmen de Matarrubilla. These also lack dividing passage slabs. There are also however western *tholoi*, as at Farisoa in the area of Reguengos de Monsaraz, with a modest orthostatic chamber and short passage and a single mid third millennium bc TL date. Rock-cut tombs too were presumably still in use and perhaps still under construction, though less attention is given to them at this stage. The monument at Praia das Maçãs near Sintra began as a rock-cut tomb and was later enlarged as a partly rock-cut passage grave with dry-stone walling and a corbelled vault. There are radiocarbon dates of the late third millennium bc for the first monument and the early second for the later monument, but none of the samples need relate to the actual construction of the respective phases.

There is also considerable variation in the distribution and density of tombs. Los Millares stands out with its concentration of 80 or more tombs, and there are smaller concentrations at El Barranquete and Cerro de Nieles, La Huelga of about 30 tombs. In the Algarve there are 13 at Alcala, but elsewhere the great majority of occurrences have only between one and five tombs. The significance and function of all tombs cannot therefore easily be assumed to be uniform, and there is also a lack of detailed information about tomb contents (quite apart from chronology). The tombs are generally assumed to have held collective burials. These certainly occur, but many tombs were disturbed or are not now well recorded. At Los Millares there is again considerable variation. For 58 of the monuments published by the Leisners some 1140 individuals are estimated, but the numbers per tomb vary from two to 100. It seems that children were largely excluded. Details of bone deposition are available for only one Los Millares tomb now, no. 21 in Almagro and Arribas' numbering. This has evidence for deliberate grouping of long bones and crania. There is similar evidence for a considerable concern for body treatment also at El Barranquete, at the Dolmen de Matarrubilla and at Praia das Maçãs.[45] The size of the sample now available for study needs little further comment by this stage, but these features do recall the discussion in chapter 6 of the British and Scandinavian tombs. Here too this kind of body treatment may be indicative of communities who were highly concerned with ordering and categorising themselves. It is worth stressing too that the numbers of people represented in the tombs can only be a fraction of contemporary populations, so that as in southern France and Italy considerable internal selection is another important general feature.

Difference and exclusiveness could also be seen in the architecture and ritual practised at many tombs, and in the nature of the grave goods. Passage slabs, where they occur, seem to emphasise the specialness of tomb interiors, which may have been reinforced by ritual practised in forecourts and baetyl enclosures. The unusual nature of many grave goods has also been noted already. Large collective burials could again as in earlier discussions be seen as the expression of an ideology serving to mask social differences. The various strands of the argument may be taken together to suggest that there was at least a considerable concern within communities by this date for internal ordering and that there was quite likely in addition real social differentiation. The Los Millares case will be discussed in this light but it is important to remember the unusual nature of this site, so that development elsewhere in southern Iberia could well have been less marked.

Chapman has suggested that an alternative approach at Los Millares to the Leisners' chronological interpretation of tomb differences is to consider these differences in terms of status variation (see Fig. 7.15). He notes that certain tombs have richer inventories than others (though this does not correlate with complexity of plan), that these tend to occur in the inner part of the cemetery, that is closer to the settlement, and that other tombs less well endowed seem to cluster around these. Thus tomb 40, of simple plan but large chamber size, has the highest number of ivory and copper objects of any tomb, while tomb 12 also of simple plan, also has the second largest number of ivory objects, some 800 ostrich eggshell beads, and the highest number of jet and amber beads, and so on in other cases. Three assumptions are implicit, that each tomb in such a cemetery can be treated as an isolated unit of study, that the final contents of a tomb reflect its status throughout its use, and that social reality is more or less directly mirrored in burials. The last assumption is perhaps the most critical, since it may not be valid to pick out the richly furnished tombs in this way, especially without further information on body treatment, ritual and chronology, and without allowance for variation in tomb complexity. It may be safer to fall back on more general features of the cemetery – the tombs themselves, associated ritual, selection of the dead, access to prestige goods, the concentration of tombs next to a probably important settlement or site and so on – in order to emphasise its special nature and the likely existence of marked social differentiation by this stage of Iberian prehistory.

The grave goods and other artefacts mentioned so far deserve some further discussion. The skill evident in pottery, bone, ivory, stone and metal may suggest craft specialisation though it is hard to take this notion further without better settlement evidence from a range of sites. Ostrich eggshell and ivory are assumed to come from North Africa, and if the various objects made of these materials were in fact status items, much of their value may derive from their exotic source.[46] Metal products may have been valuable partly because of the long process of production and distribution though these are aspects about which there is little specific evidence. There are copper ores widely distributed in southern Iberia, and finds of this period from later copper mines have been mentioned but not further highlighted. Analysis of some copper artefacts indicates an arsenical copper but it is not clear whether this reflects the use of sulphide ores or deliberate alloying, though the former possibility is more likely.[47] Working areas with crucible fragments and slag are known at Almizaraque and Vila Nova de São Pedro. Most products could have been cast in one-piece moulds, including the daggers with midrib on one side only. A number of daggers or blades – especially four from tomb 3 at Alcalá in the Algarve – have midribs on both sides, which strongly suggests the use of two piece moulds, though this has been attributed to annealing and hammering-up.[48] Copper objects were not however plentiful given the span of the Millaran phase, though there are high numbers reported at Almizaraque – over 100 – and they do occur in high proportions in rich tombs at Los Millares compared to other exotic objects.[49] Products of this stage can be seen without difficulty as the result of development from earlier Iberian practice noted above.

Artefacts can also be noted as a measure of the scale of contact between different regions within southern Iberia. There are objects held in common between the lower Tagus area and Almería, such as copper products, concave arrowheads, combs, model sandals, and *Symbolkeramik*. There are also resemblances in the construction of certain tombs and bastioned walls. For these reasons there has been much discussion in the past of 'Millaran' culture visible over the whole, or at least parts of the whole, of southern Iberia. It is however important not to exaggerate such supposed uniformity. The idea of uniformity derives largely it seems from the notion that Millaran culture itself was introduced by colonists from the eastern Mediterranean, the supposed external source of origin being in itself a self-evident source of uniformity.[50] This hypothesis itself will be reviewed and rejected below. Here it is sufficient to stress on the one hand the evident regional differences already emphasised within southern Iberia and the relatively infrequent occurrence of the diagnostic artefacts particularly in the west, and on the other hand the background of regional contact suggested for the preceding phase against which a continuation and reinforcement of regional long-range contact between elites is plausible enough in this phase. To overemphasise uniformity however is to miss the important regional differences in social development. The lower Tagus area for example does not have ivory objects, phalanges, or painted pottery, and seems to have far fewer ivory objects and baetyls. The sandal models from Alapraia are of limestone, not in ivory as from Los Millares, tomb 12. The use of plaques and limestone objects may continue into the later third millennium bc in Portugal, to further accentuate regional differences, though here the chronology lets us down again. Whatever the answer in this particular case Almería stands out in southern Iberia for the range of exotic items accessible to communities in the area. This is not to deny the great interest of bastioned enclosures occurring in Portugal as well, but if one starts from the perspective of indigenous social development, it is important to assert that one area in particular may have been provided with greater geographical opportunities for external long-range contact, which were taken up in the process of local social differentiation. The similarities and differences between regions are of complementary interest.

## Western Mediterranean developments: local or external change?

Despite the vagaries of the available chronology, the case has been presented for essentially local development in southern Iberia though at differing pace between the different regions. Older arguments for eastern Mediterranean colonists must however be noted. The suggested transformations in southern Iberia can then in turn be compared and contrasted with those in southern France and Italy.

The colonist argument stemmed from a lack of belief in the possibility of extensive local change and from a belief in the cultural superiority of the eastern Mediterranean, especially the Aegean. Key points in the argument were the bastioned walls, copper metallurgy, and collective burial in formal tombs, for which Aegean and other parallels and supposed precursors were all cited, as well as for a range of artefacts including pottery and figurines. However none of the supposed artefactual parallels is overwhelmingly similar, and there is considerable geographical diffuseness in the areas from which they are supposed to derive. Pre-Millaran indigenous development can be seen for tombs and metallurgy, and bastioned walls are not in themselves so extraordinary a development as to have originated in only one area. There is no single certain Aegean artefact or trait, and indeed no obsidian even from the west-central Mediterranean sources, which seems to emphasise the isolation of southern Iberia rather than its inclusion in wider Mediterranean networks of contact and exchange. The colonist argument also tends to ascribe any interesting development to colonists by definition, and leave the rest to natives.

Alternative approaches to Iberian development have already been suggested. The point here is to note the varied social development in the western Mediterranean as a whole. It is interesting that in Italy, southern France and southern Iberia there are significant social transformations in the earlier to mid third millennium bc and that the developments were of rather different kind in Iberia from the other two areas where the nature of change may have been more similar. It was necessary in these latter two areas also to reject explanations based on external population or on purely external factors such as climate or environment for which there is insufficient evidence of the required kind. In all three areas the social trend may have been towards differentiation. Parts of Italy stand out for their more individualised burial traditions and southern Iberia for its range of settlement types including possible regional centres, which have not so far been identified in the settlement record of the other two areas, even though suggestions were made in southern France of economic activity on a regional basis. Given their rather similar development up to around 4000 bc, it is plausible that both such convergence and divergence should be now observable.

The explanation of such change is no easier in these areas than in those covered by earlier chapters. The locus of change may lie in rather local differences, conflicts and contradictions within a wider context of social competition, which allowed certain groups to produce more and acquire more than others and which in the unfolding 'logic of situations' resulted in more established social differentiation with access to resources and status being unequally distributed within and between communities. Essentially the same trend can then be seen in most areas of Europe, even though it cannot be thought of as a uniform process. Every allowance must be made for local variation, and the nature of third millennium bc transformations is rather different in the western Mediterranean to the rest of Europe, particularly in the aspect of external contact. It is interesting that Almería developed exotic contacts with North Africa, and northern Italy limited contacts across the Alpine passes and into central Europe, but regional link-up was not, at least on present evidence, as important as in eastern, central or northern Europe.

## Northern Iberia and the Mediterranean islands

This final section briefly picks up the last point of different development within the western Mediterranean in order to make some reference – hardly adequate – to northern Iberia and the central islands. In north-east Spain burial traditions outlined earlier in the chapter may continue into this period, as also in north-west Iberia. This fact, together with the probable lack of

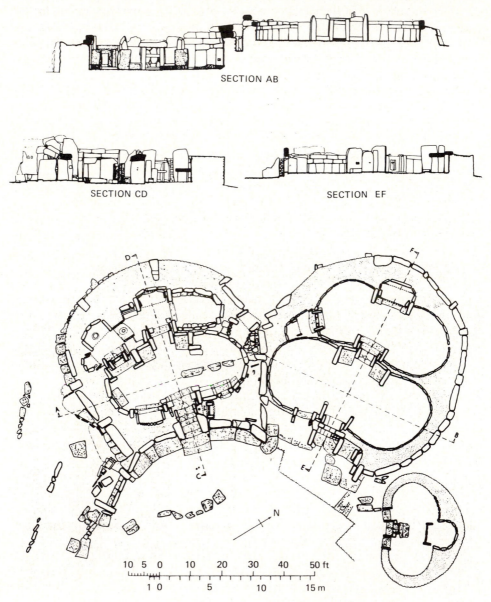

**7.16** Plans and sections of the temples at Mnajdra, Malta. *After* Evans

effective pre-Beaker penetration of the central interior, serves to emphasise the special nature of developments in the southern part of the peninsula.[51] Uneven change can also be emphasised on the islands. Sicily is distinctive in the third millennium bc as we have already seen, and Corsica and Sardinia, whose initial occupation also goes back to the sixth or fifth millennia, also had distinctive features in the fourth and third. The Sardinian Ozieri group has distinctive decorated pottery. There are also rock-cut tombs, indeed the highest density of these in the central Mediterranean, and local megaliths, but both have essentially insular traits and practices. Corsica probably lacks rock-cut tombs though it has megalithic cists and insular pottery styles. Like other small islands which offered less ecological diversity and opportunity for both hunter-gatherers and mixed farmers, the Balearic islands were perhaps colonised later than the larger islands, after around 4000 bc.[52] Close control may have been attempted of the local deer, *Myotragus balearicus*, on Mallorca, but little is yet known of other kinds of activity before the Beaker

**7.17** Temple cell, Mnajdra South, Malta. Photo: Trump

horizon, despite the proximity of the islands to south-east Spain.[53] The Maltese islands provide the best example of western Mediterranean divergence.[54] The islands are certainly smaller than the Balearics if not more isolated. They were colonised at roughly the same time, just before 4000 bc. There is some evidence for mixed farming. From before 3000 bc there is evidence based on stratigraphy and radiocarbon dating for an increasingly complex series of temples running down to around 2000 bc (Figs. 7.16 and 7.17). These are large, perhaps storeyed buildings with imposing concave facades, central courts and horseshoe-shaped structures off these, perhaps roofed. There are also local rock-cut tombs and at least one vast underground *hypogeum* or underground series of chambers, at Hal Saflieni, with architectural features carved out of the limestone and often painted, and with the remains of possibly as many as thousands of human inhumations. The temples tend to occur in pairs and are spread across Malta and Gozo, perhaps marking territories of some kind. Setting aside the possibility that the islands were used wholly for ritual purposes within the Sicilian and south Italian orbit (which the local pottery and figurine series contradict), one is left with an extraordinary localised development whose distinctive monuments cannot be paralleled elsewhere in the Mediterranean. It is a fitting final example in a book which has stressed the value of first seeking local explanations of social change, but its unique nature and isolated setting serve also to emphasise the regularity of contacts between regions and over long distances elsewhere in Europe.

# CHAPTER 8

# CONCLUSIONS

Es ist eine alte Geschichte
Doch bleibt sie immer neu.
        Heinrich Heine, *Buch der Lieder*

This book began by contrasting the great amounts of evidence available for study with the deceptively simple question of what one is to make of it all. One response could be extremely pessimistic, and suggest that we are little closer to solving or understanding any particular or general problem. Such an argument might make a distinction between the evidence and the theory available to interpret it, and stress the weaknesses of both. On the question of the nature and quality of the evidence further examples of the distortions which the archaeological record can suffer and of the often insufficient level and quality of recovery that have been achieved hardly need rehearsing; each chapter presents many. Problems of theory too have been emphasised, for example from the basic link between human action and the use of material culture to such issues as the proper interpretation of ritual and burial.

The manifest difficulties need not however lead to a creeping paralysis of our interpretative faculties. I wish to stress in conclusion that we can identify major problems in the span of the Neolithic period, that these problems are interesting, that they are connected both with specific issues of Neolithic development and with general questions of change in human society, and finally that we are in some sense closer to an understanding of these problems than say 100 or 50 years ago at earlier stages of Neolithic research. By specific issues I mean such questions as the shift in subsistence from reliance on native resources to use of cereal agriculture, the emergence and consolidation of social difference both within and between communities, or the means by which widespread changes take place, for example in the Balkans in the earlier third millennium bc or in much of central and western Europe in the later third millennium bc. By general questions of change I refer to such issues as the path or trajectory of change, kinds of change and sources of change.

The last claim – that we are in some sense closer to understanding – is the most ambitious and needs justification first. The justification however is not to be sought in overly positivist terms, tempting though that is when one contemplates the year by year accretion of surveys, excavations, reports, analyses, radiocarbon dates and the rest. The issue is not the solution of individual problems as such, but a better understanding of the nature of those problems. Progress may consist of the paradox that, as the quality of both data and theory improve, interpretation becomes more difficult.

Each area has its own questions of sequence and development. There are also major questions relevant to them all. The first chronologically is the transformation of subsistence. We are now in the position of having much more data relevant to this change, as set out in several chapters. This improvement has not in itself led to a better understanding of the problem. More important has been the willingness to speculate more widely, first about processes by which the transformation was achieved − whether by population increase and movement, or by diffusion of ideas and techniques, or indeed by a widespread parallel development − and secondly about the social context of subsistence activities. Taking the long view there is no doubting the reality and importance of the shift to cereal agriculture and animal husbandry, but one must ask oneself for each area whether the change is one of kind or one of degree in intensity of food production. One hypothesis is that agriculture spread as part of population expansion through Greece and the Balkans from the sixth millennium bc onwards, to reach parts of central and western Europe by the mid fifth millennium bc, contrasting with the diffusion of novel staples at a rather slower rate in the western Mediterranean from the sixth millennium bc onwards and in parts of western Europe from the fourth. The steppe area of eastern Europe might see both processes. More explicit alternative models than before are thus available, and indeed for all areas individual researchers still disagree as to the most appropriate. For example there are many doubters as to the external origin of the Linear pottery culture despite its often having been seen as a colonising group, and a growing number of doubters about the external origin of the first Neolithic communities in south-east Europe too. Attention is thus focused on the social context of production, its scale, organisation and purpose, in long sequences of change. For many areas the adoption of cereal agriculture may mark the end (or at least a significant marking point) rather than the beginning of interesting development. The contrast between hunter-gatherers and farmers in many areas may not have been acute.

The book has also argued for a contextual approach to subsequent developments. Intensified agriculture for example, in terms of increased clearance, plough cultivation, traction animals, wheeled transport, permanent land division and so on, has been related to wider questions of the organisation and purpose of such production, with the frequent suggestion that it was a basic means by which social difference was established and consolidated. This may be the more so if one of the motives for adopting agriculture in the first place in many areas was to exploit the social possibilities of settling down and intensifying production. For a wider view of the social context other themes such as settlement organisation, ritual, burial, exchange and material culture have been emphasised. Evidence for social difference is everywhere apparent but is extremely diverse in nature and chronological development and conflicts sharply with simple models of gradually increasing social complexity. This can best be illustrated by offering thumbnail sketches of possible social development in just three pairs of adjacent areas before suggesting certain general features of social development in the European Neolithic. The accounts are necessarily brief and schematic, and the preceding chapters provide a fuller account.

Agricultural settlement in the Balkans and Greece began in the sixth millennium bc, perhaps due to colonisation, but the sequence of subsistence change at the Franchthi cave in southern Greece or in the Danube gorges may allow for native development towards food production. Despite many limitations in the evidence the picture emerges of structured settlement from the beginning, with tell sites a notable feature in several areas. Their existence may indicate a hierarchy of settlement from the outset, and variations too in the scale and mobilisation of agricultural production. There is some emphasis on ritual within such settlements, with elements of ritual also shared over long distances. Burials are largely concentrated inside tell settlements. By the fourth millennium bc a number of changes are evident. The area and perhaps density of settlement increased. Some existing tells may be emphasised as regional centres of production and ritual. Some new foundations as in north-east Bulgaria are strongly enclosed or even defended. As well as a greater emphasis on ritual (in the form of figurines and specialised buildings), some separate cemeteries appear next to settlements or perhaps serving several settlements. Existing crafts are elaborated. Some pottery is moved long distances, and copper metallurgy rapidly developed: mines suggest a considerable scale of production, products were moved long distances and were mainly symbolic or decorative items. It is possible to see in all this an increase in conflict or tension between and within communities. The succeeding horizon of the early third millennium bc may be the result of this. The preceding cultural system ends, but with local continuity of settlement, suggesting essentially local change rather than the shock of intrusive Indo-Europeans. This is also supported by the varied dates of the changes. Less emphasis on ritual is compatible with a more openly established mode of social difference; long-range similarities in items of material culture may reflect a shift to external alliance among elites away from the pre-existing ritual ideology.

In the north Carpathian basin (northern Hungary and Slovakia) agricultural settlement begins with the Linear pottery culture in the mid fifth millennium bc, classically seen as the result of colonisation from the northern Balkans but possibly the result of indigenous transformation in connection with or in reaction to the emergence of the Vinča culture. There was a dense pattern of small settlements on favourable soils, but without the long-term continuity of individual sites seen further south. Early material uniformity was steadily replaced by regional diversity. In the early fourth millennium bc there was a horizon (early Lengyel and Tisza phases) of ritual elaboration, in the form of painted and elaborate pottery, figurines, special enclosure sites and large separate cemeteries (the latter at least in the early Lengyel area). These decline in prominence in the mid fourth millennium in the Lengyel zone. There is a decline too in the Tiszapolgár culture of elaborate pottery and figurines, but separate cemeteries (with copper among the grave goods) and perhaps more dispersed settlement emerge. It was suggested that this mid fourth millennium bc development was similar in kind to the Balkan change, just noted, but the earlier date is here of crucial interest. From the earlier third millennium both parts of the north Carpathian area are linked by the Baden culture. Other changes include wheeled transport, and pairs of oxen in burials, and initially at least much uniformity of material culture. Further consolidation of social differentiation was suggested.

The next pair of contrasts takes us to north-west Europe. Agricultural settlement begins in southern Britain probably in the earlier fourth millennium bc though whether by colonisation from the adjacent continent or by native transformation or both is still debated. Clearance and settlement may have been locally dense in the fourth millennium bc. Collective burials in megalithic and earthen tombs may indicate the existence of locally dominant groups using their ancestors as claims to land and social position. This sort of competitive situation may be increased in the earlier third millennium bc with further tomb building and the construction of enclosures for defence, ritual and the consumption of prestige goods such as imported pottery and axes. Radical material change follows in the mid third millennium bc, and earlier practices fall away. This may be consistent with a resolution of earlier competition, and by the later third millennium bc a strong emphasis emerges on material differentiation between artefact styles and groupings (along with countryside link-up in the Grooved ware complex), and some burials become more individualised. At the same time there is a notable series of ritual or ceremonial enclosures which have been seen by some as an expression of an ideology of the collective to mask social difference.

In Denmark agricultural settlement may not begin till the later or late fourth millennium bc, perhaps because of well-established patterns of production and settlement in the Ertebølle phase. One model even suggests that agriculture was not adopted until changing salinity in the Baltic led to a decline of previously important marine resources. Early agricultural settlements are small, and individually shortlived. Clearance seems to have been limited. There are some burial tombs but the number of bodies in them is small. From around 2700 bc there is a change of pace. Clearance is extended and settlements increase in number. Pottery becomes more elaborate, there is a great increase in the building of megalithic tombs and the only recently discovered enclosures belong to this horizon. The horizon is not however extended. These features fall away by the later third millennium bc with first rather plainer late TRB pottery and large settlements, then the Corded ware or Single grave culture with individual burial and inter-regional links (extending into central Europe). It is possible to see in this also a resolution of social difference into more openly defined modes after the phase of ritual elaboration and inferred competition.

Southern Italy and southern France can be used to provide further contrasts. Agricultural settlement may begin in the earlier sixth millennium bc in southern Italy. The common model is of colonisation, though this may only reflect ignorance of the full sequence. A wide range of settlements is found on the coastal plains, with ditched enclosures prominent. Set against smaller and unenclosed sites these may be interpretable as centres of local or regional social importance. Their numbers may increase in the fifth millennium. There are varied pottery styles, some of which may be exchanged regionally, along with obsidian. Burial is not a prominent feature. The settlement picture of the fourth millennium is not clear; The Tavoliere for example may or may not be occupied at this phase. Material culture is further emphasised by first elaborately decorated then plain wares, and by the scale of obsidian movement. Formal disposal begins to be more important with rock-cut tombs and cave burials. One interpretation can be that emergent social difference is accompanied by a break-up of the pre-existing settlement mode. In the third millennium bc there is some further change. Burials are further emphasised, with copper artefacts in some. But though the settlement record is incomplete, the overall picture is not one of well-defined differentiation.

In southern France the currently available sample of excavated sites suggests a slow and gradual adoption of novel artefacts and subsistence resources by the native population from the beginning of the sixth millennium bc, perhaps in that order sheep and goats, pottery and then cereals. Established patterns of subsistence and social formation may have altered rather slowly through the sixth and fifth millennia bc. Lithic styles remain in local traditions, and burial is not emphasised (though the lack of open-air settlements can again be noted). Pottery tends to be individual from region to region. By the fourth millennium bc agricultural settlement is more fully established, with an extension of activity from coastal plains to the uplands fringing them. Some large sites stand out as potentially more important than others. Burial is emphasised in specialised tombs. The Chasseen pottery is however rather plain. The succeeding horizon from the earlier third millennium bc is one of further extension in the uplands, strong regional differentiation in pottery styles (and the first copper metallurgy) and further construction of new burial monuments and continued use of existing ones. The contrasts thus offered may be between a long initial phase of a gradual change, a succeeding long phase of primary agricultural settlement and a final phase of accentuated, localised social difference.

These sketches have been presumptuously brief and selective but they serve to underline for a final time the diversity of change and development which has been emphasised throughout the book. The early agricultural communities in question presumably had much in common in terms of basic concerns for land and resources, and the operation of an agricultural economy, and in terms of basic concerns for social position through agricultural production, manipulation of burial, control of ritual and so on. Yet it is the individuality of each area which remains most striking. Many different rates and paths of development are evident. These fail to fit the simple trajectories proposed in earlier models of social development, for example from equalitarian to ranked to stratified social relations or from band to tribal to chiefdom social formations. Indeed rather than attempting such large-scale characterisations it is probably more useful as well as more interesting to attempt to understand in each specific area under consideration the potential for and focus of social conflict and contradiction. The question of 'social baseline' is important. The likely existence of social difference as far back as the early post-glacial period (the Mesolithic in conventional terminology) suggests strongly that an egalitarian baseline is not a useful concept at all.

Despite these particularising concerns, there are nonetheless features of general interest common to the development discernible in many areas. There does seem to be a general trend towards the accentuation and con-solidation of social difference though simple evolutionary models are inadequate to describe its complexity, and often more subtle features are relevant. The first is a contrast between cultural uniformity and diversity. Several Neolithic sequences begin with a certain uniformity over wide areas. The Linear pottery culture for example was discussed in terms of the role of material uniformity in a context of pioneering settlement (whether colonis-ing or not). Many sequences then have a subsequent phase of diversity and reduced geographical range. Emphasis on long-range or external factors seems often to re-emerge in subsequent periods of social change, particularly, it has been suggested, in connection with the realignment of social orders into more openly expressed difference. Dislocation of existing practices including settlement patterns often seems to accompany this kind of change. (It may be emphasised again that the book ends with different kinds of development in different areas.) The greatest emphasis on ritual (as far as this can be seen in the archaeological record) seems to occur in periods preceding such changes, when the outcome of social conflict is not yet resolved. A further contrast can be made between the permanence or otherwise of inferred changes. Social dominance must continually be reinforced; The Neolithic record suggests much variety in the timescale over which dominance was locally maintained.

The Neolithic record also encourages speculation about the wider nature of social change. One point has perhaps already been made in the preceding discussion, that the term 'social evolution', so often used in these contexts, is a very loose one, if it retains any unilinear or teleological connotations. As a synonym for social change or development it is of course perfectly acceptable. More interestingly a great amount of the evidence reviewed allows insight into both kinds and sources of change. Explanation in archaeology is subject to fashions or modes, and the history of explanation has been (at the familiar risk of over-simplification) in two phases, the first with a dominant reliance on external kinds of change, the second with a greater shift to internal kinds, coinciding roughly with the appearance of the 'new archaeology': this book has suggested examples of both, for example agricultural colonisation as a case of change in Europe initially from the outside, or the native intensifica-tion of food production, the local development of copper metallurgy and the appearance of megaliths as cases of internal change. But it has also sought to stress that in many cases, including those just cited, the dichotomy between external and internal is insufficient to cover the complexity of change. Even the hypothesis of agricultural colonisation (and more obviously the hypothesis of diffusion of new techniques and staples) involves the native population, since one must ask of a colonisation whether it was resisted, why it was successful, and so on. In other cases such as the transformation of society in the Balkans and Greece in the earlier third millennium bc or the appearance of the Corded ware complex in Europe in the later third I have argued that the focus of change is to be sought within the local regions concerned, not in population movement and disruption from the outside. But this not to deny the geographical scale over which these changes took place, and indeed explicit explanation must be sought of the existence of marked long-range similarities, a shift in the way in which social dominance was attempted or expressed being the one offered here.

The same possibilities exist in considering sources of change. This book has sought to place the main emphasis on local social conflicts and tensions as the major dynamic of change. The notion of 'egalitarian' social relations has been handled with suspicion from the outset, and examples suggested of how even at early stages of the period covered here aspects of communal activity such as food production, burial or ritual could have been the focus for competition. At the same time purely local explanations are surely unsatisfactory, since we have seen abundant evidence in several spheres, especially of material culture and ritual, for widespread connections and similarities, which suggests that even though the primary focus of social conflict was local it was resolved (or masked or accentuated, depending on the case in hand) on a far wider stage.

Finally there is the question of how change actually happens. Prehistorians often generalise from the archaeological record about trends or processes, and this book has been no exception. Very often this is an appropriate response to the uneven and sketchy nature of the evidence. Yet it may falsely encourage us to view change as something abstract and inexorable (and likewise to ignore periods of stability). The book has also offered however more particularistic concerns with individual areas, which is a useful antidote to inevitable process or trend. In some respects the archaeological record lends itself very well to a more particularising approach. We are often concerned with individual sites, structures and deposits. As local chronologies gradually improve we can begin to have greater confidence in identifying specific horizons of change. Certain features of the record could also be accorded much greater individual emphasis, and could even be seen as specific events rather than merely parts of a process. One thinks here of the construction of monuments such as barrows or enclosures, and the Danish situation c. 2700–2600 bc is a very good case in point (see chapter 6), but there are other examples involving especially foundation, such as of settlements or cemeteries. This is not to suggest that the subsequent maintenance of such sites is of no interest, but to say that here are parts of the archaeological record which can profitably be viewed in a more individual and particularising historical perspective than has often been the case in past research.

Many of the empirical and theoretical problems of the Neolithic period in Europe are unresolved. It is to be hoped that the scale of future research will match the importance of these questions. The interest of the period, which this book has sought to introduce, demands no less.

# NOTES

The notes and select bibliography are intended as a guide to the vast literature available. Most references are given in the notes but where a reference occurs more than once it is given in author and date form in the notes and in full in the select bibliography.

**Preface**

1 E.g. as formulated by E. Neustupný, 1981.
2 R. M. Clark, 1975. Note also J. Klein, *et al.*, 1982, 'Calibration of radiocarbon dates': *Radiocarbon* 24, 103–50; H. Waterbolk, 1971.

**1 Introduction: approaches to the evidence**

1 See preface.
2 This can be followed in more detail in e.g. G. Daniel, 1975, *150 years of archaeology*, London; G. Daniel (ed.), 1981, *Towards a history of archaeology*, London: O. Klindt-Jensen, 1975, *A history of Scandinavian archaeology*, London; K. Sklenar, 1983, *Archaeology in central Europe: the first 500 years*, Leicester.
3 E. Neustupný, 1971, 'Whither archaeology?', *Antiquity* 43, 34–9.
4 S. Müller, 1898, 'De jyske Enkeltgrave fra Stenalderen', *Aarbøger*, 157–202.
5 E.g. V. Childe, 1925, *The dawn of European civilisation*, London; V. Childe, 1929.
6 E.g. V. Mikov, 1939, 'Karanovo', *Antiquity* 13, 345–9; Modderman, P., 1970; B. Soudský, 1966; W. Buttler and G. Haberey, 1936.
7 E. Neustupný, 1968; 1969; C. Renfrew, 1969; 1971; 1972; cf. V. Milojčić, *et al.*, 1976.
8 E.g. J. Kruk, 1973; A. Ammerman and S. Bonardi, 1981, 'Recent developments in the study of Neolithic settlement in Calabria', in G. Barker and R. Hodges (eds.), *Archaeology and Italian society*, pp. 335–42, Oxford; P. Halstead, 1977.
9 E.g. J. G. D. Clark, 1952, *Prehistoric Europe: the economic basis*, Cambridge; E. Higgs, 1972; 1975; M. Jarman, *et al.* (eds.), 1982, *Early European agriculture*, Cambridge. This is the Cambridge tradition; note also many similar studies by various European researchers.
10 For some idea of the diversity see 'Regional patterns of archaeological research, I and II', *World Archaeology* 13, 1, 1981 and 13, 2, 1982; also J. Wiseman, 1982, 'Archaeology in Portugal', *Journal of Field Archaeology*, 9, 401–6.
11 E.g. C. Hawkes, 1954, 'Archaeological theory and method: some suggestions from the Old World', *American Anthropologist* 56, 155–68. This is fallacious

because like is not being compared with like. There are many intractable problems about the use of every technology, just as there are simple statements about social organisation, for example, to be made on the basis of common evidence such as skeletons or houses.

12  For Nilsson and Morgan, see note 2 of this chapter; for the Indo-European debate, see chapter 5.2.

13  E.g. V. Childe, 1929, p. vi. For its background see C. F. Meinander, 1981, 'The concept of culture in European archaeological literature' in G. Daniel (ed.), *Towards a history of archaeology*, pp. 100–11.

14  I. Hodder, 1982.

15  See note 14 above.

16  See papers by S. Shennan, D. Clarke and E. Neustupný, in J. Lanting and J. van der Waals (eds.), *Glockenbecher Symposion*.

17  V. Childe, 1945, 'Directional change in funerary practices during 50,000 years', *Man* 4, 13–19; P. Ucko, 1969, 'Ethnography and archaeological interpretation of funerary remains', *World Archaeol.* 1, 262–80.

18  E.g. L. Binford, 1972, 'Mortuary practices: their study and potential', in L. Binford, *An archaeological perspective*, pp. 208–43, New York; J. Tainter, 1977, 'Modeling change in prehistoric social systems, in L. Binford (ed.), *For theory building in archaeology*, pp. 327–51, New York; R. Chapman, *et al.* (eds.), 1981, *The archaeology of death*, Cambridge; cf. E. Neustupný, 1981.

19  M. Shanks and C. Tilley, 1982.

20  Evolutionary typologies have been proposed by various anthropologists, e.g. E. Service, 1962, *Primitive social organisation: an evolutionary perspective*, New York: M. Fried, 1967, *The evolution of political society*, New York; J. Gledhill and M. Rowland, 1982, 'Materialism and socio-economic process in multi-linear evolution', in C. Renfrew and S. Shennan (eds.), *Ranking, resource and exchange*, pp. 144–9, Cambridge. Note the view however in E. Leach, 1954, *Political systems of Highland Burma*, London, that political development is cyclical and the view of K. Popper, 1957, *The poverty of historicism*, London, that the 'logic of situations' is preferable to any concept of inevitable trends.

21  Formal use of the concept of contradiction is particularly associated with Marxist and neo-Marxist writings (references in C. Tilley, 1982, 'Social formation, social structures and social change' in I. Hodder (ed.), *Symbolic and structural archaeology*, pp. 26–38, Cambridge), but the concept itself has long been used as the work of such diverse historians as Thucydides and Macaulay illustrates.

## 2  Early post-glacial background, 8000–6000 bc

1  E.g. H. Tauber, 1970, 'The Scandinavian varve chronology and C14 dating', in I. U. Olsson (ed.), *Nobel symposium 12: radiocarbon variations and absolute chronology*, pp. 173–96, Stockholm. In absolute chronology the period may well be longer. There is reason to doubt the accuracy of varve chronology in the absence of further investigation of all the factors affecting the deposition of melt water silts and their correlation across space. Radiocarbon dates so far available are on associated peat samples rather than the silts themselves. More direct dating in North America (e.g. M. Stuiver, 1970, 'Long-term C14 variations', in I. U. Olsson (ed.), *Nobel symposium 12*, pp. 197–213) on lake sediments themselves suggests a substantial discrepancy between varve and radiocarbon

chronology. If calibration is necessary at this point, our period could begin much earlier in the ninth millennium.

2 J. Burdukiewicz, 1981, 'Some problems concerning the beginning of the Mesolithic in the central European lowland', in B. Gramsch (ed.), *Mesolithikum in Europe*, pp. 57–62, Berlin; R. G. West, 1969, *Pleistocene geology and biology*, London; J. Iversen, 1973; S. Indrelid, 1975; G. Jalut, 1976, 'La végétation au Pleistocène supérieur et au début de L'Holocène dans les Pyrénées', in H. de Lumley (ed.), pp. 512–16; J. Renault-Miskovsky, 1976, 'La végétation au Pleistocène supérieur et au début de l'Holocène en Provence', in H. de Lumley (ed.), pp. 496–502; S. Bottema, 1979; J. K. Kozlowski, 1979, 'La fin des temps glaciaires dans le bassin du Danube moyen et inférieur', in D. de Sonneville-Bordes (ed.), *La fin des temps glaciaires en Europe*, pp. 821–35, Paris.

3 N. Mörner, and B. Wallin, 1977; W. Dansgaard, *et al.*, 1969, 'One thousand centuries of climatic record from Camp Century on the Greenland ice sheet', *Science* 166, 377–81; N. Shackleton and N. Opdyke, 1973, 'Oxygen isotope and palaeomagnetic stratigraphy of equatorial Pacific core v 28–238: oxygen isotope temperature and ice volumes on a 105 years and 106 years scale', *Quaternary Research* 3, 39–55; M. Girard, 1976, 'La végétation . . . dans les Alpes, le Jura, la Bourgogne et les Vosges', in H. de Lumley (ed.), pp. 517–24; J. Iversen, 1973.

4 J. Bintliff, 1977; H. de Lumley, 1976; T. Van Andel and J. Shackleton, 1982, 'Late Palaeolithic and Mesolithic coastlines of Greece and the Aegean', *J. Field Archaeol.* 9, 445–54.

5 Summarised with references by E. Brinch Petersen, 1973.

6 H. de Lumley, 1976; J. Iversen, 1973; I. Simmons and M. Tooley, 1982; E. Brinch Petersen, 1973; G. Barker, 1981; J. Bintliff, 1977; J. Turner and J. Hodgson, 1979, 'Studies in the vegetational history of the northern Pennines, 1. Variations in the composition of the early Flandrian forests', *Journal of Ecology*, 67, 629–46.

7 E.g. L. Larsson, 1978, p. 154, on the conflicts between the Jessen scheme for Jutland and the Nilsson scheme for Scania.

8 G. Tromnau, 1981, 'Präborealzeitliche Fundplätze im norddeutschen Flachland', in B. Gramsch (ed.), pp. 67–71; E. Mikkelsen, 1978; J. Bay-Petersen, 1978; M. Jochim, 1976; J. G. D. Clark, 1975; L. Binford, 1978; S. Indrelid, 1975; U. Møhl, 1971.

9 A. Bolomey, 1973.

10 J. Boessneck, 1969, 'Osteological differences between sheep (*Ovis aries*. L.) and goats (*Capra hircus* L.)', in D. Brothwell and E. Higgs (eds.), *Science in archaeology*, pp. 331–58, London; J. G. Rozoy, 1978, table 70; M. Paccard, *et al.*, 1971, 'Le camp mésolithique de Gramari à Methamis-84', *Gallia Préhist.* 14, 47–137; M. Walker, 1977, 'The persistence of Upper Palaeolithic tool-kits into the early south-east Spanish Neolithic', in R. V. S. Wright (ed.), *Stone tools as cultural markers*, pp. 354–79, Canberra; G. Barker, 1981; H. P. Uerpmann, 1979; F. Poplin, 1979, 'Origine du mouflon de Corse dans une nouvelle perspective paléontologique: par marronnage', *Ann. Génét. Sél. Anim.* 11, 133–43; D. Geddes, 1980.

11 V. Boroneanţ, 1970; T. Jacobsen, 1973; R. Dennell, 1978; J. Hansen and J. Renfrew, 1978; M. Cârciumaru, 1973.

12 S. Welinder, 1978, 'The concept of ecology in Mesolithic research', in P. Mellars (ed.), pp. 11–25; J. Bay-Petersen, 1978; L. Larsson, 1981.

13 E.g. L. Keeley, 1980, *Experimental determination of stone tool use*, Chicago; C. Keller, 1966, 'The development of edge damage patterns on stone tools', *Man* 1,

501–11; N. Broadbent and K. Knutsson, 1975, 'An experimental analysis of quartz scrapers: results and applications', *Fornvannen* 3/4, 113–28.

14 J. G. Rozoy, 1978, with references to amongst others Rust's excavations in north Germany.

15 L. Larsson, 1981.

16 R. Tringham, 1973; V. Boroneanţ, 1970, 1981; D. Srejović, 1972; D. Srejović and L. Letica, 1978. The chronology of the Danube gorges sites treated in chapters 2 and 4 is difficult. For sites like Icoana there are individual or few C14 dates. Two sites, Vlasac and Lepenski Vir, have longer series, but these are internally conflicting. Vlasac I has dates from *c.* 5800–4800 bc, but Vlasac II and III have a more consistent series from *c.* 5900–5500 bc. Lepenski Vir has a coherent series *c.* 5400–4600 bc. Yugoslav specialists reject the Vlasac I and Lepenski Vir dates but I prefer the reverse, keeping Lepenski Vir and the later part of Vlasac in the later sixth/earlier fifth m.b.c.

17 J. Barta, 1981, 'Das Mesolithikum in nordwestlichen Teil das Karpatenbeckens', in B. Gramsch (ed.), pp. 395–400; T. Jacobsen, 1973; V. Milojčić, *et al.*, 1962.

18 A. Bietti, 1981; A. Broglio, 1971.

19 M. Escalon de Fonton, 1976*a*; 1976*b*; M. C. Cauvin, 1976, 'Les civilisations du Mésolithique en Périgord', in H. de Lumley (ed.), pp. 1433–5.

20 Summarised by E. Brinch Petersen, 1973. See also L. Larsson, 1978; 1981; B. Bille Henriksen, 1976.

21 R. Jacobi, 1973, 'Aspects of the Mesolithic age in Britain', in S. Kozlowski (ed.), pp. 237–66; P. Mellars, 1974, 'The Palaeolithic and Mesolithic', in C. Renfrew (ed.), *British prehistory: a new outline*, pp. 41–99, London; J. G. D. Clark, 1954.

22 R. Lee and I. DeVore, 1968; J. Yellen, 1977.

23 M. Jochim, 1976.

24 E. Mikkelsen, 1978; P. Rowley-Conwy, 1981.

25 P. Mellars, 1976*a*; J. Bay-Petersen, 1978; D. L. Clarke, 1976; L. Binford, 1978; B. Bender, 1978.

26 E.g. M. Jarman 1972, 'European deer economies and the advent of the Neolithic', in E. Higgs (ed.), pp. 125–47, *contra* L. Binford, 1978, pp. 480–2.

27 T. Jacobsen, 1969; 1973; 1976; 1981; S. Payne, 1975; J. Hansen and J. Renfrew, 1978.

28 J. Harlan, 1967, 'A wild wheat harvest in Turkey', *Archaeology* 20, 197–201.

29 A. Moore, 1975, 'The excavation of Tell Abu Hureyra in Syria: preliminary report', *PPS* 41, 50–77; J. Cauvin, 1978, *Les premiers villages de Syrie–Palestine d'IXème au VIIème millénaire avant J. C.*, Lyon.

30 A. Bietti, 1981; M. Piperao, 1981, 'La nécropole Mésolithique de la Grotte de l'Uzzo (Trapani, Sicile)', *X Congreso UISPP, Seccion V, Epipaleolitico y Mesolitico*, pp. 18–19.

31 V. Boroneanţ, 1970; 1973; 1981; A. Bolomey, 1973, 'An outline of the late Epipalaeolithic economy at the "Iron Gates": the evidence on bones', *Dacia* 17, 41–52; M. Cârciumaru, 1973.

32 R. Tringham, 1973; P. Dolukhanov, 1979; E. Comşa, 1978, 'Quelques données sur le processus de néolithisation dans le territoire de la Roumanie', *Acta Archaeol. Carpathica* 18, 69–74; A. Paunescu, 1979, 'Tardenoazianul din sud-estul României şi unele consideraţii asupra periodei cuprinse între sfrsitul paleoliticului şi inceputurile neoliticului in aceastra regiune', *Stud. Cerc. Ist. Veche. Arch.* 4, 507–26.

33 A. Bietti, 1981, and G. Barker, 1981, with individual site references; G. Barker,

1976, 'Morphological change and Neolithic economies: an example from central Italy', *Journal of Archaeological Science*, 3, 71–82; A. Broglio, 1971; L. Cardini, 1946; L. Cardini, 1970, 'Praia a Mare: relazione degli scavi 1957 bis 1970'. *Bull. Paletnologia Ital.* 79, 31–59.

34 M. Escalon de Fonton, 1970, 'Récherches sur la préhistoire dans le midi de la France', *Cahiers Ligures* 19, 97–115. For northern Spain see papers in G. Bailey (ed.), 1983, *Hunter-gatherer economy in prehistory*, Cambridge.

35 Site references in E. Brinch Petersen, 1973.

36 J. G. D. Clark, 1954; 1972; M. Pitts, 1979, 'Hides and antlers: a new look at the gatherer-hunter site at Star Carr . . .' *World Archaeol.* 11, 32–42; J. Andersen, *et al*, 1981, 'The deer hunters: Star Carr reconsidered', *World Archaeol.*, 13, 31–46; R. Jacobi, 1978, 'Northern England in the eighth millennium bc', in P. Mellars (ed.), pp. 295–332. Note also that occupation at Duvensee site VIII in Holstein now extends similarly far back: K. Bokelmann, *et al*, 1981, 'Duvensee, Wohnplatz 8: neue Aspekte zur Sammelwirtschaft im frühen Mesolithikum', *Offa*, 38, 21–40.

37 N. Noe-Nygaard, 1975, 'Two shoulder blades with healed lesions from Star Carr', *PPS* 41, 10–16; J. Hallam, *et al.*, 1973 'A late glacial elk with associated barbed points from High Furlong, Lancashire', *PPS* 39, 100–28; N. Hartz and H. Winge, 1906, 'Om Uroxen fra Vig', *Aarbøger* 21, 225–36.

38 E. Brinch Petersen, 1973, for site references; E. Brinch Petersen, 1972, 'Svaerdborg II: a maglemose hut from Svaerdborg, Zealand, Denmark', *Acta Archaeologica*, 42, 43–77; B. Bille Henriksen, 1976; K. Bokelmann, 1981, 'Eine neue Borealzeitliche Fundstelle in Schleswig-Holstein', *Köln. Jahrb.* 15, 181–8; G. Schwantes, 1939, *Die Vorgeschichte Schleswig-Holsteins*, Neumünster; E. Schuldt, 1961, *Hohen Viecheln: ein mittelsteinzeitlicher Wohnplatz in Mecklenburg*, Berlin; H. P. Blankholm, 1981, 'Aspects of the Maglemose settlements in Denmark', in B. Gramsch (ed.), pp. 401–4; C. Becker, 1945, 'En 8000-aarig Stenalderboplads i Holmegaards Mose: foreløbelig Meddelelse', *Fra Nationalmus. Arbejdsm.* 61–72; H. Broholm, 1931.

39 J. Bay-Petersen, 1978; A. Smith, 1970; H. Broholm, 1931.

40 U. Møhl, 1971.

41 E. Mikkelsen, 1978; J. G. D. Clark, 1975; I. Zagorska, 1981, 'Das Frühmesolithikum in Lettland', in B. Gramsch (ed.), pp. 73–82; K. Jaanits, 1981, 'Die mesolithischen Siedlungsplätze mit Feuersteininventar in Estland', in B. Gramsch (ed.), pp. 389–99; G. Burov, 1973, 'Die mesolithischen Kulturen im äussersten europäischen Nordosten', in S. Kozlowski (ed.), pp. 129–49.

42 H. M. Wobst, 1974; B. Bender, 1978; J. G. Rozoy, 1978.

43 U. Møhl, 1980, 'Elsdyrskeletterne fra Skottemarke og Favrbo', *Aarbøger* 1978, 5–32; J. G. D. Clark, 1975; J. G. Rozoy, 1978; V. Boroneanţ, 1973; M. Walker, 1971, 'Spanish Levantine art', *Man* 6, 553–89; also papers by C. Gamble and M. Jochim in G. Bailey (ed.), 1983, *Hunter-gatherer economy in prehistory*, Cambridge.

44 J. G. D. Clark, 1975; L. Larsson, 1978; M. Escalon de Fonton, 1976a; 1976b; A. Bietti, 1981.

45 F. Barth, 1969; I. Hodder, 1982.

46 G. Odell, 1978, 'Préliminaires d'une analyse fonctionelle des pointes microlithiques de Bergumermeer (Pays Bas), *BSPF* 75, 37–49. S. Kozlowski, 1973; J. G. Rozoy, 1978. See also P. Wiessner, 1983, 'Style and social information in Kalahari San projectile points', *American Antiquity*, 48, 253–276.

47 R. Schild, 1976; C. Renfrew, 1977.

48  J. G. Rozoy, 1978, tables 72–3 and p. 1127 for Ofnet; G. Barker, 1981; C. Corrain, *et al.*, 1976, 'La sepoltura epipaleolitico di Vatte di Zambano (Trento)', *Preist. Alpina* 12, 175–212; R. Grifoni and A. Radmilli, 1964, 'La Grotta Maritza e il Fucino prima dell' età Romana', *Riv. Sci. Preist.* 19, 25–59; L. Cardini, 1946; T. Jacobsen, 1973; V. Boroneanț, 1970; R. Schmidt, 1912, *Die diluviale Vorzeit Deutschlands*.

49  T. Ingold, 1980.

50  J. Richter, 1982, 'Adult and juvenile aurochs, *Bos primigenius* Boj, from the Maglemosian site of Ulkestrup Lyng Øst, Denmark', *J. Archaeol. Sci.* 9, 247–60.

## 3  The establishment of agricultural communities

1  R. Tringham, 1971, p. 31; M. Gimbutas, 1976; B. Frenzel, 1966; 1978; K. Kosse, 1979; J. Bintliff, 1977; P. Halstead, 1981*a*; S. Bottema, 1979; J. Greig and J. Turner, 1974, 'Some pollen diagrams from Greece and their archaeological significance', *J. Archaeol. Sci.* 1, 177–94.

2  J. Evans and C. Renfrew, 1968; A. Bolomey, 1978, 'Why no Early Neolithic in Dobrogea?', *Dacia* 22, 5–8.

3  J. Bintliff, 1976; 1977; R. Dennel and D. Webley, 1975; K. Kosse, 1979.

4  V. Dumitrescu, *et al.*, 1982; S. Weinberg, 1965; C. Tsountas, 1908, *Ai Proistorikai Akropoleis Dhiminiou kai Sesklou*, Athens; M. Garašanin, 1982; M. Gimbutas, 1976; R. Tringham, *et al.*, 1980; B. Brukner, 1971; A. Clason, 1979; W. Van Zeist, 1975; S. Bottema and B. Ottaway, 1982; M. Gimbutas, 1974*a*.

5  Only Azmak and Yasatepe in central southern Bulgaria have been fully excavated: G. Georgiev, 1965; P. Detev, 1960, 'Razkopi na selishnata mogila Yasatepe v Plovdiv prez 1959' *God. Narod. arch. mus. Plov.* 4, 5–55.

6  This requires systematic sampling and sieving: see E. Higgs, 1972. Some surprising opportunities have been presented in the past, such as the 20 cm layer of carbonised plant material at the base of Yasatepe: G. Georgiev, 1961, p. 52.

7  Azmak and Yasatepe for example remain known only through preliminary or partial reports.

8  G. Georgiev, 1961; M. Vasić; 1932.

9  V. Milojčić, *et al.*, 1962.

10  Reported in P. Halstead, 1977; J. Chapman, 1981; A. Sherratt, 1982*a*.

11  E.g. S. Weinberg, 1965; D. Theocharis, 1973; C. Ridley and K. Wardle, 1979.

12  As an example one can cite this sentence: 'By applying the vertical stratigraphy of Thessaly it can be concluded on the basis of the prevalence of the monochrome pottery that the Starcevo I phase had lasted from the proto-Sesklo to the pre-Sesklo period', in B. Brukner, *et al.*, 1974, p. 430.

13  G. Georgiev, 1961, p. 49; M. Gimbutas, 1976, fig. 9a.

14  H. Waterbolk, 1971; D. Theocharis, 1973; C. Renfrew, 1971; T. Jacobsen, 1976; M. Gimbutas, 1974; C. Ridley and K. Wardle, 1979; R. Dennell, 1978 and references; A. Benac, 1973; R. Tringham, *et al.*, 1980; N. Kalicz and J. Makkay, 1977.

15  T. Jacobsen, 1969; 1973; 1976.

16  J. D. Evans, 1971; R. Protsch and R. Berger, 1973; D. Theocharis, 1973.

17  V. Milojčić, *et al.*, 1962; D. Theocharis, 1973; M. Gimbutas, 1974.

18  V. Milojčić, *et al.*, 1962; D. Theocharis, 1973; S. Weinberg, 1965.

19  M. Gimbutas, 1974; *Radiocarbon*, 22, 1980.

20  Apart from the standard references, see J. Nandris, 1970; R. Rodden, 1962; 1965; C. Ridley and K. Wardle, 1979.

21 J. Milojčić-von Zumbusch and V. Milojčić, 1971.

22 V. Milojčić, *et al.*, 1976.

23 D. Theocharis, 1973; J. Nandris, 1970; M. Gimbutas, 1974, fig. 34.

24 M. Gimbutas, 1976.

25 N. Vlassa, 1972; B. Brukner, *et al.*, 1974; M. Garašanin, 1982, p. 94.

26 G. Georgiev, 1961; R. Tringham, 1971.

27 V. Fewkes, *et al.*, 1933; D. Garašanin, 1954; N. Kalicz, 1970; V. Dumitrescu, *et al.*, 1982; M. Garašanin, 1982; G. Georgiev, 1981; B. Nikolov, 1974.

28 V. Milojčić, 1949, *Chronologie der jüngeren Steinzeit Mittel- und Südosteuropas*, Berlin.

29 D. Garašanin, 1954; O. Trogmayer, 1968, 'A Körös csoport barbotin kerámiájáró', *Archaeologiai Ertesitö* 95, 6–12; J. Makkay, 1969 'Zur Geschichte der Erforschung der Körös-Starčevo Kultur und einigen ihrer wichtigsten Probleme', *Acta Arch. Hung.* 21, 13–31.

30 R. Tringham, 1968; 1971; N. Vlassa, 1972; J. Nandris, 1975, 'A reconsideration of the south-eastern sources of archaeological obsidian', *University of London Bulletin, Institute of Archeology* 12, 71–94; M. Gimbutas, 1976.

31 J. Nandris, 1970, figs. 1 and 2.

32 C. Renfrew, 1972; P. Halstead, 1981*b*; D. Theocharis, 1973.

33 G. Georgiev, 1961; 1965.

34 S. Milisauskas, 1978, *European prehistory*, London; V. Mikov, 1959, 'The prehistoric mound at Karanovo', *Archaeology* 12, 88–97.

35 M. Vasić, 1932; 1936; J. Chapman, 1981.

36 K. Kosse, 1979; I. Ecsedy, 1972, 'Neolithische Siedlung in Dévanványa–Katonaföldek', *Mitteil. Arch. Inst. Ung. Akad. Wiss.* 3, 59–63, 153–4.

37 V. Milojčić, *et al.*, 1962; R. Dennell, 1978; S. Bökönyi, 1974; P. Halstead, 1981*b*; G. Barker, 1975.

38 P. Halstead, 1977; R. Dennell and D. Webley, 1975; G. Barker, 1975.

39 D. Theocharis, 1973; V. Milojčić, 1960; G. Georgiev, 1961; N. Kalicz, 1970; R. Tringham, 1971; M. Gimbutas, 1976; C. Ridley and K. Wardle, 1979; O. Trogmayer, 1966, 'Ein neolithisches Hausmodellfragment von Röszke', *Acta Ant. et Arch.* 10, 11–26.

40 P. Halstead, 1981*a*, using the Naroll figure of 10 m² per person; M. Gimbutas, 1976; R. Dennell, 1978. Critical studies include J. Yellen, 1977; R. Fletcher, 1981, 'People and space: a case study in material behaviour', in I. Hodder *et al.* (eds.), *Pattern of the past*, pp. 97–128, Cambridge; P. Wiessner, 1974, 'A functional estimation of population from floor area', *Amer. Antiq.* 39, 343–50; S. Cook and R. Heizer, 1968, 'Relationships among houses, settlement areas and population in aboriginal California', in K. Chang (ed.), *Settlement archaeology*, pp. 79–116, Palo Alto.

41 R. Dennell, 1978; R. Tringham, 1971; J. Hansen and J. Renfrew, 1978; S. Payne, 1975; M. Gimbutas, 1976; S. Bökönyi, 1974; K. Kosse, 1979; S. Payne, 1972, 'On the interpretation of bone samples from archaeological sites', in E. Higgs (ed.), pp. 65–81; J. Nandris, 1978, 'Some features of Neolithic climax societies', *Studia Praehist.*, 1/2, 198–211.

42 C. Rădulesco and P. Samson, 1962, 'Sur un centre de domestication du mouton dans la grotte "La Adam" en Dobrugea', *Zeitschr. Tierzücht. Züchtungsbiol* 76, 282–320; V. Dumitrescu, *et al.*, 1982.

43 R. Protsch and R. Berger, 1973.

44 E. Higgs and M. Jarman, 1972.

45  E.g. J. Bintliff, 1976; 1977; R. Dennell and D. Webley, 1975; K. Kosse, 1979; G. Barker, 1975.

46  R. Dennell, 1978; and higher estimates in P. Halstead, 1981*b*.

47  Basic studies are R. Dennell, 1978, and G. Hillman, 1981.

48  J. Harlan, 1972, 'Crops that extend the range of agricultural settlement', in P. Ucko, *et al.*, (eds.) *Man, settlement and urbanism*, pp. 239–43, London.

49  J. Lewthwaite, 1981, 'Plains tails from the hills: transhumance in Mediterranean archaeology', in A. Sheridan and G. Bailey (eds.), pp. 57–66.

50  See note 46 above.

51  N. Kalicz, 1970; G. Georgiev, 1961.

52  A. Sherratt, 1981.

53  R. Dennell, 1978; K. Kosse, 1979.

54  E. Ardener, 1974, 'Social anthropology and population', in H. Parry (ed.), *Population and its problems: a plain man's guide*, pp. 25–50, Oxford.

55  E.g. G. Georgiev, 1961, p. 58; R. Dennell and D. Webley, 1975.

56  R. Tringham, 1971, p. 82.

57  N. Shackleton and C. Renfrew, 1970; C. Ridley and K. Wardle, 1979, p. 209.

58  J. Nandris, 1970, fig. 2; M. Gimbutas, 1974*b*; B. Bartel, 1981, 'Cultural associations and mechanisms of change in anthropomorphic figurines during the Neolithic in the eastern Mediterranean basin', *World Archaeol.*, 13, 73–86; P. Ucko, 1968, *Anthropomorphic figurines of predynastic Egypt and Neolithic Crete . . .*, London. I. Hodder, 1982; I. Hodder, 1979, 'Economic and social stress and material culture patterning', *Amer. Antiq.*, 44, 446–54; cf. F. Barth, 1969.

59  Cf. R. Dennell, 1983, *European economic prehistory*, London.

60  C. Renfrew, 1971; C. Ridley and K. Wardle, 1979; D. Theocharis, 1973.

61  M. Gimbutas, 1974*a*; V. Milojčić, 1959.

62  G. Georgiev, 1961; J. Chapman, 1981; E. Comsa, 1971.

63  Consider the sample from Divostin, Yugoslavia, split into three. Two parts gave similar dates *c.* 4000 bc (Bln-898, Z-336), but the third was six to seven centuries younger (BM-574); *Radiocarbon* 19, 1977. There is no significant inter-laboratory deviation in the Sitagroi series using Bln and BM dates.

64  J. Chapman, 1981; M. Vasić, 1936; V. Milojčić, 1949, *Chronologie der jüngeren Steinzeit Mittel- und Südosteuropas*, Berlin; M. Garašanin, 1982 and earlier references; M. Grbić, 1929, *Pločnik, äneolithische Siedlung*, Belgrade.

65  V. Dumitrescu, 1980; E. Comsa, 1971.

66  V. Childe, 1929 and references in R. Tringham, 1971, p. 1414; cf. V. Dumitrescu, 1980, p. 108 and M. Gimbutas, 1976, p. 65. Local antecedents are stressed by Tringham and Chapman.

67  N. Vlassa, 1963; M. Gimbutas, 1976; N. Makkay, 1976, 'Some stratigraphical and chronological problems of the Tărtăria tablets', *Mitt. Arch. Inst. Ung. Acad. Wiss.* 5, 13–31, and other references in R. Tringham, 1971, p. 142; V. Milojčić, 1965, 'Die Tontafeln von Tărtăria und die absolute Chronologie des mitteleuropäischen Neolithikums', *Germania* 43, 261–8; E. Neustupný, 1968; B. Nikolov, 1974. The whole assemblage has recently been suggested as the burial of a shaman, with the finds symbolising control over ritual and aracane knowledge: J. Chapman, 1983, 'Meaning and illusion in the study of burial in Balkan prehistory', in A. Poulter (ed.), *Ancient Bulgaria*, pp. 1–42, Nottingham.

68  H. Todorova, 1976; 1978.

69  C. Renfrew, 1969.

70  See references quoted earlier and J. Deshayes, 1962, 'Dikili-Tach', *Bull. Corr. Hell.* 86, 912–33; D. Berciu, 1961, 1966.

71 E.g. M. Nica and T. Niţa, 1979, 'Les établissements néolithiques de Leu et Padea de la zone d'interférence des cultures Dudeşti et Vinča', *Dacia* 23, 31–64.

72 B. Frenzel, 1966; 1978; C. Bakels, 1978; P. Dolukhanov, 1979.

73 E.g. J. G. Rozoy, 1978; S. Kozlowski, 1973; B. Gramsch, 1981; L. Vértes, 1965, 'Zur Technologie grabgerätigen Silexfunde in Nordungarn', *Folia Archaeologia*, 17, 9–36.

74 M. Sakellaridis, 1979.

75 M. Jochim, 1976.

76 S. Arora, 1976, 'Die mittlere Steinzeit im westlichen Deutschland und in den Nachbargebieten', *Rhein. Ausgrab.* 17, 1–66; M. Wobst, 1974; T. D. Price, 1981, 'Regional approaches to human adaptation in the Mesolithic of the north European plain', in B. Gramsch (ed.), pp. 217–34.

77 The German label is *Linienbandkeramik* or *Linearbandkeramik*, sometimes shortened to *Bandkeramik*, and commonly abbreviated as LBK or BK. Linear pottery is thus not a full translation but sounds better in English; the abbreviation LBK will be used also.

78 Some basic sources: B. Soudský, 1954, 'K methodice trideni volutové keramiky', *Pam. Arch.* 45, 75–105; B. Soudský, 1962; 1966; I. Pavlů, 1972, 'Das linear-keramische Ornament in der Entwicklung der böhmischen Linearkeramik', in F. Jenö and M. János (eds.), *Die Aktuelle Fragen der Bandkeramik*, pp. 131–42, Székesfehérvár; J. Lichardus, 1972; J. Pavúk and S. Šiška, 1980, 'Neolit a eneolit', *Slov. Arch.* 18, 137–58; R. Tringham, 1971; P. Modderman, 1970; M. Dohrn-Ihmig, 1979, 'Bandkeramik an Mittel- und Niederrhein', *Rhein. Ausgrab.* 19, 191–362; V. Kulczycka-Leciejewiczowa, 1970, 'The Linear and Stroked pottery cultures', in T. Wislanski (ed.), pp. 14–75; N. Kalicz and J. Makkay, 1977; G. Bailloud, 1974.

79 H. Quitta, 1960, 'Zur Frage der ältesten Bandkeramik in Mitteleuropa', *Praehist. Zeitschr.* 38, 1–38; J. Pavúk, 1973, 'Zur Chronologie und zur kulterellen Beziehung der alteren Linearkeramik', *VIIIe Congres. UISPP*, 2, 273–81.

80 J. P. Farruggia, *et al.*, 1973; R. Kuper *et al.*, 1977.

81 P. Van der Velde, 1979; S. Milisauskas, 1982, 'Stylistic change in Linear pottery culture ceramics and the distribution of obsidian artefacts at Olszanica', in J. Pavúk (ed.), pp. 173–92.

82 E.g. R. Tringham, 1968; R. Newell, in P. Modderman, 1970; L. Fiedler, 1979, 'Formen und Techniken neolithischen Steingeräte aus dem Rheinland', *Rhein. Ausgrab.*, 19, 53–190.

83 Earlier references and J. Kruk, 1973; S. Milisauskas, 1976; J. Pavúk, 1982.

84 B. Sielmann, 1972, 'Die frühneolithische Besiedlung Mitteleuropas', in *Die Anfänge des Neolithikums*, Va, pp. 1–65, Köln; J. Rulf, 1981, 'Poznamky k zemedelstvi stredoevropskeho neolitu a eneolitu', *Arch. Rozhl*, 33, 123–32; N. Starling, pers. comm.; note also some areas of intensive LBK settlement not on loess such as the Kujavia area of central Poland: P. Bogucki, 1979, 'Tactical and strategic settlements in the Early Neolithic of Lowland Poland', *Journal of Anthropological Research* 35, 238–46.

85 B. Soudský, 1969, 'Étude de la maison néolithique', *Slov. Arch.* 17, 5–96; W. Startin, 1978, 'Linear pottery culture houses: reconstruction and manpower', *PPS* 44, 143–59; P. Modderman, 1970.

86 C. Bakels, 1978, p. 75; S. Milisauskas, 1976; S. Milisauskas, 1972, 'An analysis of Linear culture longhouses at Olszanica BI, Poland', *World Archaeol.* 4, 57–74.

87 E.g. B. Soudský and I. Pavlů, 1972, 'The Linear pottery culture settlement patterns of central Europe', in P. Ucko (ed.), *Man, settlement and urbanism*,

pp. 317–28, London; C. Bakels, 1978, p. 82; I. Pavlů, 1982, 'Die Entwicklung des Siedlungsareals Bylany 1', in J. Pavúk (ed.), pp. 193–206.

88  E.g. R. Kuper, *et al.*, 1974, 'Untersuchungen zur neolithischen Besiedlung der Aldenhovener Platte, iv', *Bonn. Jahrb.* 174, 424–508; W. Schwellnus, 1982, 'Archäologische Untersuchungen im Rheinischen Braunkohlengebiet, 1977–1981', *Archäologie in den Rheinischen Lössboden*, pp. 1–31, Köln.

89  P. Modderman, *et al.*, 1959, 'Die bandkeramische Siedlung von Sittard, *'Palaeohist.*, pp. 6–7; J. Eckert, *et al.*, 1972 'Untersuchungen zur neolithischen Besiedlung der Aldenhovener Platte, ii', *Bonn. Jahrb.* 172, 344–94; W. Buttler and G. Haberey, 1936.

90  E.g. C. Bakels, 1978, figs. 16 and 17; cf. J. Kruk, 1973, map 4, and figs. 4–8; K. Wasylikowa, 1982, 'Pollen diagram from the vicinity of the Linear pottery culture site in Cracow (preliminary report)', in J. Pavúk (ed.), pp. 285–90.

91  C. Bakels, 1978; P. Willerding, 1980; K. H. Knörzer, 1967, 'Subfossile Pflanzenreste von bandkeramischen Fundstellen im Rheinland', *Archaeo-Physika* 2, 3f.; K. Kosse, 1979; A. Sherratt, 1980, 'Water, soil and seasonality in early cereal cultivation', *World Archaeol.* 11, 313–30.

92  E.g. J. Kruk, 1973; P. Modderman, 1976; P. Willerding, 1980.

93  K. Schietzel, 1965, *Müddersheim: eine Ansiedlung der jüngeren Bandkeramik im Rheinland*, Köln (cf. A. Clason in P. Modderman, 1977); H. Müller, 1964, *Die Haustiere der mitteldeutschen Bandkeramiker*, Berlin. The sites with high sheep figures are Magdeburg Prester and Barleben on the Magdeburger Börde but the samples are small. Cattle thought to be castrated on horn core evidence, but the sample is again very small. N. Starling, pers. comm.

94  D. Mania, 1973, 'Eiszeitliche Landschaftsentwicklung im Kartenbild, dargestellt am Bespiel des mittleren Elbe–Saale-Gebietes', *Jahrschr. mitteld. Vorg.* 57, 17–47.

95  F. Simmoons, 1968, *A ceremonial ox of India: the mithan in nature, culture and history*, Madison. A free-ranging bovid, living in forest, and having little regular contact with people except at salt licks. Individually owned and highly valued for consumption at feasts, ceremonies, etc.

96  J. Pavúk, 1972, 'Neolithisches Gräberfeld in Nitra', *Slov. Arch.* 20, 5–105; P. Van der Velde, 1979; H. Behrens, 1973; I. Richter, 1969, 'Die bandkeramischen Gräber von Flomborn, Kreis Alzey, und vom Alderberg bei Worms', *Mainz. Zeitschr.* 63/64, 158–79; G. Gallay and R. Schweitzer, 1971, 'Das bandkeramische Gräberfeld von Rixheim', *Arch. Korr.* 1, 15–22; M. Dohrn-Ihmig, 1983, 'Das bandkeramische Gräberfeld von Aldenhoven-Niedermerz, Kreis Duren', *Archaologie in den Rheinischen Lössboden (Rheinische Ausgrabungen 24)*, 47–189.

97  Y. Taborin, 1974, 'La parure en coquillage de l'Épipaleolithique au Bronze ancien en France', *Gallia Préhist.* 17, 101–79; G. Gallay, 1981, 'Ein verschollener Grabfund der Bandkeramik von Dijon', *Antike Welt* 12, 36–43; N. Shackleton and C. Renfrew, 1970.

98  W. Arps in C. Bakels, 1978.

99  R. Schild, 1976; R. Newell in P. Modderman, 1970.

100  D. Cahen, *et al.*, 1981, 'Éléments non-rubanés du Néolithique ancien entre les vallées du Rhin inférieur et de la Seine', *Helinium* 21, 136–75, 209–26.

101  J. Lichardus, 1972; S. Marinescu-Bîlcu, 1981; N. Kalicz, and J. Makkay, 1977.

102  K. Kosse, 1979; A. Sherratt, 1982; L. Vértes, 1965, 'The depot of silex blades from Boldogkövralja', *Act. Arch. Hung.* 17, 129–36.

103  N. Kalicz, 1970; N. Kalicz and J. Makkay, 1977.

104  E.g. R. Tringham, 1968, and J. Lichardus, 1972, 'Zur Entstehung der Linearband-

keramik', *Germania* 50, 1–15; *contra* N. Kalicz and J. Makkay, 1977; J. Pavúk, 1980, 'Ältere Linearkeramik in der Slowakei', *Slov. Arch.* 28, 5–90; P. Modderman, 1976; H. Waterbolk, 1968, 'Food production in prehistoric Europe', *Science* 162, 1093–102.

105 H. de Lumley, 1976; P. Phillips, 1975; A. Freises, *et al.*, 1976.

106 J. S. P. Bradford, 1957, *Ancient landscapes*, London; Tinè, S. (ed.), 1975, *Atti del colloquio internationale di preistoria e protoistoria della Daunia*, Firenze; S. Tinè, 1983; A. Ammerman and S. Bonardi, 1981, 'Recent developments in the study of Neolithic settlement in Calabria', in G. Barker and R. Hodges (eds.), *Archaeology and Italian society*, pp. 335–42, Oxford; S. Cassano and A. Manfredini (eds.), 1983, *Studi sul neolitico del Tavoliere della Puglia*, Oxford.

107 E.g. J. Guilaine (ed.), 1976; G. Delibrias, *et al.*, 1982 'Sommaire des datations C14 concernant la préhistoire en France, II', *Bull. Soc. Préhist. Franc.*, 79, 175–92.

108 Some basic sources: J. Guilaine, 1976 (ed.), 1976; 1979; 1980; P. Phillips, 1975; B. Bagolini and P. Biagi, 1977; P. Biagi, 1980, 'Some aspects of the prehistory of northern Italy from the final Palaeolithic to the Middle Neolithic, *PPS* 46, 9–18; G. Barker, 1981.

109 J. Guilaine, 1976; J. Coudrot, 1976, 'Repartition de la céramique cardiale dans le bassin occidental de la Méditerranée', *Cahiers Arch. Nord-Est* 34, 1–108.

110 Earlier references and J. Guilaine, *et al.*, 1981, 'Datations C14 pour le Néolithique du Tavoliere (Italie)', *Bull. Soc. Préhist. Franc.* 78, 154–60. The C14 chronology is still underdeveloped, and it remains unclear how far we may generalise from individual sites. The appearance of painted pottery might belong earlier.

111 G. Bailloud, 1969, 'Fouille d'un habitat néolithique ... à Basi ...', *Bull. Soc. Préhist. Franc.* 66, 367–84; F. Lanfranchi, 1972, 'L'abri sous roche no. l de la station de Curacchiaghiu', *Bull. Soc. Préhist. Franc.* 69 crsm 3, 70–1; Note that the Curacchiaghiu pottery may belong to the later fifth millennium; the stratigraphy is confused: Lewthwaite, pers. comm., and J. Guilaine, 1980, 'Problèmes actuels de la néolithisation et du Néolithique ancien en Méditerranée occidentale, in J. Best and N. de Vries (eds.), *Interaction and acculturation in the Mediterranean*, vol. I, 3–22, Amsterdam.

112 M. Pellicer and P. Acosta, 1982, 'El neolitico antiguo en Andalucia occidental', in *Lé Néolithique ancien Mediterranéen*, pp. 49–60, Montpellier.

113 J. Guilaine, 1970; J. Guilaine, *et al.*, 1979.

114 J. Guilaine, 1974, *La Balma de Montbolo et le néolithique de l'occident méditerranéen*, Toulouse.

115 This makes a return, on firmer evidence, to older schemes of development. Contrast R. Whitehouse, 1969, 'The Neolithic pottery sequence in southern Italy', *PPS* 35, 267–310.

116 M. Pellicer, 1964; A. Vicent and A. Muñoz, 1973; J. Morais-Arnaud, 1982, 'Le Néolithique ancien et le processus de Néolithisation au Portugal', in *Le Néolithique ancien Méditerranéen*', pp. 29–48, Montpellier.

117 S. Tinè, 1983; R. Whitehouse, 1981, 'Prehistoric settlement patterns in south east Italy', in G. Barker and R. Hodges (eds.), *Archaeology and Italian society*, pp. 157–65, Oxford; M. Cipollini Sampo, 1980, 'Le comunità neolitiche delle valli dell'Ofanto: proposta di lettura di un analisi territoriale', in E. Lattanzi (ed.), *Attività archeologica in Basilicata 1964–1977*, pp. 283–306, Matera; M. Jarman and D. Webley, 1975, 'Settlement and land use in Capitanata, Italy', in E. Higgs (ed.) pp. 177–221; S. M. Cassano and A. Manfredini, (eds.), 1983, *Studi sul neolitico del Tavoliere della Puglia*, Oxford.

118 G. Barker, 1981; G. Cremonesi, 1966, 'Il villaggio Leopardi presso Penne in

Abruzzo', *Bull. Pal. Ital.* 75, 27–49; D. Evett and J. Renfrew, 1971, 'L'agricultura neolitica italiana: una nota sui cereali', *Riv. Sci. Preist.* 26, 403–09.

119 Earlier references and: L. Barfield, 1971, *Northern Italy*, London; B. Bagolini and P. Biagi, 1975, 'Il Neolitico del Vhò di Pradena', *Preist. Alp.*, 11, 77–121; B. Bagolini, *et al.*, 1977, 'Vhò, Campo Ceresole: scavi 1977', *Preist. Alp.* 13, 67–98; G. Barker, 1977, 'Further information on the early neolithic economy of Vhò', *Preist. Alp.*, 13, 99–105.

120 J. Courtin, 1976 'Les civilisations néolithiques en Provence', in J. Guilaine, 1976 (ed.), pp. 255–66; J. Courtin, 1975, 'Le Mésolithique de la Baume de Fontbrégoua à Salernes (Var) 7', *Cahiers Lig.* 24, 109–17; P. Phillips, 1975.

121 J. Guilaine, 1970; 1976 (ed.); J. Guilaine, *et al.*, 1979; D. Geddes, 1980; A. Freises, *et al.*, 1976.

122 M. Hopf, 1964, 'Triticum monococcum L y Triticum dicoccum Schübl, en el neolitico antiguo español', *Archiv. Prehist Levant.* 11, 53–73; B. Marti Oliver, *et al.*, 1980, *Cova de l'Or* II, Valencia; A. Vicent and A. Muñoz, 1973.

123 J. Lewthwaite, 1981.

124 L. Bernabo Brea, 1957, *Sicily before the Greeks*, London.

125 L. Barfield, 1981, 'Patterns of north Italian trade, 5000–2000 bc', in G. Barker and R. Hodges (eds.), *Archaeology and Italian society*, pp. 27–51, Oxford; B. Hallam *et al.*, 1976, 'Obsidian in the west Mediterranean: characterisation by neutron activation analysis and optical emission spectroscopy', *PPS*, 42, 85–110; A. Ammerman, 1979, 'A study of obsidian exchange networks in Calabria', *World Archaeol.* 11, 95–110.

126 F. Lanfranchi and M. Weiss, 1972, 'Le Néolithique ancien de l'abri d'Araguina-Sennola (Bonifacio, Corse)', *Bull. Soc. Préhist. Franc.* 69, 376–88.

## 4  Indigenous change: the periphery from 6000 to after 4000 bc

1 D. Srejović, 1972 and see earlier references for the area in chapter 2.

2 Earlier references in chapter 2 and B. Jovanović, 1969, 'Chronological frames of the Iron Gate group of the Early Neolithic period', *Archaeol. Jugos.* 10, 23–38.

3 P. Dolukhanov, 1979; V. Danilenko, 1969, *Neolit Ukrainy*, Kiev; V. Markevich, 1974, *Bugo-Dnestrovskaya kultura na territarii Moldavii*, Kishinev.

4 V. Danilenko, 1969; P. Dolukhanov, 1979, table 8.

5 J. Roche, 1972, 'Les amas coquilliers (concheiros) mésolithiques de Muge (Portugal)', in J. Luning (ed.), *Die Anfänge des Neolithikums*, vol. 7, pp. 72–107, Köln; G. Bailey, 1978, 'Shell middens as indicators of postglacial economies: a territorial perspective', in P. Mellars (ed.), pp. 37–63.

6 Terminology too is varied. The Atlantic phase begins by the late seventh millennium bc in the scheme followed by E. Brinch Petersen, 1973 but in the earlier sixth in those followed by J. G. D. Clark, 1975. Other general references in chapter 2 notes.

7 J. Troels-Smith, 1967, 'The Ertebølle culture and its background', *Palaeohistoria* 12, 505–28; E. Brinch-Petersen, 1973; H. Tauber, 1972, 'Radiocarbon chronology of the Danish Mesolithic and Neolithic', *Antiquity* 46, 106–10.

8 S. Jørgensen, 1956, 'Kongemosen: endnu en Aamose-boplads fra den aeldre Stenalder', *Kuml*, 23–40; H. Kapel, 1969, 'En boplads fra tidlig- atlantisk tid ved Villingebaek', *Nationalmus. Arbejd.*, 85–94; T. Mathiassen, 1946; S. Andersen, 1970, 'Brovst: en kystboplads fra aeldre Stenalder', *Kuml* 1969, 67–90; C. Vedbaek, 1938, 'New finds of ornamented bone and antler artefacts in Denmark', *Acta Arch.* 9, 205–23.

9 T. Mathiassen, 1943, *Stenalderbopladser i Aamosen*, Copenhagen; S. Andersen, 1975, 'Ringkloster: en jysk inlandsoboplads med Ertebøllekultur', *Kuml* 1973–4, 10–108; H. Schwabedissen, 1967.

10 P. Rowley-Conwy, 1981.

11 H. Tauber, 1981, '13C evidence for dietary habits of prehistoric man in Denmark', *Nature* 292, 332–3.

12 E. Brinch Petersen, 1971, 'Ølby Lyng: en østsjaellands kystboplads med Ertebøllekultur', *Aarbøger* 1970, 5–42; U. Møhl, 1971; S. Andersen, 1979, 'Aggersund: en ertebølleboplads ved Limfjorden', *Kuml* 1978, 7–56; A. Madsen, *et al.*, 1900, *Affaldsdunger fra Stenalderen i Danmark*, Copenhagen; J. G. D. Clark, 1975.

13 J. Bay-Petersen, 1978; M. Degerbol and B. Fredskild, 1970, *The Urus . . . and Neolithic domesticated cattle . . . in Denmark*, Copenhagen; G. Bailey, 1978; J. G. D. Clark, 1975.

14 B. Bender, 1978; S. Albrethsen and E. Brinch Petersen, 1976; T. Mathiassen, 1946.

15 J. G. D. Clark, 1975, table 15; H. Schwabedissen, 1967; H. Schwabedissen, 1972, 'Rosenhof (Ostholstein): ein Ellerbek-Wohnplatz am einstigen Ostseeufer', *Arch. Korr.* 2, 1–8.

16 Earlier references in chapter 2 and: R. Jacobi 1976, 'Britain inside and outside Mesolithic Europe', *PPS* 42, 67–84; P. Woodman, 1978, *The Mesolithic in Ireland*, Oxford; M. Ryan, 1980, 'An Early Mesolithic site in the Irish midlands', *Antiquity* 54, 46–7; P. Mellars, 1976a, 1976b; I. Simmons and G. Dimbleby, 1974, 'The possible role of ivy in the Mesolithic economy of western Europe', *J. Archaeol. Sci.* 1, 291–6; D. L. Clarke, 1976.

17 J. Coles, 1971, 'The early settlement of Scotland: excavations at Morton, Fife', *PPS* 37 (2), 284–366; P. Mellars, 1978, 'Excavations and economic analysis of Mesolithic shell middens on the island of Oronsay (Inner Hebrides)', in P. Mellars (ed.), pp. 371–96; P. Mellars and M. Wilkinson, 1980, 'Fish otoliths as evidence for seasonality in prehistoric shell middens: the evidence from Oronsay (Inner Hebrides)', *PPS* 46, 19–44.

18 M. Péquart, *et al.*, 1937, *Téviec, station-nécropole mésolithique du Morbihan*, Paris; J. L'Helgouach, 1971; H. Case, 1969, 'Settlement patterns in the north Irish Neolithic', *Ulster Journal of Archaeology*, 32, 3–27.

19 G. Burenhult, 1981, *The Carrowmore excavations: excavation season 1980*, Stockholm; A. Lynch, 1981, *Man and environment in south-east Ireland*, 4000 BC–AD 800, Oxford.

20 Extensive series of papers in *Helinium* 16 to 19. Main sources referred to are: D. Whallon and D. Price, 1976, 'Excavations at the river dune sites s11–13', *Helinium* 16, 222–9; J. de Roever, 1976, 'Excavations at the river dune sites s21–22', *Helinium* 16, 209–21; J. de Roever, 1979, 'The pottery from Swifterbant – Dutch Ertebølle?', *Helinium* 19, 13–36; J. van der Waals, 1977, 'Excavations at the natural levée sites s2, s3–5 and s4', *Helinium* 17, 3–27; W. Casparie, *et al.*, 1977, 'The palaeobotany of Swifterbant: a preliminary report', *Helinium* 17, 28–55; A. Clason and D. Brinkhuizen, 1978, 'Swifterbant, mammals, birds, fishes: a preliminary report', *Helinium* 18, 69–82. Cf. L. Louwe Kooijmans, 1974.

## 5 Consolidation and denouement in south-east Europe

1 G. Georgiev, 1965; 1969, G. Georgiev, 'Die äneolithische Kultur in Südbulgarien im Lichte der Ausgrabungen von Tell Azmak bei Stara Zagora', *Stud. Zvesti* 17, 141–58; H. Todorova, 1976; 1978; H. Todorova, *et al.*, 1975; A. Radouncheva, 1976, *Vinitsa-eneolitno selishte i nekropol*, Sofia; V. Dumitrescu, 1954; M.

Petrescu-Dimboviţa, 1963, 'Die wichtigsten Ergebnisse der archäologischen Ausgrabungen in der neolithischen Siedlung von Truşesti (Moldau)', *Praehist. Zeitschr.* 41, 172–86; S. Marinescu-Bîlcu, 1981.

2 D. Berciu, 1966; G. Cantacuzino and S. Morintz, 1963, 'Die jungsteinzeitliche Funde in Cernica', *Dacia* 7, 27–89; G. Cantacuzino, 1969, 'The prehistoric necropolis of Cernica and its place in the Neolithic cultures of Romania and Europe in the light of recent discoveries', *Dacia* 13, 45–59; I. Ivanov, 1978; H. Todorova, 1978.

3 E. Cernych, 1978; B. Jovanović, 1979, 'The technology of primary copper mining in south-east Europe', *PPS* 45, 103–10.

4 E.g. E. Neustupný, 1968; 1969; C. Renfrew, 1969; 1971; V. Dumitrescu, *et al.*, 1982; J. Chapman, 1981.

5 Cf. G. Georgiev, 1961, and H. Todorova, 1978; 1981.

6 E.g. V. Dumitrescu, *et al.*, 1982, p. 35.

7 J. Chapman, 1981; M. Garašanin, 1982.

8 D. Theocharis, 1973 and other references in chapter 3; also V. Milojčić and H. Hauptmann, 1969, *Die Funde der frühen Dimini-Zeit aus der Arapi-Magula, Thessalien*, Bonn; H. Hauptmann, 1981.

9 T. Passek, 1961; T. Sulimirski, 1970, *Prehistoric Russia*, London; R. Tringham, 1971; E. Cernych, 1981; S. Marinescu-Bîlcu, 1981.

10 E.g. V. Dumitrescu, 1966, and references above.

11 M. Grbić, 1929, *Pločnik, äneolithische Ansiedlung*, Belgrade.

12 B. Brukner, 1971; B. Brukner, *et al.*, 1974.

13 V. Christescu, 1925, 'Les stations préhistoriques du lac de Boian', *Dacia* 2, 249–303; E. Comşa 1962, 'Sapaturi archeologice la Boian-Varasti', *Mat. Cerc. Arh.* 8, 205–12.

14 R. Popov, 1918, 'Kodza Dermenskata Mogila pri Sumen', *Izvest. Bulg. Arheol. Drvzestvo* 6, 71–156; V. Dumitrescu, 1966.

15 R. Schmidt, 1932, *Cucuteni, in der Oberen Moldau, Rumanien*, Berlin; M. Petrescu-Dimboviţa, 1965, 'Evolution de la civilisation de Cucuteni à la lumière des nouvelles fouilles archéologiques de Cucuteni–Baiceni', *Riv. Sci. Preist.* 20, 157–81; M. Petrescu-Dimboviţa, 1966, *Cucuteni*, Bucharest.

16 The basic equations between the Romanian and Russian schemes can be set out as:

| | |
|---|---|
| Pre-Cucuteni I | |
| Pre-Cucuteni II | |
| Pre-Cucuteni III | Tripolye A |
| Cucuteni A | Tripolye B1 |
| Cucuteni AB | Tripolye B2 |
| Cucuteni B | Tripolye C1/γ1 |
| Horodistea–Foltesti | Tripolye C2/γ2 |

In addition Romanian scholars claim up to four subdivisions of Cuc. A, two of Cuc. AB, and three of Cuc. B. E. Cernych, 1981 proposes numbered phases, but uses also the traditional scheme.

17 R. Tringham, 1971; T. Greeves, 1975, 'The use of copper in the Cucuteni–Tripolye culture of south-east Europe', *PPS* 41, 153–66; E. Comşa, 1980, 'Die Kupferwendung bei den Gemeinschaften der Cucuteni-Kultur in Rumänien', *Praehist. Zeitschr.*, 55, 197–219.

18 W. Kingery and J. Frierman, 1974, 'The firing temperature of a Karanovo sherd

and inferences about south-east European Chalcolithic refractory technology',
*PPS* 40, 204–5; E. Gardner, 1979, 'Graphite painted pottery', *Archaeol.* 32, 18–23.

19  S. Sergeyev, 1963, 'Rannetripolskii klad us. Karbuna', *Sov. Arch.* 1, 135–51; E.
Cernych, 1978 and references.

20  E. Comşa, 1978, 'L'utilisation du cuivre par les communautés de la culture
Gumelniţa au territoire Roumain', *Stud. Praehist.*, 1–2, 109–20.

21  I. Ivanov, 1978; 1983; H. Dumitrescu, 1961, 'Connections between the
Cucuteni–Tripolye cultural complex and the neighbouring eneolithic cultures in
the light of the utilisation of golden pendants', *Dacia* 5, 69–95; J. Makkay, 1976,
'Problems concerning Copper Age chronology in the Carpathian basin', *Acta
Arch. Acad. Sci. Hung.* 28, 251–300; B. Jovanović, 1978, 'Early gold and
Eneolithic copper mining and metallurgy of the Balkans and Danube basin', *Stud.
Praehist.* 1–2, 192–7; A. Hartmann, 1978, 'Ergebnisse der spektralanalytischen
Untersuchung äneolithischer Goldfunde aus Bulgarien', *Stud. Praehist.* 1/2,
27–45.

22  V. Dumitrescu, 1965; G. Georgiev and N. Angelov, 1957, 'Razkopko na selishnata mogila do Roussé prez 1950–1953', *Izvest. Bulg. Arch. Inst.* 21, 41–129.

23  B. Nikolov, 1978.

24  R. Tringham, 1972, 'Territorial demarcation of prehistoric settlements', in P.
Ucko *et al.* (eds.), *Man, settlement and urbanism*, pp. 463–75, London; H. and V.
Dumitrescu, 1962, 'Activitatea santierului archeologic Traian', *Mat. Cerc. Arch.*
8, 245–60.

25  A. Margos, 1978, 'Les sites lucustres dans les lacs de Varna et la nécropole de
Varna', *Stud. Praehist.* 1–2, 146–8; I. Ivanov, 1983.

26  L. Perniceva, 1978.

27  R. Tringham, *et al.*, 1980; J. Chapman, 1981, fig. 74.

28  H. Todorova, 1978, table 7.

29  L. Perniceva, 1978; D. Galbenu, 1963.

30  E.g. M. Gimbutas, 1974.

31  H. Todorova, 1976; 1978; H. Todorova, 1974, 'Kultszene und Hausmodell aus
Ovčarovo, Bez Targovishte', *Thracia* 3, 39–46.

32  M. Makarevich, 1960, 'Ob ideologicheskikh predstyarlenijakh u tripolskikh
plemen', *Odess. Arkh. Obsh. Zap.* 34, 290–301.

33  M. Gimbutas, 1980, 'The temples of old Europe', *Archaeol.* 33, 41–50.

34  V. Dumitrescu, 1965; V. Dumitrescu, 1970, 'Édifice destiné au culte découvert
dans la couche Boian–Spanţov de la station-tell de Căscioarele', *Dacia* 14, 5–24.

35  R. Galović, 1975, 'Neolitska ritualna grupa iz Smederevska Palanka', *Zborn.
Rad. Narod. Muz. Beograd.* 8, 21–30.

36  H. Dumitrescu, 1968, 'Un modèle de sanctuaire découvert dans la station
énéolithique de Căscioarele', *Dacia*, 12, 318–94.

37  M. Gimbutas, 1974*b*; J. Chapman, 1981, p. 75.

38  H. Moore, 1982, 'The interpretation of spatial patterning in settlement residues',
in I. Hodder (ed.), *Symbolic and structural archaeology*, pp. 74–9, Cambridge.

39  Earlier references and D. Galbenu, 1963.

40  V. Markevich, 1970, 'Mnogosloynoe poselenie Novye Ruseshty 1', *Krat. Soob.
Inst. Arkh.* 123, 56–68.

41  See references earlier in this chapter to these cemeteries especially in notes 1
and 2.

42  C. Renfrew, 1972.

43  For Gomolava and Greece, see references in chapter 3. K. Kanchev, 1978,

'Microwear studies of weapons and tools from the Chalcolithis necropolis at the city of Varna', *Stud. Praehist.* 1–2, 46–9.

44  V. Dumitrescu and T. Banateanu, 1965; J. Chapman, 1981; C. Mateescu, 1975.

45  C. Renfrew, 1978, 'Space, time and polity', in J. Frierman and M. Rowlands (eds.), *The evolution of social systems*, pp. 89–114, London.

46  E.g. V. Dumitrescu, 1966; V. Dumitrescu, 1960, 'A new statuette of Thessalian type discovered at Gumelniţa', *Dacia* 4, 443–53; S. Marinescu-Bîlcu, 1981; J. Lavessi, 1978, 'Prehistoric investigations at Corinth', *Hesperia* 47, 402–51; W. Bray, 1966, 'Neolithic painted ware on the Adriatic', *Antiquity*, 40, 100–6.

47  E.g. H. Hauptman, 1981, fig. 7; V. Milojčić, 1959.

48  C. Renfrew, 1971; 1972; D. Theocharis, 1973; E. Hanschmann and V. Milojčić, 1976, *Die deutschen Ausgrabungen auf der Argissa-Magula in Thessalien, III: die frühe und beginnende mittlere Bronzezeit*, Bonn.

49  G. Georgiev, *et al.*, 1979; V. Mikov, 1971; H. Todorova, 1981, p. 205; L. Ghetov, 1980, 'Sur le problème des sceptres zoomorphes en pierre', *Stud. Praehist.* 3, 91–6.

50  D. Berciu, 1961; S. Morintz and P. Roman, 1969, 'Über die Chronologie der Übergangszeit vom Äneolithikum zur Bronzezeit in Rumänien', *Dacia* 13, 61–71; H. Todorova, 1981; P. Roman, 1981, 'Forme de manifestare culturala din Eneoliticul tîrziu si perioada de tranzitie spre epoca bronzului', *SCIVA* 32, 21–41; M. Mirtchev, 1961, 'Trois sépultures de l'époque Néolithique', *Bull. Soc. Arch. Varna* 12, 117–25; E. Comşa, 1974.

51  D. Berciu, 1961; V. Dumitrescu, *et al.*, 1982; N. Tasic, 1979, 'Bubanj-Salcuţa-Krivodol Kompleks', in N. Tasic (ed.), *Praistorija Jugoslavenskih Zemalja, III: Eneolitsko Doba*, pp. 87–114, Sarajevo; M. Garašanin, 1982; P. Roman, 1977, *The Late Copper Age Coţofeni culture of south-east Europe*, Oxford; B. Nikolov, 1978; B. Nikolov, 1975, *Zaminets*, Sofia; P. Roman and I. Neméti, 1978, *Cultura Baden în România*, Bucharest.

52  Data summarised in J. Mallory, 1977.

53  E.g. V. Dumitrescu, *et al.*, 1982, *contra* T. Passek, 1961.

54  H. Dumitrescu, 1945, 'La station préhistorique de Horodiştea sur le Pruth', *Dacia*, 9–10, 127–63; M. Petrescu-Dimboviţa, *et al.*, 1951, 'Sapaturile de la Folteşti', *Stud. Cerc. Ist. Vech.* 2, 249–65; M. Petrescu-Dimboviţa and D. Marin, 1974, 'Nouvelles fouilles archéologiques à Folteşti (dep. de Galaţi)', *Dacia* 18, 19–72; A. Dodd-Opritescu, 1981, 'Ceramica ornamentată cu şnurul din ana culturilor Cucuteni şi Cernavodă 1', *SCIVA* 32, 511–28.

55  E.g. N. Kalicz, 1963, *Die Badener (Péceler) Kultur und Anatolien*, Budapest.

56  E. Hajnalova, 1980, 'Palaeoethnobotanical findings from the multi-layer Nova Zagora settlement', *Stud. Praehist.* 4, 98; R. Dennell, 1978.

57  P. Halstead, 1981b.

58  M. Dinu, 1980. A little further north, in eastern Hungary, the first horses appear in Tiszapolgár graves of the mid-fourth mbc, but then disappear till the Baden phase: S. Bökönyi, 1978; S. Haimovici, 1979, 'Caracteristicile paleofaunei din aşezările perioadei de tranziţie de la Eneolitic la epoca bronzului din Moldova', *SCIVA* 30, 11–20.

59  A. Sherratt, 1981; A. Sherratt, 1983, 'The secondary exploitation of animals in the Old World', *World Archaeol.* 15, 90–104.

60  For the Halafian situation, G. Hillman, pers. comm.; V. Dumitrescu and T. Banateanu, 1965; C. Mateescu, 1975; M. Dinu, 1980; A. Bolomey, 1979, 'Gospodărirea animaleler în aşezarea neolitica de la Fărcaşu de Sus', *SCIVA* 30, 3–10; S. Piggott, 1983, *The earliest wheeled transport*, London.

61  M. Gimbutas, 1973, 'The beginning of the Bronze Age in Europe and the Indo-Europeans: 3,500–2500 BC', *J. Indo-Eur. Studs*, 1, 163–214; T. Greeves, 1975, 'The use of copper in the Cucuteni–Tripolye culture of south-east Europe', *PPS* 41, 153–66; A. Sherratt, 1976, 'Resources, technology and trade: an essay in early European metallurgy', in G. Sieveking (eds.), *et al.*, *Problems in economic and social archaeology*, pp. 557–82, London.

62  C. Renfrew, 1972; D. Theocharis, 1973: V. Dumitrescu, *et al.*, 1982; J. Mallory, 1977; M. Dinu, 1980; V. Mikov, 1971; R. Katincharov, 1981; I. Ecsedy, 1979, *The people of the pit-grave Kurgans in eastern Hungary*, Budapest; M. Dinu, 1974, 'Le problème de tombes à ocre dans les régions orientales de la Roumanie', *Preist. Alp.* 10, 261–75; G. Tonceva, 1978, 'Nècropole tumulaire de l'àge du bronze ancien prîs du village Belogradec', *Stud. Praehist.* 1–2, 228–37; G. Tonceva, 1981, 'Monuments sculpturaux en Bulgarie du Nord-Est de l'âge du bronze', *Stud. Praehist.*, 5–6, 129–45; D. Popescu, 1940 'La tombe à ocre de Casimcea (Dobrogea)', *Dacia* 7–8, 85–91.

63  A. Sherratt, 1981, fig. 10.15; A. Dodd-Opritescu, 1980, 'Consideraţii asupra ceramicii Cucuteni C', *SCIVA* 31, m 547–57; T. Sulimirski, 1968; and see chapter 6.

64  J. Mallory, 1976; 1977; M. Gimbutas; 1977, 'The first wave of Eurasian steppe pastoralists into Copper Age Europe', *Journal of Indo-European Studies* 5, 277–331; M. Garašanin, 1971, 'Nomades des steppes et autochtones dans le Sud-Est européen à l'époque de transition du néolithique à l'âge du bronze', in V. Georgiev (ed.), *L'ethnogénèse des peuples balkaniques*, pp. 9–14, Sofia; D. Garašanin, 1971, 'Problèmes de l'appartenance linguistique des populations néolithiques dans le centre des Balkans', in V. Georgiev (ed.), *L'ethnogénèse des peuples balkaniques*, pp. 15–19; E. Comşa, 1974; E. Comşa, 1980, 'Contribution à la connaissance du processus d'indo-européanisation des régions carpato-danubiennes', in R. Vulpe (ed.), *Actes du IIe congrès international de Thracologie*, pp. 29–33, Bucharest; P. Roman, 1977.

65  H. Todorova, 1973, 'Zur Frage des Überganges vom Äneolithikum zur Frühbronzezeit in Bulgarien', in B. Chropovský (ed.), *Symposium über Entstehung und Chronologie der Badener Kultur*, pp. 435–47, Bratislava; H. Todorova, 1981; V. Mikov, 1971. Continuity stressed by R. Katincharov, 1981 and G. Georgiev, 1972, 'Die Gemeinsamkeit der Kulturen Südbulgariens und Nordgriechenlands während des Neolithikums, Äneolithikums und der Frühbronzezeit', *Acta 2nd Int. Colloq. Aegean Prehistory*, pp. 115–28.

66  C. Renfrew, 1973, 'Problems in the general correlation of archaeological and linguistic data in prehistoric Greece: the model of autochthonous origin', in R. Crossland and A. Birchall (eds.), *Bronze Age migrations in the Aegean*, pp. 263–79, London; M. Sakellariou, 1977, *Peuples préhelléniques d'origine indo-européene*, Athens.

67  D. L. Clarke, 1968, *Analytical archaeology*, London; F. Barth, 1969; J. Mallory, 1976, with references to linguistic views.

68  V. Georgiev, 1966, *Introduzione alla storia delle lingue indoeuropee*, Rome.

## 6  The central and western European mosaic

1   A. Medunová-Benešová, 1972; M. Wosinszky, 1888.

2   E.g. I. Simmons and M. Tooley, 1981, and references; F. Schweingruber, 1976, *Prähistorisches Holz*, Bern; B. Becker, 1978, 'Dendrochronological evidence for Holocene changes in the drainage system of southern central Europe', in J.

Fletcher (ed.), *Dendrochronology in Europe*, pp. 289–90, Oxford; B. Frenzel, 1978; J. Iversen, 1973; H. de Lumley, 1976; L. Louwe Kooijmans, 1974.

3  N. Kalicz, 1970; I. Bognár-Kutzián, 1963; 1972. There are current Hungarian–Russian excavations at Herpaly itself.

4  J. Pavúk, 1981; J. Pavúk, 1969, 'Chronologie der Zeliezovce-Gruppe', *Slov. Arch.* 17, 269–367; A. Tocik, and J. Lichardus, 1966, 'Staršia fáza slovensko-moravskiej malovanej keramiki na juhozópadnam Slovensku', *Pam. Arch.* 57, 1–90; V. Němejcová-Pavúková, 1964, 'Sidlisko bolerzskeho tipu v Nitrianskom Hrádu', *Slov. Arch.* 12, 163–268; J. Pavúk and S. Šiška, 1980, 'Neolit e eneolit (Vorschlagder Chronologie der Vor- und Frühgeschichte in der Slowakei)', *Slov. Arch.* 18, 137–58; I. Pavlů and M. Zápatocká, 1979, 'Současný stav a úkoly studia neolitu v Čechach', *Pam. Arch.* 70, 281–318; J. Dombay, 1960; V. Podborský, *et al.*, 1977, *Numericky Kod Moravske Malovane Keramiky*, Brno.

5  M. Zápatocká, 1970, 'Die Stichbandkeramik in Böhmen und in Mitteleuropa', in H. Schwabedissen (ed.), *Die Anfänge des Neolithikums*. vol. 2 (Sonderdruck) Köln; D. Kaufmann, 1976, *Wirtschaft und Kultur der Stichbandkeramiker im Saalegebiet*, Berlin; T. Wislanski, 1970.

6  W. Meier-Arendt, 1974, 'Zur Frage der Genese der Rössener Kultur', *Germania* 52, 1–15; W. Meier-Arendt, 1975, *Die Hinkelstein Gruppe*, Berlin; F. Niquet, 1937, 'Die Rössener Kultur im Mitteldeutschland', *Jahr. Vorg. Sachs. Thur. Land.* 26, 1–111; H. Behrens, 1973; K. Mauser-Goller, 1972, 'Die Rössener Kultur in ihrem südwestlichen Verbreitungsgebiet', in *Die Anfänge des Neolithikums*, pp. 259–68, Köln; K. Brandt, 1967.

7  G. Bailloud, 1974; M. Boureux, and A. Coudart, 1978; C. Constantin, and J. Demoule, 1982, 'Groupe de Villeneuve–Saint–Germain', *Helinium* 22, 255–71; J. L'Helgouach, 1971; J. L'Helgouach and J. Lecornec, 1976, 'Le site mégalithique "Min Goh Ru" près Larcuste à Colpo (Morbihan)', *Bull. Soc. Préhist. Franc.* 73, 370–97; A. Whittle, 1977 and references; A. ApSimon, 1976; H. Bamford, 1979, 'Briar Hill Neolithic causewayed enclosure', *Northamptonshire Archaeology* 14, 3–9.

8  Earlier references to A. Sherratt, 1982a; S. Bökönyi, 1974; 1978.

9  J. Makkay, 1978 'Excavations at Bicske, 1. The Early Neolithic – the earliest linearband ceramic', *Alba Regia* 16, 9–60; V. Němejcová-Pavúková, 1980, 'Ergebnisse der systematischen Grabung in Svodín', *Arch. Vysk. Nal. Slov. Rok.* 1979, 147–8; J. Pavúk, 1982, 'Die Hauptzuge der neolithischen Besiedlung in der Slowakei in Bezug zu Naturbedingungen', *Metodologické problémy československé archeologie*, 40–8, Praha.

10  J. Neustupný, 1950, 'Neolitická opevnená osada v Hlubokych Mašuvkách u Znojma', *Cas. Narod. Mus. Praha* 117–19, 11–49; R. Tichy, 1965, 'Die dritte Grabungssaison auf der befestigten neolithischen Siedlung in Křepice bei Znojmo', *Prehled Vyzkumu AU Brno* 1964, 28–9; V. Podborský, 1976, 'Erkenntnisse auf Grund der bisherigen Ausgrabungen in der Siedlung mit mährischer bemalter Keramik bei Těšetice–Kyjovice', *Jahr. Mitteldeutsch. Vorg.* 60, 129–48; H. Behrens, and E. Schröter, 1980.

11  M. Wosinszky, 1888; J. Dombay, 1960; N. Kalicz, 1976, 'Siedlung und Gräber der Lengyel-Kultur in Aszód (Jahresbericht 1972)', *Mitt. Arch. Inst. Ung. Akad. Wiss.* 5, 33–9.

12  J. Pavúk, 1981; J. Lichardus and J. Vladar, 1970, 'Neskorolengyelske sidliskové a hrobove nalezy z Nitry', *Slov. Arch.* 18, 373–419.

13  Earlier references, and J. Kruk, 1973.

14  B. Soudský, 1966; P. Modderman, 1977.

15  I. Pavlů, 1982, 'Die Neolithischen Kreisgrabenanlagen in Böhmen', *Arch. Rozhl.* 34, 176–89; R. Maier, 1962, 'Fragen zu neolithischen Erdwerken Südbayerns', *Jahresber. Bay. Boden.*, 5–21; H. Behrens, 1973.

16  B. Soudský, 1969, 'Étude de la maison néolithique', *Slov. Arch.* 17, 5–96. This has been doubted by P. Modderman, 1973, 'Bespiegelingen over de constructie van een bandceramisch huis', in W. van Els (eds.), *et al.*, *Archaeologie en historie*, pp. 131–40, Bussum.

17  P. Bogucki and R. Grygiel, 1981*a*.

18  Earlier references and A. Whittle, 1977.

19  A. Jürgens, 1979, 'Die Rössener Siedlung von Aldenhoven, Kreis Düren', *Rhein. Ausgrab.* 19, 385–506; R. Kuper and W. Piepers, 1966, 'Eine Siedlung der Rössener Kultur in Inden (Kreis Jülich) und Lamersdorf (Kreis Düren). Vorbericht', *Bonn. Jahrb.* 166, 370–6; K. Günther, 1973, 'Eine neue Variante der mittelneolithischen Trapezhauses', *Germania* 51, 41–53; K. Brandt, 1960, 'Einzaunungen an bandkeramischen und altrössener Bauten', *Germania* 38, 418–23; J. Eckert, *et al.*, 1972, 'Untersuchungen zur neolithischer Besiedlung der Aldenhovener Platte, II', *Bonn. Jahrb.* 172, 344–94; A. Whittle, 1977 and references.

20  G. Bailloud, 1974; M. Boureux and A. Coudart, 1978; J. L'Helgouach, 'Le tumulus de Dissignac à Saint-Nazaire . . .', in S. de Laet (ed.), *Acculturation and continuity in Atlantic Europe*, pp. 142–9, Brugge; P. R. Giot, *et al.*, 1965, 'Le site du Curnic en Guissèny', *Ann. Bret.* 72, 49–70.

21  P. Bogucki, and R. Grygiel, 1981*b*.

22  H. de Lumley 1976; J. Guilaine, 1976 (ed.); K. H. Knörzer, 1971, 'Pflanzliche Grossreste aus der rössenzeitliche Siedlung bei Langweiler, Kr Jülich', *Bonn. Jahrb.* 171, 9–33.

23  Note that the increase is inferred from the expansion of settlement and character of sites, not their numbers. In fact there are regularly more LBK sites than later ones in well-studied areas. In central Germany, the LBK : Stich BK : Rössen/Gatersleben ratio is approximately and consistently 100 : 60 : 30 (N. Starling, pers. comm.).

24  A. Whittle, 1977; I. Simmons and M. Tooley, 1981; A. ApSimon, 1976; G. Wainwright, 1972, 'The excavation of a Neolithic settlement on Broome Heath, Ditchingham, Norfolk', *PPS* 38, 1–97; and other references earlier and in chapter 4.

25  J. Banner and J. Korek, 1949, 'Negyedik és ötödik ásatás a Hódmezövásáhelyi–Kökenydombon', *Arch. Ert.* 76, 9–25; A. Sherratt, 1982*b*.

26  P. Patay, 1978, 'A Tiszavalk–Tetetsi rezkovi temetö es telep', *Fol. Arch.* 29, 21–58; A. Sherratt, 1982*a*; P. Patay, 1970, 'A javarezkor nehany etnkikai es idorendi kerdeserol', *Fol. Arch.*, 21, 7–26; J. Vizdal, 1977 *Tiszapolgarske pohrebisko vo Vel'kých Raškovciach*, Košice.

27  J. Chapman, 1981 and see chapter 5.

28  J. Chapman, 1983, 'Meaning and illusion in the study of burial in Balkan prehistory', in A. Poulter (ed.), *Ancient Bulgaria*, pp. 1–42, Nottingham.

29  M. Zápatocká, 1981, 'Bi-ritual cemetery of the Stroked-pottery culture at Miskovice, district of Kutna Hora', in J. Hrala (ed.), *Nouvelles archéologiques dans la république socialiste tchèque*, pp. 26–31, Prague; D. Kaufmann, 1976, map 8.

30  A. Jodlowski, 1969, 'Problem eksploatacji soli w okolicach krakowa w starozytnosci i we wczesnym sredniowieczu', *Arch. Pol.* 14, 137–65; H. Burch-

ard, 1967, 'Czy w neolicie eksploatowano solanki na Podkaspaciu polskim?', *Act. Arch. Carpath.* 9, 5–10.

31  C. Pellet, 1978, 'La nécropole rubanée de "L'étang David" à Chichery (Yonne)', *Rév. Arch. Est.* 29, 65–84.

32  J. L'Helgouach, 1965; J. Arnal, *et al.*, 1955, 'Les tumulus de Bougon', *Rév. Arch.* 46, 129–64; G. Burenhult, 1981, *The Carrowmore excavations: excavation season 1980*, Stockholm.

33  E.g. H. Case, 1969, 'Settlement patterns in the north Irish Neolithic', *Ulster Journal of Archaeology* 32, 3–27; P. Ashbee, 1970.

34  A. Fleming, 1973; C. Renfrew, 1976; C. Tilley, 1981, 'Conceptual frameworks for the explanation of sociocultural change', in I. Hodder *et al.* (eds.), *Pattern of the past*, pp. 363–86, Cambridge.

35  E.g. W. Pape, 1979; H. Tauber, 1972; J. Bakker, 1979; J. Bakker, *et al.*, 1969, 'TRB and other C14 dates from Poland'; *Helinium* 9, 209–38; J. Guilaine 1976 (ed.); A. Whittle, 1977, etc.

36  E.g. B. Huber and W. Merz, 1963; B. Becker, 1978, 'Dendroecological zones of central European forest communities', in J. Fletcher (ed.), *Dendrochronology in Europe*, pp. 101–14, Oxford; B. Becker and A. Delorme, 1978, 'Oak chronologies in central Europe: their extension from medieval to prehistoric times', in J. Fletcher (ed.), *Dendrochronology in Europe*, pp. 59–64; E. Hollstein, 1980, *Mitteleuropäische Eichenchronologie*, Mainz; J. Pilcher, *et al.*, 1977, 'A long subfossil oak tree-ring chronology from the north of Ireland', *New Phytologist* 79, 713–29; R. Morgan, 1979, 'Tree ring studies in the Somerset Levels: the Drove site of the Sweet Track', *Somerset Levels Papers* 5, 65–75.

37  Earlier references and P. Patay, 1974; J. Banner, 1956, 'Die Péceler Kultur', *Arch. Hung.* 35; E. Neustupný, 1973; T. Wislanski, 1970; V. Němejcová-Pavúková, 1981.

38  J. Pavúk, 1981; T. Wislanski, 1970; H. Behrens, 1973. Jordanowa in central Germany is called Jordansmühl, but is peripheral.

39  H. Behrens, 1973; J. Bakker, 1979; C. Becker, 1955, 'Die mittelneolithischen Kulturen in Südskandinavien', *Acta Arch.* 25, 49–150; T. Wislanski, 1970; M. Zápatocký, 1957, 'K problému počátků kultury nálevkovitých pohárů', *Arch. Rozhl.* 9, 206–35.

40  E.g. S. Müller, 1918, *Stenalderens Kunst i Denmark*, Copenhagen; J. Winther, 1943; T. Mathiassen, 1939m 'Brundsø, eu yngre Stenalders Boplads paa Als', *Aarboger*, 1–55; T. Mathiassen, 1943, *Stenalderbopladses i Aamosen*, Copenhagen; N. Andersen and T. Madsen, 1978, 'Skale og baegre med storvinkelband fra yngre Stenalder', *Kuml* 1977, 131–60.

41  H. Tauber, 1972; J. Bakker, 1979, fig. 75; N. Andersen, 1981; A. Gebauer, 1979, 'The Middle Neolithic Funnel beaker culture in south-west Jutland: an analysis of the pottery', *Kuml* 1978, 117–58.

42  J. Bakker, 1979; A. van Giffen and W. Glasbergen, 1964, 'De vroegste faze van de TRB-cultuur in Nederland', *Helinium* 4, 40–8; W. Van Zeist, 1955, 'Some radiocarbon dates from the raised bog at Emmen (Netherlands)', *Palaeohist.* 4, 113–18.

43  H. Behrens, 1973. Chronology is uncertain. The Salzmünde group could be a regional variation on the basis of its restricted distribution, and also connected largely with *Höhensiedlungen* (N. Starling, pers. comm.).

44  K. Brandt, 1957; T. Wislanski, 1970; K. Randsborg, 1980, 'Resource distribution and the function of copper tools in Early Neolithic Denmark', in M. Ryan (ed.), *The origins of metallurgy in Atlantic Europe*, pp. 303–18, Dublin.

45  J. Lüning, 1967; J. Lüning, 1969, 'Die Entwicklung der Keramik beim Übergang vom Mittel – zum Jungneolithikum im süddeutschen Raum', *BRGK* 50, 1–98; R. Koch, 1971, 'Zwei Erdwerke der Michelsberger Kultur aus dem Kreis Heilbronn', *Fundber. aus Schwaben* 19, 51–67.

46  J. Driehaus, 1960, *Die Altheimer Gruppe und das Jungneolithikum in Mitteleuropa*, Mainz; J. Winiger, *Das Fundmaterial von Thayngen-Weier im Rahmen der Pfyner Kultur*, Basel; B. Ottaway and C. Strahm, 1975; E. Pleslova-Stikova, 1977, 'Die Entwicklung der Metallurgie auf dem Balkan, im Karpatenbekken und in Mitteleuropa, unter besonderer Berucksichtigung der Kupferproduktion im ostalpenländischen Zentrum', *Pam. Arch.* 68, 56–73.

47  M. Sakellaridis, 1979; E. Vogt, 1964, 'Der Stand der neolithischen Forschung in der Schweiz', *Jahrb Schweiz. Ges. Urg.* 51, 7–27; A. Furger, *et al.*, 1977.

48  B. Huber and W. Merz, 1963; H. Bandi, 1967; W. Guyan, 1967; H. Waterbolk and W. van Zeist, 1978; W. Mook, *et al.*, 1972.

49  G. Bailloud, 1974; J. Thévenot, 1969, 'Elements chasséens de la céramique de Chassey', *Rev. Arch. East. Centre-Est.* 20, 7–96; J. C. Blanchet and A. Decormeille, 1980, 'Le site du Coq Galleux et du Hazoy à Compiégne (Oise)', *Cahiers Arch. Picardie* 11, 3–12; J. Guilaine, 1976 (ed.); J. L'Helgouach 1971; C. Burnez, 1976, *Le Néolithique et le Chalcolithique dans le centre-ouest de la France*, Paris.

50  I. Smith, 1974, 'The Neolithic', in C. Renfrew (ed.), *British prehistory: a new outline*, pp. 100–36, London; H. Green, 1979, *The flint arrowheads of the British Isles*, Oxford; J. Coles, *et al.*, 1973, 'Prehistoric roads and tracks in Somerset: 3. The Sweet Track', *PPS* 39, 256–93, especially p. xxx.

51  S. Bökönyi, 1974; 1978; A. Sherratt, 1981; 1982a; J. Korek, 1951, 'Ein Gräberfeld der Badener Kultur bei Alsónémedi', *Act. Arch. Hung.*, 1, 35–91; N. Kalicz, 1976, 'Ein neues kupferzeitliches Wagenmodell aus der Umgebung von Budapest', in H. Mitscha-Märheim (eds.), *Festschrift für Richard Pittioni*, pp. 188–207 (Arch. Austr. Beiheft 13); J. Pavelčík, 1981, 'The hilltop settlement of the Channelled-ware people at Hlinsko by Lipník', in J. Hrala (ed.), *Nouvelles archéologiques dans la république socialiste tchèque*, pp. 46–8, Prague.

52  H. Thrane, 1982; S. Milisauskas and J. Kruk, 1982, 'Die Wagendarstellung auf dem Trichterbecher aus Bronocice in Polen', *Arch. Korr.* 12, 141–4.

53  J. Skaarup, 1975, *Stengade: ein langeländerischer Wohnplatz mit Hausresten aus der frühneolithischen Zeit*, Rudkøbing; T. Madsen, 1979; H. Zürn, 1965, *Das jungsteinzeitliche Dorf Ehrenstein (Kr. Ulm). I: Die Baugeschichte*, Stuttgart; H. Reinerth, 1929, *Das Federseemoor als Siedlungsland der Vorzeitmenschen*, Leipzig; R. Schmidt, 1936, *Jungsteinzeit-Siedlungen im Federseemoor*, vol. 2, Stuttgart; R. Schmidt, 1937, *Jungsteinzeit-Siedlungen im Federseemoor*, vol. 3, Stuttgart; P. Modderman, 1977.

54  K. Spång, *et al.*, 1976.

55  J. Kruk, 1973; S. Milisauskas and J. Kruk, 1978; J. Kruk, and S. Milisauskas 1981; M. Dabrowski, 1971 'Pollen analysis of cultural layers from Sarnowo', *Prace i Mat.* 18, 163–4.

56  E.g. J. Winther, 1943; J. Winther, 1935, 1938, *Troldebjerg, en bymaessig Bebyggelse fra Danmarks yngre Stenalder*, vols. 1, 2, Rudkøbing; H. Berg, 1951, 'Klintebakke, en boplads fra mellem neolitisk tid', *Medd. Langelands Mus.*, 7–18.

57  J. Lüning, 1967; N. Andersen, 1981; H. Hingst, 1971, 'Ein befestigtes Dorf aus der Jungsteinzeit in Büdelsdorf (Holstein)', *Arch. Korr.* 1, 191–4; H. Behrens, 1973; H. Behrens and E. Schröter, 1980; E. Pleslová–Štiková, *et al.*, 1980, 'A square

enclosure of the Funnel beaker culture at Makotřasy (Central Bohemia): a palaeoastronomic structure', *Arch. Rozhl.* 32, 3–35; F. Hubert, 1971, 'Fossés néolithiques à Spiennes', *Arch. Belg.* 136.

58  T. Madsen, 1982, 'Settlement systems of early agricultural societies in east Jutland, Denmark: a regional study of change', *Journal of Anthropological Archaeology* 1, 197–236; K. Kristiansen, 1982; K. Ebbesen and E. Brinch Petersen, 1973; H. Thrane, 1982; A. Sherratt, 1981.

59  H. Waterbolk and W. van Zeist, 1978; W. Guyan, 1967; H. Bandi, 1967; E. Vogt, 1951, 'Das steinzeitliche Uferdorf Egolzwil 3 (Kt. Luzern)', *Zeitschr. Schweiz. Arch. Kunstgeschichte* 12, 193–215; R. Wyss, 1976, *Das jungsteinzeitliche Jäger-Bauerndorf von Egolzwil 5 im Wauwilermoos*, Zürich.

60  A. Furger *et al.*, 1977; M. Sakellaridis, 1979; J. Troels Smith, 1955, 'Pollen-analytische Untersuchungen zu einigen schweizerischen Pfahlbauproblemen', in W. Buyan (ed.), *Das Pfahlbauproblem*, pp. 11–58, Basel; K. Brunnacker, *et al.*, 1967, *Seeberg, Burgäschisee-Süd, 4: Chronologie und Umwelt*, Bern; W. Mook, *et al.*, 1972.

61  B. Ottaway and C. Strahm, 1975.

62  Earlier references and C. and D. Mordant, 1972, 'L' enceinte néolithique de Noyen-sur-Seine', *Bull. Soc. Préhist. Franc.* 69, 554–69; R. Agache, 1971, 'Un camp néolithique à accès multiples découvert dans la Somme', *Archaeologia* 43, 84–5; M. Marsac, and C. Scarre, 1979, 'Recent discoveries of Neolithic ditched camps in west-central France', *Aerial Archaeology* 4, 37–57; C. Scarre, 1982, 'Settlement patterns and landscape change: the Late Neolithic and the Bronze Age of the Marais Poitevin area of western France', *PPS* 48, 53–73; C. Burnez and H. Case, 1966, 'Les camps néolithiques des Matignons à Juillac-le-Coq (Charente)', *Gallia Préhist.* 9, 131–245.

63  Earlier references and J. Clark, *et al.*, 1960, 'Excavations at the Neolithic site of Hurst Fen, Mildenhall, Suffolk', *PPS* 26, 202–45; S. O'Nuallain, 1972, 'A Neolithic house at Ballyglass, Co. Mayo', *Journal of the Royal Society of Antiquaries of Ireland* 102, 49–57; F. Pryor, 1974, *Excavation at Fengate, Peterborough, England: the first report*, Ontario; F. Pryor, 1976; A. Whittle, 1982, 'Scord of Brouster and early settlement in Shetland', *Archaeologia Atlantica* 3, 35–55; J. Coles and B. Orme, 1979, 'The Sweet Track: Drove Site', *Somerset Levels Papers* 5, 43–64; S. O'Riordain, 1954, 'Lough Gur excavations: Neolithic and Bronze Age houses on Knockadoon', *Proceedings of the Royal Irish Academy* 56C, 297–459.

64  R. Mercer, *Hambledon Hill*, Edinburgh; P. Dixon, 1979, 'A Neolithic and Iron Age hillfort in southern England', *Scientific American* 241, 142–50; J. Hedges and D. Buckley, 1978, 'Excavations at a Neolithic causewayed enclosure, Orsett, Essex, 1975', *PPS* 44, 219–308; I. Smith, 1965, *Windmill Hill and Avebury*, Oxford; O. Bedwin, 1981, 'Excavations at the Neolithic enclosure on Bury Hill, Houghton, West Sussex 1979', *PPS* 47, 69–86.

65  A. Legge, 1981, 'Aspects of cattle husbandry', in R. Mercer (ed.), *Farming practice in British prehistory*, pp. 169–81, Edinburgh; R. Dennell, 1976, 'Prehistoric crop cultivation in southern England: a reconsideration', *Antiquaries Journal* 56, 11–23; P. Ashbee, *et al.*, 1979, 'Excavation of three long barrows near Avebury, Wiltshire', *PPS* 45, 207–300; J. Evans, 1972, *Land snails in archaeology*, London; I. Simmons and M. Tooley, 1981; J. Pilcher, and A. Smith, 1979, 'Palaeoecological investigations at Ballynagilly, a Neolithic and Bronze Age settlement in Co. Tyrone, N. Ireland', *Philosophical Transactions of the Royal Society of London*

B, 286, 345–69; M. Bell, 1978, 'Excavations at Bishopstone', *Sussex Archaeological Collections* 115; A. Whittle, 1978, 'Resources and population in the British Neolithic', *Antiquity* 52, 34–42.

66 O. Rackham, 1977, 'Neolithic woodland management in the Somerset Levels: Garvin's, Walton Heath and Rowland's Tracks', *Somerset Levels Papers* 2, 65–71; R. Morgan, 1978, 'Tree ring studies in the Somerset Levels: the Drove site of the Sweet Track', *Somerset Level Papers* 5, 65–75.

67 A. Sherratt, 1981; E. Neustupný, 1968; N. Kalicz, 1963, *Die Badener (Péceler) Kultur und Anatolien*, Budapest.

68 H. Behrens and E. Schröter, 1980.

69 K. Jazdzewski, 1965, *Poland*, London; K. Jazdzewski, 1973, 'The relations between Kujavian barrows in Poland and megalithic tombs in northern Germany, Denmark and western European countries', in P. Kjaerum and G. Daniel (eds.), *Megalithic graves and ritual*, pp. 63–74, Copenhagen; E. Sprockhoff, 1966, 1967, 1975, *Atlas der Megalithgräber Deutschlands*, vols. 1–3, Berlin.

70 I. Pleinerová, 1980, 'Kultovní objekty z pozdní doby kamenné v Březné v Loun', *Pam. Arch.* 71, 10–60.

71 T. Wislanski, 1970.

72 K. Elliott, *et al.*, 1978, 'The simulation of Neolithic axe dispersal in Britain', in I. Hodder (ed.), *Simulation studies in archaeology* pp. 79–97, Cambridge.

73 J. Bakker, 1979; J. Preuss, 1980, *Die altmärkische Gruppe der Tiefstichkeramik*, Berlin; H. Behrens, 1973; U. Fischer, 1956, *Die Gräber der Steinzeit im Saalegebiet*, Berlin; K. Günther, 1979, 'Die neolithischen Steinkammergräber von Atteln, Kr. Paderborn (Westfalen)', *Germania* 57, 153–61.

74 K. Kristiansen, 1982; T. Madsen, 1979; J. Brøndsted, *Nordische Vorzeit*, vol. 1, Neümunster, and references.

75 M. Strömberg, 1971; M. Shanks and C. Tilley, 1982.

76 P. Kjaerum, 1967.

77 C. Becker, 1959, 'Flint mining in Neolithic Denmark', *Antiquity* 33, 87–93; T. Sulimirski, 1960, 'Remarks concerning the distribution of some varieties of flint in Poland', *Swiatowit* 23, 281–307.

78 K. Randsborg, 1975, 'Social dimensions of Early Neolithic Denmark', *PPS* 41, 105–18. The method of land classification used however is not without problems since it relies on the nineteenth century situation.

79 E. Munck, 1886–7, 'Exposé des principales découvertes archéologiques faites à Obourg dans le courant des années 1879–86', *Bull. Soc. Anthrop. Bruxelles* 5; J. Verheylewghen, 1963, 'Evolution chronologique du néolithique au "Camp à Cayaux" de Spiennes . . .', *Helinium* 3, 3–38; F. Hubert, 1969, 'Fouilles au site minier néolithique de Spiennes', *Arch. Belg.* 111.

80 R. Caillaud and E. Lagnel, 1972, 'Le cairn et le crématoire néolithiques de la Hoguette, Fontenay-le-Marmion, Calvados', *Gallia Préhist.* 15, 137–98.

81 P. R. Giot, 1964, 'Résultats de l'identification pétrographique des materiaux des haches polies en France septentrionale', *Studien aus Alteuropa* 1, 123–33; C. T. Le Roux, 1971, 'A stone axe-factory in Brittany', *Antiquity* 45, 283–8; C. T. Le Roux, and G. Cordier, 1974, 'Etude petrographique des haches polies de Touraine', *Bull. Soc. Préhist. Franc.* 71, 335–54.

82 H. Case, 1973, 'A ritual site in north-east Ireland', in P. Kjaerum and G. Daniel (eds.), *Megalithic graves and ritual*, pp. 173–96, Copenhagen.

83 F. Pryor, 1976; R. Atkinson, 1965, 'Wayland's smithy', *Antiquity* 39, 126–33; P. Ashbee, 1970; J. Corcoran, 1969, 'The Cotswold-Severn group', in T. Powell (ed.),

*Megalithic enquiries in the west of Britain*, pp. 13–104, Liverpool; I. Kinnes, 1979; P. Ashbee, 1966; S. Piggott, 1962; cf. M. Shanks and C. Tilley, 1982.

84  A. Fleming, 1972; C. Renfrew, 1976; I. Kinnes, 1975, 'Monumental function in British Neolithic burial practices', *World Archaeol.* 7, 16–29; M. Shanks and C. Tilley, 1982.

85  W. Grimes, 1939, 'The excavation of Ty-Isaf long cairn, Brecknockshire', *PPS* 5, 119–42.

86  C. Renfrew, 1979; M. Herity, 1974, *Irish passage graves*, Dublin; T. Darvill, 1979, 'Court cairns, passage graves and social change in Ireland', *Man* 14, 311–27; M. O'Kelly, 1982; E. Twohig, 1981; G. Eogan, 1969, 'Excavations at Knowth, Co. Meath, 1968', *Antiquity* 49, 8–14; G. Eogan, 1974, 'Report on the excavations of some passage graves, unprotected inhumation burials and a settlement site at Knowth, Co. Meath', *Proc. Roy. Ir. Acad.* 74C, 11–112.

87  T. Clough and W. Cummins, 1979, and references; G. Sieveking, *et al.*, 1970, 'Prehistoric flint mines and their identification as sources of raw material', *Archaeometry* 14, 151–76.

88  Coles *et al.*, 1976; D. Peacock, 1969; A. Whittle, 1977.

89  J. Lanting and J. van der Waals, 1976; C. Malmros and H. Tauber, 1977, 'Kulstof–14 dateringer af dansk enkeltgravskultur', *Aarbøger* (1975) 78–95; W. Pape, 1978, 1979; V. Němejcová-Pavúková, 1981; C. Strahm, 1981, 'Der Stand der Erforschung der Schnurkeramik in der Schweiz', *Jahrschr. Mitteldeutsch. Vorq.* 64, 167–75.

90  R. Schmidt, 1945; E. Neustupný, 1973; B. Brukner, *et al.*, 1974; A. Medunová-Benešová, 1972; V. Němejcová-Pavúková, 1981; R. Ehrich and E. Pleslová-Štiková, 1968.

91  J. Kruk and S. Milisauskas, 1981; H. Behrens, 1973; H. Behrens, 1981, 'Der Walternienburger und der Bernburger Keramikstil und die Walternienburg-Bernburger Kultur', *Jahres. Mitteldeutsch. Vorg.* 63, 11–16; T. Wislanski, 1970; J. Machnik, 1981, 'Der Stand der Erforschung der schnurkeramischen Gruppen im Gebiet der VR Polen', *JMV* 64, 189–210.

92  M. Malmer, 1967.

93  K. Struve, 1955, *Die Einzelgrabkultur in Schleswig-Holstein und ihre kontinentale Beziehung*, Neumünster; M. Buchvaldek, 1966, 'Die Schnurkeramik in Mitteleuropa', *Pam. Arch.* 57, 126–171; H. Behrens, 1981, 'Radiokarbon- Daten für das Neolithikum des Mittelelbe-Saale-Gebietes', *JMV* 63, 189–93.

94  S. Müller, 1898, 'De jyske Enkeltgrave fra Stenalderen', *Aarbøger*, 157–202; P. Glob, 1945.

95  E.g. T. Sulimirski, 1968; K. Jażdżewski, 1965, in contrast to the views expressed by the authors in *JMV* 64, 1981.

96  C. Becker, 1950, 'Den Grubenkeramische Kultur i Danmark', *Aarbøger*, 153–274; K. Davidsen, 1978; C. Becker, 1981, 'Probleme der ältesten Phase der Einzelgrabkultur in Dänemark', *JMV* 64, 109–16.

97  K. Spång, *et al.*, 1976; L. Kaelas, 1976.

98  R. Ehrich and E. Pleslová-Štiková, 1968; E. Pleslová-Štiková, 1981, 'Chronologie und Siedlungsformen des Řivnáč-Kultur und Kugelamphorenkultur Böhmens', *JMV* 63, 159–71; R. Schmidt, 1945.

99  J. Kruk, 1973; T. Wislanksi, 1970; E. Jørgensen, 1977; F. Schlette, 1969, 'Das Siedlungwesen der Becherkulturen', in H. Behrens and F. Schlette (eds.), *Die neolithischen Becherkulturen in Gebiet der DDR und ihre europäischen Beziehungen*, pp. 155–68, Berlin; E. Neustupný, 1969, 'Economy of the Corded ware cultures', *Arch. Rozhl.* 21, 43–67.

100 M. Malmer, 1967; H. Behrens and E. Schröter, 1980; P. Modderman, 1977; S. Milisauskas and J. Kruk, 1978.
101 T. Mathiassen, 1939, 'Brundsø, en yngre Stenalders Boplads paa Als', *Aarbøger*, 1–55; J. Winther, 1926–8, *Lindø: en boplads fra Danmarks yngre Stenalder*, Rudkøbing; C. Becker, 1954, 'Stenalderbebyggelsen ved Store Valby; Vestsjaelland'. Problemer omkring tragtbaegerkulturens aeldste og ungste fase', *Aarbøger*, 127–97; P. Rowley-Conwy, 1979, 'Forkullet korn fra Lindebjerg', *Kuml* 1978, 159–71.
102 H. Waterbolk, 1956, 'Pollen spectra from Neolithic grave monuments in the northern Netherlands', *Palaeohistoria* 12, 39–51; H. Waterbolk, 1961, 'Preliminary report on the excavations at Anlo in 1957 and 1958', *Palaeohistoria* 8, 59–90.
103 L. Kaelas, 1976; S. Welinder, 1975, 'Agriculture, inland hunting, and sea hunting in the western and northern region of the Baltic, 6000–2000 BC', in W. Fitzhugh (ed.), *Prehistoric maritime adaptations of the circumpolar zone*, pp. 21–39, The Hague; N. Broadbent, 1979, *Coastal resources and settlement stability*, Uppsala.
104 J. van der Waals, 1964; H. Rostholm, 1978.
105 O. Frödin, 1910, 'En svensk palbyggnad fran stenaldern', *Fornvännen* 5, 29–77; M. Stenberger, 1977, *Nordische Vorzeit*, Neumünster.
106 M. Sakellaridis, 1979; A. Sherratt, 1981; H. Rostholm, 1978.
107 Earlier references and D. V. Clarke, 1976; S. Caulfield, 1978; D. Simpson, 1976, 'The Later Neolithic and Beaker settlement site at Northton, Isle of Harris', in C. Burgess and R. Miket (eds.), *Settlement and economy in the 3rd and 2nd millennia BC*, pp. 221–31, Oxford; G. Hillman, 1981; F. Pryor, 1978, *Excavations at Fengate, Peterborough, England: the second report*, Toronto.
108 R. Feustel and H. Ullrich, 1965, 'Totenhütten der neolithischen Walternienburger Gruppe', *Alt-Thüringen* 7, 105–202; D. Müller and H. Stahlhofen, 1981, 'Zwei Kollektivgräber der Bernburger Keramik aus dem Nordharzvorland', *JMV* 63, 27–65.
109 H. Behrens, 1964; 1973.
110 J. Kruk and S. Milisauskas, 1982, 'A multiple Neolithic burial at Bronocice, Poland', *Germania* 60, 211–16.
111 P. Kjaerum, 1967; H. Tauber, 1972; C. Becker, 1973, 'Problems of the megalithic "mortuary houses" in Denmark', in P. Kjaerum and G. Daniel (eds.), *Megalithic graves and ritual*, pp. 75–80, Copenhagen.
112 M. Strömberg, 1971; K. Ebbesen and E. Brinch Petersen, 1973; K. Ebbesen, 1975.
113 H. Behrens and E. Shröter, 1980.
114 W. Matthias, 1956, 'Ein schnurkeramisches Gräberfeld von Schafstadt, Kreis Merseburg', *JMV* 40, 51–108; M. Buchvaldek and D. Koutecky, 1970; E. Neustupný, 1978; E. Neustupný, 1983, 'The demography of prehistoric cemeteries', *Pam. Arch.* 74, 7–34.
115 E. Jørgensen, 1977; W. Pape, 1979.
116 M. Helms, 1980, 'Succession to high office in pre-Columbian circum-Caribbean chiefdoms', *Man* 15, 718–31.
117 J. Bakker, 1979; J. Lanting and J. Van der Waals, 1976; A. Sherratt, 1976, 'Resources, technology and trade: an essay in early European metallurgy', in G. Sieveking *et al.* (eds.), *Problems in economic and social archaeology*, pp. 557–82, London.
118 R. Ricquet, 1970, *Anthropologie du Néolithique et du Bronze Ancien*, Poitiers; K. Gerhardt, 1976, 'Anthropotypologie der Glockenbecherleute in ihren Ausschwärmelandschaften', in J. Lanting and J. Van der Waals (eds.), *Glockenbecher*

*Symposion*, pp. 147–64, Bussum; M. Henneberg, *et al.*, 1978, 'Natural selection and morphological variability: the case of Europe from Neolithic to modern times', *Current Anthropology* 19, 67–82.

119  E.g. S. Shennan, 1982; K. Kristiansen, 1982.

120  G. Bailloud, 1974; C. Masset, 1972, 'The megalithic tomb of La Chaussée-Tirancourt', *Antiquity* 46, 297–300.

121  R. Bradley, 1976, 'Maumbury Rings, Dorchester: the excavations of 1908–13', *Archaeologia* 105, 1–97; R. Atkinson, 1955, 'The Dorset cursus', *Antiquity* 29, 4–9; C. Renfrew, 1979; I. Kinnes, 1979; A. Thom, 1967, *Megalithic sites in Britain*, Oxford; A. Thom, 1971, *Megalithic lunar observatories*, Oxford.

122  I. Kinnes, 1979, and references.

123  S. Shennan, 1982.

## 7  Paths of change in the Mediterranean regions, 4000–before 2000 bc

1  E.g. H. de Lumley, 1976; P. Phillips, 1975; 1982; R. Chapman, 1978.

2  J. Guilaine, 1976; J. Guilaine, *et al.*, 1981, 'Datations C14 pour le Néolithique du Tavoliere (Italie)', *Bull. Soc. Préhist. Franc.* 78, 154–60; L. Bernabo Brea and M. Cavalier, 1960, *Meligunís-Lipára*, vol. 1, Palermo; P. Phillips, 1975. As earlier, the detail of the sequence remains to be finally established; Serra d'Alto for example may go earlier.

3  G. Barker, 1981; L. Barfield, 1971; B. Bagolini and P. Biagi, 1977; B. Bagolini, *et al.*, 1979, *Le Basse di Valcalaona*, Brescia; G. Guerreschi, 1967, *La Lagozza di Besnate e il Neolitico superiore Padano*, Como.

4  J. Guilaine, 1976 (ed.); 1976; P. Phillips, 1975; 1982.

5  J. Guilaine, 1976; 1980; J. Guilaine, *et al.*, 1982, 'Prehistoric human adaptations in Catalonia (Spain)', *J. Field Archaeol.* 9, 407–16; H. Savory, 1968; A. Muñoz 1965, *La cultura neolitica Catalana de los sepulcros de fosa*, Barcelona; P. Acosta, 1976; M. Pellicer, 1963; G. Leisner and V. Leisner, 1951; E. Whittle and J. Arnaud, 1975.

6  R. Whitehouse, 1981; G. Barker, 1981; L. Barfield, 1971; L. Barfield and A. Broglio, 1976, 'Die neolithische Siedlung von Fimon-Molino Casarotto', *Arch. Austriaca* 13, 137–57.

7  J. Guilaine, 1976 (ed.); 1976; P. Phillips, 1975; 1982; J. Courtin, 1974, *Le Néolithique de la Provence*, Paris; L. Méroc and G. Simonnet, 1969, 'Le village néolithique Chasséen de Saint-Michel-du-Touch, commune de Toulouse (Haute-Garonne)', *Bull. Soc. Mérid. Spéléol. Préhist*, 14–15, 27–37.

8  J. Guilaine, 1976; R. Whitehouse, 1972, 'The rock-cut tombs of the central Mediterranean', *Antiquity* 46, 275–81; U. Rellini, 1925, 'Scavi preistorici a Serra d'Alto', *Notiz. Scavi* (series 6) 1, 257–95; A. Mosso, 1910, 'La necropoli di Molfetta', *Monumenti Antichi* 20, 237–56; for cave deposits paper by R. Whitehouse, Deya conference 1983, and e.g. S. Tinè and F. Isetti, 1982, 'Culto neolitico delle acque e recenti scavi nella Grotta Scaloria', *Bull. Paletnol. Ital.* 82, 31–70.

9  B. Hallam, *et al.*, 1976, 'Obsidian in the west Mediterranean: characterisation by neutron activation analysis and optical emission spectroscopy', *PPS* 42, 85–110; L. Barfield, 1981, 'Patterns of north Italian trade, 5000–2000 bc', in G. Barker and R. Hodges (eds.), *Archaeology and Italian society*, pp. 27–51, Oxford.

10  L. Barfield, 1971; 1981, and earlier references.

11  L. Mèroc and G. Simonnet, 1979, 'Les sépultures chasséennes de Saint-Michel-du-Touch (Haute Garonne)', *Bull. Soc. Préhist. Franc.* 76, 379–403.

12  Earlier references and P. Acosta, 1976; M. Hopf, and M. Pellicer, 1970, 'Neolit-
    ische Getreidefunde in der Höhle von Nerja (prov. Malaga)', *Madrid. Mitteil.* 11,
    17–34; J. Arnaud, 1971, 'Os povoados "neo-eneoliticos" de Famaõ e Aboboreira
    (Ciladas, Vila Vicosa). Noticio preliminar', *Act. 11 Cong. Nac. Arqueol.* 199–221;
    J. Arnaud and T. Gamito, 1972, 'O povoado fortificado neo-eneolitico da Serra das
    Bautas (Carenque, Belas)', *Arq. Port.* (series 3) 6, 119–61; J. Arnaud, *et al.*, 1971.

13  R. Chapman, 1981*a*; G. Leisner and V. Leisner, 1943; 1951; 1956; 1965; C.
    Marquez, *et al.*, 1952.

14  Earlier references and V. Leisner, 1967.

15  G. Leisner and V. Leisner, 1951; E. Whittle and J. Arnaud, 1975.

16  H. Savory, 1968; C. Renfrew, 1967, for local development.

17  P. Bosch-Gimpera, 1967, 'Civilisation mégalithique portugaise et civilisations
    espagnoles', *L'Anthrop.* 71, 1–48; H. Savory, 1968.

18  M. Cipollini Sampò, 1982, 'Ambiente, economia e societa dall 'eneolitico all' età
    del bronzo in Italia sun-orientale', *Dialoghi di archeologia* 4, 27–38; C. Renfrew
    and R. Whitehouse, 1974, 'The Copper Age of peninsular Italy and the Aegean',
    *Ann. Brit. School Athens* 69, 343–90; F. Biancofiore, 1967; J. Guilaine, 1976;
    G. Barker, 1981; L. Barfield, 1971; G. Colini, 1900; P. Phillips, 1975; 1982.

19  R. Whitehouse, 1981.

20  G. Barker, 1981; S. Puglisi, 1965, 'Sulla facies protoappenninica in Italia', *Att 6
    Congresso UIPP 1962* 2, 403–7.

21  L. Barfield, 1971; F. Zorzi, 1953, 'Resti di un Abitato capannicolo Eneolitico alle
    Colombare di Negrar', *Act IV Congr. Int. Quaternaire 1953*.

22  J. Guilaine, 1976 (ed.); 1976; P. Phillips, 1975; P. Phillips, 1982, especially p. 65 on
    rainfall.

23  F. Biancofiore, 1967; H. Müller-Karpe, 1974, *Handbuch der Vorgeschichte, III,
    Kupferzeit: 2, Regesten*, Munich; R. Whitehouse 1967, 'The megalithic monu-
    ments of south-east Italy', *Man* 2, 267–310; P. Sestieri, 1947, 'Nuovi resultati
    degli scavi nella necropoli preistorica di Paestum', *Riv. Sci. Preist.* 2, 283–90; G.
    Voza, 1964, 'Gli ultimi scavi della necropoli del Gaudo', *Atti 8 e 9 Riunione UIPP*,
    265–74; G. Onerato, 1960 *La Ricerca archeologica in Irpinia*, Avellino; R.
    Holloway, (ed.) 1973, *Buccino: the Eneolithic necropolis of San Antonio*, Rome;
    G. Barker, 1981.

24  G. Barker, 1981; G. Colini, 1903, 'Tombe eneolitiche del Viterbese (Roma)', *Bull.
    Paletnol. Ital.* 29, 150–86; L. Pernier, 1905, 'Tombe eneolitiche del Viterbese
    (Roma)', *Bull. Paletnol. Ital.* 31, 145–53.

25  L. Barfield, 1971; G. Colini, 1900.

26  E.g. D. Trump, 1965, *Central and southern Italy*, London; B. Barich, *et al.*, 1968,
    'Trovamenti eneolitici presso Tarquinia', *Origini* 2, 173–246; A. Radmilli, 1974,
    *Popoli e civiltà dell' Italia antica, vol. 1: dal Paleolitico all' Età del Bronzo*,
    Rome; K. Branigan, 1966, 'Prehistoric relations between Italy and the Aegean',
    *Bull. Paletnol. Ital.* 75, 97–109.

27  L. Barfield, 1971; A. Gallay, 1972, 'Récherches préhistoriques au Petit-Chasseur,
    Sion', *Helvetia Archaeol.* 3, 35–61; G. Gallay and K. Spindler, 1972, 'Le Petit
    Chasseur – chronologische und kulturelle Probleme', *Helvetia Archaeol.* 3,
    62–87.

28  J. Crowfoot, 1926, 'Note on excavations in a Ligurian Cave, 1907–09', *Man* 26,
    83–8.

29  J. Guilaine, 1976; O. Roudil and G. Bérard, 1981, *Les sépultures mégalithiques du
    Var*, Paris; G. Daniel, 1960, *The prehistoric chamber tombs of France*, London; S.

Gagnière, 1968, 'Informations archéologiques. Circonscription des antiquités préhistoriques, Provence-Côte d'Azur-Corse', *Gallia Préhist.* 11, 493–528.

30 J. Arnal, 1976, 'L'art protohistorique: les statues menhirs de France', in J. *Guilaine (ed.), Le préhistoire française,* vol. 2, pp. 211–21.

31 J. Guilaine, 1976.

32 P. Phillips, 1975.

33 L. Siret, 1893, 'L'Espagne préhistorique', *Révue Questions Scient.*; L. Siret, 1913, *Questions de chronologie et d'ethnographie ibériques,* vol. 1, Paris; H. Siret and L. Siret, 1887, *Les premiers âges du métal dans le sud-est de l'Espagne,* Anvers; G. Leisner and V. Leisner, 1943; M. Almagro and A. Arribas, 1963; A. Arribas, *et al.,* 1979, 'Excavaciones en los Millares (Santa Fe, Almería): campanas de 1978 y 1979', *Cuadernos Prehist. Univ. Granada* 4, 61–110; A. Arribas and F. Molina, 1982, 'Los Millares: neue Ausgrabungen in der kupferzeitlichen Siedlung (1978–1981)', *Madrider Mitteil.,* 23, 9–32; R. Chapman, 1981a; 1981b; 1981c; R. Chapman, forthcoming 'Los Millares y la cronologia relativa de la Edad del Cobre en el S. E. de España', *Cuadernos Prehist. Univ. Granada* 6, 1983.

34 F. Gusi, 1976, 'Resumen de la labor en el Yaciamento de Tabernas (Almería)', *Notic. Arq. Hisp. Prehist.* 5, 201–5; M. Almagro Gorbea, 1973, *El poblado y la necropolis de El Barranquete (Almería),* Madrid; M. Almagro Gorbea, 1977, 'El recientemente destruido poblado de 'El Tarajal', *XIV Congresso Nac. Arq. (Vitoria 1975),* pp. 305–18; A. Arribas, *et al.,* 1977, 'El poblado eneolitico de "El Malagon" de Cullar-Baza (Granada)', *XIV Congresso Nac. Arq.* (Vitoria, 1975), 319–324; J. Guilaine, 1980; W. Schüle, 1980, *Orce und Galera,* Mainz. Note also the site of Cabezo de la Cueva del Plomo (Mazarron, Murcia), recently investigated and with C14 dates *c.* 3000 bc. This has a bastioned stone wall and a second internal wall. If the dates are valid, the enclosed type of site goes back to the beginning of the third mbc at least: A. Muñoz, lecture to 1983 Montpellier conference, and R. Chapman, pers. comm.

35 E.g. V. Leisner, 1967; H. Savory, 1968; A. do Paço and E. Sangmeister, 1956.

36 J. Guilaine, 1976, p. 203; E. Sangmeister and H. Schubart, 1981.

37 E.g. C. Renfrew, 1967.

38 R. Chapman, 1978; A. Arribas, 1968, 'Las bases economicas del Neolitico al Bronce', in M. Tadurell (ed.), *Estudios de economia antiqua de la peninsula Iberica,* pp. 33–60, Barcelona.

39 R. Chapman, 1978.

40 It may be argued however that a range of site locations and types was one means of coping with aridity, and indeed the sparse evidence from before the third millennium bc in Almeria could suggest that it was in some ways marginal for agricultural settlement before such suggested developments as water control and storage and site hierarchy (R. Chapman, pers. comm.).

41 A. do Paço and E. Sangmeister, 1956; H. Savory, 1968, and fig. 41 for the surrounding area.

42 E. Sangmeister and H. Schubart, 1972; 1981.

43 J. Arnaud, *et al.,* 1971; E. Whittle and J. Arnaud, 1975.

44 R. Chapman, 1981a, and references.

45 M. Almagro and A. Arribas, 1963, fig. 118; G. Leisner and V. Leisner, 1943; 1965; F. Collantes de Terán, 1969, 'El Dolmen de Matarrubilla', *Tartessos y sus problemas: V Symposion Internacional de Prehistoria Peninsular,* pp. 47–62, Barcelona.

46 R. Harrison and A. Gilman, 1977, 'Trade in the second and third millennia B.C.

between the Maghreb and Iberia', in V. Markotić (ed.), *Ancient Europe and the Mediterranean*, pp. 90–104.

47 H. Savory, 1968, p. 165; R. Harrison, 1974, 'A reconsideration of the Iberian background to Iberian metallurgy', *Palaeohist.* 63–105. There are suggestions of copper mining as far back as the fourth mbc in Huelva in south-west Spain (B. Rothenberg and A. Blanco-Freijeiro, (eds.), 1981, *Ancient mining and metallurgy in south-west Spain*, London) but radiocarbon dates from the area are so far all later Bronze Age. R. Chapman, pers. comm.

48 C. Renfrew, 1967, p. 278.

49 R. Chapman, 1981*b*, table 4.

50 E.g. B. Blance, 1961, 'Early Bronze Age colonists in Iberia', *Antiquity* 35, 192–202; M. Almagro and A. Arribas, 1963; H. Savory, 1968. And behind these lies V. Childe, 1957, *The dawn of European civilisation*, London, p. 284: 'The urbanization of the Almerian economy . . . is presumably a reflection, however indirect, of Oriental cities' demand for metal.'

51 For an emergent sequence in Catalonia, see J. Guilaine, *et al.*, 1982, 'Prehistoric human adaptations in Catalonia (Spain)', *J. Field Archaeol.* 9, 407–16. For the interior, J. Guilaine, 1976, p. 205.

52 J. Lewthwaite, 1981; J. Cherry, 1981, 'Pattern and process in the earliest colonisation of the Mediterranean islands', *PPS* 47, 41–68.

53 M. Fernandez-Miranda and W. Waldren, 1974, 'El abrigo de Son Matge (Valdermosa) y la periodizacion de prehistoria mallorquina mediante los analisis de carbono-14', *Trabajos de Prehistoria* 31, 297–304. Both fortifications and rock-cut tombs in the Balearics may go back to the third millennium; J. Lewthwaite, pers. comm.

54 D. Trump, 1966, *Skorba*, London; J. D. Evans, 1971, *The prehistoric antiquities of the Maltese Islands*, London; C. Renfrew, 1973, *Before civilisation: the radiocarbon revolution and prehistoric Europe*, London.

# SELECT BIBLIOGRAPHY

Acosta, P., 1976. Excavaciones en el yaciamento de El Garcel, Antas (Almería). *Noticario Arqueologia Hispanica Prehistoria* 5, 187–91.

Albrethsen, S. E. and Brinch Petersen, E., 1976. Excavation of a Mesolithic cemetery at Vedbaek, Denmark. *Acta Archaeologica* 47, 1–28.

Almagro, M. and Arribas, A., 1963. *El poblado y la necropolis megaliticos de Los Millares*, Bibliotheca praehistorica Hispana III. Madrid: Instituto español de prehistoria.

Andersen, N. H., 1981. Sarup: befaestede neolitiske anlaeg og deres baggrund. *Kuml* 1980, 63–103.

ApSimon, A. M., 1976. Ballynagilly and the beginning and end of the Irish Neolithic. In S. de Laet (ed.), *Acculturation and continuity in Atlantic Europe*, pp. 15–30. Brugge: de Tempel.

Arnaud, J., De Oliveira, V. and Jorge, V., 1971. O povoado fortificado neo-eneolitico do Penedo de Lexim (Mafra): campanha preliminar de escavaçõe – 1970. *Arqueologo Portugues* 5, 97–131.

Ashbee, P., 1966. The Fussell's Lodge long barrow excavations, 1957. *Archaeologia*, 100, 1–80.

  1970. *The earthen long barrow in Britain.* London: Dent.

Bagolini, B. and Biagi, P., 1977. Current culture history issues in the study of the Neolithic of northern Italy. *Bulletin of the Institute of Archaeology of London* 14, 143–66.

Bailloud, G., 1974. *Le Néolithique dans le Bassin Parisien*, Paris: CNRS.

Bakels, C. C. 1978. *Four Linearbandkeramik settlements and their environment: a palaeoecological study of Sittard, Stein, Elsloo and Hienheim.* (Analecta praehistorica Leidensia XI). Leiden: Leiden University Press.

Bakker, J. A., 1979. *The TRB West Group: studies in the chronology and geography of the makers of Hunebeds and Tiefstich pottery.* Amsterdam: Universiteit van Amsterdam, Subfaculteit der pre-en protohistorie.

Bandi, H., 1967. Die Auswertung von Ausgrabungen im neolithischen Uferdorf Seeberg, Burgäschisee-Süd, Kt. Bern. *Palaeohistoria* 12, 17–32.

Barfield, L., 1971. *Northern Italy.* London: Thames and Hudson.

Barker, G., 1975. Prehistoric territories and economies in central Italy. In E. Higgs (ed.), *Palaeoeconomy*, pp. 111–75. Cambridge: Cambridge University Press.

Barker, G., 1981. *Landscape and society: prehistoric central Italy.* London: Academic Press.

Barth, F., 1969. *Ethnic groups and boundaries: the social organization of culture difference.* Boston: Little, Brown and Company.

Bay-Petersen, J., 1978. Animal exploitation in Mesolithic Denmark. In P. Mellars (ed.), *The early postglacial settlement of northern Europe*, pp. 115–45. London: Duckworth.

Behrens, H., 1964. *Die neolithischen-frühmetalzeitlichen Tierskelettfunde der Alten Welt*. (Veröffentlichungen des Landesmuseums für Vorgeschichte in Halle 19). Berlin: VEB Deutscher Verlag der Wissenschaften.

1973. *Die Jungsteinzeit im Mittelelbe–Saale Gebiet*. Berlin: VEB Deutscher Verlag der Wissenschaften.

Behrens, H. and Schröter, E., 1980. *Siedlungen und Gräber der Trichterbecherkultur und Schnurkeramik bei Halle (Saale)*. (Veröffentlichungen des Landesmuseums für Vorgeschichte in Halle 34). Berlin: VEB Deutscher Verlag der Wissenschaften.

Benac, A., 1973. *Obre II: a Neolithic settlement of the Butmir group at Gornje Polje'*, Wissenschaftliche Mitteilungen des Bosnisch-Herzegowinischen Landesmuseums (Sarajevo) 3, Heft A, pp. 5–91.

Bender, B., 1978 Gatherer-hunter to farmer: a social perspective. *World Archaeology*. 10, 204–22.

Berciu, D., 1961. *Contribuţii la problemele Neoliticului în Rominîa în lumîna noilor cercetări*. Bucharest: Editura Academiei Republicii Populare Romîne.

1966. *Cultura Hamangia*. Bucharest: Editura Academiei Republicii Populare Romîne.

Biancofiore, F., 1967. La necropoli eneolitica di Laterza: origini e sviluppo dei gruppi 'protoappenninici' in Apulia. *Origini* 1, 195–300.

Bietti, A., 1981. The Mesolithic cultures in Italy: new activities in connection with Upper Palaeolithic cultural traditions. In B. Gramsch (ed.), *Mesolithikum in Europa*, pp. 33–50. Berlin: VEB Deutscher Verlag der Wissenschaften.

Bille Henriksen, B., 1976. *Svaerdborg I. Excavations 1943–44*. Copenhagen: Akademisk Forlag.

Binford, L. R., 1978. *Nunamiut Ethnoarchaeology*. New York: Academic Press.

Bintliff, J., 1976. The plain of western Macedonia and the site of Nea Nikomedeia. *PPS* 42, 241–62.

1977. *Natural environment and human settlement in prehistoric Greece*. Oxford: BAR s 28.

Bognár-Kutzián, I., 1963. *The Copper Age cemetery of Tiszapolgár–Basatanya*. Budapest: Akadémiai Kiadó.

1972. *The Early Copper Age Tiszapolgár culture in the Carpathian basin*. Budapest: Akadémiai Kiadó.

Bogucki, P. I. and Grygiel, R., 1981*a*. The household cluster at Brześć Kujawaski 3: small site methodology in the Polish lowlands. *World Archaeology*. 13, 59–72.

1981*b*. Early Neolithic site at Brześć Kujawski, Poland: preliminary report on the 1976–79 excavations. *Journal of Field Archaeology* 8, 9–27.

Bökönyi, S., 1974. *History of domestic mammals in central and eastern Europe*. Budapest: Akadémiai Kiadó.

1978. The earliest waves of domestic horses in east Europe. *Journal of Indo-European Studies* 6, 17–70.

Bolomey, A., 1973. The present state of knowledge of mammal exploitation during the Epipalaeolithic and the earliest Neolithic in the territory of Romania. In J. Matoksi (ed.), *Domestikationsforschung und Geschichte der Haustiere*, pp. 197–203. Budapest: Akademiai Kiado.

Boroneanţ, V., 1970. La période épipaléolithique sur la rive roumaine des Portes de Fer du Danube. *Praehistorische Zeitschrift* 45, 1–25.

1973. Recherches archéologiques sur la culture Schela Cladovei de la zone des Portes de Fer. *Dacia* 17, 5–39.

1981. Betrachtungen über das Epipaläolithikum (Mesolithikum) in Rumänien. In B.

Gramsch (ed.), *Mesolithikum in Europa*, pp. 289–94. Berlin: VEB Deutscher Verlag der Wissenschaften.

Bottema, S., 1979. Pollen analytical investigations in Thessaly (Greece). *Palaeohistoria* 21, 19–20.

Bottema, S. and Ottaway, B. S., 1982. Botanical malacological and archaeological zonation of settlement deposits at Gomolava. *Journal of Archaeological Science* 9, 221–46.

Boureux, M. and Coudart, A., 1978. Implantations des premiers paysans sédentaires dans la vallée de l'Aisne. *Bull. Soc. Préhist. Franc.* 75, 341–60.

Brandt, K., 1967. *Studien über steinerne Axte und Beile der jüngeren Steinzeit und der Stein-Kupferzeit Nordwestdeutschlands*. Hildesheim: Lax.

Brinch Petersen, E., 1973. A survey of the Late Palaeolithic and Mesolithic of Denmark. In S. K. Kozlowski (ed.), *The Mesolithic in Europe*, pp. 77–127. Warsaw: Warsaw University Press.

Broglio, A., 1971. Risultati preliminari delle ricerche sui complessi epipaleolitici della valle dell' Adige. *Preistoria Alpina* 7, 135–241.

Broholm, H., 1931. Nouvelles trouvailles du plus ancien âge de la pierre: les trouvailles de Holmegaard et de Svaerdborg. *Mem. Antiq. Nord* 1926–31, 1–128.

Brukner, B., 1971. Gomolava à Hrtkovci, site préhistorique à plusieurs couches. In G. Novak (ed.), *Époque préhistorique et protohistorique en Yougoslavie: recherches et résultats*, pp. 175–6. Beograd: Société archéologique de Yougoslavie.

Brukner, B., Jovanovic, B. and Tasic, N., 1974. *Praistorija Vojvodine*. Novi Sad: Institut za izucavanje istorije vojvodine.

Buchvaldek, M. and Koutecky, D., 1970. *Vikletice: ein schnukeramisches Gräberfeld*. Praha: Universita Karlova.

Buttler, W. and Haberey, W., 1936. *Die bandkeramische Ansiedlung bei Köln–Lindenthal*. Berlin and Leipzig: Walter de Gruyter.

Cârciumaru, M., 1973. Analyse pollinique des coprolithes livrés par quelques stations archéologiques des deux bords du Danube dans la zone des Portes de Fer. *Dacia* 17, 53–60.

Caulfield, S., 1978. Neolithic fields: the Irish evidence. In C. Bowen and P. Fowler (eds.), *Early land allotment*, pp. 137–44. Oxford: BAR 48.

Cardini, L., 1946. Gli strati mesolitici e paleolitici della Caverna delle Arene Candide. *Rivista di Studi Liguri* 12, 29–37.

Cernych, E., 1978. Aibunar – a Balkan copper mine of the fourth millennium B.C. *PPS* 44, 203–17.

1981. Formyrovanye Tripolyisko–Cucutensko kulturnae obshnoste. *Studia Praehistorica* 5–6, 5–47.

Chapman, J., 1981. *The Vinča culture of south-east Europe*. Oxford. BAR s 117.

Chapman, R., 1978. The evidence for prehistoric water control in south-east Spain. *Journal of Arid Environments* 1, 261–74.

1981*a*. The megalithic tombs of Iberia. In B. Cunliffe *et al.* (eds.), *Antiquity and man*, pp. 93–106. London: Thames and Hudson.

1981*b*. The emergence of formal disposal areas and the 'problem' of megalithic tombs in prehistoric Europe. In R. Chapman *et al.* (eds.), *The archaeology of death*, pp. 71–81. Cambridge: Cambridge University Press.

1981*c*. Archaeological theory and communal burial in prehistoric Europe. In I. Hodder *et al.* (eds.), *Pattern of the past*, pp. 387–411. Cambridge: Cambridge University Press.

Childe, V., 1929. *The Danube in prehistory*. Oxford: Clarendon Press.

Chropovský, B., (ed.), 1973. *Symposium über die Enstehung und Chronologie der Badener Kultur.* Bratislava: Slovak Academy of Sciences Press.

Clark, J. G. D. 1954. *Excavations at Star Carr.* Cambridge: Cambridge University Press.

1972. *Star Carr: a case study in bioarchaeology.* McCaleb Module 10 in Anthropology. Reading, Mass.: Addison-Wesley Modular Publications.

1975. *The Earlier Stone Age settlement of Scandinavia.* Cambridge: Cambridge University Press.

Clark, R. M., 1975. A calibration curve for radiocarbon dates. *Antiquity* 49, 251–66.

Clarke, D. L., 1976. Mesolithic Europe: the economic basis. In G. de G. Sieveking, I. H. Longworth, and K. E. Wilson (eds.), *Problems in social and economic archaeology*, pp. 449–82. London: Duckworth.

Clarke, D. V., 1976. *The Neolithic village at Skara Brae, Orkney. 1972–3 excavations: an interim report.* Edinburgh: HMSO.

Clason, A. T., 1979. The farmers of Gomolava in the Vinča and La Tenè period. *Palaeohistoria* 21, 41–82.

Clough, T. H. M. and Cummins, W. A. (eds.), 1979. *Stone axe studies.* London: CBA (Res. Rep. 23).

Colini, G. A., 1900. Il sepolcreto di Remedello Sotto nel Bresciano e il periodo eneolitico in Italia. *Bull. Paletnologia Italiana* 26, 57–101, 202–67.

Comşa, E., 1971. Données sur la civilisation de Dudeşti. *Praehistorische Zeitschrift* 46, 195–249.

1974. Quelques données concernant le commencement du processus de l'indo-européisation dans le nord-est de la péninsule Balkanique. *Thracia* 3, 15–20.

Davidsen, K., 1978. *The final TRB culture in Denmark.* Copenhagen: Akademisk Forlag.

De Lumley, H., (ed.) 1976. *La préhistoire française*, 1, 2. Paris: CNRS.

Dennell, R., 1978. *Early farming in Bulgaria from the VI to the III millennia BC.* Oxford: BAR s 45.

Dennell, R. W. and Webley, D., 1975. Prehistoric settlement and land-use in southern Bulgaria. In E. Higgs (ed.), *Palaeoeconomy*, pp. 97–109. Cambridge: Cambridge University Press.

Dinu, M., 1980. Le complexe Horodiştea–Folteşti et le problème de l'indo-européanisation de l'éspace carpato-danubien. In R. Vulpe (ed.), *Actes 2 Congrès Int. Thracologie*, pp. 35–48. Bucharest: Editura Academiei Republicii Socialiste România.

Dolukhanov, P. M. 1979. *Ecology and economy in Neolithic eastern Europe.* London: Duckworth.

Dombay, J., 1960. *Die Siedlung und das Gräberfeld in Zengövárkony: Beiträge zur Kultur des Aeneolithikums in Ungarn.* Budapest: Ungarische Akademie der Wissenschaften.

Do Paço, A. and Sangmeister, E., 1956. Vila Nova de S. Pedro, eine befestigte Siedlung der Kupferzeit in Portugal. *Germania* 34, 211–30.

Dumitrescu, V., 1954. *Hăbăşeşti.* Bucharest: Editura Academiei Republicii Populare Romîne.

1965. Căscioarele: a Late Neolithic settlement on the lower Danube. *Archaeology* 18, 34–40.

1966. New discoveries at Gumelniţa. *Archaeology* 19, 162–72.

1980. *The Neolithic settlement at Rast (South-west Oltenia, Romania).* Oxford: BAR s 72.

Dumitrescu, V. and Banateanu, T., 1965. À propos d'un soc de charrue primitive, en bois de cerf, découvert dans la station néolithique de Căscioarele. *Dacia* 9, 59–67.

Dumitrescu, V., Bolomey, A. and Mogosanu, F., 1982. The prehistory of Romania from the earliest times to 1000 BC. *Cambridge Ancient History* III, part 1, 1–74. Cambridge: Cambridge University Press.

Ebbesen, K., 1975. *Die jüngere Trichterbecherkultur auf den danischen Inseln*. Copenhagen: Akademisk Forlag.

Ebbesen, K. and Brinch Petersen, E. B. 1973. Fuglebaeksbanken, en jaettestue pa Stevns. *Aarbøger*, 73–106.

Ehrich, R. W. and Pleslová-Štiková, E., 1968. *Homolka: an Eneolithic site in Bohemia*. American School of Prehistoric Research Bulletin 26.

Escalon de Fonton, M. E., 1976a. Les civilisations de l'Epipaléolithique et du Mésolithique en Provence littorale. In H. de Lumley (ed.), *La préhistoire française*, 1, 2, pp. 1367–8. Paris: CNRS.

1976b. Les civilisations de l'Epipaléolithique et du Mésolithique en Languedoc oriental. In H. de Lumley (ed.), *La préhistoire française*, 1, 2, pp. 1382–9. Paris: CNRS.

Evans, J. D., 1971. Neolithic Knossos – the growth of a settlement. *Proceedings of the Prehistoric Society* 37 (2), 95–117.

Evans, J. D. and Renfrew, C., 1968. *Excavations at Saliagos near Antiparos*. BSA Supplement, 5. London: Cambridge University Press.

Farruggia, J. P., Kuper, R., Lüning, J. and Stehli, P., 1973. *Der bandkeramische Siedlungsplatz Langweiler 2, Gem. Aldenhoven, Kr. Düren*. Rheinische Ausgrabungen 13. Bonn: Rheinland-Verlag GMBH.

Fewkes, V. J., Goldman, H. and Ehrich, R. W., 1933. Excavations at Starčevo, Yugoslavia, seasons of 1931 and 1932: a preliminary report. *Bulletin American School Prehistoric Research* 9, 33–54.

Fleming, A., 1971. The genesis of pastoralism in European prehistory. *World Archaeology* 4, 179–91.

1973. Tombs for the living. *Man* 8, 177–93.

Freises, A., Montjardin, R. and Guilaine, J., 1976. Le gisement cardial de l'Île Corrège à Port-Leucate (Aude). *Actes XXe Congrès Préhist. France*, 277–94.

Frenzel, B., 1966. Climatic change in the Atlantic–Sub Boreal transition on the northern hemisphere: botanical evidence. In J. Sawyer (ed.), *Proceedings of the first international symposium on world climate 8000–0 BC* pp. 99–123. London: Royal Meterological Society.

1978. Postglaziale Klimaschwankungen im südwestlichen Mitteleuropa. In B. Frenzel (ed.), *Dendrochronologie und postglaziale Klimaschwankungen in Europa*, pp. 297–322. Wiesbaden: Steiner.

Furger, A., Orcel, A., Stöckli, W. and Suter, P., 1977. *Die neolithischen Ufersiedlungen von Twann. Vorbericht*. Bern: Stampfli.

Galbenu, D., 1963. Neolitičeskaya masterkaya dlya obrabotki ukrašenii v Hîrşove. *Dacia* 7, 501–9.

Garašanin, D., 1954. *Starčevačka kultura*. Ljubljana.

Garašanin, M., 1978. Betrachtungen zum Salcuţa–Krivodol–Bubanj–Komplex auf dem mittleren Balkan. *Studia Praehistorica* 1–2, 101–8.

1982. The Stone Age in the central Balkan area; the Eneolithic period in the central Balkan Area. *Cambridge Ancient History* III, part 1, pp. 75–162. Cambridge: Cambridge University Press.

Geddes, D., 1980. De la chasse au troupeau en Mediterranée Occidentale. *Archives d'Écologie Préhistorique* 5. Toulouse: Ecole de Hautes Études en Sciences Sociales.

Georgiev, G. I., 1961. Kulturgruppen der Jungstein – und der Kupferzeit in der Ebene von Thrazien (Südbulgarien). In J. Böhm and S. J. de Laet (eds.), *L'Europe à la fin de l'âge de la pierre*, pp. 45–100. Prague: Editions de l'Académie tchéchoslovaque des Sciences.

1965. The Azmak mound in southern Bulgaria. *Antiquity* 39, 6–8.

Georgiev, G. I., Merpert, N. J., Katincharov, R. V. and Dimitrov, D. G., 1979. *Ezero, Rannobronzovoto Selishe*. Sofia: Bulgarian Academy of Sciences.

Gimbutas, M., 1974a. Achilleion: a Neolithic mound in Thessaly. *Journal of Field Archaeology* 1, 277–302.

1974b. *The gods and goddesses of Old Europe*. London: Thames and Hudson.

Gimbutas, M. (ed.), 1976. *Neolithic Macedonia as reflected by excavation at Anza, south east Yugoslavia*. Monumenta Archaeologica, 1. Los Angeles: Institute of Archaeology, University of California, Los Angeles.

Glob, P. V., 1945. Studien over den jyske Enkeltgravskultur. *Aarbøger* 1944, 1–283.

Gramsch, B. (ed.), 1981. *Mesolithikum in Europa* (2. Internationales Symposium Potsdam 1978). Berlin: VEB Deutscher Verlag der Wissenschaften.

Guilaine, J., 1970. Les fouilles de la grotte de Gazel (Salèlles-Cabardès, Aude). *Bull. Soc. Études Scient. Aude* 70, 61–73.

1976. *Premiers bergers et paysans de l'occident Méditerranéen*. Paris: Mouton.

1979. The earliest Neolithic in the west Mediterranean: a new appraisal. *Antiquity* 53, 22–30.

1980. La chronologie du Néolithique Ibérique. *Travaux de l'institut d'art préhistorique* (Toulouse) 22, 231–44.

Guilaine, J., (ed.), 1976. *La préhistoire française*, 11. Paris: CNRS.

Guilaine, J., *et al.*, 1979. *L'abri Jean Cros*. Toulouse: Centre d'anthropologie des sociétés rurales.

Guyan, W. U., 1967. Die jungsteinzeitlichen Moordörfer im Weier bei Thayngen. *Zeitschrift für Schweizerische Archäologie und Kunstgeschichte* 25, 1–39.

Halstead, P., 1977. Prehistoric Thessaly: the submergence of civilisation. In J. Bintliff (ed.), *Mycenaean geography*, pp. 23–32. Cambridge: British Association for Myceaean Studies.

1981a. From determinism to uncertainty: social storage and the rise of the Minoan palace. In A. Sheridan and G. Bailey (eds.), *Economic archaeology*, pp. 187–213. Oxford: BAR s 96.

1981b. Counting sheep in Neolithic and Bronze Age Greece. In I. Hodder *et al.* (eds.), *Pattern of the past*, pp. 307–39. Cambridge: Cambridge University Press.

Hansen, J. and Renfrew, J., 1978. Palaeolithic–Neolithic seed remains at Franchthi Cave, Greece. *Nature* 271, 349–52.

Hauptmann, H., 1981. *Die deutschen Ausgrabungen auf der Otzaki-Magula in Thessalien, III: das späte Neolithikum und das Chalkolithikum*. Bonn: Rudolf Habelt.

Higgs, E. (ed.), 1972. *Papers in economic prehistory*. Cambridge: Cambridge University Press.

1975. *Palaeoeconomy*. Cambridge: Cambridge University Press.

Higgs, E. S. and Jarman, M. R., 1972. The origins of animal and plant husbandry. In E. Higgs (ed.), *Papers in economic prehistory*, pp. 3–13. Cambridge: Cambridge University Press.

Hillman, G., 1981. Reconstructing crop husbandry practices from charred remains of crops. In R. Mercer (ed.), *Farming practice in British prehistory*, pp. 123–62. Edinburgh: Edinburgh University Press.

Hodder, I., 1982, *Symbols in action*. Cambridge. Cambridge University Press.

Huber, B. and Merz, W., 1963. Jahrringchronologie Synchronisierung der jung-steinzeitlichen Siedlungen Thayngen-Weier und Burgäschisee-Süd und -Süd-west. *Germania* 41, 1–9.

Indrelid, S., 1975. Problems relating to the Early Mesolithic settlement of southern Norway. *Norwegian Archaeological Review* 8, 1–18.

Ingold, T., 1980. *Hunters, pastoralists and ranchers*. Cambridge: Cambridge University Press.

Ivanov, I. S., 1978. Les fouilles archéologiques de la nécropole chalcolithique à Varna (1972–1975). *Studia Praehistorica* 1–2, 13–26.

1983. Le Chalcolithique en Bulgarie et dans la nécropole de Varna. In A. Poulter (ed.), *Ancient Bulgaria*, pp. 154–63. Nottingham: Department of Classical and Archaeological Studies, University of Nottingham.

Iversen, J., 1973. *The development of Denmark's nature since the last glacial*. Danmarks Geologiske Undersøgelse v, 7-c. Copenhagen.

Jacobsen, T. W., 1969. Excavations at Porto Cheli and vicinity, preliminary report 11: the Franchthi Cave 1967–1968. *Hesperia* 38, 343–81.

1973. Excavations at the Franchthi Cave 1969–1971. *Hesperia* 42, 45–88, 253–83.

1976. 17000 years of Greek prehistory. *Scientific American* 234 (6), 76–87.

1981. The Franchthi Cave and the beginnings of settled village life in Greece. *Hesperia* 50, 303–19.

Jażdżewski, K., 1965. *Poland*. London· Thames and Hudson.

Jochim, M., 1976. *Hunter-gatherer subsistence: a predictive model*. New York and London: Academic Press.

Jørgensen, E., 1977. *Hagebrogård–Vroue–Koldkur, neolithische Gräberfeld aus Nord-west-Jutland*. Copenhagen: Arkaeologiske Studier IV.

Kaelas, L., 1976. Pitted ware culture – the acculturation of a food-producing group. In S. de Laet (ed.), *Acculturation and continuity in Atlantic Europe*, pp. 130–41. Brugge: De Tempel.

Kalicz, N., 1970. *Clay gods: The Neolithic period and Copper Age in Hungary*. Budapest: Corvina Press.

Kalicz, N. and Makkay, J., 1977. *Die Linienbandkeramik in der Grosser Ungarischen Tiefebene*. Budapest: Akadémiai Kiadó.

Katincharov, R., 1981. État des recherches sur l'âge du bronze en Bulgarie du sud-est. *Izvestija* 36, 117–40.

Kinnes, I., 1979. *Round barrows and ring-ditches in the British Neolithic*. London: British Museum Occasional Paper 7.

Kjaerum, P., 1967. The chronology of the passage graves in Jutland. *Palaeohistoria* 12, 323–34.

Kosse, K., 1979. *Settlement ecology of the Early and Middle Neolithic Körös and Linear pottery cultures in Hungary*. Oxford: BAR s 64.

Kozlowski, S. K. (ed.), 1973. *The Mesolithic in Europe*. Warsaw: Warsaw University Press.

Kristiansen, K., 1982. The formation of tribal systems in later European prehistory: northern Europe, 4000–500 BC. In C. Renfrew *et al.* (eds.), *Theory and explanation in archaeology*, pp. 241–80. London: Academic Press.

Kruk, J., 1973. *Studia Osadnicze nad Neolitem Wyzyn Lessowych*. Wrocław: Polska Akademia Nauk.

Kruk, J. and Milisauskas, S., 1981. Chronology of Funnel-Beaker, Baden-like and Volynian settlements at Bronocice, Poland. *Germania*, 59, 1–19.

Kuper, R., Löhr, H., Lüning, J., Stehli, P. and Zimmerman, A. 1977. *Der Bandkeramische Siedlungsplatz Langweiler 9, Gem. Aldenhoven, Kr Düren*, Rheinische Ausgrabungen 18. Bonn: Rheinland-Verlag GMBH.

Lanting, J. N. and Van der Waals, J. D., 1976. Beaker culture relations in the Lower Rhine basin. In J. N. Lanting and J. D. van der Waals (eds.), *Glockenbecher Symposion Oberried 1976*, pp. 1–80. Bussum and Haarlem: Fibula-van Dishoek.

Larsson, L., 1978. *Ageröd I:B – Ageröd I:D. a study of early Atlantic settlement in Scania*. Acta Archaeologica Lundensia, series 4, no. 12. Lund: CWK Gleerup.

1981. The early Atlantic settlement of southern Sweden. In B. Gramsch (ed.), *Mesolithikum in Europa*, pp. 405–17. Berlin: Deutscher Verlag der Wissenschaften.

Lee, R. and DeVore, I. (eds.), 1968. *Man the hunter*. Chicago: Aldine.

Leisner, V., 1967. Die verschiedenen Phasen des Neolithikums in Portugal. *Palaeohistoria* 12, 363–72.

Leisner, G. and Leisner, V., 1943. *Die Megalithgräber der Iberischen Halbinsel, 1: der Suden*. Berlin: Walter de Gruyter.

1951. *Antas do Concelho de Reguengos de Monsaraz*. Lisbon: Instituto para a Alta Cultura.

1956. *Die Megalithgräber der Iberischen Halbinsel: der Westen*. Berlin: Walter de Gruyter.

1965. *Die Megalithgräber der Iberischen Halbinsel: der Westen*. Berlin: Walter de Gruyter.

Lewthwaite, J., 1981. Ambiguous first impressions: a survey of recent work on the Early Neolithic of the west Mediterranean. *Journal of Mediterranean Anthropology Archaeology* 1, 292–307.

L'Helgouach, J., 1965. *Les sépultures mégalithiques en Armorique*. Rennes: Laboratoire d'Anthropologie Préhistorique.

1971. Les débuts du Néolithique en Armorique au quatrième millénaire et son développement au commencement du troisième millénaire. In J. Lüning (ed.), *Die Anfänge des Neolithikums von Orient bis Nordeuropa*, vol. 6 (Fundamenta Reihe A Band 3) pp. 178–200. Köln: Bohlau Verlag.

Lichardus, J., 1972. Beitrag zur chronologischen Stellung der östlichen Linearbandkeramik in der Slowakei. In F. Jenö and M. János (eds.), *Die aktuelle Fragen der Bandkeramik*, pp. 107–22. Székesfehérvár: Az. I. Pannonia Konferencia Aktái.

Louwe Kooijmans, L. P., 1974. *The Rhine/Meuse Delta* (Analecta Praehistorica Leidensia VII). Leiden: Leiden University Press.

Lüning, J., 1967. Die Michelsberger Kultur. *BRGK* 48, 1–50.

Madsen, T., 1979. Earthen long barrows and timber structures: aspects of the Early Neolithic practice in Denmark. *PPS* 45, 301–20.

Mallory, J. P., 1976. The chronology of the early Kurgan tradition (part 1). *Journal of Indo-European Studies* 4, 257–94.

Mallory, J. P., 1977. The chronology of the early Kurgan tradition (part 2). *Journal of Indo-European Studies* 5, 339–68.

Malmer, M. P., 1967. The correlation between definitions and interpretations of Neolithic cultures in north-western Europe. *Palaeohistoria* 12, 373–8.

Marinescu-Bîlcu, S., 1981. *Tîrpeşti: from prehistory to history in eastern Romania*. Oxford: BAR s 107.

Marquez, C. C., Leisner, G. and Leisner, V., 1952. *Los Sepulcros Megaliticos de Huelva*. Madrid.

Mateescu, C. N., 1975. Remarks on cattle breeding and agriculture in the Middle and Late Neolithic on the lower Danube. *Dacia* 19, 13–18.

Mathiassen, T., 1946. En boplads fra stenalder ved Vedbaek Boldbaner. *Sollerødbogen*, 19–35.

Medunová-Benešová, A., 1972. Jevišovice–Starý Zamek: Schicht B – Katalog der Funde. *Fontes Archaeologicae Moraviae* 6.

Mellars, P. A. 1976a. Fire ecology, animal populations and man: a study of some ecological relationships in prehistory. *PPS* 42, 15–46.

    1976b. Settlement patterns and industrial variability in the British Neolithic. In G. Sieveking *et al.* (eds.), *Problems in economic and social archaeology*, 375–99. London: Duckworth.

Mellars, P. (ed.), 1978. *The early postglacial settlement of northern Europe*. London: Duckworth.

Mikkelsen, E., 1978. Seasonality and Mesolithic adaptation in Norway. In K. Kristiansen and C. Paludan-Müller (eds.), *New directions in Scandinavian archaeology*, pp. 79–119. Copenhagen: National Museum of Denmark.

Mikov, V., 1971. La Bulgarie à l'âge du bronze. In V. Georgiev (ed.), *L'ethnogénèse des peuples balkaniques*, pp. 51–61. Sofia: Academie Bulgare des Sciences.

Milisauskas, S., 1976. *Archaeological investigations on the Linear culture village of Olszanica*. Wroclaw: Polska Akademia Nauk.

Milisauskas, S. and Kruk, J., 1978. Bronocice: a Neolithic settlement in southeastern Poland. *Archaeology* 31, 44–52.

Milojčić, V., 1959. Ergebnisse der deutschen Ausgrabungen in Thessalien 1953–1958. *Jahrbuch des Römisch-Germanischen Zentralmuseum Mainz* 6, 1–56.

    1960. *Hauptergebnisse der deutschen Ausgrabungen in Thessalien 1953–1958*. Bonn: Rudolf Habelt.

Milojčić, V., Boessneck, J. and Hopf, M., 1962. *Die deutschen Ausgrabungen auf der Argissa-Magula in Thessalien, I: das präkeramische neolithikum sowie die Tier- und Pflanzenreste*. Bonn: Rudolf Habelt.

Milojčić, V., von den Driesch, A., Enderlek, Milojčić-Von Zumbusch, J. and Kilian, K., 1976. *Die deutschen Ausgrabungen auf Magulen um Larisa in Thessalien 1966*. Bonn: Rudolf Habelt.

Milojčić-von Zumbusch, J. and Milojčić, V., 1971. *Die deutschen Ausgrabungen auf der Otzaki-magula in Thessalien, I: das fruhe Neolithikum*. Bonn: Rudolf Habelt.

Modderman, P. J. R., 1970. Linearbandkeramik aus Elsloo und Stein. *Analecta Praehistorica Leidensia* 3.

    1976. Theorie und Praxis bei der Erforschung des Niederrheins und der Maas. *Jahresschrift für Mitteldeutsche Vorgeschichte* 60, 49–60.

    1977. Die neolithische Besiedlung bei Hienheim, Ldkr Kelheim, I: Die Ausgrabungen am Weinberg 19165–70. *Analecta Praehistorica Leidensia* 10.

Møhl, U., 1970. Fangstdyrne ved de danske strande. *Kuml* 1970, 297–330.

Mook, W., Munaut, A. and Waterbolk, H., 1972. Determination of age and duration of stratified bog settlements. *Proceedings of the 8th International Radiocarbon Dating Conference*, vol. 2, F27–40. Wellington: Royal Society of New Zealand.

Mörner, N. A. and Wallin, B., 1977. A 10,000 year temperature record from Gotland, Sweden. *Palaeogeography, Palaeoclimatology, Palaeoecology* 21, 113–38.

Nandris, J., 1970. The development and relationships of the earlier Greek Neolithic. *Man* 5, 191–213.

Němejcová-Pavúková, V., 1981. Nacrt periodizacie Badenskej kultury a jej chronologickych vztahov k juhovchodnej Europe. *Slovenská Archeológia* 29, 261–96.

Neustupný, E., 1968. Absolute chronology of the Neolithic and Aeneolithic periods in central and south-eastern Europe. *Slovenská Archeológia* 16, 19–60.

1969. Absolute chronology of the Neolithic and Aeneolithic periods in central and south-east Europe II. *Archeologické Rozhledy* 21, 783–810.

1973. Die Badener Kultur. In B. Chropovský (ed.), *Symposium über die Entstehung und Chronologie der Badener Kultur*, pp. 317–52. Bratislava: Verlag der Slowakischen Akademie der Wissenschaften.

1978. Mathematical analysis of an Aeneolithic cemetery. *Studia Praehistorica* 1–2, 238–43.

1981. Das Äneolithikum Mitteleuropas. *Jahresschrift für mitteldeutsche Vorgeschichte* 63, 177–87.

Newell, R., 1970. The flint industry of the Dutch Linearbandkeramik. *Analecta Praehistorica Leidensia* 3, 144–83.

Nikolov, B., 1974. *Gradeshnitsa*. Sofia: Isdatelstvo 'Nauka y Izkustvo'.

1978. Développement du Chalcolithique en Bulgarie de l'ouest et du nord-ouest. *Studia Praehistorica* 1–2, 121–9.

O'Kelly, M., 1982. *Newgrange*. London: Thames and Hudson.

Ottaway, B. and Strahm, C., 1975. Swiss Neolithic copper beads: currency, ornament or prestige items. *World Archaeology* 6, 307–21.

Pape, W., 1978. *Bemerkungen zur relativen Chronologie des Endneolithikums am Beispiel Südwestdeutschlands und der Schweiz*. Tubingen: Verlag Archaeologica Venatoria, Institut für Urgeschichte der Universität Tubingen.

1979. Histogramme neolithischer 14C-Daten. *Germania* 57, 1–51.

Passek, T. S., 1961. Problèmes de l'Enéolithique du sud-ouest de l'Europe occidentale. In J. Böhm and S. de Laet (eds.), *L'Europe à la fin de l'âge de la pierre*, pp. 137–160. Prague: Editions de l'Académie Tchécoslovaque des Sciences.

Patay, P., 1974. Die hochkupferzeitliche Bodrog–Keresztúr-Kultur. *BRGK* 55, 1–71.

Pavúk, J., 1981. Súčasný stav štúdia Lengyelskej kultúry na Slovensku. *Památky Archeologické* 72, 255–99.

Pavúk, J. (ed.), 1982. *Siedlungen der Kultur mit Linearkeramik in Europa*. Nitra: Archäologisches Institut der Slowakischen Akademie der Wissenschaften.

Payne, S., 1975. Faunal change at Franchthi Cave from 20,000 BC to 3,000 BC. In A. T. Clason (ed.), *Archaeozoological Studies*, pp. 120–31. Amsterdam, Oxford and New York: North Holland Publishing Co. and American Elsevier Publishing Co.

Peacock, D. F. S., 1969. Neolithic pottery production in Cornwall. *Antiquity* 43, 145–49.

Pellicer, M., 1963. Estratigrafia prehistorica de la cueva de Nerja. *Excavaciones Arqueologicas en Espana* 16.

1964. El Neolitico y el bronce de la Cueva de la Cariguela de Pinar (Granada). *Trabajos de Prehistoria* 15.

Perniceva, L., 1978. Sites et habitations du Chalcolithique en Bulgarie. *Studia Praehistorica* 1–2, 163–9.

Phillips, P., 1975. *Early farmers of west Mediterranean Europe*. London: Hutchinson University Library.

1982. *The Middle Neolithic in southern France*. Oxford: BAR s 142.

Piggott, S., 1962. *The West Kennet Long Barrow: excavations 1955–6*. London: HMSO.

Protsch, R. and Berger, R., 1973. Earliest radiocarbon dates for domesticated animals. *Science* 179, 235–9.

Pryor, F., 1976. A Neolithic multiple burial from Fengate, Peterborough. *Antiquity* 50, 232–3.

Renfrew, C., 1967. Colonialism and megalithismus. *Antiquity* 41, 276–88.

1969. The autonomy of the south east European Copper Age. *PPS* 35, 12–47.

1971. Sitagroi, radiocarbon and the prehistory of south-east Europe. *Antiquity* 45, 275–82.

1972. *The emergence of civilisation: the Cyclades and the Aegean in the third millennium B.C.* London: Methuen.

1976. Megaliths, territories and populations. In S. de Laet (ed.), *Acculturation and continuity in Atlantic Europe*, pp. 198–220. Brugge: De Tempel.

1977. Alternative models for exchange and spatial distribution. In T. K. Earle and J. E. Ericson (eds.), *Exchange systems in prehistory*, pp. 71–90. New York: Academic Press.

1979. *Investigations in Orkney*. London: Society of Antiquaries.

Ridley, C. and Wardle, K. A., 1979. Rescue excavations at Servia, 1971–1973; a preliminary report. *Annals British School Athens* 74, 185–230.

Rodden, R. J., 1962. Excavations at the Early Neolithic Site of Nea Nikomedeia, Greek Macedonia. *PPS* 28, 267–88.

1965. An Early Neolithic village in Greece. *Scientific American*, 212 (April), 82–92.

Rostholm, H., 1978. Neolitiske Skivehjul fra Kideris og Bjerregarde i Midttylland. *Kuml* 1977, 185–222.

Rowley-Conwy, P., 1981. Mesolithic Danish bacon: permanent and temporary sites in the Danish Mesolithic. In A. Sheridan and G. Bailey (eds.), *Economic archaeology*, pp. 51–5. Oxford: BAR s 96.

Rozoy, J. G., 1978. *Les derniers chasseurs. l'Epipaléolithique en France et en Belgique.* Bulletin de la soc. arch. champenoise (Reims), numéro special. Charleville.

Sakellaridis, M., 1979. *The economic exploitation of the Swiss area in the Mesolithic and Neolithic periods*. Oxford: BAR s 67.

Sangmeister, E. and Schubart, H., 1972. Zambujal. *Antiquity* 546, 191–7.

1981. *Zambujal: die Grabungen 1964 bis 1973*. Madrider Beilage 5. Mainz: Philipp von Zabern.

Savory, H. N., 1968. *Spain and Portugal*. London: Thames and Hudson.

Schild, R., 1976. Flint mining and trade in Polish prehistory as seen from the perspective of the chocolate flint of central plant: a second approach. *Acta Archaeologica Carpathica* 16, 147–77.

Schmidt, R. R., 1945. *Die Burg Vučedol*. Zagreb: Ausgabe der Kroatischen Archäologischen Staatsmuseums in Zagreb.

Schwabedissen, H., 1967. Ein horizontierter 'Breitkeil' aus Satrup und die mannigfachen Kulturbindungen der beginnenden Neolithikums im Norden und Nordwesten. *Palaeohistoria* 12, 409–68.

Shackleton, N. and Renfrew, C., 1970. Neolithic trade routes realigned by oxygen isotope analysis. *Nature* 228, 1062–4.

Shanks, M. and Tilley, C., 1982. Ideology, symbolic power and ritual communication: a reinterpretation of Neolithic mortuary practices. In I. Hodder (ed.), *Symbolic and structural archaeology*, pp. 129–54. Cambridge: Cambridge University Press.

Shennan, S., 1982. Ideology, change and the study of the European Early Bronze Age. In I. Hodder (ed.), *Symbolic and structural archaeology*, pp. 155–61. Cambridge: Cambridge University Press.

Sheridan, A. and Bailey, G. (eds.), 1981. *Economic archaeology: towards an integration of ecological and social approaches.* Oxford: BAR s 96.

Sherratt, A. G., 1981. Plough and pastoralism: aspects of the secondary products revolution. In N. Hammond, *et al.* (eds.), *Pattern of the past*, pp. 261–305. Cambridge: Cambridge University Press.

   1982*a*. The development of Neolithic and Copper Age settlement in the Great Hungarian plain. Part 1: The regional setting. *Oxford Journal of Archaeology* 1, 287–316.

   1982*b*. Mobile resources: settlement and exchange in early agricultural Europe. In C. Renfrew and S. Shennan (eds.), *Ranking, resource and exchange*, pp. 13–26. Cambridge: Cambridge University Press.

Simmons, I. and Tooley, M. (eds.), 1981. *The environment in British prehistory.* London: Duckworth.

Smith, A. G., 1970. The influence of Mesolithic and Neolithic man on British vegetation: a discussion. In D. Walker and R. G. West (eds.), *Studies in the vegetational history of the British Isles*, pp. 81–96. Cambridge: Cambridge University Press.

Soudský, B., 1962. The Neolithic site of Bylany. *Antiquity* 36, 190–200.

   1966. *Bylany: osada nejstarsich zemedelcu z mladzi doby kamenne.* Prague: Academia nakladatelstvi Czechoslovenske akademie ved.

Spång, K., Welinder, S. and Wyszomerski, B., 1976. The introduction of the Neolithic Stone Age into the Baltic area. In S. de Laet (ed.), *Acculturation and continuity in Atlantic Europe*, pp. 235–50. Brugge: De Tempel.

Srejović, D., 1972. *Europe's first monumental sculpture: new discoveries at Lepenski Vir.* London: Thames and Hudson.

Srejović, D. and Letica, L., 1978. *Vlasac: a mesolithic settlement in the Iron Gates, I: Archaeology.* Beograd: Serbian Academy of Sciences and Arts (Monographies 512, Dept of Historical Sciences, vol. 5).

Strömberg, M., 1971. *Die Megalithgräber von Hagestad.* Lund: CWK Gleerups Verlag.

Sulimirski, T., 1968. *Corded ware and Globular amphorae north-east of the Carpathians.* London: Athlone Press.

Tauber, H., 1972. Radiocarbon chronology of the Danish Mesolithic and Neolithic. *Antiquity* 46, 106–10.

Theocharis, D. R., 1973. *Neolithic Greece.* Athens: National Bank of Greece.

Thrane, H., 1982. Dyrkningsspor fra yngre stenalder i Danmark. *Skrifter fra Historisk Institut, Odense Universitet* 30, 20–8.

Tinè, S., 1983. *Passo di Corvo e la civiltà neolitica del Tavoliere.* Genoa: Sagep.

Todorova, H., 1976. *Ovčarovo.* Sofia: Izdatelstvo 'Septemviri'.

   1978. *The Eneolithic period in Bulgaria in the fifth millennium B.C.* Oxford: BAR s 49.

   1981. Das Chronologiesystem von Karanovo im Lichte der neuen Forschungsergebnisse in Bulgarien. *Slovenská Archeológia* 29, 203–16.

Todorova, H., Ivanov, S., Vasilev, V., Hopf, M., Quitta, H. and Kohl, G., 1975. *Selishnata mogila pri Golyamo Delchevo.* Sofia: Razkopki i prouchvaniya, v.

Tringham, R., 1968. A preliminary study of the Early Neolithic and latest Mesolithic blade industries in southeast and central Europe. In J. M. Coles and D. D. A. Simpson (eds.), *Studies in ancient Europe*, pp. 45–70. Leicester: Leicester University Press.

   1971. *Hunters, fishers and farmers of eastern Europe, 6000–3000 BC.* London: Hutchinson University Library.

1973. The Mesolithic of south-eastern Europe. In S. K. Kozlowski (ed.), *The Mesolithic in Europe*, pp. 551–72. Warsaw: University Press.

Tringham, R., Krstic, D., Kaiser, T. and Voyter, B., 1980. The early agricultural site of Selevac, Yugoslavia. *Archaeology* 33, 24–32.

Twohig, E. S., 1981. *The Megalithic art of western Europe*. Oxford: Clarendon Press.

Uerpmann, H. P., 1979. *Probleme der Neolithisierung des Mittelmeerraumes*. Wiesbaden: Reichert.

Van der Velde, P., 1979. The social anthropology of a Neolithic cemetery in the Netherlands. *Current Anthropology* 20, 37–58.

Van der Waals, J. D., 1964. *Prehistoric disc wheels in the Netherlands*. Groningen: JB Wolters.

Van Zeist, W., 1975. Preliminary report on the botany of Gomolava. *Journal of Archaeological Science* 2, 315–25.

Vasić, M. M., 1932. *Preistoriska Vinča*. Belgrade.

1936. *Preistoriska Vinča II–IV*. Belgrade.

Vicent, A. M. and Muñoz, A. M., 1973. Secunda campana de excavaciones: la Cueva de Los Murcielagos, Zuheros (Cordoba) 1969. *Excavaciones Arqueologicas en Espana* 77.

Vlassa, N., 1963. Chronology of the Neolithic of Transylvania in the light of the Tărtăria settlement's stratigraphy. *Dacia* (new series) 7, 485–94.

1972. Eine frühneolithische Kultur mit bemalter Keramik der Vor-Starčevo–Körös-Zeit in Cluj–Gura Baciului, Siebenburgen. *Praehistorische Zeitschrift* 47, 174–97.

Waterbolk, H. T., 1971. Working with radiocarbon dates. *PPS* 37 (2), 15–33.

Waterbolk, H. T., and van Zeist, W., 1978. *Niederwil, eine Siedlung der Pfyner Kultur, vol. 1: die Grabungen*. Academica Helvetica 1. Bern and Stuttgart: Paul Haupt.

Weinberg, S. S., 1965. The Stone Age in the Aegean. *Cambridge Ancient History*, rev. edn, vol. 1, p. x. Cambridge: Cambridge University Press.

Whitehouse, R., 1981. Prehistoric settlement patterns in south-east Italy. In G. Barker and R. Hodges (eds.), *Archaeology and Italian society*, pp. 157–65. Oxford: BAR s 102.

Whittle, A. W. R., 1977. *The earlier Neolithic of southern England and its continental background*. Oxford: BAR s 35.

Whittle, E. H. and Arnaud, J. M., 1975. Thermoluminescent dating of Neolithic and Chalcolithic pottery from sites in central Portugal. *Archaeometry* 17, 5–24.

Willerding, U., 1980. Zum Ackerbau der Bandkeramiker. *Materialhefte Ur- und Frühgeschichte Niedersachsens* 16, 421–56.

Winther, J., 1943. *Blandebjerg*. Rudkøbing: Eget Forlag.

Wislanski, T. (ed.), 1970. *The Neolithic in Poland*. Wroclaw: Nauk.

Wobst, H. M., 1974. Boundary conditions for Palaeolithic social systems: a simulation approach. *American Antiquity* 39, 147–78.

Wosinszky, M., 1888. *Das prähistorische Schanzwerk Lengyel*. Budapest: F. Kilian.

Yellen, J. E., 1977. *Archaeological approaches to the present: models for reconstructing the past*. New York: Academic Press.

**Suggestions for further reading**

Like the unfortunate victim in the advertisement for a certain newspaper some years ago, one constantly wishes to be better informed. There is no slackening in the pace of publications and even at this book goes to press, new works are appearing which will be relevant to the study of this period and area. For those who wish to keep up with this process, there is no substitute for the hard graft of following the appropriate journals, conference proceedings, monographs and books. This requires a first-rate library. Those seeking more general orientation are more easily served. There are useful general introductions to European prehistory such as *Ancient Europe* by S. Piggott (Chicago, 1965), *European prehistory* by S. Milisauskas (New York, 1978), or *Prehistoric Europe* by T. Champion *et al.* (New York, 1984). There are regional surveys for the western Mediterranean by P. Phillips, *Early farmers of the western Mediterranean* (London, 1975), and by J. Guilaine, *Premiers bergers et paysans de l'occident méditerranéen* (Paris, 1976) and for south-east Europe by R. Tringham, *Hunters, fishes and farmers of eastern Europe, 6000–3000 BC* (London, 1971), but central and western Europe are not well served at this level. Surveys of smaller areas are more common, but are too numerous to mention here individually; details of many can be found in the notes and select bibliography. Recent examples are *The Eneolithic period in Bulgaria in the fifth millennium B.C.* (Oxford, 1978) and *La préhistoire française*, the relevant volumes of which are edited by H. de Lumley and J. Guilaine (Paris, 1976).

# INDEX
References to figures are in italics